HOW

ST. PETERSBURG

LEARNED TO

STUDY ITSELF

STUDIES OF THE HARRIMAN INSTITUTE:
SELECTED TITLES IN RUSSIAN LITERATURE AND HISTORY

THE PENNSYLVANIA STATE UNIVERSITY PRESS
UNIVERSITY PARK, PENNSYLVANIA

HOW

ST. PETERSBURG

LEARNED TO

STUDY ITSELF

The Russian
Idea of
Kraevedenie

EMILY D. JOHNSON

Studies of the Harriman Institute, Columbia University

The Harriman Institute, Columbia University, sponsors the Studies of the Harriman Institute in the belief that their publication contributes to scholarly research and public understanding. In this way, the Institute, while not necessarily endorsing their conclusions, is pleased to make available the results of some of the research conducted under its auspices.

Library of Congress Cataloging-in-Publication Data

Johnson, Emily D., 1966–
   How St. Petersburg learned to study itself : the Russian idea
   of kraevedenie / Emily D. Johnson.
      p.   cm. — (Studies of the Harriman Institute)
Includes bibliographical references and index.
ISBN 978-0-271-05865-8 (pbk : alk. paper)
1. Saint Petersburg (Russia)—History—Study and teaching—History.
2. Saint Petersburg (Russia)—Historiography—History.
3. Local history—Study and teaching—Russia (Federation)—Saint Petersburg.
4. Saint Petersburg (Russia)—Civilization.
I. Title.
II. Title: How Saint Petersburg learned to study itself.
III. Series.

DK561.J647 2006
947'.210072047—dc22
2005037526

Copyright © 2006 The Pennsylvania State University
All rights reserved
Printed in the United States of America
Published by The Pennsylvania State University Press,
University Park, PA 16802-1003

The Pennsylvania State University Press is a member of the Association of American University Presses.

It is the policy of The Pennsylvania State University Press to use acid-free paper. This book is printed on stock that meets the minimum requirements of American National Standard for Information Sciences—Permanence of Paper for Printed Library Material, ANSI Z39.48–1992.

CONTENTS

List of Illustrations   vii
Preface and Acknowledgments   ix
A Note on Transliteration and Translations   xiv
List of Abbreviations   xv

Introduction
Ways of Knowing: Russian Local Studies as an Identity Discipline   1

1   The Eighteenth- and Nineteenth-Century Tradition   17
2   The Art Journals of the Silver Age, St. Petersburg Preservationism, and the Guidebook   45
3   Old Petersburg After the Revolution   73
4   The Excursion Movement and Excursion Methodology   97
5   Excursion Primers and Literary Tours   125
6   *Kraevedenie* in St. Petersburg   155
7   Literary *Kraevedenie*   183

Conclusion   215

Notes   229
Selected Bibliography   273
Index   288

ILLUSTRATIONS

1. Map of St. Petersburg, from Karl Baedeker, *Russia with Teheran, Port Arthur, and Peking: Handbook for Travelers* (Leipzig: Karl Baedeker, 1914)   viii

2. A view of St. Isaac's bridge and the area of St. Petersburg from the Admiralty to Senate Square. Engraving from a drawing by Paterssen (1794), from M. Pyliaev, *Staryi Petersburg: Rasskazy iz byloi zhizni stolitsy*, 2nd ed. (St. Petersburg: Izdanie A. S. Suvorina, 1889)   42

3. A procession featuring elephants given to the Russian tsar by the Persian shah. Engraving from a watercolor by Vorobiev, from M. Pyliaev, *Staryi Peterburg: Rasskazy iz byloi zhizni stolitsy*, 2nd ed. (St. Petersburg: Izdanie A. S. Suvorina, 1889)   44

4. The opening of Étienne-Maurice Falconet's monument to Peter I, *The Bronze Horseman*, in 1782. Engraving by Melnikov, made from a drawing by Davidov, from M. Pyliaev, *Staryi Petersburg: Rasskazy iz byloi zhizni stolitsy*, 2nd ed. (St. Petersburg: Izdanie A. S. Suvorina, 1889)   48

5. Evgeny Lanceray, frontispiece for *World of Art*, no. 1 (1902), a special issue commemorating St. Petersburg's bicentennial   55

6. Anna Ostroumova-Lebedeva, view of the river Fontanka, from *Petersburg: Avtolitografii A. P. Ostroumovoi* (St. Petersburg: Komitet populiarizatsii khudozhestvennykh izdanii, 1922)   195

7. Erikh Gollerbakh, frontispiece to Erikh Gollerbakh, *Gorod muz*, 2nd ed. (Leningrad, 1930)   205

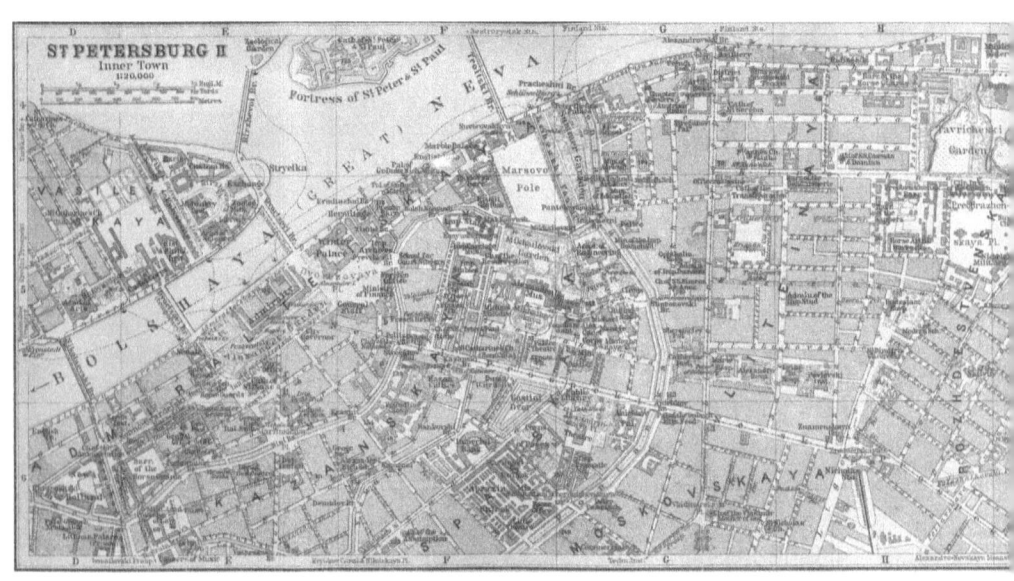

FIG. 1 Map of St. Petersburg from Karl Baedeker's 1914 guide to Russia.

PREFACE AND ACKNOWLEDGMENTS

In the early 1990s, I spent several years working for the Academy of Sciences in St. Petersburg, Russia, as a translator and interpreter. I arrived in country a month after the August 1991 abortive coup, witnessed the collapse of the Soviet Union firsthand, and had the disconcerting experience of living amidst hyperinflation. For a while, as I recall, food prices doubled every week. As they rose, the shelves of official grocery stores, which at one point had contained little except powdered cake mix and canned seaweed, slowly filled again.

Paper money, in the volatile new economy, suddenly emerged as the chief deficit good. As prices shot up, the banks ran out of currency. Organizations, even if they theoretically had funds in their accounts, often could not meet their payroll. Salary delays of six months to a year were not uncommon, particularly in the public sector. Given the rate at which the ruble was losing its value, by the time Russian employees received the money they were owed, it was often almost worthless.

In this economic climate, everyone began to look for extra sources of income. Russian scholars with international reputations, curators and restoration experts from major museums, well-known poets, the editors of important literary journals, and local political figures all agreed with alacrity to speak to groups of foreign undergraduates in exchange for very modest sums of hard currency. For a while, I spent much of my time providing consecutive interpreting for prestige lectures and guided tours: multi-week courses on pre-Revolutionary history, the development of Russian architecture, or post-Soviet political culture; back-corridor visits to architectural monuments that for one reason or another remained closed to the public; tours of the Petersburg of Brodsky and Mandelstam led by prominent literary historians.

As I grew more comfortable in my job, my Russian employers began to encourage me to take on additional responsibilities. When specialists failed to show up for scheduled excursions, when arrangements at museums and monuments suddenly fell through, I was sometimes pressed into service, called upon to deliver an impromptu tour myself. With some regularity, I found myself perched in the jump seat of a red tour bus, microphone in hand, reciting general facts about the city. Eventually it occurred to me that I needed to prepare for such situations. I began frequenting both used and new bookstores and bought everything I could find on the history and culture of St. Petersburg.

Certainly there was no shortage of material to buy. A great boom in the publication of literature about St. Petersburg and, for that matter, Russian territory as a whole had begun almost as soon as the old Soviet censorship restrictions started to lift. New studies describing monuments demolished by the Soviet authorities, preliminary efforts to document sites connected with the biography of writers long out of official favor, anthologies on urban folklore, and lovingly assembled facsimile editions of classic sketch collections and pre-Revolutionary guidebooks all found their way onto bookstore shelves in the late 1980s and early 1990s. By most accounts, these books seem to have sold quite well. Publishing runs, particularly for reprints of pre-Revolutionary works, often reached 50,000; 150,000; or even 500,000 copies and quickly disappeared. These books appealed to Russian readers because they offered access to long-suppressed and, in many cases, almost wholly forgotten facts concerning Russia's national heritage. They invested familiar landscapes with "new" significance and hence represented powerful tools in the struggle to de-Sovietize geographic space.

Nowhere did this process seem more important than in the old imperial capital. The view that Moscow had specifically targeted the area for persecution—attacking its intelligentsia with particular ferocity in the purges of the Stalin era and callously abandoning its population to famine in World War II—had always enjoyed a certain measure of popularity among local residents. The city chronically lacked funding for key restoration projects; its much-celebrated architectural ensembles were obviously crumbling. Many inhabitants resented the old imperial capital's decline in status and, with its three-hundredth anniversary only a dozen years away, longed to see it recapture at least some of its former glory. In 1991 residents voted to rename the city, known for much of the Soviet era as Leningrad, restoring the original toponym St. Petersburg. Public debate before the referendum helped to focus attention on the area's unique heritage and excited renewed interest in all aspects of local history. Reclaiming the legacy of old Petersburg emerged as an enormously popular preoccupation.

Of all the material I read as part of my effort to improve my knowledge of the city where I lived and worked, one particular kind of publication captured my imagination: the old guidebooks that Russian publishers were reprinting. These books struck me as enormously culturally significant and entirely unexpected. More varied and readable than the Western guides with which I was familiar, they seemed an important complement to the famous descriptions of Petersburg from classic Russian poetry and fiction by authors such as Pushkin, Gogol, and Dostoevsky. Studying them added something new to my understanding of the Petersburg myth and cult, giving me a better sense of what the city meant for Russian culture as a whole. When I finally left Russia for New York and graduate school, I took an entire suitcase of facsimile editions of old guidebooks with me. They might, I thought, make a good subject for a dissertation.

In 1997 funding from the American Council of Teachers of Russian and the Harriman Institute of Columbia University made it possible for me to return to St. Petersburg for fifteen months to conduct dissertation research. Soon after I arrived, I went to the National Library of Russia to ask a reference librarian for help with my topic. I wanted, I explained to her, to find background information on classic Petersburg guidebooks and on the men and women who had written them, including, most specifically, the early-twentieth-century scholars of the city Nikolai Antsiferov, Petr Stolpiansky, and Vladimir Kurbatov. She handed me five long drawers of index cards containing bibliographic citations, all of them labeled with a single word, *kraevedenie*, roughly translated as local or regional studies (*krai*, region or local administrative district, and *vedenie*, study or knowledge of). My dissertation topic, I gradually came to understand over the course of the next several months, represented in part an exercise in disciplinary history. I was studying the foundation texts and founding fathers of a minor discipline that, by most accounts, had taken shape at the beginning of the twentieth century.

In 1997, when I arrived in St. Petersburg to conduct dissertation research, I had a general idea of what the word *kraevedenie* meant, but I knew very little about the discipline's history or significance. I had noticed that the guidebooks I liked so much were often shelved in sections labeled with this disciplinary term in bookstores, but I had never paused to think about the relevance of the category per se to my project. How did guidebooks become so firmly associated with *kraevedenie*? In what terms should the relationship between this minor textual form and Russian local studies as a field of inquiry be understood? As I read through sources in the library, these questions began to seem increasingly important to me. Another issue also emerged as paramount as my work progressed. Many of the written sources and individual authorities I consulted described St. Petersburg as the "theoretical center" and/or site of the leading school of Russian *kraevedenie*. These designations seemed incongruous given the fact that the discipline itself had, as I learned from my reading, often been understood in the 1920s as purely provincial in scope. Although St. Petersburg is situated on the periphery of Russian territory and lost much of its political influence during the Soviet period, most Russians continue to view it as a major cultural center and would hesitate to label it as provincial. How, I wondered, had St. Petersburg acquired a reputation as a leading center of *kraevedenie*?

How St. Petersburg Learned to Study Itself represents the ultimate product of my efforts to answer this basic question. In it, I trace the history of *kraevedenie*, looking both at how meanings of the term have changed over time and at the role that Petersburg-based scholars and institutions played in the evolution of the discipline. In conjunction with this effort, I also examine the way in which experts in local studies have traditionally understood and used guidebooks, consider the significance of *kraevedenie* within Russian society today, and draw some tentative comparisons between this field of inquiry and other Russian and Western knowledge systems.

This book is part of a substantial wave of recent studies that examine the image, myth, development, historical role, and significance of Russia's old imperial capital. The celebration of St. Petersburg's three-hundredth anniversary in 2003 inspired both Russian and Western scholars to produce many important new works about the city, to reconsider accepted truisms, and to begin to analyze long-neglected caches of material. Julie A. Buckler's *Mapping St. Petersburg*, Alexander Schenker's *The Bronze Horseman*, Anna Lisa Crone and Jennifer Day's *My Petersburg/Myself*, and Moisei Kagan's *Peter's City* (*Grad Petrov*) seem particularly worthy of mention. In its focus on *kraevedenie*, my book differs from these and other scholarly works about St. Petersburg published in anticipation of and immediately following the city's 2003 jubilee.

Many individuals and institutions have helped me in my work on this project. My friends and former employers Nikita Lomagin and Arkady Poliarus deserve credit for first introducing me to the exciting world of excursion work and hence for inspiring my interest in both *kraevedenie* and guidebooks. Robert

Maguire, my dissertation advisor at Columbia University, was a constant source of advice and support. His guidance at every stage of this process was invaluable. I feel very fortunate to have had the chance to work under the direction of such a superb scholar and teacher. Few people in my life have influenced me as much. Cathy Nepomnyashchy and Carol Ueland have played a key role in my life as mentors since shortly after I entered graduate school. I am very grateful for the encouragement and support that they have offered me over years. Richard Gustafson, Elizabeth Valkenier, Irina Reyfman, Julie Buckler, Julie Cassiday, Anne Lounsbery, Larry Holmes, and Tom Beyer all read and commented on various versions of this text, making many helpful suggestions. Olga Semenovna Ostroi provided me with key advice on basic sources when I first began conducting archival research in St. Petersburg. The National Library of Russia remains my favorite place in the world to work; its staff always made me feel at home.

I would like to thank Peter Potter of Penn State Press for believing in this project and for his help in refining the text. I am indebted to Ron Meyer, the publications editor at the Harriman Institute, for his valuable editorial suggestions and advice concerning the publication process.

Funding for this project was provided by the American Council of Teachers of Russian, the U.S. Department of State Program for Research and Training on Eastern Europe and the Independent States of the Former Soviet Union, the Slavic Department of Columbia University, the Harriman Institute, and the University of Oklahoma. I would like to express special appreciation to the University Seminars at Columbia University for their help in publication. Material in this work was presented to the University Seminar on Slavic History and Culture.

Part of Chapter 7 of this book appeared in a slightly different form in Ian Lilly, ed., *Moscow and Petersburg: The City in Russian Culture* (Nottingham: Astra Press, 2002). My thanks to Ian Lilly and Garth Terry for helping me to refine this material.

A NOTE ON TRANSLITERATION AND TRANSLATIONS

I have used a slightly modified version of the Library of Congress system for transliterating Russian. For aesthetic reasons I have omitted most diacriticals and have shortened the endings *-skii* and *-nyi*, when they appear at the end of Russian names and place names, to *-sky* and *-ny* respectively. I have also generally used the traditional English spelling for the names of well-known Russian cultural figures, substituting the familiar Alexander Benois, for instance, for Aleksandr Benua. In the notes and bibliography, I have chosen to adhere somewhat more strictly to the Library of Congress System than I have in the text on the theory that accurately rendering Russian spelling was of primary importance in the scholarly apparatus of the book. Although authors' names are still given in a simplified form, titles have been transliterated fully, and soft and hard signs are indicated. All translations, unless otherwise noted, are my own.

ABBREVIATIONS

Aktsentr	The Academic Center of Narkompros
Glavnauka	The Central Scientific Administration of Narkompros
Glavprofobr	The Central Administration for Professional Education of Narkompros
Gosizdat	State Publishing House
Gubispolkom	Gubernia (Party) Executive Committee
Gubotkomkhoz	Leningrad Gubernia Department of Communal Management
GUS	State Academic Council of Narkompros
Komsomol	The Young Communists' League
LOIMK	The Leningrad Society for the Study of the Local Region
Narkompros	The Commissariat of Enlightenment
NEP	New Economic Policy
OKRAM	The Society of Marxist Kraevedy at the Communist Academy
OPTE	The Society of Proletarian Tourism and Excursions
Politprosvet	The Department of Political Enlightenment at Narkompros
Proletkult	Proletarian Cultural and Educational Organizations
Prompartiia	The Industrial Party. A 1930 show trial
RKP	Russian Communist Party
Sovnarkom	Council of People's Commissars
TSBK	The Central Bureau of Kraevedenie
Tsentrarkhiv	The Central State Archive
TSNIMKR	The Central Scientific Research Institute on the Methods of *Kraevedenie*

Introduction
Ways of Knowing: Russian Local Studies as an Identity Discipline

Disciplines are cultural constructs. They arise in specific places at particular moments in time, and they either flourish or fade depending on the extent to which they are perceived as intellectually viable, useful, fashionable, and/or compatible with the needs and aspirations of influential social groups. Like styles of music, trends in fashion, and political theories, disciplines can be exported. They can cross boundaries, spreading from their culture of origin to other countries and continents. Sometimes disciplines change substantially when placed in new surroundings: their aims, boundaries, and theoretical underpinnings, the basic vocabulary employed by practitioners, can all evolve in response to local conditions. Often, however, disciplines may seem, at least superficially, to pass unaltered from one culture to the next.

Strong nations and empires, unsurprisingly, export academic disciplines more successfully than weaker states. In recent decades environmental engineering, gender studies, and ethnic studies, emerging disciplines that enjoy significant popularity in Western Europe and the United States, have all begun to gain ground in other areas of the globe. Leading universities in countries as far-flung as Argentina, Uganda, Slovenia, and Yemen regularly issue promotional material filled with references to new academic units, programs, and courses that, to a contemporary American educator, may well sound familiar. The similarities are at times so striking that one might reasonably presume that, thanks to modern tools of communication and Western economic and cultural dominance, a single homogeneous system for the organization and classification of approaches to learning has taken hold throughout the world and that regional trends in the composition of intellectual life that originate outside the great democracies of the West are of little real significance.

However, despite the unquestionable influence of Western universities, scientific societies, and grant-giving agencies, substantial diversity continues to exist in the organization of learning and scholarship. Disciplines that are largely or entirely unknown in the United States flourish in other areas of the globe. They can easily escape the notice of American academics, because they do not fit into our system of disciplinary classification: no words exist for them in the English language; they overlap with and yet do not entirely coincide with accepted Western fields of specialization; to us they seem sometimes like one thing and sometimes like another, but never distinct and important in and of themselves. As a result, American specialists tend to translate foreign disciplinary terms either reductively or situationally. In the first case, they render the name of a foreign discipline in English literally and then, noting that it sounds roughly equivalent to one of its well-known Western counterparts, assume, without regard to coverage or methodology, that the two approaches to learning are essentially identical. In the second case, they ignore the existence of the unfamiliar category entirely and reclassify individual works of scholarship in the foreign discipline according to Western norms: they might label some pieces as history, identify others as political science, and list a third group under cultural anthropology. The set as such disappears, leaving in its place only disparate items. Both reductive and situational translations of foreign disciplinary terms tend to reinforce our cultural blindness; false equations and hastily conceived comparisons reduce our already limited ability to perceive unfamiliar categories and structures.

Should our disregard for foreign disciplines concern us? Are categories and labels at all important or is it just individual works of scholarship that matter? In this age of interdisciplinary studies, it would be foolish to regard the lines that divide fields of specialization as inherently fixed or impermeable, but does that mean that disciplines as such are wholly irrelevant? I would argue no: the ways in which human beings organize scholarship, the categories and approaches developed in various parts of the globe, deserve our attention. By studying them we can learn a great deal about ourselves and our neighbors, about what is constant and immutable in the universal quest for knowledge, and about what varies according to the culture and the age.

This book focuses on a disciplinary tradition that will be unfamiliar to most Americans and to many Western Europeans: the system of inquiry that in Russian is called *kraevedenie*. Best translated into English as regional or, perhaps, local studies (*krai*, region or local administrative district, and *vedenie*, study or knowledge of), this field took shape in central Russia in the early twentieth century, combining elements drawn from a variety of domestic and foreign antecedents. As it developed, *kraevedenie* grew and changed in response to local historical conditions, acquiring, over time, functions, a theoretical base, and social significance that render it distinct from all obvious precursors. Popular from the beginning, *kraevedenie* rapidly spread throughout Soviet territory and, in the decades following World War II, even played a certain role in some of the U.S.S.R.'s East European satellites.[1] Following the collapse of communism, *kraevedenie* appears to have ceased expanding geographically, but it remains a vibrant and important force throughout the former Soviet Union. In Russia, in particular, it has flourished in recent years, in no way overshadowed or diminished by recently imported Western disciplines and modes of thinking. Since the early 1990s, Russia has seen—in addition to the creation of new departments, centers, and schools of gender studies, public relations, and marketing—a significant increase in the number of academic units and institutions devoted to *kraevedenie*.

What exactly is *kraevedenie*? Contemporary Russian lexicographers generally define the term as "the study of the natural environment, population, economy, history, or culture of some part of a country, such as an administrative or natural region, or a place of settlement."[2] As such a definition implies, *kraevedenie* represents a synthetic field that draws upon the methodological and theoretical legacies of various scholarly traditions. In it, approaches, terminology, and tools typical of fields as diverse as anthropology, sociology, history, art history, economics, and soil science are brought together to produce a new holistic science of place. *Kraevedy* (practitioners of *kraevedenie*) investigate and describe both natural and man-made landscapes, study the ways in which human society and the environment affect each other, and decipher the semiotics of space. They deconstruct local myths, analyze the conventions governing the depiction of specific regions and towns in works of art and literature, and dissect both outsider and insider perceptions of local population groups. The notion that people are shaped and defined by the environment in which they live is fundamental to modern *kraevedenie*. *Kraevedy* believe that geographic factors play an active role both in human history at large and in the lives of individual men and women. They maintain that long-term residence in a specific town or region—exposure to a particular aesthetic and social environment, to a certain set of symbols, myths, stereotypes, and historical conceptions—can influence our options, choices, points-of-view, and to some extent even our character. For this reason, *kraevedy* tend to see the exploration of geographic space as a means of studying human consciousness and culture.

In terms of the range of issues it explores, one might perhaps reasonably compare *kraevedenie* to modern human geography. Structurally, however, the two disciplines differ in a number of significant respects. Most important, while geographers investigate both large and small units of territory and explore places both close to and distant from their own personal experiences, *kraevedy* almost invariably study discrete localities (cities, parishes, administrative regions) in which they have at one time lived or that are in some other way associated with family history, such as a long-lost patrimony or the site of a parent's death. It is highly unusual for *kraevedy* to write about places to which they have no clear personal connection. As lexicographers struggling to define *kraevedenie* sometimes acknowledge, "for the most part" this form of research represents the work of individuals who could under some rubric be classified as "local inhabitants."[3]

In this respect, *kraevedenie* closely resembles German *Heimatkunde* (literally: homeland studies), a tradition of local activism and regional geographic inquiry to which it owes a particularly obvious debt of inspiration and from which it might in a limited sense even be said to have derived. As I will explain in more detail later in this manuscript, the word *kraevedenie* entered the Russian language at the beginning of the twentieth century as one of three possible translations of *Heimatkunde*. Significantly less popular than the competing calques *rodinovedenie* (motherland studies) and *stranovedenie* (country studies), *kraevedenie* appeared in Russian publications only sporadically until the 1920s, at which time it became associated with an emerging network of provincial scientific societies that was loosely affiliated with the Academy of Sciences. Over the course of the next several decades, definitions of *kraevedenie* gradually expanded to include other institutions and the forms of regional scholarship that they practiced. In the process, the resemblance of this mode of inquiry to *Heimatkunde* significantly decreased. Compared to its German predecessor, *kraevedenie* became less exclusively provincial in character, and it gained new academic pretensions and ambitions.⁴ However, most researchers continued, even as Russian local studies to some extent professionalized, to investigate the areas in which they lived or to which they felt a personal connection. They explored landscapes that they believed had shaped their own characters and, thereby, in investigating space also worked to define the self.

Like *Heimatkunde* and, for that matter, gender studies, gay and lesbian studies, and various forms of ethnic studies in the United States, *kraevedenie* might reasonably be described as an "identity discipline." By this I mean a field dominated by scholars who strongly identify with the subject of their scholarship, perceiving it as "self" rather than "other." In such areas of specialization, the distinction between researcher and researched remains blurred at best. Historically and culturally contingent notions of identity often function as key determinants of disciplinary boundaries, and investigators frequently view their academic activities as part of a larger quest for certain political and social rights, the rectification of past injustices, self-fulfillment, self-awareness, and protection from oppression. As a result, scholarship can easily merge with activism.⁵

Scholars interested in the problem of disciplinarity often argue that identity fields do not constitute real disciplines at all. They note that such areas of specialization are marred by too much subjectivism and lack real cohesion. What, critics sometimes charge, do all the practitioners of women's studies have in common except that they work on projects that in some way involve women or notions of femaleness? They do not necessarily share the same training or even hold the same degrees; they may have vastly different interests and methodological biases. Perhaps all this to some extent represents a valid point, but it seems worth noting that the same kinds of criticism can also be leveled at a host of more traditional fields of specialization. If intellectual coherence represents the primary measure of disciplinarity, then how many areas meet the standard? Does English? Would economics, history, anthropology, medicine, or physics? In publications from the last twenty years, scholars who view "unity" as the primary benchmark of disciplinary status have labeled (or have come close to labeling) each of these fields as nondisciplines.⁶

Approaches to the study of knowledge systems that emphasize external features rather than internal consistency as the key measure of disciplinarity tend to be more inclusive and often can accommodate contemporary identity disciplines. Fields like women's studies, African American studies, and gay and lesbian studies generally exhibit most of the functional characteristics associated with disciplinary status. An elaborate academic infrastructure exists to support them: they have their own departments, professional societies, conferences, journals, grants, endowed chairs, and textbooks. They also are at least to some extent associated with specific theories, methods, techniques, and discursive strategies.[7] Scholars working in them employ a specialized vocabulary and propagate themselves by training, examining, and accrediting successors. They review each other's articles and monographs; submit and judge applications for funding; and build upon the work of their predecessors.[8] Although it would be ludicrous to argue that identity disciplines possess the degree of formalization characteristic of established fields like biology, denying them disciplinary status outright seems to ignore a significant trend: many of these areas of specialization are rapidly professionalizing and in certain cases even arguably becoming more cohesive.

In this book, I intend to treat Russian *kraevedenie* as an identity discipline, a field of specialization that combines a certain amount of external structure with substantial internal diversity; in which scholars tend to identify strongly with the subject they study; and where the pursuit of knowledge can easily merge with political and social activism. Just as women's studies throughout the globe in many respects remains bound to the feminist movement and racial and ethnic studies tied to the struggle for tolerance and equality, *kraevedenie* in Russia has always been strongly associated with the historical and ecological preservation movements, various forms of local boosterism, and, to a real extent, anticentrist sentiment. Scholars who work in institutes and centers of local studies, teach courses in *kraevedenie,* and author important textbooks in the field also often belong to nongovernmental organizations that agitate for the enforcement of restrictions on development, press for stricter pollution controls, and fight to gain or retain funding for regional museums and parks. They mix comfortably and sense themselves to have common interests with various kinds of local activists. In general, it would be fair to say that most *kraevedy* perceive themselves as part of a vibrant regional community whose unique character and voice both merits and requires protection. Interested in encouraging the growth of interest in local studies among the population at large and inclined to value many forms of speech on regional affairs, they will often include amateurs with little formal scholarly training or experience in their conferences and publishing projects: instructors who introduce material related to local studies into their elementary-schools courses, high-school students who have written exceptionally fine papers on regional history, artists whose work depicts local monuments and landscapes, as well as various sorts of enthusiasts and collectors.

A willingness to allow certain nonacademic community members to participate in scholarly forums on a limited basis represents a typical feature of identity disciplines.[9] How can fields in which research and the quest for self-knowledge are regularly equated rigidly exclude beginners and enthusiasts? Practitioners often feel impelled to encourage nonacademics starting off on what they view as the path toward self-realization and fulfillment. Moreover, many value untrained speech on identity issues for another reason: they view it as an important primary source, an example of the way in which the self they study is popularly understood and experienced. Because of their relative inclusiveness, identity disciplines often continue to resemble popular movements even after they have substantially professionalized. They remain inextricably tied to the social and political crusades from which they evolved.

What explains the popularity of *kraevedenie* in Russia today? What factors have contributed to the growth of interest in this essentially native-born identity discipline over the course of the last fifteen years? Social and political turmoil, the collapse of the Soviet Union, and the emergence of a host of new nation-states and regional entities have no doubt played a role. As borders throughout Eastern Europe have shifted, old ways of imagining and understanding the self geographically have necessarily lost much of their relevance. Suddenly no longer part of a larger Soviet population group, Russians have had to redefine themselves as a people in a number of essential ways: they have needed to revise their national historical narrative; establish ethnic, linguistic, and behavioral boundaries between themselves and their neighbors; lay claim to new symbols; and reassess their country's role on the international stage. What, they ask themselves, does it mean to be Russian? Where does Russianness begin and end? As a discipline that deals with both identity and geographic space, *kraevedenie* represents an ideal forum for the contemplation of such questions. It offers Russians today the chance to forge regional identities that are at least potentially unmarred by the nationalist (and internationalist) excesses of the Soviet period. Will all the local identities fashioned through *kraevedenie* ultimately contribute to the growth of a new national sense of belonging that tolerates and even embraces regional differences as important reflections of Russianness? Will *kraevedenie* help to draw post-Soviet Russia together much as, according to Alon Confino, *heimat* ideas and symbols did in Germany following the unification of 1871?[10] Perhaps, but it is just as easy to read contemporary Russian regionalism in general and *kraevedenie* specifically as profoundly anticentrist in orientation, more conducive to continued division than to the reemergence of a strong and relatively untroubled sense of nationhood.

Shifting borders and the need to forge new post-Soviet collective identities go far to explaining the growth of interest in local studies in Russia today. Another less obvious historical factor has also almost certainly contributed to the current boom, however. Modern Russian *kraevedenie* emerged out of the confluence of several small intellectual and cultural movements, all of which were viciously purged in the late 1920s and the early 1930s. Leading researchers ended up in prisons and camps, institutes and associations closed, and journals folded. These events proved central to the self-conception of later generations of *kraevedy*. After Stalin's death in 1953, restrictions on free speech and fear of persecution eased enough to allow *kraevedy* to rediscover their heritage. Young researchers combed through both public and private libraries and archives in search of forgotten sources; they read the books and manuscripts written by their early-twentieth-century predecessors and met with purge survivors. Inspired by what they learned, many ultimately came to understand the history and purpose of *kraevedenie* in allegorical terms. They eulogized the time just before the purge as a lost "golden age"; mourned the fallen as "martyrs," savagely slaughtered by a centralized Soviet state that in terms of its rapaciousness was wholly comparable to Rome; and identified themselves as "survivors," destined to bear a special form of enlightenment forward into the world. In the decades that followed Stalin's death, *kraevedy* worked hard to disseminate knowledge and expand the practice of *kraevedenie,* but, even when most successful, tended to perceive themselves as somehow "marginal," operating outside or even against leading social trends, and, for this reason, as possible targets for official persecution. In a sense, Russia's *kraevedy* ultimately embraced one of the central charges leveled against them in purge-era diatribes: in the post-Stalin era many practitioners came to regard *kraevedenie* as fundamentally anti-establishment.[11]

Kraevedenie's history as a martyred discipline and its countercultural self-conception in the post-Stalin years paved the way for its rapid expansion after the collapse of the Soviet Union. In the early 1990s, as other fields struggled to shake off the legacy of seventy years of communism, *kraevedenie* reveled in its heroic past. It had relatively little institutional baggage and could respond rapidly to political and social changes. Veteran investigators had often led such marginal existences during the Soviet period that they could not easily be accused of complicity in abuses of power. Strongly associated with various forms of regional activism and relatively inclusive by its very nature, *kraevedenie* seemed more democratic than many older and more established fields. When conflict between Russia's national government and local interests intensified and emerged as a key political issue in the mid-1990s, *kraevedenie* resumed its traditional function as a forum for the expression of regionalist ideas. Even as it expanded and put down new institutional roots, it remained a viable avenue for airing minority views on important issues and hence at least potentially an organizing point for new political parties and groups.[12]

I discuss the role of *kraevedenie* in post-Soviet Russia in somewhat more detail in the conclusion to this book. Earlier sections of this monograph focus on an issue that I see as more primary: the question of *kraevedenie*'s origin. I do not believe that one can fully grasp the present form of Russian local studies without tracing the history of the discipline. One must, to put the problem in more Foucaultian terms, first show how this particular discursive formation emerged out of a web of relations between centralized state government and various regional interests; the public and the private spheres; art and literary criticism, the educational profession, the scientific community, and central planning authorities; and advocates of old and new aesthetic standards and value systems.[13]

The account of the origin of modern *kraevedenie* that I provide here will center almost exclusively on a single Russian city: St. Petersburg.[14] In this sense my work resembles the studies of the German *heimat* idea in the Palatinate by Celia Applegate and in Württemberg by Alon Confino: I look at the way in which a phenomenon that existed throughout an entire country manifested itself in a single locality.[15] It is worth noting, however, that by choosing Russia's old imperial capital, I have opted to describe a regional school of *kraevedenie* that is influential as opposed to typical, the discipline's leading edge rather than its norm.[16] No other Russian city or region can claim the same kind of developed cult of place as St. Petersburg. Founded by Tsar Peter the Great in 1703 as part of an ambitious modernization and Westernization campaign, St. Petersburg from the very first represented symbolic space. It was Russia's window on Europe; the location of the country's largest port, most lavish palaces, and greatest cultural institutions. It was the self-consciously Western-looking capital of a half-Asiatic empire. During much of the last three centuries Russian writers and social commentators have used descriptions of St. Petersburg as a means of articulating views on their country's history and destiny. The city obsessed both the Slavophile and the Westernizer camps in the 1840s, most of the great polemicists of the 1860s, and many early-twentieth-century intellectuals. Depending on one's point of view, Petersburg could represent a symbol of much-needed and entirely natural progress or an "artificial" city erected in defiance of Russia's intrinsic character, the capital of a fallen empire or the cradle of the revolution. Speech about St. Petersburg almost inevitably touched upon the central problems of Russian identity. Were Russianness and Europeanness at all compatible? Should Russia strive to emulate the West? Was it behind England, Germany, and France? If so, how could it catch up? Did Russia have some special contribution to make to the world? What constituted the essential characteristics of the Russian people? Were these traits at all in evidence in St. Petersburg?

St. Petersburg's history and symbolic importance in Russian culture made it a natural site for the emergence of a strong school of local studies. In the early twentieth century, a whole series of popular associations and cultural institutions arose that sought to study Russia's northern capital and/or preserve the city's most valuable historical and architectural monuments. Profoundly innovative in many respects, they developed new techniques for the investigation and description of local landscapes; came up with concepts, programs for organizing research activity, and academic standards; coined terminology; and established far-reaching scholarly objectives. *Kraevedy* from all over Russia today acknowledge these structures as essential wellsprings from which the discipline they practice evolved. Because of both the historical contributions of these early-twentieth-century institutions and the vibrancy of local studies initiatives within St. Petersburg today, the city is widely regarded by contemporary Russian *kraevedy* as the "theoretical center" of modern *kraevedenie*. It boasts a huge number of self-professed *kraevedy* and produces more publications classifiable as works of *kraevedenie* than any other city or town in Russia. Trends that develop within its regional studies community continue, even now, to spread rapidly to scholarly collectives in other areas.

Nonetheless, my decision to write about *kraevedenie* in the context of St. Petersburg might, at least from a certain point of view, appear surprising. Although accepted as a truism by most contemporary *kraevedy,* the designation of St. Petersburg as the "theoretical center" of modern *kraevedenie* sometimes sounds paradoxical to both Russians outside the discipline and foreign observers with some knowledge of Slavic languages. The etymology of the term *kraevedenie* doubtless plays a role in fueling such reactions. In Russian, the word *krai* has a number of different meanings. It can refer to a local region or administrative district, as I noted a few pages ago, but it also calls to mind a host of other, more primary associations. It most frequently signifies the edge or furthest limit of some object or substance (*krai stola, krai odezhdy;* the edge of a table, the hem on a piece of clothing) and hence, when used in reference to units of territory, tends to suggest location on the periphery; distance from the center (*krai sela, krai sveta;* the outskirts of the village, the world's end). Given this pattern, the term *kraevedenie,* if broken down into its constituent elements, might reasonably be understood to mean the study of the hinterlands, of those areas that lie farthest from the capital. It smacks of provincialism and, as a result, when used in reference to research projects centered in and on the seat of the old imperial government sounds incongruous to many speakers of Russian. Although geographically St. Petersburg does lie on the edge of Russian territory and in the spring of 1918 the city ceased to serve as the nation's capital, it remains, in the minds of many Russians, of supreme cultural importance and hence far from provincial in character.

In this book I intend to explore those aspects of the history of *kraevedenie* that helped, despite the apparent etymological incongruity, facilitate the emergence of St. Petersburg as the discipline's "theoretical center and principal place of origin. I will look in detail at three cultural movements that were, to one extent or another, based in St. Petersburg and that contributed to the formation of modern *kraevedenie.* Chapters 2 and 3 will discuss the historical preservation movement that emerged at the very beginning of the twentieth century and that was, at least initially, loosely associated with the World of Art circle (*Mir iskusstva*). In Chapters 4 and 5, I will focus on the pedagogical excursion movement, emphasizing the work of the St. Petersburg excursion theorist Ivan Grevs and his disciple Nikolai Antsiferov. Chapter 6 will look at the network of local studies organizations that was affiliated with the Central Bureau of *Kraevedenie* (*Tsentral'noe biuro kraevedeniia* [TsBK]) of the Academy of Sciences in the 1920s. In Chapter 7, I will attempt to show how the meaning of the term *kraevedenie* shifted and expanded over time by examining a single subfield: literary *kraevedenie.* In the case of each of the three movements I discuss in this book, I will provide fairly substantive accounts of the history of specific cultural institutions and will comment on the lives and work of individual scholars. This information represents an important part of the prehistory and mythology of modern *kraevedenie* and is essential to any understanding of the discipline's current self-conception. As I have already implied, contemporary Russian *kraevedy* tend to define themselves through comparison to early twentieth-century people and institutions: as the followers of Benois, Grevs, and Antsiferov; the heirs to the traditions of the Society for the Study and Preservation of Old Petersburg, the Petrograd Excursion Institute, and the Central Bureau of *Kraevedenie.* Tremendously self-reflective as a discipline, *kraevedenie* today devotes significant energy to discussions of its emergence and evolution. Virtually every collection of scholarly essays on *kraevedenie* contains a substantial section on the careers and fate of earlier generations of regional investigators; at conferences, papers on similar topics abound. St. Petersburg preservationists, excursionists, and scholars associated with the Central Bureau of *Kraevedenie* invariably figure prominently in accounts of *kraevedenie*'s past.

Aside from an interest in the scholarly investigation of discrete geographic areas and the experience of persecution, what did early-twentieth-century preservationism, the pedagogical excursion movement, and the kind of organized local studies research promoted by the Academy of Sciences in the 1920s share? What ultimately allowed them to be perceived, at least in hindsight, as part of a single disciplinary tradition, as cornerstones of modern *kraevedenie*? Each movement had its own concerns and biases, a unique approach to the study of geographic space, and a distinct identity. Early-twentieth-century preservationists and excursionists did not, as a rule, think of themselves as *kraevedy*: until the 1930s, many Russians understood the term *kraevedenie* quite narrowly, as referring exclusively to the kind of local research promoted by the Central Bureau of *Kraevedenie*. I argue that one of the primary linkages that helped to bind the movements I study together, ultimately allowing them to be subsumed within a single disciplinary category, was *literary*. Preservationists, excursionists, and researchers associated with the Central Bureau's *kraevedenie* organizations all shared an interest in a class of descriptive texts known commonly as *putevoditeli* (roughly, guidebooks or written guides).[17] Scholars associated with these movements read these texts, drew factual information from them, collected them, wrote about them, and promoted their dissemination. Emulating the men and women they revere as "forefathers," modern *kraevedy* have continued this tradition. They consider old *putevoditeli* such essential texts that in the last fifteen years they have taken steps to reprint many classic works. Moreover, they work assiduously to promote the continued evolution of this textual form today, composing countless new *putevoditeli* every year. Although *kraevedy*, like other scholars, do write traditional book- and article-length studies, much of their most important and characteristic research reaches print in *putevoditel'* form.

What exactly is this mode of expression that is so closely associated with *kraevedenie* today? Broken down into its constituent parts, the word *putevoditel'* quite literally means "an instrument (thing) that leads or guides one (*voditel'*) along a path or route (*put'*)" and hence, viewed from an etymological perspective, is, as I have already suggested, equivalent to the English-language terms "guidebook" and "guide," in the sense of a written document. As used by most contemporary Russian readers, bibliographers, and publishers, however, the word has a somewhat broader meaning than its most obvious English-language translations tend to suggest. When applied to descriptions of geographic areas, it can refer not just to standard surveys of sights and places to stay for tourists or business travelers, but also to other, more sophisticated textual forms: inventory-like catalogs of the wonders contained in a particular Russian palace or city; multivolume compendiums of historical anecdotes, statistics, and facts about a particular area; popular surveys of architectural history; and books that provide routes and sample monologues for group tours.[18] Publications that in their titles contain the terms *opisanie* (description, in this case of a geographic area), *ekskursiia* (excursion primer), *progulka* (stroll), and sometimes even *ocherk* (sketch)—each one of which could designate a separate genre—are often referred to today as *putevoditeli,* provided they describe a geographic area and its major landmarks or the way of life of its inhabitants. In fact, in the case of at least geographic descriptions and excursion primers, this trend is so pervasive that it would be fair to say that both are generally viewed by Russian readers as subcategories within the larger category of the *putevoditel'.* A geographic description might well be defined as a *putevoditel'* that, in certain respects, resembles an inventory or catalog; the excursion primer as a *putevoditel'* that provides those planning to lead a tour to a certain site with necessary background information and a sample route.

Some of the books that contemporary Russians classify as *putevoditeli* obviously cater to the needs of tourists, business travelers, or new residents. They provide basic factual information about a particular region, city, or sight and offer helpful tips for visitors: notes on where and how to secure services; lists of hotels, restaurants, and clubs; sample itineraries; and estimated costs. A surprising number of texts, however, seem geared more to the interests of long-term local residents. They assume a high level of familiarity with the area and include little practical information. Moreover, although they may contain basic historical facts (when buildings were constructed, the names and nationalities of leading architects, the significance of various monuments), they are often not organized to allow readers to locate the answers to specific questions quickly. In many works termed *putevoditeli* today, the notion that the book itself represents an immediately useful portable tool, a kind of verbal compass that can lead the reader through physical space, holds true only on the level of metaphor. Authors, as I will explain in more detail in the next chapter, invariably imply that the landscape they survey merits our attention; they often take great pains to point out its most beautiful and interesting features; they may arrange part of their material geographically or use inclusive forms of speech that place both narrator and reader at successive locations so as to create the illusion that, as we read, we also advance through physical space. The guides they write, however, are frequently too heavy to carry on walks and make unwieldy references.

Like certain forms of biography in the West, the *putevoditel'* in Russia today appeals to a broad readership with diverse interests and requirements. Although, as I have already suggested, authors can and do craft texts with particular audiences in mind, a single well-written and researched book can attract various categories of readers: visitors to the area being described; new arrivals eager to learn about the city or region to which they have just moved; long-time local residents with an interest in history, geography, or culture; enthusiastic armchair travelers; and specialists in *kraevedenie*. As a result, such books often sell well. Works that describe Russia's two modern capitals Moscow and St. Petersburg enjoy particular popularity, no doubt for fairly obvious reasons: each city has a large population, a strong tradition of local patriotism, and a developed myth; each has played an exceptionally important role in Russian history, provides the setting for many important works of Russian literature, and represents the focus of the desires and aspirations of much of Russia's population. As Americans dream of life in New York and Hollywood, Russians fantasize about Moscow and St. Petersburg. Guidebooks about smaller regional centers and provincial areas, although they can sell well enough to justify publication, necessarily attract smaller audiences: with rare exceptions, they appeal primarily to residents (or former residents) and visitors.

Identity issues play an important role in the *putevoditel'*. In these works writers do not just describe cities, regions, and countries, they also generally strive to characterize their inhabitants. Working from either an insider's or an outsider's perspective, depending on their personal loyalties and target audience, authors consider what it means to be a Petersburger, a Muscovite, a Siberian, or a resident of some other area. They struggle to define the personality traits, behavior patterns, and attitudes that, in general, represent manifestations of Russianness. In this sense, the *putevoditel'* meshes well with both modern *kraevedenie* and many of its most obvious precursors; as a genre the guidebook intrinsically seeks to define the self (and in some cases its counterpart, the other) geographically. Early-twentieth-century preservationists, excursionists, and researchers associated with the Central Bureau of *Kraevedenie* were, no doubt, drawn to the *putevoditel'* in part because the natural tendencies of this form mirrored their own proclivities. These geographic descriptions offered the forefathers of modern *kraevedenie* the opportunity to explore two issues that particularly fascinated them: space and identity. Semipopular in tone, they could be used to communicate with both other specialists and the public at large, something that suited the activist spirit of all three movements.

Because the *putevoditel'* played such an important role in the formation of modern *kraevedenie*, because I see this textual form as a central element that helps to hold the discipline I am writing about together, I will devote considerable space in this volume to discussions of such texts. I will explain why early-twentieth-century preservationists, excursionists, and scholars associated with the Central Bureau of *Kraevedenie* saw the guidebook as an important form, show how they used old geographic descriptions as sources, and describe the way in which they both innovated and built upon preexisting descriptive traditions in the guides they authored. In order to facilitate this discussion, in Chapter 1 of this text I provide readers with some basic background information about the kinds of geographic descriptions that were written in Russia in the eighteenth and nineteenth centuries, focusing as in the body of my book on material relating to the St. Petersburg area.

Before launching into this discussion, I want to point out that, although a comparatively young city, St. Petersburg has what in Russian terms counts as an old guidebook tradition. Topographic descriptions of the city began to appear in print soon after it was founded in 1703 and quickly evolved, acquiring, in the space of a single century, many of the attributes of modern guides. By the beginning of the nineteenth century, St. Petersburg had the most developed descriptive tradition in all of Russia. Books written about the capital influenced those composed about other Russian cities and areas. In other words, in guidebook-writing as well as in local studies in general, St. Petersburg represented an important locus of innovation. Trends that appeared in this region frequently spread, prompting similar developments in other cities several years later. Therefore, although the account I provide here of the emergence and evolution of the *putevoditel'* will focus on St. Petersburg writers and texts, many of the more general observations I make will also be relevant to the examination of the guidebook's history as a national literary form.

I

The Eighteenth- and Nineteenth-Century Tradition

The first extensive topographic description of St. Petersburg appeared in print a decade after the city was founded, in the year 1713. It was written in German and published in Leipzig anonymously.[1] Historians have long speculated about the provenance and authorship of this document, proposing various theories about who composed it and how the anonymous writer came to travel to St. Petersburg. Some commentators have suggested that the text represents a translation or reworking of an original Russian manuscript, which has since been lost. It seems more likely, however, that, like most comparable works about the area from the early eighteenth century, it was composed by a foreigner: either a German traveler or, as Iurii Bespiatykh has suggested, a German employee of the Russian court, perhaps commissioned by Peter I himself to write a flattering description of the new capital for Western European consumption.[2] For the tsar, St. Petersburg represented a showcase for ongoing reforms, a material demonstration of the vast wealth and military might of the empire he governed. The city's carefully crafted Western look identified Russia as a European power and suggested that the state aspired to play an increasingly significant role in continental affairs. Disseminating accounts of the city's rapid rise amounted to a political imperative: descriptions of St. Petersburg served to highlight Russia's new ambitions and, inasmuch as they detailed the growth of military installations and defensive fortifications, might also reasonably have been presumed to deter incursions from abroad.[3] Perhaps for this reason both Peter I and his immediate successors tended to encourage Western curiosity about the area and, in order to ensure that overwhelmingly positive accounts predominated, sometimes even commissioned court employees to write about the city.[4]

Secular literary culture remained underdeveloped in Russia during the first decades of the eighteenth century. Nonecclesiastical printing houses and newspapers were only beginning to emerge; Russia had few experienced native-born writers and, particularly outside Moscow and St. Petersburg, few readers; its literary language remained largely uncodified. Given these facts, it is not surprising that most topographic descriptions of St. Petersburg dating back to this period were written by foreign-born employees of the Russian crown or European visitors and targeted audiences abroad. Swedish prisoners of war stranded in Russia during the long Northern War (1700–1721), Polish diplomats, English governesses, and Scottish doctors and army officers all wrote detailed accounts of the time they spent in Russia's new northern capital. In many cases they succeeded in getting their work published in Western Europe, and their impressions of the city attracted considerable attention.[5] Only a small number of geographic descriptions of St. Petersburg written by Russian authors during this period exist. Those that do are relatively brief and, because they either languished in archives for many years or appeared in obscure publications, had only limited circulation. The earliest and probably the most important Russian work is quite typical in this respect. It was written by an anonymous author around 1725, is five pages long, and provides a concise account of how St. Petersburg was founded. It also lists several important events, including floods, that took place during the first two decades of the city's history. This text appeared in print for the first time in the journal *The Russian Archive* (*Russkii arkhiv*) in 1863.[6]

Most other topographic descriptions of St. Petersburg composed by Russian authors in the early eighteenth century represent fragments of larger texts. Feofan Prokopovich, for instance, in his *History of the Emperor Peter the Great*, includes a few pages on the founding of Petersburg.[7] Similarly, the poet Antiokh Kantemir briefly describes the new capital in a larger work he published in Frankfurt and Leipzig in the German language in 1738.[8] At the time, Kantemir was serving as a diplomat in Western Europe. He learned that a volume entitled *Moscow Letters,* which portrayed Russia in an extremely negative light, had recently appeared in several European capitals. Concerned that the book might damage the image of Russia abroad, Kantemir, after an exchange of correspondence with Tsarina Anna Ioannovna, decided to publish a substantial rebuttal for the benefit of Western readers. Although in the original offending text St. Petersburg was barely mentioned, Kantemir included a short description of it in his treatise, no doubt assuming that a portrait of the city, which had been hailed by so many visitors as "the eighth wonder of the world," could only help in a propaganda war.

Regardless of how interesting they may seem to historians today, such descriptions of St. Petersburg did not exert a major influence on later works about the capital. They were too fragmentary and by and large inaccessible—being published in German or not at all—to make effective models for Russian writers. These brief accounts do, however, anticipate later Russian topographic descriptions of St. Petersburg in two important respects. First, all are profoundly adulatory and depict the new capital as the miraculous creation of a mighty tsar. Until well into the nineteenth century, paying homage to Peter I and to his successors represented one of the chief purposes of most geographic descriptions written about the capital.[9] To anyone who accepted the official ideology, Petersburg represented one of the Romanov dynasty's most magnificent accomplishments. Praising it, just like extolling the magnificence of the body of the tsar, represented a standard way to express loyalty to the regime.

Second, although these early descriptions often compare St. Petersburg to Western or classical cities and may note the contributions of foreign architects to the new capital's construction, they also typically represent its creation as a supremely important stage in the fulfillment of Russia's divinely foreordained and much heralded historic destiny. Detailing providential signs that appeared during the first period of the capital's construction and, in many cases, summarizing old prophesies that seem relevant to the events of the early eighteenth century, Petersburg's first chroniclers anticipate future influence and glory.[10] Just as Moscow, following the fall of Byzantium in the fifteenth century, was touted in official Russian pronouncements as the "third Rome," Christianity's new and most ardent protector, so Petersburg in these early-eighteenth-century topographic descriptions emerges as a new center from which Russia's contributions to the world will surely emanate. The tendency to view Europeanness and Russianness as mutually exclusive opposites, which gained popularity in high Russian culture as a result of the Slavophile-Westernizer debates of the 1830s, is not really anticipated in these texts: in them St. Petersburg's European look remains unproblematic and in no way undermines the city's ability to serve as a focal point for Russian messianism. As Christopher Ely points out in his study of the evolution of Russian landscape painting, concepts of national identity remained relatively diffuse in Russia throughout the eighteenth century. Discourse centered on the state's international significance rather than on the "innate" characteristics of its territory or people and, as a result, the view that Europeanization represented a natural process, the pursuit of Russia's destiny as opposed to divergence from it, tended to predominate, at least in the written documents produced by Russia's small educated elite.[11]

The first book-length topographic description of St. Petersburg written by a Russian author builds on both of these traditions. It was composed between 1749 and 1751 by Andrei Bogdanov, the assistant librarian at the Academy of Sciences Library. Bogdanov had apparently been asked to prepare a brief explanatory key to a new map of the capital that was supposed to be formally presented to the Empress Elizabeth.[12] Once he began collecting research for the project, however, Bogdanov seems to have gotten carried away. By the time he submitted the final version of his text to the Academy of Sciences in June 1752, it had ballooned into a 341 folio (*list*) long manuscript with a separate map, an index, portraits of tsars Peter I and Elizabeth, and a large number of drawings of the old city.[13] Despite the fact that Bogdanov had clearly strayed from the assignment he had been given, he apparently continued to hope that his manuscript would be presented to the empress. He opened the text with a lengthy dedication to her in which he explicitly compared her current building campaigns to the enormous construction projects carried out under her father.

> Everyone knows, Most Gracious Majesty, how vast and magnificent this city of Tsars [*Tsarstvuiushchii Grad*], St. Petersburg, has been since the beginning of its construction. Your parent, who is Dearly remembered and Eternally Worthy of Glory, His Imperial Majesty, the Lord and Emperor Peter the Great, amidst his most arduous and unceasing military labors, deigned to found it to the glory of his name. But if one were to compare its former condition to its current, then there would be as much of a difference as between a first foundation and perfection. For by the zealous diligence of Your Imperial Majesty, this city has now so

expanded and is adorned and exalted with such glorious new buildings that it is superior in this respect to many glorious European cities that are renowned for their antiquity. This [brings] indescribable glory to the Founder himself and particularly to Your Imperial Majesty.[14]

Throughout much of his description, Bogdanov maintains this panegyric tone. He compares the ascension of Peter I to the Russian throne to the sudden appearance of the sun in a sky that previously was dark with clouds. He repeatedly reminds his reader that the founding of St. Petersburg represented the result of both Peter's ceaseless striving and the will of God. Peter, we are told, was as wise as Solomon, as adept at military matters as Cyrus the Great, and erected as many fine buildings as the French King Louis the XIV. He is explicitly referred to as a "Second Constantine" who founded for himself a *Tsarstvuiushchii Grad*—a city of tsars, of caesars—in which he could rule so "merrily, with such love and delight" that it was almost as if he were ruling in "Holy Zion." His successors, particularly his daughter Elizabeth, are worthy of praise for continuing to carry out his policies and making St. Petersburg more glorious with each passing day. The city itself, although only recently created, already surpasses the great cities of Europe by many measures and promises to continue to grow in beauty and international significance with each passing year.[15]

Despite all these fine sentiments, Bogdanov's manuscript, perhaps because of its length, was not published as a supplement to the official map for which it had been commissioned. Instead, a smaller text written by an anonymous author took its place, and Bogdanov ended up depositing his manuscript in the Academy of Sciences Library. It remained there for several decades, periodically attracting the attention of visitors. Several copies were made, and one of these apparently caught the eye of poet Vasily Ruban. In 1776 he published a note in the monthly journal *A Collection of Various Compositions and News* (*Sobranie raznykh sochinenii i novostei*), stating that in the near future he intended to publish Andrei Bogdanov's description of the city of St. Petersburg.[16] Three years later, Ruban fulfilled this promise to the public. He printed Bogdanov's 1749–51 manuscript, but with a number of significant changes.[17] He added new material to the manuscript in an effort to bring it up to date and also made a number of "corrections" to the original text, changing dates and facts that he felt to be inaccurate. By and large contemporary historians have been critical of these changes.[18] They acknowledge, however, that Ruban's edition of Bogdanov's manuscript, regardless of how flawed, played an enormous role in increasing the Russian reading public's interest in the history of St.

Petersburg. It encouraged many other would-be entrepreneurs to go out and look for similar texts, raw accounts of Russia's recent past by eyewitnesses that could either be printed as is or used as sources for more modern descriptions of the city.

It also brought Bogdanov a measure of posthumous glory. Underpaid and little appreciated during the decades he spent working for the Academy of Sciences, Bogdanov was promptly forgotten following his death in 1766. Almost no one remembered that he had once played a key role in managing day-to-day operations at the Academy of Sciences Library, helped supervise a Japanese language school, and contributed to various academic publications. Ruban's edition of Bogdanov's long-forgotten manuscript established the author as St. Petersburg's first great chronicler and generated interest in his life and work. In the early nineteenth century, researchers discovered a second text about St. Petersburg by Bogdanov. After turning in his first manuscript to the Academy of Sciences in 1751, Bogdanov, it seems, had continued to collect information about the city and had composed a supplement to his original work covering the period from 1751 to 1762. An excerpt from this text appeared in the periodical *Son of the Fatherland* (*Syn Otechestva*) in 1839.[19] The entire manuscript was finally published in time for St. Petersburg's two-hundredth anniversary in the year 1903.[20]

Aside from Bogdanov's work, the most important book-length topographic description of St. Petersburg from the eighteenth century to be published in the Russian language is undoubtedly Johann Gottlieb Georgi's *Description of the Russian Imperial Capital City St. Petersburg and the Memorable Sites in Its Suburbs, with a Map* (*Opisanie rossiissko-imperatorskogo stolichnogo goroda Sankt-Peterburga i dostopamiatnostei v okrestnostiakh onogo s planom*). Born in Pomerania and educated in Sweden, Georgi was invited to Russia in the 1770s to participate in a scientific expedition to Siberia that was being led by the German naturalist Peter Simon Pallas. He ended up staying on in St. Petersburg after returning from the expedition. He served as head of the Chemistry Laboratory at the Academy of Sciences and practiced medicine. Fascinated with his adopted home, he also soon began to collect information about St. Petersburg and, in 1791, published a book-length German-language topographic description of the city at a St. Petersburg publishing house. In 1793, a second German-language edition of this book appeared in Riga, and a French translation was issued in St. Petersburg. In the following year, the book was translated into Russian and published in a significantly amended form in St. Petersburg. Georgi made changes to his original text for the Russian-language edition, as he explains in the preface he wrote to the volume, because he realized that he was suddenly targeting a new readership. His first edition had been aimed primarily at an audience of "foreigners—either living here or in other states." With his 1794 edition, he was trying instead "to satisfy the Russian public."[21] Hence, he omitted a great deal of information about local traditions and living conditions that native inhabitants would not have found interesting or helpful. He also took the opportunity to correct mistakes that he had discovered in his earlier work and to update it significantly.

Although written by a foreigner and originally published in German, Georgi's description deserves more than passing mention here because it influenced so many later Russian works about the capital. To the present day, it remains the great encyclopedic guide to eighteenth-century Petersburg. Aside from a description of each of the five main sections of the city (the St. Petersburg Side, Vasilievsky Island, the Admiralty Side, the Vyborg Side, and the Liteinaia District), it also includes a whole variety of other useful resources: a discussion of the Hermitage and a list of the treasures it contained; information about schools, hospitals, churches, and charitable institutions; lists of government departments and individuals holding prominent posts at court; and accounts of state and popular holidays. Bogdanov had included a good deal of factual material of this kind in his description as well, but the portrait Georgi provided of the city was infinitely more complete. Unlike Bogdanov who, as a true pioneer, largely had to forge ahead on his own, collecting information as best he could, Georgi had clear models to work from. He mentions in his introduction that he patterned his book after a German guide to Berlin and also that he used both Bogdanov's work and an assortment of foreign travel accounts as sources. In addition, he thanks a large number of high-ranking officials for helping him to gain access to archives and for allowing him to tour institutions normally inaccessible to the public. Empress Catherine II herself is specifically thanked for permitting him to view and write about the Hermitage.[22]

The introduction to the Russian edition of Georgi's work, in fact, is so packed with acknowledgments that it leaves one with the impression that the production of this amended version represented something of a state priority. "The imperial capital of St. Petersburg," Georgi announces in the opening of his introduction, "by virtue of its size, grandeur, and the many sites it contains, is at least no less worthy of an exact description . . . than any of the major cities in Europe." Despite all the difficulties entailed in assembling such a description, Georgi adds, "knowing the *usefulness* [italics mine] a topographical description of St. Petersburg would have," he had willingly invested a considerable amount of time and effort in the initial German-language edition of his book. For similar reasons, when he was asked by certain "lovers of literature" (*liubiteli slovesnosti*) to put together a Russian-language version of his book in 1793, he had immediately agreed and began collecting additional information on the city.[23]

Why did Georgi and his unnamed backers see producing an adequate description of St. Petersburg for Russian readers as such an essential task? The text of Georgi's book does not provide a direct answer to this question. Judging by the amount of factual information about specific institutions and regulations included in the book, however, it seems likely that at least in part they did envision the volume as a useful reference tool, a resource to which both residents and visitors from the provinces might turn in search of answers to specific practical questions. Georgi's description also, however, fulfilled a variety of other functions. Like Bogdanov's earlier work, it served in part as a record of the accomplishments of the Romanov tsars. Although somewhat less florid in his praise of the ruling dynasty than his predecessor, Georgi does continually acknowledge the role that various rulers, particularly Peter I and Catherine II, played in the growth of the city. Each time he mentions a charitable institution or an improvement in local services, he is careful to note Her Majesty's involvement in the project and to detail any specific contributions she may have made. Furthermore, like Bogdanov, Georgi takes pains to emphasize the enormous changes that are continuously taking place in the landscape of the capital. At one point, after recommending that readers try to look out upon the city from several different elevated points so that they might get a better sense of its varied and constantly evolving appearance, Georgi concludes: "Comparing the current condition of the capital with its previous inhospitableness and wildness, taking into account its brief existence and keeping in mind the fact that only two rulers really assisted in its adornment and return [to splendor] one's soul is filled with rapture."[24] Reminding readers of the almost miraculous changes that had taken place in the area in the course of a single century seems to have been an important part of the mission of these eighteenth-century topographic descriptions. Petersburg's rapid development, all the new architectural marvels, parks, and cultural institutions, stand in these texts as proof of the Russian Empire's growing wealth, power, and importance in the world. The assistance Georgi apparently received from the tsarist regime while preparing the Russian-language edition of his description highlights the fact that inculcating this basic message in domestic audiences often represented as much of a priority for Russia's rulers as spreading it abroad.

In a number of important respects, Georgi's 1794 description of St. Petersburg much more closely resembles a modern Russian guide than Bogdanov's earlier effort. Unlike Bogdanov, who consistently structured his text thematically, devoting discrete chapters to topics such as islands, rivers, palaces, and trading rows, Georgi organized at least certain sections of his book geographically. Such an approach is the norm in contemporary works and often helps, even in the case of unwieldy volumes, to sustain the illusion that the guidebook might conceivably be used as a practical aid to navigation. Although his description is quite large and too encyclopedic to make a convenient portable reference, Georgi clearly hopes the book will inspire his readers to go out and explore the physical city. He frequently points out "noteworthy sights" and "marvelous spectacles" in a tone that seems calculated to encourage visits.[25] As I have already noted, in one place in his description he specifically recommends that readers make an effort to inspect the city from an elevated point like the Admiralty. In the nineteenth century, lists of landmarks readers should visit, detailed notes on routes that might be used as the basis for walking or carriage tours, and long descriptions of the city's panorama from a bird's-eye view all became standard features of Russian guides.

Does Georgi's description deserve to be classified as a *putevoditel'*? That, of course, depends on how one defines the term. Georgi himself employs the word only once in his 1794 description. In the introduction to his book, he writes that he hopes the work will serve as a "substitute for a guidebook [*putevoditel'*] when one goes out to inspect and observe the sites, the excellent features [of the area] and so forth."[26] As the Russian researcher Olga Ostroi has pointed out, this statement suggests that Georgi believed the work he had penned, although capable of fulfilling some of the same functions as a guidebook, did not fully meet what he perceived as the standards of the genre.[27] In all likelihood Georgi understood the guidebook as a simple, utilitarian textual form, written with the sole intent of helping travelers navigate their way through an unfamiliar city. Such a view was probably typical for the time. The term *putevoditel'*, which first appeared in the title of a Russian geographic description in 1792, was, until relatively late in the nineteenth century, most frequently applied to relatively concise pragmatic texts.[28] When referring to longer and more ambitious works of geographic description like Georgi's book, Russian writers and publishers tended to employ the term *opisanie,* which they perceived as more general in meaning. The difference in usage was, however, very slight and not always observed perfectly. Even in the early nineteenth century books appeared with the word *putevoditel'* in their titles that were four volumes long and contained far more detailed historical information than the average sightseer could be assumed to need.²⁹ Works referred to by their authors as *opisaniia* often included the same kinds of references to strolls and sights that characterized *putevoditeli.*

Two books written about St. Petersburg in the first decades of the nineteenth century can help to illustrate the potential for and problems endemic to defining the *putevoditel'* and the *opisanie* as separate genres even in this early period: Pavel Svinin's five-part *Noteworthy Sights in St. Petersburg and Its Environs* (*Dostopamiatnosti Sanktpeterburga i ego okrestnostei;* 1816–1828), a work generally described by its creator as an *opisanie,* and Fyodor Shreder's 1820 *Newest Guidebook to St. Petersburg* (*Noveishii putevoditel' po Sankt-Peterburgu*), the first description of Russia's northern capital to contain the word *putevoditel'* in its title. At first glance, the books appear to differ markedly, exemplifying, on a basic physical level, the distinction that many late-eighteenth-century and early-nineteenth-century Russian-speakers seem to have perceived between the terms *opisanie* and *putevoditel'.* Extant copies of Svinin's description are bound into either four or five lavishly illustrated volumes, each of which is more than ten inches high and far too heavy for readers to carry conveniently on strolls. Shreder's one-volume guide is comparatively small and light.³⁰ Aside from a single inserted map, it contains no illustrations and hence could be sold relatively cheaply to a mass audience. Compared to Svinin's work, Shreder's guide seems terse and pragmatic: descriptions of individual sights and accounts of the achievements of members of the ruling family are generally short, and more practical information is provided, including tips on how to enroll a child in a military academy, find a hotel, report a dishonest carriage-driver, and register a passport.

If one looks beyond these obvious differences, however, the books, in many respects, appear quite similar. Both Svinin and Shreder aimed to reach a fairly broad audience, including to some extent, longtime residents of St. Petersburg as well as domestic and foreign travelers.³¹ Both suggest places readers might visit, indicate which elevated points offer the best panoramic views of the city, and sketch out, in at least a fragmentary form, routes for sight-seeing tours.³² Despite the seemingly prohibitive size of his description, Svinin, like Shreder, at times even suggests that readers might, at least on certain occasions, carry individual volumes along on jaunts, relying upon them as a kind of printed *cicerone.*³³

Over time the similarities between *opisaniia* and *putevoditeli* no doubt came to seem more important than their differences. Today writers, publishers, and, in some cases, scholars often group the books I have discussed by Georgi, Svinin, Shreder, and even Bogdanov together, labeling them all with the now general term *putevoditel'*, because they see them as fulfilling the same functions and as part of a single expressive tradition. All of these books represent important precursors to modern Russian guides; all exercised an important influence on later written representations of St. Petersburg. In this monograph, I accept the loose contemporary definition of the word *putevoditel'*, understanding the term as encompassing both the late eighteenth-century and early nineteenth-century book-length descriptions that I have discussed here and their obvious descendants. I classify as guidebooks all primarily nonfictional descriptive texts that aid (or claim to aid) the reader in navigating physical space, list noteworthy sights, and sketch out routes for strolls or tours in at least a rudimentary form. The category, as I see it, includes both brief, practical texts designed to meet the needs of travelers and longer, less utilitarian works that might appeal to longtime residents of the areas they describe; volumes that might, even under the most restrictive definition of the word, be safely categorized as *putevoditeli* and those originally viewed by their authors as *opisaniia*.

In one other respect, the topographic descriptions written by Svinin and Shreder merit note in the context of a survey of the development of the guidebook as a genre and of depictions of St. Petersburg specifically. In keeping with the pattern set by their eighteenth-century precursors, both authors take a strong patriotic position. They continually extol the achievements of the Romanov dynasty, noting the empire's fine cultural and social institutions; low crime rate; polite, efficient state bureaucracy; and growing influence abroad.[34] Moreover, these texts also reflect a new kind of ethnic nationalism that, as many scholars have noted, began to gain currency in Russian culture during the early nineteenth century as a result of both the influence of European romanticism and the new sense of cultural unity that emerged as Russians from all social classes fought together to defeat Napoleon.[35] After the War of 1812, statements on Russian identity increasingly involved, in addition to assertions of the empire's equivalence or superiority to the great powers of the West, attempts to isolate virtues, traits, and popular traditions distinctive of the Russian people as an *ethnos*. In keeping with this trend, Shreder and, even more obviously, Svinin identify certain positive behaviors as typically Russian. Svinin, for instance, writes that, besides Russia, "no other nation has such a fortunate talent for the arts or is endowed with such intelligence." When drunk, he notes, "Russians do not seethe and curse, but embrace, ask forgiveness, and make vows of friendship—this is the distinctive tendency of our people just as the inhabitants of southern countries are distinguished by their brutality when they are drunk!"[36] Although generally more restrained in his rhetoric, Shreder also on occasion calls attention to positive Russian traits and traditions, noting, for instance, the politeness, helpfulness, and love of art displayed by all classes of society in the empire's capital.[37] Once again treated as a fundamentally Russian city despite its European look, St. Petersburg in these texts emerges as both the center of imperial power, the locus from which Russia's messianic energy radiates out into the world, and a site in which virtues peculiar to Russians as an ethno-cultural group might reasonably be detected.[38] Imperial identity and tentative efforts to characterize the Russian people as an ethnos blend together here, producing a vision of Russianness that remains diffuse enough to encompass Peter's modern capital.

Readers familiar with the history of Russian literature will doubtless sense parallels between the descriptive norms employed in the guidebooks I have discussed thus far and the representations of St. Petersburg provided in a host of classic literary works from approximately the same period, including, most notably, a series of odes by Mikhail Lomonosov, Alexander Sumarokov, and Gavrila Derzhavin that are often hailed by literary scholars as the first true masterpieces of St. Petersburg description. Like Bogdanov, Georgi, Svinin, and Shreder, these poets tended to depict St. Petersburg in overwhelmingly positive terms and often used descriptions of the capital as opportunities for the expression of gratitude and fealty to the ruling Romanov dynasty. For them, St. Petersburg represented "the empress of cities."[39] Building upon the notion of Moscow as the Third Rome, they argued in their work that the new capital had superseded not only this ancient metropolis but also Athens, Venice, Amsterdam, and Paris. In one ode, Lomonosov compares St. Petersburg to the heavens, noting that the city appears to emit a continuous stream of light: the water in the Neva river, the gilding and polished marble on the palaces all shine and sparkle.[40] This simile, in addition to hinting at the notion of St. Petersburg as a holy, celestial city, a New Jerusalem, calls to mind the sun imagery used in representations of Louis XIV in seventeenth-century France. Like the court of Versailles, we are led to believe, St. Petersburg represents the chief residence of a supreme monarch who beneficently provides her subjects with light, warmth, and order.[41] The comparisons between the Russian imperial capital and foreign cities that fill eighteenth-century verse are invariably positive in tone: writers consistently describe St. Petersburg as equaling or surpassing potential rivals; as in early topographic descriptions of the northern city, the fact that such comparisons can be posited in no way undermines the imperial capital's capacity to serve as the focus of Russia's historical aspirations.

Poetic paeans to St. Petersburg as seat of imperial power began to fall out of fashion at the end of the eighteenth century as the state ode, the literary genre most characteristically used for the expression of political panegyrics, went into decline. In the 1810s and 1820s depictions of St. Petersburg grew markedly more diverse. In rapidly evolving forms, like the lyric poem and the essay, some authors continued to speak, albeit with somewhat more restraint, about the city's majestic prospects; the stately facades of its palaces, churches, and other public buildings; and the role of past and reigning emperors in promoting new construction. They wondered at St. Petersburg's brief history, noting that the capital had reached its present state in the space of scarcely more than a hundred years.[42] Other writers, however, began to depict the city in strikingly different terms. Young poet-officers who had returned from the Napoleonic Wars hungry for political reform, those who supported or sympathized with the abortive rebellion staged on Senate Square in December 1825, often made reference in their work to the dampness and unhealthfulness of the local climate; the capital's grim darkness during the long northern winters; and the pettiness, ignorance, and idle malice of court society. For them St. Petersburg represented the chief bastion of intractable autocracy, the city in which the tyranny that characterized all of Russian life was most keenly felt.[43] Imported architectural styles and improvements in urban planning could not, they believed, mask the fact that in terms of essential political freedoms Russia remained far behind its Western European rivals.

The negative trend in the depiction of St. Petersburg that emerged at the beginning of the nineteenth century developed rapidly and, as early as the 1830s and 1840s, might reasonably be regarded as dominant in high literature. In these decades, Russian writers produced a whole series of masterpieces in which the city at least at times appeared bleak, frightening, and, in some cases, potentially malevolent, a hostile environment in which individual citizens might easily come to ruin. Alexander Pushkin's *The Bronze Horseman* (written in 1833; published in 1837) is often identified as a key turning point. Many scholars have noted that although in the introduction to this poem Pushkin describes St. Petersburg in a celebratory tone that seems deliberately to recall the great panegyric odes of the eighteenth century, he shifts register as he moves into the body of his narrative and ultimately presents a far less positive view of the capital. Describing the cataclysmic flood of 1824 in meticulous detail, he notes the gloom that overshadowed the city and the "thunderous fury" of the river Neva. In the last section of the poem, Pushkin's hero Evgenii, an impoverished ex-civil servant who loses his mind after his beloved perishes in the disaster, shakes his fist at the statue of the city's founder "whose will, implacable as doom, had chosen seashore for his city."[44]

Soon after the composition of *The Bronze Horseman,* a string of other works depicting St. Petersburg in strikingly dark tones appeared: Nikolai Gogol's "Nevsky Prospect," "The Portrait," "Diary of a Madman," "Nose," and, most important, "The Overcoat"; Fyodor Dostoevsky's *Poor Folk;* and various pieces by Mikhail Lermontov and Vladimir Odoevsky.[45] In many of these works, as in Pushkin's *The Bronze Horseman,* "little men" take center stage. Petty clerks subsisting on meager salaries see their dreams of happiness dashed; oppressed by the harsh conditions prevailing in the capital, they go mad or take to drink. Signs of the devil's influence on events (or at least the wrath of God) abound; St. Petersburg often appears a hellish, accursed place that arose with unnatural speed and might just as quickly disappear. In this last respect, texts from this period build upon an important element in the Russian folk tradition: opposition to the Petrine reforms in the early eighteenth century gave rise to a host of anecdotes, prophesies, and curses that labeled Peter I the Antichrist and his new capital an unholy seat.[46] In the 1830s and 1840s, while the great debates between the Slavophiles and Westernizers were taking place, this aspect of the city's image and myth at last began to find more regular and prominent reflection in high literature. As leading intellectual figures spoke out for and against Westernization, as they argued about the ultimate effect of Peter's modernization campaign, St. Petersburg, the principal locus of the great reforms of the early eighteenth century, necessarily emerged as supremely problematic space. For Slavophiles the city represented an artificial creation, fundamentally alien to Russia's true nature, and, as such, exemplified all the mistakes of the eighteenth century, including the abandonment of indigenous traditions and of Russia's destiny as an Orthodox Slavic state. For Westernizers it served as a constant reminder of how far the Empire still had to go; the city's neat facades and orderly grid of streets, if anything, made the contradictions and inequities present in every aspect of Russian social life all the more glaring. Neither group could look at the city at all complacently.

Because conventions for describing the city of St. Petersburg in guidebooks and canonical literary texts largely coincided in the eighteenth and early nineteenth centuries, one might reasonably expect similar patterns of development to prevail in later periods as well. To some extent, certainly, they do. In the 1830s and 1840s a new generation of guidebook writers appeared who, in keeping with the trend toward the depiction of "little men" in poetry and fiction, began to craft descriptions of the St. Petersburg that accorded unprecedented attention to less prosperous segments of the city's population. Alexander Bashutsky, for instance, in his innovative 1834 *Panorama of St. Petersburg* (*Panorama Sanktpeterburga*) divides the residents of the capital into five separate categories (high society, the educated public, the third estate, foreigners, and the lower classes) and then spends dozens of pages characterizing the living habits and appearance typical for members of each group.[47] Similarly, in his 1841 *Description of St. Petersburg and the Chief Towns of the Regions of the St. Petersburg Gubernia* (*Opisanie Sanktpeterburga i uezdnykh gorodov S. Peterburgskoi gubernii*), Ivan Pushkarev devotes substantial space to the habits of the petty manufacturers, street tradesmen, and common swindlers of the capital.[48]

The introduction of such sociological material in guidebooks, while undoubtedly significant, did not, however, coincide with or herald the kind of shift in tone, the consistent darkening of mood, common to both poetic and fictional descriptions of St. Petersburg from this period. The reasons for this are no doubt in part generic. The central trope of the guidebook, the notion of the reader as real or would-be sightseer and the text as functional navigational aid, encourages a primarily positive orientation. By selecting a particular city or site for description, the guidebook writer labels it as a worthwhile destination and nourishes the reader's desire to explore; the reader will, he implies, by surveying the area, gain pleasure, enlightenment, or some other tangible benefit. Although guidebook writers can and do acknowledge flaws in the landscapes they describe, although they may provide information on unpleasant or tragic aspects of local history and life, they must shape this material so as not to diminish interest in touring the area or they risk stripping the text of its functionality and purpose. In order to place themselves properly in the narrative, in order to become fully engaged in the book, readers must want to move along the route the writer has prescribed; they must retain their enthusiasm for the process of regional exploration. For this reason, in guidebooks, natural disasters, scandals, failures of governance, and other negative events often appear as setbacks that have or can be overcome, lessons from which the reader can learn, or mildly titillating episodes that, if anything, lend piquancy to the region's image. Poverty, crime, and other social problems rarely evoke the extreme notes of horror and pathos so often found in works of nineteenth-century poetry and fiction.[49] In many instances, descriptions of lower-class inhabitants serve primarily as local color.

Much like the state ode, the guidebook as a form might be said to have innate panegyric tendencies. In it the subject described is generally elevated rather than cast down. Writers strive to isolate the unique characteristics and features of the place they have chosen to depict; they argue for its importance; they seek to instill in their readers an appreciation for its peculiar merits and charms. Just as state odes tend to highlight and reinforce the bonds between the subject and autocrat, populace and motherland, guidebooks will, whether written for outsiders or residents, in most instances promote the development and growth of some form of geographic attachment.[50] Because this core orientation never changes, because in all periods guidebook writers will tend to apotheosize if not the present then at least the past or future potential of the area they survey, in St. Petersburg such works will often seem, even as they evolve and broaden their focus, in a limited sense, to remain true to eighteenth-century and early-nineteenth-century descriptive tradition. Like Georgi and Svinin, guidebook writers from the 1830s and 1840s aim, in addition to providing readers with practical tips about how to get around the capital, to instill in them an appreciation for St. Petersburg's many fine architectural monuments, dramatic past, and unique role as a center of Russian political life and culture.[51] With great pride and enthusiasm, they detail the workings of the capital's most important social, educational, and administrative institutions, describe panoramic views glimpsed from observation decks and church spires, and sketch out routes for tours through the city. Although, by this time, writers no longer seem to view guidebooks chiefly as vehicles for praise of the Romanov dynasty, most authors continue to pay homage to at least certain members of the imperial family in their descriptions. Peter I strides through most guides like a demigod—all-powerful, inscrutable, and ceaselessly laboring for the good of the fatherland. Maria Fyodorovna, the widow of the doomed emperor Paul, is singled out for special praise in connection with her many charitable efforts. As ruling monarch, Nicholas I receives at least a certain measure of attention. St. Petersburg's creation is invariably understood in positive terms. When acknowledged at all, hardships connected with the city's rapid construction and harsh climate serve to enhance appreciation for St. Petersburg's current glory.

The literary forms that the guidebook most closely resembles in the mid-nineteenth century are the sketch (*ocherk*) and the feuilleton. Like guidebooks, sketches and feuilletons frequently describe geographic areas. In them a first-person narrator often strolls through a city, remarking on specific scenes, sites, and sounds. The literary critic Gary Saul Morson argues in his book *The Boundaries of Genre* that sketches and feuilletons seem at once to belong to real life and to art, to display characteristics of both journalistic reporting and of great literature, of traditionally aesthetic and nonaesthetic communicative forms.[52] Something similar might be said about guidebooks. In the 1830s and 1840s, such texts began, on occasion, to incorporate fictional elements and literary flourishes. Victor Burianov's 1838 *A Stroll with Children Through St. Petersburg and the Surrounding Regions* (*Progulka s det'mi po S.-Peterburgu i ego okrestnostiam*) represents a particularly striking example of this trend. A semifictionalized account of a multiweek tour of the capital, it is broken up into a series of "days," each one of which constitutes a separate stroll or jaunt. The first-person narrator moves about St. Petersburg in the company of a group of young charges, commenting in the present tense on everything they see or experience. The text is replete with references to weather, helpful acquaintances, and the minor inconveniences of travel. The use of first- and second-person plural pronouns and verb forms throughout the narrative, the constant repetition of "we" and "you," invites the reader to consider himself or herself as part of the happy collective and to set out on a jaunt, following the routes so carefully documented in the book. For all the fictional flourishes that embellish the narrative, Burianov's *Stroll* seems intended, at least in part, for use as a practical guidebook. In the first pages of the text, the author takes pains to inform the presumably provincial children preparing to join him on his stroll of what documents and supplementary bibliographic resources they should assemble before departing for St. Petersburg. Throughout the book he gives his reader precise instructions for navigating his or her way through the city; he also sometimes notes shopping opportunities, suggests places to stay in the suburbs, and provides information about available means of transportation.[53]

Although for the most part nonfictional in tone, Bashutsky's *Panorama of St. Petersburg* also might in certain respects be termed literary in its tendencies. It contains, in addition to a lengthy account of the city panorama from a bird's-eye view and fragmentary descriptions of walking tours, one section that obviously represents a fictional composition. In a chapter entitled "A Petersburg Day in 1723," the author imagines how, in that particular year, a series of fictional characters might have celebrated Peter I's saint's day. He describes a visit to a tavern, the drunken revelry of the Prince-Pope (*kniaz'-papa*), and a ball (*assambleia*).[54] At the end of the day, the principal hero of the tale, a young nobleman who has long refused to adapt to the new Western norms of social behavior, finally shaves off his beard and wins the hand of his sweetheart.

If guidebooks, sketches, and feuilletons resemble each other in so many respects, if all three genres are often used to explore geographic space, employ the trope of the stroll, and straddle the boundary between traditionally aesthetic and nonaesthetic modes of communication, then what makes each form unique? In what way does the *putevoditel'* differ from other descriptive texts? A number of factors make it difficult to draw rigid distinctions. Each category includes significant variation—the terms *ocherk* and *putevoditel'*, in particular, are arguably very broad. In certain cases genres clearly overlap—sometimes a portion of a guide may, for example, reasonably be said to constitute a sketch or a feuilleton. In a number of instances individual authors contributed to the development of more than one descriptive form.[55] Some generalizations can, however, be productively advanced. Unlike sketches and feuilletons, guidebooks do not depend on the trope of fragmentariness and the illusion of haphazard spontaneity.[56] Although in some cases writers may affect a discursive air, the form itself by no means necessitates such a manner. Guidebooks are often relatively long; feuilletons and sketches tend to brevity. In written guides the reader always plays the role of prospective sightseer, and the text itself is at least imagined as a kind of navigational aid. Typically writers draw us in with strings of first- and second-person pronouns, they give practical tips for easing our passage through a site or area, and they suggest we follow in their footsteps along the routes outlined in the guide. Although many guidebooks are too heavy to carry along on jaunts, and may include more background information than ordinary sightseers and travelers tend to require, they can at least in general terms be understood to assist the reader in the practical work of exploring physical space by facilitating the planning of travel and/or strolls.

In feuilletons and sketches, the narrator most often serves as our proxy rather than as a guide or companion. Armed with leisure time and, at least potentially, special skills, insight, connections, and savoir-faire, he or she visits and reports on realms in many cases far removed from our experience. We are not assumed to possess the capacity or even want to duplicate these adventures. The narrator in many cases seems to wander almost aimlessly, following personal whim, chasing after transitory stimuli and current news, as opposed to moving along a carefully conceived model route. The narrator's travels lead to discoveries about people and places that he or she graciously agrees to share, thereby freeing us from the obligation to cover the same territory ourselves. Often a sketch will function as a kind of journalistic exposé: it will reveal hidden or unsavory aspects of local life. Unlike in guidebooks, writers do not necessarily evaluate or promote the sites and areas they describe as potential destinations for tours and strolls.

Sketches and feuilletons achieved significant popularity in Russia in the 1830s and the 1840s, just as the image of St. Petersburg in poetry and fiction was beginning to darken. The semijournalistic character of both forms made them ideal vehicles for ruminations on contemporary Russian life and social problems. Seized upon by talented writers and critics associated with various literary and philosophical camps, they quickly evolved into key forums for partisan sallies and debate. The great dispute that raged between the Westernizers and Slavophiles in this period, for instance, played out partly in the pages of sketches. Most notably, in 1845 a group of writers associated with *Notes of the Fatherland* (*Otechestvennye zapiski*), the principal publication organ of the Westernizers and home to the radical critic Vissarion Belinsky, released a tremendously influential sketch anthology entitled *A Physiology of Petersburg* (*Fiziologiia Peterburga*). Replete with witticisms at the expense of the rival Slavophile camp in Moscow, the collection played an important role in popularizing the physiological sketch, a subgeneric form introduced in Russia at the beginning of the decade on the basis of French models. Authors of physiological sketches characteristically sought to study and classify man scientifically by crafting detailed portraits of typical representatives of individual professions, social castes, and nationalities. They also showed an interest in the functional analysis of geographic space. In some cases explicitly equating cities to living organisms, they broke them down into their constituent parts and attempted to understand the mechanisms that supported their existence. They looked at the streets, rivers, and forms of transportation that bound them together (circulatory system); the markets and stores that fed them (digestive tract); the organs of mass communication and cultural institutions that simultaneously shaped the taste and expressed the character of local citizens (personality/mind/spirit/soul). Many physiological sketches focused on the lower strata of society and seemed to have progressive political implications suited to the views of leading Westernizers. They depicted the deplorable conditions in which the poor lived so vividly that they read as a clarion call to social action.

In the introduction that he penned for *A Physiology of Petersburg*, Belinsky challenged Russian writers to take the collection as an example and devote more attention to describing Russian territory. He noted that despite scattered efforts in the 1830s, Russian society continued to suffer from a lack of good

> belletristic works in the form of travel narratives [*puteshestviia*], accounts of tours [*poezdki*], sketches, stories, and geographic descriptions [*opisaniia*] that would acquaint [the public] with the various parts of boundless and diverse Russia that includes within itself so many climates,

so many peoples and tribes, so many faiths and customs; the indigenous Russian population of which seems such an enormous mass with such a multiplicity of contrasting and varied layers and strata, all endlessly variegated and shaded.[57]

Although, when he composed his introduction, Belinsky doubtless aimed primarily to promote the physiological sketch as a form, his remarks also suggest support for other kinds of descriptive literature, including categories of texts that today are often casually classified as guidebooks. When, later in his introduction, he surveys earlier efforts to describe Russian territory, Belinsky singles out Bashutsky's *Panorama* for special praise.[58]

Perhaps predictably, given the polemical sallies the volume contained, Slavophiles reacted negatively to *A Physiology of Petersburg*. Konstantin Aksakov penned a scathing review of the anthology for the periodical *The Muscovite* (*Moskvitianin*) in which he derided selected passages in Belinsky's introduction as illogical and charged that the collection as a whole lacked originality, representing little more than a blind imitation of a foreign literary trend.[59] It seems worth noting, however, that Aksakov did not dispute Belinsky's assessment of the need for more literature describing Russian territory.[60] In the years that followed the publication of *A Physiology of Petersburg*, Slavophiles as well as Westernizers supported efforts to study and produce verbal portraits of the Russian Empire and its people. Writers sympathetic to the views of each group and, in some cases, leading ideologues themselves drafted works that surveyed specific cities and units of territory, highlighting social phenomena and trends that seemed particularly relevant to a discussion of the problem of national development. For many authors the habits, attitudes, and behavior of various segments of the population; living conditions in urban and rural areas; the current state of agriculture, industry, journalism, and artistic production; even local landscape features and climatic conditions represented evidence, useful in posing comprehensive answers to the great questions of the day. Had the reforms of the early eighteenth century helped Russia shed some of its backwardness and approach a Western level of development or did they represent a disastrous mistake? Did the country need to find native solutions for its problems or should it continue to follow in the footsteps of the West? How could Russianness best be defined? With what features was it most closely associated? Because Moscow and St. Petersburg had particular significance within the context of the Slavophile-Westernizer debate, they tended to attract disproportionate attention. Many authors struggled to define the character of one or both of Russia's capitals. Time and time again writers touched upon the problem of St. Petersburg's seeming foreignness: they asked themselves if the Western-looking capital that Peter I had so hastily erected as the centerpiece of his reform campaign represented modern Russia's greatest hope and achievement or a betrayal of the country's true nature.[61]

As Russian writers began to spend increasing amounts of time crafting belletristic descriptions of geographic space, as the value the literary world assigned to sketches, feuilletons, and other short descriptive forms soared, one might think that guidebooks would have flourished. In fact, however, the production of guidebooks to St. Petersburg declined sharply in the late 1840s and remained low until the end of the 1860s. The Central Statistical Committee of the Ministry of Internal Affairs (*Tsentral'nyi statisticheskii komitet Ministerstva vnutrennikh del*) and other administrative agencies did release some important compendiums of statistical information on St. Petersburg in this period, but these collective efforts offer little in the way of narrative and hence are useful almost solely as factual references.[62]

Several factors probably discouraged writers from producing guides to St. Petersburg in the mid-nineteenth century. First, as I have already suggested, the wave of fictional work, sketches, and feuilletons about St. Petersburg that appeared in print in the late 1830s and early 1840s gradually changed public perceptions of the city. Northern Palmyra lost much of its sheen; it came to seem darker and more phantasmagoric, a site of profound social misery where vice and crime were allowed to rage rampant. The great classical architectural ensembles that dominated the center of the city fell out of fashion. Gradually many Russians came to view the rows of uniform yellow facades that lined so many streets and squares as somehow emblematic of the rigid and tyrannical habits of the Romanov dynasty, of the regime's love of military order and persistent refusal to implement real democratic reforms. As a result, fewer and fewer people came to perceive St. Petersburg as a place of architectural marvels and noteworthy sites, the inspection of which would necessarily lead to the development of artistic taste and personal enrichment. An important component of the need for guidebooks focusing on historical and cultural landmarks (as opposed to simple directories and compendiums of geographic facts) to some extent fell away.

Second, by the middle of the 1840s Russian readers faced a glut of texts about St. Petersburg: physiological sketches, short stories and novels composed by writers of the natural school, and feuilletons and works of fiction in the new realist style. As new forms and manners of description proliferated, guidebooks must inevitably have come to seem old-fashioned and increasingly irrelevant.

The journalistic role that they had once helped to fill now seemed more than adequately executed by the city's many sketch-writers. In an era when most of educated Russian society yearned to discuss contemporary social problems—serfdom, poverty, the need for reforms—the panegyric mode of exposition with which guidebooks were associated to many must have appeared inappropriate. Interest in written guides plummeted.[63]

New guidebooks began to emerge in large numbers only relatively late in the century and then at least in part thanks to another cultural trend. In the late 1850s and the early 1860s, after the death of Tsar Nicholas I, archives that had long been almost entirely closed to researchers slowly began to open up. Censorship also loosened considerably. An official directive issued in the year 1860 gave Russian historians the right to report freely on all events that had taken place before the death of Peter I in 1725. If they wished to write about more recent history, then they did have to follow established censorship procedures, but they no longer found themselves automatically banned from attempting to describe the personalities and private lives of members of the imperial family. Looking back on this period of liberalization during which he first began to work as a historian, Mikhail Semevsky, the primary force behind the journal *Russian Olden Times* (*Russkaia starina*), later recalled:

> Sixteen years have passed since the appearance of my first historical sketches, and, from a certain point of view, I find them . . . rather weak. But I will never say that these works were useless to our public. . . . When I began to publish, most people . . . were completely ignorant about their native land. And then suddenly monographs started to appear in the literary journals that were quite lively, and . . . treated all historical personages and particularly the representatives of the regime in the eighteenth century in the simplest way, taking them off of their pedestals. The new monographs made these personages . . . come to life for the reader. All of their flaws, both great and small; all of their human weaknesses; all of the effects the environment that surrounded them in childhood and later life had had on their characters and their actions were clearly depicted.[64]

The change in the censorship regime and access to a broader range of archival documents revolutionized Russian historical writing. Noteworthy articles began to appear much more regularly in the thick journals of the capital during the late 1850s and early 1860s. Moreover, the interest generated by this material was so great that soon it became feasible to open up popular journals devoted solely to the publication of historical studies and materials. *Russian Olden Times,* founded in 1870, was the most prominent and successful of these journals. It ran for twenty-two years and generally had between five and six thousand subscribers.[65]

Publishing success stories like that of *Russian Olden Times* suggested that Russians were interested in learning more about their own recent national history. This in turn led to the emergence of a new kind of guidebook: publications that seemed decidedly less journalistic, that focused more on the city's past than on the lives of present-day inhabitants. In them, authors rarely offered information on contemporary social norms, administrative procedures, and holiday traditions; they also did not, as a rule, devote much space to chronicling the achievements of current tsars or expound at length upon the importance of recent construction projects and reforms. Instead they offered accounts of the construction and renovation of particular monuments and areas; depicted how key buildings, streets, and squares looked in the late eighteenth and early nineteenth centuries; and described abandoned traditions, norms of behavior, regulations, and rules. To some extent, of course, Russian guidebooks had always included such materials. In this period, however, the past began to receive more attention. Depicting it, rather than the present, became the principal aim of many writers.[66]

In some cases, the Romanov dynasty itself seems to have played a role in encouraging the composition of these new historical guides. In the late 1860s and the 1870s several guidebooks were published that described the imperial palace and park complexes in the suburbs around St. Petersburg. These books could not have appeared without at least the consent, if not the active support, of the Romanovs. Alexander Geirot, who at one point ran the Peterhof palace administration, issued a book about Peterhof in 1868 that included both a great deal of historical information and fairly detailed descriptions of the various ornaments and structures in the parks.[67] A decade later, Grand Prince Konstantin Nikolaevich asked Mikhail Semevsky to assemble a considerably more ambitious description of Pavlovsk in connection with the hundredth anniversary of the palace complex. After the volume was completed and printed, a copy was presented to Tsar Alexander II. He enjoyed the book enormously and made corrections in the margins in places where he felt the author had made minor errors regarding dates and other factual information. When Grand Prince Konstantin Nikolaevich gave the corrections to Semevsky, he suggested that they could be inserted into the book as footnotes if a new edition were ever released.[68]

In part no doubt because they focus on bucolic suburban palace complexes rather than the city of St. Petersburg proper, the guides that Geirot and Semevsky wrote provide little information on Russia's lower classes. Peasants, guards, and even servants appear in them primarily as the objects of Romanov charity and concern.[69] In this respect, it might be tempting to label these guides throwbacks to an earlier era. It is worth noting, however that in tone they differ markedly from the descriptions written by authors like Bogdanov, Georgi, and Svinin in the late eighteenth and early nineteenth centuries. They are more scholarly, making use of a vast array of documents, held partly in palace archives. They give far fuller accounts of construction projects and more detailed descriptions of individual architectural monuments. They also, on balance, provide a more intimate view of court life. Members of the Romanov family appear in them not just as representatives of the ruling dynasty, public benefactors who inspire awe and deserve glorification, but also as loving wives, mothers, and sons; as individuals who can experience both great love and personal loss.[70] As a result, these works read less like formal hymns of praise: although a divide still separates the Tsars from their subjects, the former no longer resemble deities—they have taken on human characteristics.

In the context of the time, Geirot and Semevsky's guides do seem conservative at least in one key respect. Perhaps, in part, because each author worked to some extent at the pleasure of the imperial family, neither chose to devote much space to the peccadilloes and romantic escapades of past representatives of the Romanov dynasty. Their guides to Peterhof and Pavlovsk appear particularly tame when compared to an average issue of Semevsky's periodical *Russian Olden Times*, which published a great deal of sensational material in the 1870s and 1880s, including copies of Potemkin's correspondence, notes on eighteenth-century torture techniques, and legends surrounding various imperial pretenders. Excluding such titillating material probably had a negative impact on sales. Semevsky's guide to Pavlovsk, at least, did not fly off bookstore shelves.[71]

By far the most popular late-nineteenth-century writer on the landscape and history of St. Petersburg and its suburbs was Mikhail Pyliaev. He began his career as a journalist, writing short articles and sketches for the newspapers and magazines of the capital, including *New Times* (*Novoe vremia*) and *The Historical Herald* (*Istoricheskii vestnik*). He later reworked many of the sketches he wrote, combining them together into collections that he then issued as separate books. The two great works he wrote about St. Petersburg were compiled in this way. *Old Petersburg* (*Staryi Peterburg*) and *The Forgotten Past of the Suburbs* of Petersburg (*Zabytoe proshloe okrestnostei Peterburga*) both represent, in effect, anthologies of material originally published as sketches. The books are broken into chapters and organized according to temporal and geographic principles. They were wildly successful and went through multiple editions.

Readers loved Pyliaev's works not so much because he provided important new factual material—he culled many of the facts he used in his books from old sources and sometimes relied on documents or oral informants who were not entirely accurate—but because he was so entertaining. Pyliaev knew how to tell an anecdote. Out of a profusion of seemingly isolated details—descriptions of imperial banquets and balls, outlandish ladies' fashions, the eccentric behavior of elderly generals, and the personal foibles of the tsars; accounts of savage drinking rituals, forgotten public amusements, and mysterious deaths; notes on the care of the elephants that were once housed in the Summer Gardens; and sketches of long lost palaces, dachas, and parks—he constructed a romanticized version of the capital's past that was at once vivid and enticing. Heavily ornamented and eroticized, Pyliaev's St. Petersburg reads almost as an Orientalist fantasy. Master-servant (slave) relationships, the intimacies of the boudoir, and oddly lush vegetation (given the capital's northern location) are everywhere. Describing the daily life of one mid-eighteenth-century Empress, Pyliaev writes: "As she was drifting off to sleep, Elizabeth loved to listen to stories told by old women and tradeswomen who had been collected for her from city squares. While she listened to their stories and fairy tales, someone would scratch the soles of Elizabeth's feet, and she would slowly fall asleep."[72] Pyliaev's account of the great ball thrown by Prince Potemkin at the Tauride Palace in 1791 includes the following passage of ecstatic description:

> From the great hall, there was an exit leading out into the winter garden. The garden was a wonder of luxury and artifice, six times larger than that in the Hermitage. There was a green turf slope, which was densely planted with flowering Seville orange trees, fragrant jasmine, and roses. In the shrubbery one could glimpse the nests of nightingales and other birds that filled the garden with their singing. Between the bushes various incense burners had been discretely placed for [the pleasure of] strollers. A fountain gushed forth lavender water.[73]

As in a classical fairy tale, the atmosphere of enchantment can all too quickly give way to the grotesque or horrible. Pyliaev recounts a drunken orgy staged by a tax collector that ultimately led to four hundred deaths, the hideous

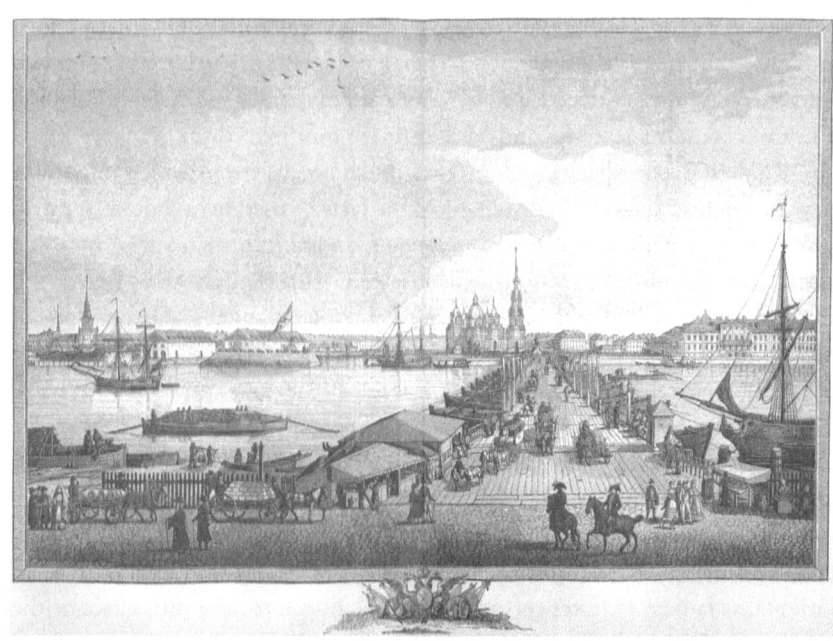

FIG. 2 A view of St. Isaac's bridge and the area of St. Petersburg from the Admiralty to Senate Square.

tortures inflicted on those arrested in the reign of Anna Ioannovna, and the alabaster statues on the riverview property of one wealthy eccentric that, painted flesh-pink, resembled naked revelers.[74] In Pyliaev's work, words like "remarkable" (*zamechatel'nyi*), "curious" (*kur'eznyi*), "fairytale/fabulous" (*skazochnyi*), "marvels" (*dikovinki*), "originals" (*originaly*), "eccentrics" (*chudaki*), "inordinate" (*nepomernyi*), and "unparalleled" (*besprimernyi*) abound. The author alludes continually to legends, myths, and anecdotes, to the reports of various unidentified witnesses, to what people say or assume.

Along with popular historical journals like Semevsky's *Russian Olden Times,* Pyliaev's books promoted the emergence of a new form of nostalgic nationalism. By consistently calling attention to the most fantastic and curious episodes in Russian history, to the empire's most notorious eccentrics, to its strangest cultural traditions, they encouraged Russians to perceive themselves as residents of a land in which the unbelievable had, at least until the very recent past, regularly occurred. In them a familiar and often galling Western European stereotype, the notion of Russia as exotic other, a land of voluptuous Asiatic excess and unheard-of wonders, was effectively transformed into a positive self-conception. Fleshed out in glorious historical detail, an almost Gogolian vision of Russian landscapes and Russian life emerged as the ultimate object of collective nostalgic yearning. The idealized vision of Russia's past presented in the pages of Pyliaev's books differed markedly from the nostalgic reveries of the Slavophiles of the 1840s and their later followers and sympathizers. Most of Pyliaev's published work focuses on the post-Petrine age and urban areas instead of on peasant life and pre-Petrine Russian traditions. Like the guidebook writers I discussed earlier in this chapter, he treats Petersburg as an integral and characteristic part of Russia's cultural landscape rather than as a foreign metropolis, profoundly alien to the country in which it arose.

More than any other writer, Pyliaev deserves credit for popularizing the term "old Petersburg," which had appeared only irregularly in printed works in the early- and mid-nineteenth century and must, throughout this period, have seemed almost oxymoronic to many Russian intellectuals.[75] How could anything related to St. Petersburg be described as old? The capital still seemed so new that in the 1840s Alexander Herzen had famously termed it "a city without a history."[76] Along with Semevsky's journal *Russian Olden Times*, Pyliaev helped to teach Russians to see St. Petersburg as a historic city. He transformed the capital's past into something to daydream about, a place to explore in one's imagination with a book as a guide. Pyliaev's works generated interest in the history of the imperial capital. They inspired a host of imitators and, in a certain sense, might be said to have paved the way for the great boom in local research that took place in St. Petersburg at the beginning of the twentieth century. Redefined in the first years of the twentieth century, the term Pyliaev popularized—old Petersburg—came to serve as a rallying cry for historical preservationism, one of the three great early-twentieth-century St. Petersburg-based cultural movements that I will link to the rise of modern *kraevedenie* in this monograph.

The growth of interest in historical preservation work in Russia in the early twentieth century is closely linked to the activities of the World of Art circle, a loosely defined and continually evolving consortium of artists and critics that played a dominant role in Russian and, to a real extent, European cultural life in the period. Participants included Sergei Diaghilev, the entrepreneur who would later go on to found the legendary Ballets Russes; Alexander Benois, a talented painter and perhaps the greatest Russian art critic of the twentieth century; Dmitrii Filosofov, the critic and eventual cofounder of the St. Petersburg Religious-Philosophical society; the renowned architectural historian Igor Grabar; and the artists Mstislav Dobuzhinsky, Konstantin Somov, and Leon Bakst. The group coalesced around and received its name

FIG. 3 A procession featuring elephants given to the Russian tsar by the Persian shah.

from *World of Art* (*Mir iskusstva*), the thick journal devoted to art, philosophy, and literature that Diaghilev organized with the help of other participants in 1898. This vastly influential periodical introduced the Russian public to a host of new styles and trends (symbolism, cubism, primitivism, the early-twentieth-century revival of neoclassical architecture) and published plans for the reform of many of Russia's most respected cultural institutions. After it collapsed in 1904, participants dispersed to work on a host of different projects.

Because so much good scholarship already exists on World of Art, this book does not include a complete account of the group's history or cultural contributions. Instead, the next two chapters offer a focused treatment of those aspects of World of Art ideology and activities that seem most obviously connected to the rise of modern *kraevedenie*. They consider the way in which World of Art participants understood and applied the term old Petersburg, the organs of publication that group members used as forums for the discussion of preservation work, and the institutions they founded to advance preservationist aims. Most important, these chapters show how World of Art efforts to study and protect the monuments of the capital lead to the creation of a new generation of gudebooks.

2

The Art Journals of the Silver Age, St. Petersburg Preservationism, and the Guidebook

> *I will return to Petersburg in my memoirs on every possible occasion—like a man in love to the object of his adoration.*
>
> —Alexander Benois, *Moi vospominaniia v piati knigakh*, 1:15

When late-nineteenth-century writers like Mikhail Pyliaev spoke about old Petersburg, they generally had in mind the eighteenth century, particularly the glamorous reigns of Elizabeth and Catherine the Great: the balls, the dresses, the fireworks, the staggering opulence of life at court. The first dozen years following the ascension of Alexander I to the throne in 1801 were sometimes included in this golden age. Writers might wistfully describe the handsome young tsar, the optimistic atmosphere that prevailed throughout society, and the uniformed officers marching off to fight in the Napoleonic Wars. For the chroniclers of the nineteenth century, old Petersburg, however, ended with the return of Russia's troops from abroad in 1815. The second half of Alexander's reign already seemed to be a part of the modern age and hence did not inspire the same sort of nostalgia. The atmosphere of the period, its social rituals, and its look were still too easily recalled, its problems too immediate. More time had to pass, another generation of commentators had to appear, before the late 1810s and the 1820s could be at all warmly remembered.

Alexander Benois is often and quite correctly credited with expanding the temporal boundaries of old Petersburg to include the second half of Alexander's reign and, to a certain extent, even the decades spent under the rule of Nicholas I.[1] From 1899 on, Benois and a number of other critics who contributed to the journal *World of Art* worked to change public perceptions of the great age of Russian imperialism, arguing in a series of articles that, for all its Roman severity, formality, and order, the epoch was not without its charms.[2] Aside from expanding the meaning of the term "old Petersburg" to include a new period of time, the critics who wrote for *World of Art* also redefined the concept in another significant respect. Unlike Pyliaev and the writers who contributed nostalgic pieces to the journal *Russian Olden Times*, Benois and his confreres tended to focus almost exclusively on art and architecture in their discussions of the past. They might occasionally recount a titillating anecdote about the imperial family or describe a picturesque scene, but, for the most part, historical events and the spectacle of daily life in the capital interested them relatively little. In an early article on Peterhof's Monplaisir, for instance, Benois noted critically:

> Most people look at our suburban palaces from an exclusively historical point of view. With rare exceptions, it never occurs to anyone to notice that all of these "great" and "small" palaces are of enormous artistic interest: the Marlies, the Monplaisirs, the hermitages, the grottos, the summer houses, aviaries, Turkish and Chinese cottages. These charming creations of the eighteenth century are known to the public only because in one of them Peter loved to feast with his protégés [*ptentsy*]; in another his ink-well, dressing gown and shoes are kept; in a third, he supposedly carved out the droll decorations with his own hands; in a fourth Catherine II conducted state affairs on hot summer days; in a fifth there is a table with a special, curious mechanism.[3]

The World of Art group argued for a new kind of nostalgic retrospection. They hoped that the public would move beyond a simple "*engouement historique*," a mere appreciation of the "charms of antiquity"; they wanted Russians to value the monuments of old Petersburg on purely aesthetic grounds, as something "truly good" and "eternally beautiful."[4] They challenged the negative assessments of the capital's look that had predominated in literary and critical texts throughout much of the nineteenth century.

Benois and his collaborators treated the capital as a successful work of art. They believed that, at least until the mid-nineteenth century, when a trend toward eclecticism in architecture had begun to spoil the general panorama, St. Petersburg had been "in its own way splendid and integrated, with a distinct style."[5] In one of his most influential articles, "Picturesque Petersburg" (*Zhivopisnyi Peterburg*), Benois urged the public to take a closer look at the older sections of the city, pointing out that the capital was, for all the coldness recent generations of Russian writers and critics had so often noted, tremendously seductive.

> If it [St. Petersburg] is beautiful, it is so in its entirety or, more accurately, in vast segments, in great ensembles, broad panoramas, executed in a certain character: stiff, but splendid and majestic. All these pictures are not very cheerful. If one compares views of Petersburg to certain views of Paris, the comparison of a stern Roman senator to a ravishing Greek bacchante unwittingly comes to mind. But, after all, the Roman senator is no less beautiful, no less charming, than the bacchante, otherwise the Roman senator would not have subjugated the whole world and that same bacchante. Petersburg has that same stern Roman spirit, the spirit of order, the spirit of formally perfect life, which is unbearable to Russian slovenliness, but, indisputably, is not without its charms.[6]

This description of the capital seems calculated to call to mind two separate sets of associations. First and foremost, Benois is clearly personifying St. Petersburg, identifying the northern capital with its magnetic, overbearing founder. Peter I, the merciless historical opponent of all forms of "Russian slovenliness," had often been depicted in official portraits and sculptures as an ancient "Roman." Both of the great equestrian monuments to the tsar built in St. Petersburg during the course of the eighteenth century, for example, show Peter I in some form of antique dress.[7] "Roman sternness" and a "love of order" are qualities that can be understood in either positive or negative terms. For Benois, they are clearly preferable to the obvious alternative, "Russian slovenliness," and hence, by extension, both Peter I and St. Petersburg, the city that was the locus of the tsar's reforms, deserve praise rather than censure.

In this passage Alexander Benois is doing more, however, than simply taking sides in the great debate over the effects of the Petrine reforms, which

FIG. 4 The opening of Étienne-Maurice Falconet's monument to Peter I, the *Bronze Horseman*, in 1872.

had raged ceaselessly throughout the nineteenth century and had given rise to the rival Slavophile and Westernizer camps in the 1830s. Each of the key phrases in the citation provided above can be read not just as an allusion to the figure of Peter I, but also as a reference to a particular architectural style. Benois's description of St. Petersburg seems calculated to call to mind a specific set of local monuments: the "great ensembles" built in the Empire style at the beginning of the nineteenth century. Carlo Rossi's spectacular redesign of Palace Square, the area surrounding the Mikhailovsky Palace, the stretch of territory between the Alexandrine Theater and Lomonosov Square, and Zakharov's Admiralty, more than anything else in the city, are truly "Roman in scale and grandeur.[8] In the second half of the nineteenth century, such construction projects fell out of favor and were criticized in the press. A new generation of architects and clients appeared on the scene, rejecting the standards of the past. They typically dismissed the Empire style as too "stern," "severe," and "boring."[9] Instead, they preferred buildings that were more ornate and a little warmer, embellished with some composite of Venetian and Arabic decorative motifs, or in any of a dozen other eclectic forms. The neo-Russian style attracted a particularly vocal group of proponents, including the country's last two tsars, Alexander III and Nicholas II. These romantic nationalists characteristically rejected St. Petersburg and its classical buildings as too European. Convinced that the great Petrine reforms, which had led to the creation of Russia's "window on the West," were fundamentally against the national interest, they looked back wistfully and tried to revive the traditions of seventeenth-century Muscovy.[10]

In "Picturesque Petersburg," Benois worked to counter anticlassical sentiment. He spoke out against the past fifty years of construction, against what he viewed as botched restoration projects and ill-conceived additions to the city's orderly panorama. Disliking both the new Western styles and the popular neo-Russian look, he argued that residents should stop trying to spruce up older structures by adding "cheap, loathsome molded 'decorations,'" "motley, gaudy tiles," or "roosters . . . and other 'Russian' details."[11] He wanted them to learn to cherish the unique look of historic St. Petersburg, to recognize that constructions built in both the currently unpopular classical style and the earlier baroque manner represented, in many cases, priceless national treasures. Architects like Rastrelli, Quarenghi, Rossi, and Thomon, although foreign by birth, had quickly adapted to the unique conditions of their new homeland. The buildings they designed may not have resembled traditional Russian structures, but they should not be dismissed as mere Western borrowings. They were something fundamentally new: Russia's vast open spaces and the enormous financial resources of its nobility had allowed these men to implement their ideas and theories in a way that had never been possible in Italy or France. Petersburg could boast of having the finest and most fully realized examples of a variety of eighteenth-century and early nineteenth-century architectural trends. The failure of Western European specialists to discuss these buildings in their studies of the period represented, Benois believed, an "unpardonable oversight"; the neglect and abuse that the characteristic landscape of St. Petersburg suffered at the hands of the Russian public counted as an even greater tragedy.[12]

For all he played up the seeming foreignness of classical St. Petersburg in the extravagant descriptions he included at the beginning of "Picturesque Petersburg," Benois ultimately called upon his fellow countrymen to acknowledge the ensembles in the center of the capital as something quintessentially Russian, an aesthetic marvel of worldwide significance that arose as a direct result of Russia's unique geography (boundless space) and essentially unlimited financial resources. In the last section of "Picturesque Petersburg," Benois urged Russia's artists, in particular, to take pride in the northern capital and to try, in their work, to capture its unique beauty. By doing so, he believed, they could teach the public to cherish the city's many monuments and its majestic panoramas. They could save St. Petersburg "from ruin, stop the barbarous distortion of it," and "protect its beauty from the encroachments of coarse ignoramuses." In recent decades, he argued, Russia's artists had failed to fulfill this important task. The city that had been portrayed by both painters and poets in the eighteenth and early nineteenth centuries as a glorious "Northern Palmyra" had been largely forgotten by later generations. "At present," Benois claimed, "one can find quite a few artists who are occupied with Moscow and who are truly able to convey its beauty and its character. But there is not a single one who wants to pay serious attention to Petersburg." Russia's writers, similarly, had been derelict: "Not a single one of the great poets of the second half of the nineteenth century interceded for Petersburg."[13]

Benois criticized the writers of the late nineteenth century for failing to acknowledge the physical beauty of the capital, but that does not mean that he wanted them to renounce a hundred years of literary history and return to drafting panegyric odes in the manner of Lomonosov and Derzhavin.[14] Benois clearly accepted the descriptions of the capital penned by Pushkin, Gogol, and Dostoevsky. He realized that there was a dark side to the city, that it represented something more than just a collection of "magnificent" classical facades; St. Petersburg was also "fantastic," "gloomy," and even a little "horrible."[15] In fact, for Benois, the potentially menacing aspects of the capital's character apparently contributed to its appeal.

> In this stiffness, in what, to all appearances is just philistine "bon ton," there is even something fantastic, a certain fairy tale about a sorcerer who is wise but not good-hearted and who wanted to create an entire city in which, in the place of living people and living life, there would be robots, irreproachably fulfilling their roles, a grandiose, never slackening music-box spring. The fairy tale is rather gloomy, but one can't say that it is completely disagreeable. I repeat—in this mechanicalness there is some and perhaps even a great deal of charm, in any case, a greater charm than there is in the bourgeois, sensible, diligent life of Berlin.[16]

This Hoffmanesque description of the city almost seems deliberately recall the work of Pushkin, Gogol, and at least early Dostoevsky. Benois may have had little interest in the social issues purportedly explored by these authors, their meticulous accounts of "little men" and squalid living conditions, but he found the horrifying atmosphere that infused their descriptions of the capital fascinating from an aesthetic point of view. He seems to have understood "fantastic," "spectral" St. Petersburg—the city where collegiate assessors were transformed into helpless automatons, where noses, portraits, and reflections acquired unnatural powers, as a kind of symbolist puppet show. Benois had a talent for theatrical decoration, and he no doubt intuitively sensed that horror and magnificence were artistically compatible. The standard plot of nineteenth-century St. Petersburg fiction, the story of a helpless victim caught up in the maw of a hostile supernatural entity (representing on some level, of course, the capital itself), appeared to great advantage when acted out in front of an endless row of classical facades.

Of all the writers of the nineteenth century, Benois probably had the greatest affinity for Pushkin. Both men had the capacity to perceive St. Petersburg simultaneously in two ways: as the miraculous creation of the Russian tsar, a delight and wonder worthy of the grandest hymn of praise, and as a strange and ominous place, a natural setting for great tragedies. In "Picturesque Petersburg," Benois urged writers to include descriptions of both aspects of the city's nature in their compositions. They could continue to probe the dark underbelly of the northern capital, but they should also not forget to pause occasionally and, like Pushkin in the first part of "The Bronze Horseman," acknowledge the city's external charms.

Preserving the look of the northern capital and saving the glorious central sections of the city from destruction began to obsess Benois very early in the *World of Art* period. In 1899, three years before the publication of "Picturesque Petersburg," he had begun contributing short articles on the northern capital to the journal on a regular basis. By all accounts, these pieces had quickly captured the attention of at least a certain segment of the reading public. With the two-hundredth anniversary of the founding of St. Petersburg rapidly approaching, a surge of interest in the city's history and its architectural monuments was, perhaps, entirely predictable. Benois's anguished protests against recent acts of architectural vandalism aroused sympathy; his brief descriptions of local landmarks created a demand for more detailed and systematic studies. *World of Art,* in many respects, however, was not ideally suited to the task of satisfying this growing interest. The journal was relatively encyclopedic in nature and, in general, could accommodate no more than a single brief article on the capital or a handful of photographs in a given month. Its editorial staff was committed to providing readers with broad coverage of the contemporary arts scene in both Russia and abroad and therefore could not afford to set aside a large number of the pages for coverage of a single problem. Each issue was expected to contain exhibit reviews; news about recent auctions; translations of promising studies in art history; a substantial literary section with contributions by Russia's leading symbolists; enthusiastic descriptions of new schools of painting and aesthetic trends; and polemics against and projects for the reform of conservative cultural institutions like the Academy of the Arts, the Hermitage, and the Imperial Society for the Encouragement of the Arts.

Occasionally the staff at *World of Art* did vary the journal's format, moving away from a strictly encyclopedic approach and devoting at least a significant section of an issue to the exposition of a single theme. Such topical issues, however, were produced relatively rarely. One appeared in 1899 in connection with the hundredth anniversary of the birth of Pushkin; several more came out between 1902 and 1904. Moreover, on all occasions except in the case of the Pushkin issue, these nominally thematic issues included, alongside text and illustrations pertaining to the featured topic, a good deal of material on unrelated subjects. The sole topical number devoted to St. Petersburg, the first issue of 1902, is in this sense typical. It opens with a frontispiece emblazoned with the word "Petersburg" and an image of the Peter and Paul Fortress. The issue contains an extended series of photographs and reproductions depicting the architecture of the northern capital. Benois's seminal article "Picturesque Petersburg" appears in its "Chronicle" section. These contributions occupy about a third of the magazine. The remaining pages are filled with articles on other subjects. As this description shows, even in issues that focused theoretically on a single theme, *World of Art* tended to remain encyclopedic. One brief article on St. Petersburg and a series of illustrations was the best that could be expected.

Perhaps because he wanted to escape from this encyclopedic format, to write at greater length about both the artistic culture of the past in general and specifically about old Petersburg, Benois was willing to consider other publishing opportunities even relatively early in the World of Art period.[17] In the summer of 1900, Pavel Marser, a member of the governing committee of the Imperial Society for the Encouragement of the Arts, met Benois in Paris at the World's Fair and offered him the post of editor of the society's magazine. Benois quickly accepted despite the fact that the proposal was surprising; at the time, *Art and Art Industry* (*Iskusstvo i khudozhestvennaia promyshlennost*), the publication Marser hoped to turn over to Benois, represented one of *World of Art*'s principal polemical opponents. Within two days, Benois had worked out a concrete proposal for revamping the society's journal. He suggested abandoning *Art and Art Industry*'s current format and creating a slim monthly magazine modeled in part on the popular European periodicals *L'art pour tous, Formenschatz, Bilderschatz,* and *Skulpturenschatz,* which relied on illustrations to educate their readership. Each issue would consist primarily of high-quality reproductions of works of art supplemented, when necessary, by concise but accurate historical commentary. Moreover, Benois argued that the journal might reasonably confine itself to cataloging cultural treasures located on Russian soil. The country's museums, palaces, churches, and private collections contained many beautiful pieces, fine examples of a variety of national and foreign artistic styles. Because few people had access to these places, the publication of reproductions would itself represent a significant public service. If the society approved his plan, Benois suggested giving the magazine an appropriate, new name: *Art Treasures of Russia* (*Khudozhestvennye sokrovishcha Rossii*).

In his memoirs, Benois later noted that while devising the proposal for the new journal, he was very conscious of the need to make it as unlike *World of Art* as possible. He did not want to compete with the publication that he and his friends had been working on for two years. No doubt this concern helped shape the suggestions that he sent to the Society for the Encouragement of the Arts. When Benois decided not to cover Western Europe at all and, in general, to de-emphasize the importance of text, he may well have had the interests of *World of Art* foremost in his mind. For the most part though, despite the fact that he was working under certain self-imposed restrictions, Benois seems to have been delighted at the final shape of his project for *Art Treasures of Russia*. As he notes in his memoirs, by the time that he was ready to submit the proposal, he had realized that he "really wanted to get control of this enterprise."[18] This sudden burst of enthusiasm, no doubt, stemmed in part from the thought that the proposed publication would allow him to research a set of topics that had long fascinated him: he would be able to explore Russia's finest collections and to assemble information on its lovely palaces and parks. Benois may also, however, have appreciated the fact that, as editor of the society's publication, he was likely to have considerable independence. *World of Art* was a cooperative venture and hence had always reflected the interests and tastes of various individuals, including, first and foremost, those of its editor, Sergei Diaghilev. The new magazine would give Benois a platform of his own; he would personally have final say in all editorial decisions. In his memoirs, Benois always refers to *Art Treasures of Russia* as "my" publication, *World of Art* he labels "ours."[19]

Benois passed on only one significant demand to the society's governing committee along with his proposal for revamping the organization's magazine. He had to be free to conduct himself as he saw fit when not acting in his capacity as editor and to publish whatever he chose in other publications. The organization's board quickly agreed to everything, adding only one significant stipulation of its own: all materials for *Art Treasures of Russia*, including paper and reproductions, had to be obtained domestically. Although he recognized that this would significantly complicate his work, Benois acquiesced.

Benois spent the fall of 1900 laying groundwork for the new publication and placing preliminary orders. With the first issue of the journal slated to appear at the beginning of 1901, he had to move quickly, negotiating deals with printers and securing a reliable supply of high-quality paper. Moreover, because he knew that lack of sunlight would make it difficult to take good pictures in St. Petersburg after early autumn, he wanted to put together a supply of photographs that would last through the long winter season. He spent weeks traveling around the city with photographers and capturing a wide range of images on film. For the commentary that would accompany these illustrations, Benois relied mostly on his own expertise. He later claimed to have personally composed "at least three-quarters of the printed text" that appeared in *Art Treasures of Russia*, including not only the descriptive notes that accompanied the illustrations but also most of the contributions to the monthly chronicle and the reviews of other periodicals and books.[20] When he did not feel competent to comment on a topic himself, Benois generally turned to one of his old friends in the World of Art circle or, in extreme situations, to outside experts: professors at St. Petersburg University and the heads of various departments at the Hermitage regularly contributed commentary to the magazine.

Art Treasures of Russia received very favorable reviews when it first appeared and quickly gained popularity with Russian readers.[21] Although it did not engage in the kind of fiery polemics that had made *World of Art* so notorious and therefore played, in some respects, a far less prominent role in the cultural scene, the magazine was innovative in its own way. By the middle of 1901, Benois had gained considerable skill as editor and had begun to pay careful attention to the selection and arrangement of material for each issue. He began to group illustrations thematically and placed explanatory texts within reasonable proximity of the pictures to which they referred. Although this may seem like an obvious organizational strategy now, it had not been the practice at *World of Art*. There, particularly during the first two years of publication, text and pictures had often been distributed erratically, with illustrations for one article running through the next or a string of reproductions appearing in the middle of a text for no discernible reason.[22] In addition, the vignettes and other decorations used to dress up *World of Art*'s pages frequently did not correspond to the pieces they accompanied; the artists working on *World of*

FIG. 5 Evgeny Lanceray, frontispiece for *World of Art*, no. 1 (1902), a special issue commemorating St. Petersburg's bicentennial.

Art selected motifs almost at whim, rarely thinking of the articles that would eventually appear on the pages they were decorating.

Benois worked very differently. He clearly viewed each issue of *Art Treasures of Russia* as a single work of art and organized the text and pictures to make a unified impression on the reader. As soon as the journal had established itself, he began putting together ambitious thematic issues devoted to a single topic. The Chinese Palace in Oranienbaum, Petr Semenov-Tian-Shansky's Dutch painting collection, and the Stroganov Palace in St. Petersburg all received in-depth coverage in 1901. Each thematic issue contained spectacular groups of reproductions and photographs, including pictures taken in places that often still remained largely closed to visitors. Benois also typically chose to vary his journal's format for these special numbers and included longer articles that were rather scholarly in nature. A 1902 issue devoted to Peterhof, for instance, featured a substantial piece by Benois, an essay by the popular historian Ivan Bozherianov, and an article containing information gathered in the Archive of the Ministry of the Court by Alexander Uspensky. For a thematic issue on the age of Peter I that was published at the beginning of 1903, Benois wrote a brief article describing an old plaster mask that he had found forgotten in the storage cabinets of the Hermitage's Petrine gallery. Research suggested, he argued, that the casting had been made from the face of the tsar and that it had been done while Peter I was still alive.[23]

Effectively, several times a year Benois was sending his readers elaborate illustrated books in the place of ordinary issues, special volumes that often described sites and objects located in St. Petersburg and sometimes contained legitimate scholarly discoveries. These monographic numbers proved immensely popular with the public and quickly began to attract the attention of other editors and journalists. By early 1902, even *World of Art,* at times, seemed inclined to emulate Benois's approach. While Diaghilev, for the most part, remained committed to producing a journal that was encyclopedic in nature, he did put together several issues during 1902 and 1903 where at least the bulk of the text in the art section and most of the illustrations focused on a single topic.[24] The thematic approach would also later be employed in a more elaborate form at the popular magazine *Bygone Years* (*Starye gody*). Each summer between 1907 and 1916, this journal put out a huge triple issue, generally devoted almost entirely to the exploration of one aspect of Russian art and culture, such as the art of the eighteenth century, art in the age of Alexander I, or the palace and park complex at Gatchina, for instance.[25] Single and double thematic issues often appeared at other times of year.

The implementation of Benois's system, using entire issues to explore specific topics, necessarily entailed changes in the way art journals operated. Putting together an illustrated scholarly monograph of anywhere from two hundred to five hundred pages, depending upon the number and size of the issues it was meant to replace, represented a daunting task. Writers, photographers, and designers had to collaborate extraordinarily closely in order to ensure consistency. If they wanted to follow Benois's lead and say something of scholarly significance instead of just recapitulating commonly accepted facts, then they needed to conduct extensive field research and familiarize themselves with both printed sources and archival records. Writers for these journals were particularly interested in learning about old Petersburg: somewhere between one-third and one-half of the material published in *Art Treasures of Russia* and *Bygone Years* focused on the art and architecture of the northern capital. They explored the shelves of the St. Petersburg Public Library and many of the city's archives, hunting for old guidebooks, maps, memoirs, and the inventories of palaces and museums. Works by Bogdanov, Georgi, Bashutsky, Svinin, and Pyliaev were rediscovered, dusted off, and declared important historical resources.

Contributors to *Art Treasures of Russia* and *Bygone Years* cited these volumes constantly in their articles. They appreciated the wealth of factual information that the books contained and the wit and style with which they had been written. They also, however, detected significant shortcomings in these old descriptions of St. Petersburg. The men who wrote guides to St. Petersburg in the eighteenth and nineteenth centuries paid very little attention to aesthetic issues. Art history and criticism had been underdeveloped as disciplines in Russia until the beginning of the twentieth century. As a result, most chroniclers working in earlier periods had not really understood the importance of accurately documenting the appearance of architectural monuments. Even if they appreciated the splendor of the city's sweeping panoramic views, they lacked the specialized vocabulary to describe the buildings they admired in real detail. Historical facts and simple lists of the expensive trinkets on display at various palaces and institutions represented their true forte, not classifying and evaluating works of art with scientific precision. Moreover, those who had written about the city in the eighteenth and nineteenth centuries had often failed to provide their readers with even the most basic information about the sources used in their research. They did not explain how they had dated a particular construction or where they had learned the names of owners and architects. As Igor Grabar noted in annoyance, writers either did not bother to include any citations at all or, like Petr Petrov, they seemed to have "purposely mixed up all traces of their sources so that others would not be able to use them."²⁶ Anecdotal information, the vague recollections of elderly city residents, and the writer's own conjectures were often thrown haphazardly together with very valuable pieces of information culled from little-known and entirely reliable sources. Finally, the old books about the city often did not meet the special needs of various groups of modern scholars, visitors, and residents. Convenient pocket guides to many important local sites did not exist, most local museums did not have accurate and up-to-date catalogs available for specialists, and basic information that should long ago have made it into print often remained locked away in archives. As Benois remarked in a book review in 1904,

> One testimony to our low cultural level is our lack of decent guidebooks. It is strange to say, but Petersburg, this city, which is so tremendously rich in treasures of art, up to now has not had a decent *cicerone*. A Russian who wanted to get to know his capital has had to fall back on the foreign Baedeker. But the Baedeker for Petersburg is not at all as well composed as the classical guidebooks to Germany and Italy by the same publisher. It is no surprise considering the poverty of sources. We still have not had our Naglers, Burkharts, Pasavans, Kavalkasals—[those sources], which Baedeker is able to use so effectively. In most of our museums there aren't even any explanatory catalogues. True, the most significant of them, the Hermitage, is an exception, but the catalogues in the Hermitage alone represent an entire library, which the ordinary tourist can hardly use.²⁷

If St. Petersburg was ever to be properly understood, Benois implies here, practical new guidebooks for the sightseer and a host of other, more basic resources had to be composed.

The writers working for St. Petersburg's major art magazines did more than just publicly bemoan the lack of literature on the city in their articles and reviews; they largely took it upon themselves to solve the problem. Moving beyond journal articles and thematic issues, they quickly began to dream of independent publishing ventures and vast programs of research. A whole generation of young writers who had cut their teeth working for Benois's magazine or for the journal *Bygone Years*—men like Vladimir Kurbatov, Petr Stolpiansky, and Georgy Lukomsky—went on to write important monographs about Petersburg on their own in the 1910s and 1920s. They published basic guidebooks to the northern capital and its suburbs, major studies of park landscaping as an art form, and important annotated bibliographies. They often chose to emphasize in their work a basic complex of ideas that had been heavily promoted in preservationist periodicals: the cultural heritage of the past should be viewed as a priceless treasure; significant monuments must at all costs be protected against decay, development, and misguided renovation projects; despite its apparently European look, St. Petersburg constituted a uniquely Russian phenomenon of tremendous aesthetic importance, which, as of yet, had not received adequate scholarly attention; even seemingly inconsequential details such as the choice of colors of paint or the alteration, addition, or removal of small ornamental flourishes on the exterior of a single historic building could significantly affect an urban area as a whole and hence merited careful consideration.[28] Guidebooks played a particularly important role in conveying preservationist views and priorities to the Russian public, because the form appealed to a relatively broad and diverse audience.

The first great thematic issues on old Petersburg put together by Benois at his journal *Art Treasures of Russia* inaugurated a new era in the study and description of Russia's northern capital. Although interest in the city had been growing steadily since Benois first spoke out against the "vandalism" of local monuments in *World of Art* in 1899, it was only when he accepted the post of editor of the new journal for the Society for the Encouragement of the Arts in 1901 that the preservation movement really came into its own. Benois and his allies acquired a platform from which they could continuously express their views. With a new expanse of empty pages waiting for them every month, they had a real incentive to immerse themselves completely in the study of the city they loved. Intent on providing the Russian public with basic information in a convenient and accessible form, they would eventually begin to craft a new kind of guidebook that focused greater attention on the aesthetic issues that absorbed them.

Benois's tenure as the editor of *Art Treasures of Russia* ended acrimoniously at the beginning of 1903, shortly after he published an extremely negative review of an exhibit organized by the Society for the Encouragement of the Arts under his own name in the journal *World of Art*. Although Benois's employment agreement theoretically allowed him complete freedom to print whatever he chose in publications other than *Art Treasures of Russia*, the society felt betrayed. The members of its governing committee objected to being lambasted in the press by their own employee and voted to send Benois a formal letter of reprimand, threatening him with dismissal if he ever publicly criticized the society again. Five days later Benois submitted his resignation. The Society appointed Adrian Prakhov, a much older art critic, to replace him.[29]

Under Prakhov's leadership, *Art Treasures of Russia* continued to exist for another five years. In his memoirs, Benois repeatedly lambastes his replacement, suggesting that, as soon as Prakhov took over as editor, publication standards at the society's journal began to decline precipitously.[30] Although, *Art Treasures of Russia* did gradually lose some of its polish, fading into mediocrity in its later years, the change took place far less abruptly than Benois liked to pretend. At least initially Prakhov got on fairly well, partly by making use of material that Benois had left behind in the magazine's editorial office after his sudden departure. Prakhov viewed the archival data Benois had collected, his ideas for future issues, and even the contacts he had cultivated during the years he spent working on *Art Treasures of Russia* as the property of the journal. In 1903 and 1904 he went ahead and realized his predecessor's plans for thematic issues on Pavlovsk and Tsarskoe Selo.

Although Benois might have implemented these projects a little differently, each issue represents a remarkable achievement in the form in which Prakhov released it. The thematic issue on Pavlovsk, which appeared in 1903, remains an important source for art historians to the present day.[31] Aside from a large article by Uspensky and a breathtaking series of photographs, it contains a number of important documents, such as old inventories and descriptions of the main palace, including one written out by the Grand Princess Maria Fyodorovna in her own handwriting in 1795. These records had never been available to the public at large before, and, naturally, their publication represented an event of real significance. The material that appeared in *Art Treasures of Russia* in the following year concerning Tsarskoe Selo was, in many respects, equally important.[32] Benois's old contact Uspensky once again composed most of the text. He had access to the archives of the Ministry of Court, to which it was notoriously difficult to gain entry, and, as a result, his articles were always filled with wonderful facts and citations culled from the correspondence of empresses, architects, and engineers. In future years, Uspensky would collect information for Prakhov on a variety of other sites, including the Marble Palace, the Anichkov Palace, and the Winter Palace. Thanks largely to his participation, *Art Treasures of Russia* was able to continue publishing good thematic issues on the wonders of old Petersburg almost up until it folded.

By stressing the importance of the thematic issues released by *Art Treasures of Russia* under Prakhov's supervision, I do not mean to suggest that the journal was not hurt by the departure of Benois. Although Prakhov clearly tried to maintain as much continuity as possible during the first years of his tenure, many veteran contributors refused to work for *Art Treasures of Russia* after

Benois left, including, most notably, the members of the World of Art group. Artists like Evgeny Lanceray, Dobuzhinsky, and Bakst, who had willingly agreed to help Benois on numerous occasions, had no real ties to Prakhov. Vladimir Kurbatov and Stepan Iaremich, the two young men who had worked most consistently on the society's publication, also disappeared.[33]

After leaving *Art Treasures of Russia*, Benois turned his attention to other projects, including, first and foremost, *World of Art*. Although he had never stopped contributing to Diaghilev's publication entirely, in 1901 and 1902 Benois had quite understandably been preoccupied with the affairs of his own magazine.[34] He devoted far more of his time and energy to *World of Art* in 1903 and 1904, eventually assuming the post of co-editor. By mutual agreement, six of the twelve issues of *World of Art* that appeared in 1904 were edited by Diaghilev; six by Benois.[35] Perhaps predictably the numbers assembled by Benois in some respects resemble issues of *Art Treasures of Russia:* they focus on the art of the past rather than on modern works, include few literary and philosophical contributions, and are predominantly thematic rather than encyclopedic in style. Topics included the "Arkhangelskoe" estate, a recent historical exhibit of objets d'art, medieval illustrated manuscripts, Moscow classicism, the patriarch's sacristy in Moscow, and the folk art of the Russian North.

Interestingly enough, none of the issues of *World of Art* that Benois edited in 1904 deals at any length with the architecture of old Petersburg. Perhaps Benois believed Prakhov had preempted him, or perhaps he simply felt that he needed to move on to new topics after the disappointments of the preceding year. His plans to describe Pavlovsk and Tsarskoe Selo had, as far as he was concerned, been taken from him and imperfectly realized; he may well have decided that there was no sense in trying to resurrect them. Regardless of what motivated Benois's decision, he had clearly put aside the idea of using art journals and thematic issues as a medium for exploring old Petersburg, at least for a time.[36]

World of Art folded at the beginning of 1905. With the Russo-Japanese War under way, state spending on culture was sharply declining, and the publication lost its government subsidy. Although Diaghilev looked for alternative funding sources for the journal, he ultimately was not able to reach an agreement with anyone.[37] In any case, the journal's main contributors had already begun to drift apart, developing a variety of independent projects and interests. As Benois states pointedly in his memoirs: "All three of us, Diaghilev, Filosofov, and I, had grown tired of fussing over the journal. It seemed to us all that everything that needed to be said and shown had been said and shown. For that reason, everything that followed would just be repetition, marching in place, and that was particularly distasteful to us."[38] In the end, they decided that it was time to move on to other projects.

Art Treasures of Russia folded three years later, also at least in part because of financial difficulties. The budgetary commission of the Second State Duma had voted to eliminate its yearly 10,000 ruble subsidy to the magazine in the middle of 1907, arguing that, as a publication "intended for the privileged classes," the journal did not deserve to receive financial assistance from the government.[39] Although in the last issue of *Art Treasures of Russia* in 1907, Prakhov spoke optimistically about his magazine's future, claiming to have found new sources of funding for the coming year, the journal did not appear in 1908.[40] In any case, it had by this point already ceased to play a meaningful part in the cultural life of the capital. A new art publication had arisen in January 1907 that had largely superseded Prakhov's magazine, taking upon itself the role of serving as a mouthpiece for the city's preservation movement.

Bygone Years, the periodical that probably did the most to promote the cult of old Petersburg in early-twentieth-century Russia, was created by a group of men who, for the most part, had not played significant roles at either *World of Art* or Benois's publication *Art Treasures of Russia:* Vasily Vereshchagin and Iakov Ratkov-Rozhnov, members of the circle of Lovers of Russian Fine Editions (*Kruzhok liubitelei russkikh iziashchnikh izdanii*); Sergei Troinitsky and Alexander Trubnikov, the founders of the recently created publishing house "Sirius"; Petr Veiner, the famous Petersburg collector; and Sergei Makovsky, the art historian and poet. These men effectively represented a second wave of preservationist-journalists, admirers of Benois's earlier campaigns to save Russia's monuments, who felt inspired, after the disappearance of the journal *World of Art* and the decline of *Art Treasures of Russia,* to organize their own high-quality art publication.

Sometime during the middle of 1907, the first year in which *Bygone Years* appeared, this core editorial group expanded slightly to include Baron Nikolai Vrangel, a young critic who had helped Diaghilev organize an important portraiture exhibit in 1905, and finally Benois himself. According to published staff lists, Benois served on the editorial board of *Bygone Years* from the middle of 1907 until the journal closed in 1916. He did not, however, ever exercise primary control over the magazine. In his memoirs, Benois always speaks of *Bygone Years* as a publication run by other individuals, as a periodical that was edited first by Vereshchagin and then by Veiner, but which perhaps was intellectually dominated by Vrangel, the "heart and soul," according to Benois, of the new collective.[41]

Despite the fact that *Bygone Years* was run by a group of people who, for the most part, had never played significant roles at either *World of Art* or *Art Treasures of Russia,* in many ways the journal followed the lead of its predecessors. It pursued a similar agenda toward the culture of the past, adopting a program that in many respects recalls Benois's original proposal for *Art Treasures of Russia.* In the editorial statements and subscription announcements included in the first few issues of *Bygone Years,* the journal's organizers promised that the new periodical would acquaint its readers with "a variety of issues concerning the art of the past, both Russian and foreign."[42] It would describe works of art from public and private collections; publish information about forgotten architects, artistic schools, and techniques; and provide regular bulletins on current preservation work, recent museum acquisitions, and exhibits relating to the culture of the past.

Some distinctions can be made, of course, between the program proposed for the journal *Bygone Years* in the winter of 1907 and the policies pursued by Benois at *Art Treasures of Russia,* but they probably reflect a difference in the circumstances in which the two journals were created rather than a real discrepancy in their goals. *Bygone Years* was free from many of the outside pressures that had shaped *Art Treasures of Russia.* Its organizers did not have to take into account the needs of a second publication, and therefore could afford to dispense with some of the artificial restrictions that Benois had imposed on his magazine in order to keep it from competing with *World of Art.* No formal policy, for instance, ever existed at *Bygone Years* restricting coverage to events and objects located on Russian territory. Although in practice the journal did tend to focus on such topics, articles on certain aspects of Western European artistic life appeared fairly regularly. Substantial, scholarly pieces were also never discouraged. From the very first, *Bygone Years* was envisioned by its organizers as a full-fledged journal rather than an illustrated magazine.

Aside from these differences, *Bygone Years* resembles Benois's magazine closely in both format and approach. Similarities in the way that each journal covered St. Petersburg are particularly obvious. Like *Art Treasures of Russia, Bygone Years* published a great deal of material on the monuments of the capital and the need for their preservation. Enthusiastic descriptions of architectural masterpieces and reports of recent acts of "vandalism"—the apparently "senseless" destruction of beloved structures and facades—appeared every month. The writers who composed these pieces tended overwhelmingly to echo Alexander Benois, borrowing both basic vocabulary and ideas from his famous essays on the landscape of the capital. They praised St. Petersburg for its "grand" and "splendid" look, noted the significance of its ensembles, spoke about the importance of keeping its central squares from becoming cluttered, and, perhaps most important, promoted the view that historical St. Petersburg deserved recognition as a uniquely Russian cultural phenomenon.[43] Once the new periodical had established itself, writers who had regularly contributed retrospective pieces to *World of Art* and *Art Treasures of Russia,* began to send in articles. Vladimir Kurbatov, Ivan Fomin, Stepan Iaremich, Igor Grabar, and Alexander Uspensky all periodically submitted work. The participation of these well-known scholars and critics no doubt made *Bygone Years* seem even more like a continuation of the earlier preservationist magazines.

In at least one respect, however, the coverage of St. Petersburg provided in *Bygone Years* could be considered truly innovative. As I noted earlier in this chapter, when contributors to the journals *World of Art* and *Art Treasures of Russia* spoke about saving old Petersburg, they primarily meant the monuments and sections of the capital that had been built during the reigns of Peter I, Elizabeth, Catherine II, Paul, and Alexander I, that is, constructions in the baroque, early classical, and Empire styles. Examples of later trends in architecture, the neo-Gothic, pseudo-Renaissance, and rococo structures that had begun to appear in the capital during the reign of Nicholas I, did not receive favorable attention at either *World of Art* or *Art Treasures of Russia*. In this early period, both Benois and his most prominent sympathizers generally dismissed these buildings as part of the disastrous decline into eclecticism that marked the end of the golden age of Russian architecture, and therefore did not consider them worthy of preservation. During the decade in which *Bygone Years* appeared, at least a certain faction of the preservation movement began to reconsider this assessment.

In the summer of 1913, *Bygone Years* put out a triple issue in honor of the three-hundred-year jubilee of the Romanov dynasty. It contained several articles that focused on the artistic legacy of Nicholas I. The centerpiece of the number was a long, thoughtful essay by Alexander Benois and his old *World of Art* associate Nikolai Lanceray that effectively proposed a new, inclusive approach to preservation work. "Not so long ago," the two critics noted at the beginning of their article, "everything remaining from the era that precedes us by sixty to eighty years seemed the height of tastelessness, something entirely devoid of artistic meaning and charm. . . . Recently, however, it is possible to detect an inevitable change of attitude in respect to all of this. In some incomprehensible way, that which just ten years ago seemed repulsive has started now to seem touching and dear."[44] For Benois and Lanceray, this recent shift in both their own personal taste and prevailing critical attitudes testified to an important fact: artistic standards inevitably change with the passage of time. Styles and trends popular in a given age eventually fall out of favor, becoming subject to ridicule and abuse. Often, however, after a while, they begin to attract admirers again. This process, Benois and Lanceray suggest, represents a kind of natural law of artistic development: "The past only begins to seem attractive to us when we, with all our being, feel that it is really past, that it has slipped away into the abyss of the ages and will bother us no more."[45]

The notion that change is a natural law, that beauty is not an absolute, clearly undermines the validity of any exercise in urban planning and "purification" that bases its decisions solely on the likes and dislikes of current experts. If our appreciation for the art of the recent past can improve, then preservation groups should try to save the best examples of every style and period: they should plan for and anticipate the enthusiasms of their children. The greatest change in preservationist ideology that can be detected in the pages of *Bygone Years* is a movement away from absolute evaluations of the merits of periods and styles and toward a more expansive definition of old Petersburg. Although some writers like Vladimir Kurbatov and Georgy Lukomsky continued, at least for a time, to adhere to the old standards, maintaining the absolute primacy of the Empire style and railing against eclecticism, many others quickly adopted the new, softer approach suggested by Benois and Lanceray in their 1913 article. They tried to maintain intact the great Empire ensembles that they loved so much and fought against the construction of objects that might obscure them, but outside the central areas of the city, quietly tolerated a good deal of eclecticism.[46]

Bygone Years enjoyed considerable success with the reading public, eventually becoming, according to some calculations, one of the most popular journals in all of Europe. The number of subscribers grew from 1,000 in 1907 to 5,000 in 1914.[47] During World War I, despite publishing delays and problems with delivery, these figures continued to rise. Even in the best years, however, the journal's sponsors do not appear to have made any money. The cost of reproductions remained too high to allow them to generate any real return. Instead, organizers allowed themselves to be contented with flattering reviews and public acclaim. Petr Veiner, the principal financial backer of *Bygone Years*, its publisher, and, from 1908 on, its editor, received a Pushkin Medal from the Academy of Sciences for his efforts in 1911. In 1912 he was elected a full member of the Academy of the Arts. Other key figures at the magazine also went on to occupy prominent posts in the cultural world of the capital. During the years in which the journal appeared, its principal organizers worked for a number of art museums; they cataloged collections, put together sensational art exhibits, and organized new magazines.[48] Even more important from the point of view of this book, they spearheaded the drive to create and presided over a number of private organizations devoted to protecting Russia's architectural heritage. With regard to this last form of involvement in particular, St. Petersburg preservationism deserves to be considered as part of a larger trend identified by many scholars in late imperial Russia: the gradual emergence of civil society in at least a rudimentary form.

Frustrated by what they perceived as the indifference, ineffectiveness, and conservatism of the ruling Romanov house, many educated Russians in the late nineteenth and early twentieth centuries began to look to private initiative to solve pressing problems and provide much needed services. If the state could or would not take decisive action to improve living conditions among the poor, modernize Russia's educational and medical systems, protect monuments, and create museums and libraries, then perhaps, such individuals tended to believe, educated society itself (*obshchestvennost*) should step into the breach. It could play an important role in bringing culture and enlightenment to the common people (*narod*), who, two centuries after the Petrine reforms, still remained all too obviously mired in darkness and ignorance.[49] The creation of voluntary associations of various sorts represented one important marker of this trend toward the emergence of a civil society. As Joseph Bradley has noted, following the great reforms of the 1860s and 1870s, regulations concerning nongovernmental institutions and voluntary associations relaxed, leading ultimately to an exponential increase in the number of organizations in existence.[50] By the end of the century Russia had, in addition to the local assemblies known as zemstvos created by the reforms themselves, a well-developed network of professional associations; societies of nature lovers, art lovers, and collectors; and sporting clubs, charitable groups, and self-education circles. Many of these organizations aimed to serve not just their own membership and/or natural constituency but also Russia at large: they saw themselves as accomplishing social and cultural tasks long neglected by the government.

In the case of preservationism, one widely publicized legislative debacle played a particularly important role in fueling interest in cultural activism in the decade before the October Revolution: the government's failure to pass a viable law protecting artistic and historical monuments. When the journal *Bygone Years* was founded in 1907, regulations governing the preservation of

Russia's architectural treasures remained quite primitive and, particularly in regard to eighteenth- and nineteenth-century constructions, were largely ineffectual. Although theoretically both the Academy of Arts and the Archeological Commission had the right to intervene in certain situations and block projects that threatened to disfigure or destroy major landmarks, they rarely exercised their authority.[51] Acknowledging the problems, in 1901 the government had launched an effort to draft a more effective statute, but deliberations had dragged on endlessly. For twelve years the project passed from one committee to another, gradually evolving to accommodate a whole series of conflicting interests. When a draft of the legislation finally reached the Duma in 1912, leading preservationists spoke out against it, arguing that it was so poorly conceived that it might actually impede conservation efforts. They noted derisively that the proposed statute called for the creation of an oversight committee composed almost entirely of bureaucrats, allocated little funding to preservation work, and did not even apply to church property. Although the Duma ultimately revised the legislation to address some of these concerns, coverage of the law in *Bygone Years* remained overwhelmingly negative.[52]

Disillusioned by all the bungling and delays, long before 1912, many preservationists had largely lost faith in the regime's efforts at legislative reform. They had come to believe that unless the government's priorities, procedures, and, quite possibly, composition changed dramatically, its agencies and the public institutions it supported would never take the measures necessary to protect Russia's architectural heritage. In the years preceding the February Revolution, men like Benois, Petr Veiner, and Baron Nikolai Vrangel were more inclined to pin their hopes on society than on the state. In their public statements, they consistently stressed that the educated public could make a tremendous difference if it would just take up the cause. As Vrangel remarked in a 1910 article, "All of cultured Russia must solicitously care for the artistic and historical treasures of the country." Vrangel urged volunteers to band together, forming associations to study and preserve local historical monuments. He believed "a network of such leagues, distributed across the entire country would represent a powerful force for preventing acts of vandalism, destruction, and the export [of antiquities]."[53]

Some of the preservationist organizations that emerged in the years before the Revolution did indeed, in keeping with the grand vision that Vrangel articulated in his 1910 article, pursue an agenda that was truly national in scope. Most notably, the Society for the Protection and Preservation in Russia of Monuments of Art and Antiquity (*Obshchestvo zashchity i sokhranenie v Rossii pamiatnikov iskusstva i stariny*), which Vrangel himself founded in 1910, although based in St. Petersburg, quickly gave rise to a network of provincial affiliates. Other nongovernmental institutions and associations, however, operated primarily within the confines of greater St. Petersburg, an area that, it would be fair to say, remained the principal focus of the preservation movement's efforts right up until the Revolution. The organizational models they adopted and forms of activism they pursued proved extraordinarily influential, attracting imitators in both the early Soviet and post-Soviet periods.

One of the most important pre-Revolutionary organizations dedicated to preserving the architectural heritage of Russian northern capital was the Commission for the Study and Description of Old Petersburg (*Komissiia izucheniia i opisaniia Starogo Peterburga*). Created as an affiliate of the Society of Architect-Artists in 1907, it was initially headed by Benois and had an active membership that included a host of other individuals prominent in preservationist circles: Vrangel, Vladimir Kurbatov, Mstislav Dobuzhinsky, Nikolai Roerich, Konstantin Somov, Vladimir Shchuko, and Ivan Fomin.[54] Although, from a legal point of view, the commission had no power to prevent the demolition or renovation of older buildings, it tried through carefully orchestrated media campaigns to influence public opinion and to shame property owners into complying with its recommendations. Because so many of its members held positions on the editorial board of *Bygone Years* or at least contributed regularly to the journal, the commission received a great deal of free publicity from the popular magazine. Bulletins on its activities and concerns appeared in the chronicle section of *Bygone Years* almost every month. These reports listed the commission's recent successes and failures and frequently reminded members of the public that the organization would gratefully welcome any information they might have on old buildings, including reports of vandalism, relevant sketches, and photographs. For the most part, this kind of agitation seems to have paid off. The threat of bad publicity was often enough to convince both public institutions and private landowners to follow the commission's recommendations and leave the structures in their care untouched or at least to reach some acceptable compromise.[55]

If it could not save a particular monument from destruction, the commission usually tried to convince the building's owners to allow its members to take measurements and photographs and to lay claim to any unusual or historically significant decorative details before the arrival of the wrecking crews. Fragments of molding work, ceiling murals, cast iron grates, and old tile stoves were all carefully removed and hauled away to an institution called the Museum of Old Petersburg (*Muzei Starogo Peterburga*). Created by the Commission for the Study and Description of Old Petersburg in 1907, this private cultural repository quickly came to play an important role in local preservation work. It inventoried and stored the architectural details and documents collected through the commission's constant efforts; solicited additional donations from state archives, government departments, and private individuals; eagerly displayed its collections to visitors; and, like its parent organization, continuously agitated for the preservation of the capital's architectural monuments.

The museum was initially governed by a council made up of the members of the Commission for the Study and Description of Old Petersburg.[56] Although, according to the bylaws of the institution, this council could, if it chose, expand, extending voting privileges to prominent local artists, critics, or others sympathetic to the aims of the preservation movement, for the most part the museum and the commission continued to be run by similar groups of individuals right up until the Revolution.[57] At its first meeting, the museum's council elected from its own midst a board to handle day-to-day operations for the next three years: a director, two assistants, a secretary, and four fellows. Most were members of the commission; many wrote for or edited *Bygone Years*. The first director of the museum was Benois; Ivan Fomin served as secretary; Petr Veiner, Vladimir Kurbatov, Vladimir Shchuko, and Vrangel accepted posts as fellows. A. F. Guash, the artist and well-known collector, became the museum's curator, taking responsibility for its rapidly expanding collections.

Before the museum had even opened officially, several major St. Petersburg collectors began to offer important pieces to the new repository.[58] Vladimir Argutinsky-Dolgoruky gave the museum a huge collection of drawings, engravings, and lithographs, depicting the individual buildings and the streets of the capital. The gift included works by the well-known landscape artists and original sketches by some of the capital's most famous architects. Petr Veiner, Nikolai Vrangel, Ivan Fomin, and the museum's curator, A. F. Guash, also made important contributions. As these donations flowed in and as the museum gradually convinced state archives and government departments to turn over documents and plans that had long been in their possession, the collection grew. By 1911, the museum claimed to own approximately 1,000 separate exhibits; by 1912 the figure had jumped to 1,457, including twenty antique carriages contributed by the Ministry of Court.[59] Holdings continued to grow in later years, reaching a total of slightly more than 3,000 separate items on the eve of the Revolution.[60] All of this material had to fit into a block of rooms in the home of Pavel Siuzor, the permanent chairman of the Society of Architect-Artists. Because no suitable building could be found for the museum when it was first created in 1907, Siuzor had offered to allow the institution to move into part of his three-story home on a temporary basis. Despite the continuous efforts of the society to find some other space for the collection, the museum remained in Siuzor's home until 1917. Initially open only two days a week, it expanded its hours to accommodate increasing numbers of visitors in 1912.

Funding for the Museum of Old Petersburg came from a variety of sources, including allocations made by the Society of Architect-Artists, private donations, entry and membership fees, and money raised at exhibits, concerts, and auctions. In addition, like many other privately run cultural institutions in the late imperial period, the museum regularly received subsidies from the government as well as occasional donations of material artifacts from individual state ministries and members of the Romanov family. This last fact points to an interesting paradox. As scholars such as Samuel D. Kassow have pointed out, although the juxtaposition of the wonders wrought by the educated public and the inaction or inefficiency of the Tsarist regime represented something of a "stock theme" in Russian political discourse until the Revolution, the relation between state and society was, in reality, far from simple and cannot be understood in purely oppositional terms. For all they may have railed against misplaced imperial priorities, the reactionary attitudes of Russia's last tsars, and official incompetence and malfeasance, civic-minded private groups in late imperial Russia often remained, in many respects, dependent on the government. They relied upon the regime "to create essential preconditions for purposeful social action" and would collaborate, when they felt it would advance a favorite cause, with its agencies and officials.[61] Moreover governmental elites often viewed private cultural and social undertakings positively, recognizing, particularly in periods when resources were stretched thin, that such efforts could supplement official programs.

A similar pattern of ties persisted and in some respects even grew more pronounced in the first few years after the October Revolution. Intent on meeting what they viewed as pressing cultural and social needs and also desperate, in many cases, to secure a reliable source of income, veteran cultural workers often volunteered to help the Bolshevik regime even if their political views were relatively conservative. The authorities initially welcomed such assistance. In the post-Revolutionary period and the first difficult years following the Civil War, the government needed experienced administrators and specialists and recognized that it shared some interests and goals with certain members of the old educated elite. Commissariats encouraged and even provided funding for voluntary associations; they also sometimes pressed nongovernmental organizations to coordinate their activities with official agencies. As a result, distinctions between private and state undertakings grew increasingly blurry over time. Voluntary associations became used to petitioning the state for support. Making one small compromise after another, they worked to secure or retain the financing, administrative status, and privileges they needed to operate effectively. In the mid and late 1920s, when state agencies began increasingly to view independent cultural associations as potential competitors and old specialists as too unreliable to make a positive contribution, veteran activists were often unprepared. Focused, understandably, on immediate problems, they tried at all cost to keep the institutions and organizations they had created intact, often fighting among themselves over resources. Many failed to perceive the hopelessness of their situation until very late. As the Stalinist system solidified, they had the exquisitely painful experience of watching as much of what they had built either disappeared entirely or was co-opted (and from their perspective warped) by the state. Ultimately, of course, for all its early promise and achievements, the civil society that had emerged in Russia in the late imperial period proved too weak and fragmented to stave off the rise of totalitarianism. Chapter 3 considers the way in which this process played out in the case of preservatioism.

3

Old Petersburg After the Revolution

After the collapse of the tsarist government in February 1917, the preservationists of Petrograd began to play, if anything, an even more important role in Russian cultural affairs. Two days after the abdication of Nicholas II, a group of fifty prominent artists and critics, including many veteran contributors to the journals *World of Art* and *Bygone Years,* gathered at Maxim Gorky's Petrograd apartment to discuss the new political situation and its implications for the arts. All agreed that given the risk of looting and riots, measures urgently needed to be taken to protect the imperial palaces in and around the capital and other vulnerable local monuments. The group voted to create a Commission on Artistic Affairs (*Komissiia po delam iskusstva*), charged with bringing this matter to the attention of the new authorities. Delegates initially included Alexander Benois, Nikolai Lanceray, Ivan Fomin, Georgy Lukomsky, Nikolai Roerich, Mstislav Dobuzhinsky, Ivan Bilibin, Kuzma Petrov-Vodkin, Maxim Gorky, and Fyodor Shaliapin.[1] With the exception, perhaps, of Gorky, all those elected had at one time or another been associated with the World of Art group and its enterprises.

Over the next few days, this commission entered into negotiations with both the Provisional Government and the Petrograd Soviet of Workers' and Soldiers' Deputies, offering in each case to help the new authorities design and implement an effective cultural policy. Both rival organs of government quickly voted to grant the group official mandates; each also gave it a new name. The Petrograd Soviet called the volunteers its Commission on Artistic Issues (*Komissiia po voprosam iskusstva*). The Provisional Government dubbed its new affiliate the Special Advisory Board on Artistic Affairs (*Osoboe soveshchanie po delam iskusstva*). Although theoretically separate entities, the Provisional Government's board and the Petrograd Soviet's commission had essentially the same members, aims, and priorities. Within the art world, they were generally seen as a single organization; both were popularly referred to as the Gorky Commission.

The mandates that the Gorky Commission received early in March 1917 effectively transformed it into an official entity. As agents of the Provisional Government and the Petrograd Soviet, members could gain access to buildings that were closed to the public; they had the authority to conduct inspections and could make direct recommendations to local officials on the basis of what they saw. To many commission members this position must have seemed at once novel and exciting. Although the tsarist government had occasionally provided the preservation movement with various forms of assistance, leading activists had always tended to perceive themselves as outsiders, private citizens struggling to solve problems caused or at least left unaddressed by a negligent, hopelessly inefficient political regime. Suddenly they had the chance to operate from within the system and play a direct role in setting official cultural policy. The members of the Gorky Commission, in early March at least, looked on the future hopefully. They began to think in terms of progressively more ambitious projects and, both in private and at public forums, spoke enthusiastically about everything the government might soon begin to accomplish in the arts.

At the first organizational meeting in Gorky's apartment, even before contact had been made with the new authorities, Benois had introduced the idea of creating a ministry of fine arts as one possible long-term goal. Once negotiations with the Provisional Government and the Petrograd Soviet were underway, the members of the Gorky Commission began to discuss Benois's proposal seriously. On March 7, 1917, a special meeting was held at the Institute of Art History (*Institut istorii iskusstva*) to consider how a ministry of fine arts might be organized and what its responsibilities should be. Many members of the Gorky Commission, including Benois, were in attendance. Thanks partly to their influence, the plan that emerged at the meeting in many ways reflected the priorities and views of the Petersburg preservation movement and the World of Art group. The ministry, it was declared, would take charge of the nation's theaters, conservatories, and the Academy of Arts. It would protect existing works of art and try to encourage the creation of new ones, set up both permanent museums and traveling exhibits, develop educational programs for the masses, organize popular festivals, and work to improve the appearance of buildings, streets, and squares. Most important, perhaps, the ministry would free artists and cultural institutions from their dependence on wealthy patrons. It would presumably receive budgetary allocations from the treasury each year and could use these funds to finance worthwhile endeavors.

Those assembled at the meeting on March 7 asked Benois to head the commission that would work out the details of the project. It met on March 10 and, in hopes of quickly moving forward, created seven specialized subcommittees, each of which was staffed by experts on a particular field of art or form of cultural work. Predictably, World of Art loyalists dominated many of the subcommittees, particularly those that focused on painting, graphics, and sculpture; architecture; theater; and preservation work.[2] When, toward the end of the meeting, the commission discussed possible candidates for the post of Minister of Fine Arts, Sergei Diaghilev, the editor of the old journal *World of Art*, was immediately mentioned.

The members of the Gorky Commission became so absorbed in their plans and projects in early March that they appear not to have noticed that many people within the artistic community took exception to their approach. Opponents objected to the fact that individuals they perceived as belonging to a single, narrow artistic group had gone and volunteered their services to the authorities; they accused the Gorky Commission of attempting, in effect, to "seize control" of the nation's cultural life.[3] The aesthetic views of men like Benois, Fomin, Lukomsky, and Dobuzhinsky were by no means uncontroversial in revolutionary Petrograd. Many avant-gardists, in particular, found the stylistic affectations of the World of Art group utterly appalling; Benois's nostalgic sketches of Louis XIV at Versailles, Konstantin Somov's paintings of court masquerades and leering cavaliers, and the whole notion of neoclassical architecture struck many in 1917 as utterly reactionary, a strange homage to autocratic tyranny and the excesses of the old aristocracy. Wasn't it time to move on? Instead of fetishizing the past and organizing yet another string of preservation campaigns, shouldn't the artists of Petrograd turn their attention to new and revolutionary forms of activity? Instead of placing themselves under the authority of a government ministry, shouldn't they, at least for a while, revel in their autonomy, in their sudden freedom from tsarist censorship and hidebound imperial institutions?

On March 9, less than one week after the Gorky Commission was organized, a consortium of Petrograd artistic institutions, societies, and groups issued a statement calling for a citywide meeting of all those involved in the arts. The gathering took place three days later in the Mikhailovsky Theater and attracted an unexpectedly large number of participants; 1,400 individuals assembled to discuss the current situation on the cultural front and to decide upon an appropriate course of action. Early in the meeting, Gorky gave a report on the activities of the Gorky Commission in which he described with enormous pride the organization's first successful preservation projects and its contacts with the new authorities. To his surprise and to the shock of the other members of the commission who were present in the auditorium, this brief speech provoked a storm of criticism. I. Zdanevich, Vladimir Mayakovsky, and Vsevolod Meyerhold all took stands later in the meeting against the program of the Gorky Commission, accusing its members of "usurping power" and questioning the wisdom of their campaign to preserve the architectural relics of imperialism. Many others in the audience seemed inclined to agree with them. At the end of the meeting, those assembled passed a resolution in which it was officially noted that the Gorky Commission did not speak for the artistic community as a whole. They called for the immediate creation of an alternative representative body, an artists' union (*Soiuz deiatelei iskusstva*), that would more accurately reflect the interests of the Russian art world. They hoped that this new organization would in time provide "answers to all of the artistic questions posed by life, answers that would serve as the foundation for deciding upon all government measures in the field of art."[4]

As a result of the meeting at the Mikhailovsky Theater, a twelve-man organizational committee was created to lay the groundwork for the formation of an artists' union. During the spring of 1917 this entity lodged a barrage of petitions against the Gorky Commission with the Provisional Government and regularly criticized its rival in the press. The Gorky Commission, however, managed to fend off most attacks and remained active throughout March and April, contributing, in particular, to preservation efforts in the Petrograd area.[5] The commission sent a panel of experts, including Benois, Nikolai Lanceray, and Georgy Lukomsky, out to Peterhof and Oranienbaum to inspect the palaces, and, when they discovered minor damage and evidence of theft, took steps to secure the premises. In hopes of preventing similar problems in the future, the commission began working on a plan to inventory all the palaces in the Petrograd area. It drafted appeals to the militia, asking them to guard local architectural monuments, and voted to hang posters on some of the most vulnerable structures with the text: "This building belongs to the people. Protect it."[6] Such slogans aimed to instill pride of ownership in the lower classes. They encouraged workers and peasants to claim for themselves and hence accord some value to physical structures that, as Richard Stites notes, many seemed inclined to regard solely as artifacts of an alien way of life, graphic representations of the inequality, coerciveness, and uninclusiveness of the old system.[7]

The museums of the northern capital also benefited from the efforts of the Gorky Commission. Members found a new facility to house the Museum of Old Petersburg, which had been recently forced to leave the home of Pavel Siuzor; lobbied for the preservation of the city's lapidary factories and museums; took steps to increase the amount of exhibition space at the Museum of Alexander III (the Russian Museum); and worked to save the Museum of the Society for the Encouragement of the Arts.[8] They drafted proposals suggesting that the government buy the country's most valuable private collections, or at least move them into temporary storage facilities where they could be adequately protected until the political situation in Russia stabilized. All of these projects and proposals, even those that the Gorky Commission did not succeed in implementing during the two months in which it was active, were valuable as models for the efforts of other, later organizations.

At the end of April, after weeks of conflict with the group organizing the Artists' Union, the Gorky Commission finally collapsed. Its members had been, as Benois later recalled, "mortally offended" by the charge that they were merely out to usurp power, that the organization they had worked so hard to create was fundamentally "undemocratic." They had grown tired of countering the distorted accounts of their actions and motives that appeared so regularly in the press.[9] On April 20, Gorky sent a letter to the Provisional Government informing the authorities that the Special Advisory Board on Artistic Affairs had disbanded. Shortly thereafter Dobuzhinsky released a similar statement to the press.[10] For a while the Gorky Commission continued to operate under the protection of the Petrograd Soviet, but there too it found itself under attack. In the end, it seemed easier to give in to the demands of the Artists' Union and leave the field entirely. Benois and his old colleagues from World of Art retreated for a time to their old offices and studios, and citywide preservation efforts ground to a halt. In May and June, despite attempts by both the

Provisional Government and the Artists' Union to create new structures that would take the place of the Gorky Commission, nothing much got done.

A promising new organization finally appeared in July 1917. On the first of that month, in response to a scandalous rash of break-ins at the palaces in and around Petrograd, F. A. Golovin, the commissar of the former Ministry of the Imperial Court for the Provisional Government, announced the creation of a new agency: the Artistic-Historical Commission for Inventorying the Movable Property of the Petrograd Palaces of the Former Palace Administration. As the name suggests, Golovin hoped this entity would complete one of the Gorky Commission's more ambitious projects: he wanted it to catalog the contents of the imperial palaces of the capital, writing up accurate scholarly descriptions of everything of any artistic or historical significance and photographing objects that seemed particularly valuable. Until this basic inventory work was completed, Golovin understood, there was little hope of even monitoring security at the palaces, let alone catching thieves or recovering lost property. In order to expedite the process as much as possible, Golovin approached one of the most prominent preservationists in the city, Vasily Vereshchagin, and asked him to chair the new commission. Vereshchagin had played an instrumental role in founding both the journal *Bygone Years* and the Society for the Protection and Preservation in Russia of Monuments of Art and Antiquity. His connections and experience made him, in many respects, an ideal candidate to head the new commission.

Aside from Vereshchagin, the Petrograd Artistic-Historical Commission at least initially appears only to have had two other members, neither of whom was particularly prominent.[11] The modest size of the new agency and the fact that it had a clearly defined and initially relatively limited mission to complete may have played in its favor. Unlike the Gorky Commission, it managed for a time to steer clear of controversy and accomplished a great deal. By mid-August, members had made significant progress toward inventorying the contents of the Winter Palace and had begun to put together a list of specific items that appeared to have been stolen from the collection in the spring and early summer. These preliminary results pleased everyone concerned. By the end of the summer, three more artistic-historical commissions had appeared: one in Tsarskoe Selo, another in Gatchina, and a third in Peterhof. All were small-scale operations and were staffed by both relative newcomers and well-known older preservationists. Several men who had in the past worked with Vereshchagin on the journal *Bygone Years* accepted positions on the suburban commissions including, most notably, Georgy Lukomsky and Petr Veiner.[12] Their presence helped to ensure that the new agencies inherited the spirit and the traditions of the old preservation movement and that they had the same basic aesthetic sensibilities and reverence for old Petersburg.

Under the Provisional Government, the artistic-historical commissions primarily conducted inventory work and, as the German army approached Petrograd, packed up valuables for evacuation to Moscow. After the October Revolution, they took on additional functions. The commissions were the only structures within the former Ministry of the Imperial Court that immediately agreed to cooperate with the Bolshevik government after the October coup and, as a result, they quickly won the trust of Anatoly Lunacharsky, the Commissar of Enlightenment. Placed in charge of both the old Ministry of Education and the former Ministry of the Imperial Court on October 30, Lunacharsky at first desperately needed qualified assistants and hence was eager to accept whatever help the artistic-historical commissions could give him. Aside from working on their catalogs, they began to make regular sweeps of antique stores and art galleries in search of property that had been stolen in recent months from the palaces. They expanded their field of activity, gradually taking on responsibility for securing and protecting new buildings, monuments, and collections. In addition, as their first inventory projects approached completion, the commissions began transforming the most important palaces in Petrograd and its immediate suburbs into museums. They decided which interiors and furnishings to display to the public, trying in the case of each imperial residence to focus on a distinct period and/or a particularly characteristic style. In the main palace at Peterhof, the artistic-historical commission chose to emphasize the age of Peter I and, to a lesser extent, the reign of Nicholas I; the first exhibit in the Catherine Palace in Tsarskoe Selo gave the public the opportunity to admire both mid-eighteenth-century baroque and early Russian classicism; and at Gatchina displays focused on the time of Paul and Alexander III. In this sense the commissions were, as some activists later acknowledged, engaged as much in the construction of a national past as in its protection.[13] Preservation work inevitably involved an element of selection. In the Petrograd area as a whole, members of the movement fought to protect what they judged to be especially fine or at least representative of a particular period or stylistic trend; at individual sites, they worked to create interior displays and exterior vistas that would provide the public with a clear picture of a specific historic moment and/or stage in Russia's aesthetic development. They cleared away whatever did not fit: evidence that fell outside the focus designated for the exhibit; decorative touches that they considered incompatible with the vision they had chosen to project.

From July 1917 to June 1918, the artistic-historical commissions represented the primary mechanism for conducting preservation work in the Petrograd area. Shortly thereafter they began to disappear, superseded by or merging with other, more permanent organizations. For a brief period of time, however, they had played a tremendously important role both in preserving the cultural treasures of the past and in deciding how they would initially be displayed to the Russian populace. Why did the members of Golovin's commissions agree to cooperate with Lunacharsky so quickly? Why did they not boycott the Bolshevik regime like so many other government officials and members of the intelligentsia? Quite a few commission members, including, most notably, Vereshchagin, were from wealthy or aristocratic families and held relatively conservative political views.[14] They had no natural reason to sympathize with the Bolsheviks, so when they began to collaborate with the new authorities in the days after the Revolution, it came as a surprise to many. In June 1918, Petr Veiner made a belated effort to explain the motivation behind the decision of the commission members: "When, right after the October coup, we started to work to preserve monuments of art and antiquity, we didn't hesitate at all to enter into cooperation with a party that was alien to us. We believed that our tasks in this affair lay outside the realm of politics and knew, on the other hand . . . that no later action of any kind, not even the most intensive labor, would return what was lost."[15]

The basic attitude to power that Veiner describes, this willingness to collaborate with even an unsympathetic political regime in the interests of short-term preservation goals, was in many ways typical of the old preservationists of Petrograd. The men who had once contributed to the journals *World of Art* and *Bygone Years* liked to think of themselves and the movement that they led as "apolitical."[16] They prided themselves on the fact that they did not take sides, that they had never tied themselves to a particular political party or ideological point of view. In the pre-Revolutionary era, leading preservationists had often put aside their distaste for the tsarist government and accepted official posts, committee appointments, and material aid when they felt it to be in the interest of their cause. Similarly, preservationists had by and large refused to choose sides in the chaos that had followed the abdication of the tsar in the spring of 1917. Although, no doubt, the natural sympathies of most of those who had gathered at Gorky's Petrograd apartment on March 4 lay with the Provisional Government, they had opted to send delegations with approximately the same appeal to both this institution and its rival, the Petrograd Soviet of Workers' and Soldiers' Deputies. Following the October coup, once again, many preservationists, even if they disliked the new Bolshevik regime, had started collaborating relatively quickly.[17]

Because they began to cooperate with the Bolsheviks at a time when the regime still desperately needed qualified specialists, the preservationists of Petrograd, in many cases, ascended to positions of real importance in the first years after the Revolution. Benois, Vereshchagin, Troinitsky, and Veiner all served on a variety of commissions at the Commissariat of Enlightenment (*Narodnyi komissariat prosveshcheniia*, abbreviated Narkompros) and helped run major cultural institutions during the Civil War period.[18] From these positions, they managed to introduce a whole series of significant reforms, acting on proposals that, in many cases, had repeatedly been made over the preceding two decades in the pages of *World of Art* and *Bygone Years*. Benois and his friends worked to raise standards for urban planning, restoration, and museum curatorship. As members of the new preservation commissions organized by the Commissariat of Enlightenment, they tried, as much as possible, to protect both individual monuments and historic districts of the capital from destruction while at the same time allowing for necessary improvements in housing and sanitation.

Of course, even in the first few years after the October Revolution, the preservationists faced significant frustrations: conflict between rival governmental structures, poor communication, and shortages of key resources often made it impossible for them to safeguard fragile monuments even when they theoretically had the backing of key Bolshevik officials. No amount of hollering could prevent most of the northern capital's remaining eighteenth-century wooden buildings from being demolished for firewood during the worst days of the Civil War. Military troops and delegations of peasants from the provinces continued to be billeted in palaces from time to time. Museums all too frequently disappeared just as swiftly as they had been created, freeing up valuable space for other uses. As time went on, the old contributors to the journals *World of Art* and *Bygone Years* faced disappointments like these more frequently and found themselves increasingly at odds with the emerging Soviet state. By the second half of the 1920s, official emphasis on party-mindedness had made the "apolitical" stance they favored untenable; the government's ruthless campaigns to industrialize, modernize, and sovietize Russian society in many cases precluded the protection of older monuments. Some preservationists, like Benois and Georgy Lukomsky, ultimately chose to emigrate. Others retreated to their offices in the hope of waiting out the storm of cultural revolution.

In many respects, the approach to preservation work employed by Benois and his friends changed remarkably little in the first years following the Revolution. They continued to engage in the same activities and often relied on familiar organizational strategies. Two organizations that they helped to create in Petrograd in the first few years after the Revolution, in particular, seem like conscious attempts to resurrect and expand upon pre-Revolutionary structures: the Museum of the City (*Muzei Goroda*) and the Society for the Study, Popularization, and Artistic Preservation of Old Petersburg (*Obshchestva izucheniia, populiarizatsii i khudozhestvennoi okhrany Starogo Peterburga*). In hindsight both of these entities would come to be identified as major centers of *kraevedenie*. Because they figure prominently in the mythic narrative that many present-day Russian *kraevedy* accept as a true account of their discipline's origin and history, these institutions merit some discussion here.

The Museum of the City was created in the fall of 1918. In May of that year, after the former Ministry of Provisions was evacuated to Moscow, the Anichkov Palace, an imperial residence located on the corner of Nevsky Prospect and the Fontanka River, had been turned over to Cultural Enlightenment Department of the Petrograd Municipal Authority (*Kul'turno-prosvetitel'nyi otdel Petrogradskoi gorodskoi upravy*).[19] Unsure as to how best to use the buildings, the head of the Cultural Enlightenment Department, Vera Menzhinskaia, asked the veteran preservationist Vladimir Kurbatov for advice. A minor figure at *World of Art* and a regular contributor to both *Art Treasures of Russia* and *Bygone Years,* Kurbatov was, by this time, widely acknowledged as a leading expert on the cultural monuments and heritage of St. Petersburg. In the years just before the October Revolution, he had composed some of the first pocket guides to the suburban palace-park complexes outside the northern capital, written a popular architectural history of St. Petersburg that exercised a profound influence on all later descriptions of the city, and published a pioneering study of the history of landscape and park design.[20] One of the first preservationists to volunteer his services to the Bolshevik regime, Kurbatov was already contributing to a variety of Narkompros projects related to preservation work and landscape design when Menzhinskaia approached him.[21]

Despite his busy schedule, Kurbatov responded favorably to Menzhinskaia's request and went to look at the Anichkov Palace facilities with his old acquaintance, the architect Lev Ilin. Both men quickly agreed that it was ill-suited to the needs of a teaching institution. The majestic facade of the main palace and its many ornate interiors, the configuration of the service buildings on the site, and the central location of the complex as a whole made the new facility perfect, however, they believed, for a major museum. In the report that they later made to Menzhinskaia, Kurbatov and Ilin suggested creating a new museum within the palace complex that would examine the city of Petrograd and problems of urban life. Although two repositories already existed that might, in a sense, be considered to fulfill a similar purpose, each, they argued, suffered from obvious deficiencies. The City Museum on Kronverksky Prospect had an unimpressive collection and lacked the space to expand. The Museum of Old Petersburg had been unable to mount a proper exhibit since the February Revolution and, in any case, had always focused exclusively on the capital's past, emphasizing primarily art and architecture. Kurbatov and Ilin felt that in the vast Anichkov Palace a municipal museum could be created that would address a broader range of concerns.

Menzhinskaia agreed to this suggestion and assembled a commission to draw up a specific plan. Members included Kurbatov, Ilin, and a host of other less illustrious figures, many of them engineers involved in local planning work. In the space of a few months, they drafted a detailed proposal that won the approval of Narkompros. On October 4 Lunacharsky signed a decree that officially brought the new museum into being and simultaneously confirmed the repository's right to use not just the Anichkov Palace itself, but also a whole array of adjacent structures, including the palace of Grand Prince Sergei Aleksandrovich, the Serebriakov house, several apartment buildings, and the Office of His Majesty (*Kabinet ego velichestva*).[22] Effectively, the Museum of the City gained possession of an entire square block of real estate in the center of Petrograd.[23] Menzhinskaia's commission, which had by this time evolved into a permanent administrative board, began setting up exhibits immediately, enabling the museum to open its doors to the public in the space of only a few weeks.[24] Although initially displays were modest, the collection quickly grew. By 1923, the museum would boast eight separate departments, each with its own library and offices for receiving visitors as well as exhibition facilities.[25]

From the first, the museum's administration aimed to create something of truly national or even international significance—not just a museum of Petrograd, but a repository that would illustrate the history and structural nature of urban areas in general. The word *city* in Museum of the City, board members noted, was meant to be understood in "the collective sense," not as a reference to Petrograd specifically.[26] In keeping with this broad purpose, universal and comparative issues represented the focus of the museum's displays. Many exhibits illustrated problems of organization, service, and supply that had plagued urban areas for thousands of years and contemporary efforts to arrive at effective solutions. The repository boasted a huge Department of Communal and Social Hygiene, a Technical Department that focused on energy systems and transportation, and extensive materials relating to city planning.[27] Grand displays outlined the evolution of human settlements from ancient times up to the modern era and depicted utopian models for the garden cities of the future.

Despite this emphasis on universal issues, the study of Petrograd always represented an important focus of activity for the staff of the Museum of the City. No doubt this was inevitable: the repository could not reasonably ignore the metropolitan area that surrounded it. Even in relatively early statements, members of Menzhinskaia's commission had admitted that the northern capital would doubtless serve as "the primary example, a base for study" in many departments and displays.[28] They knew that material on Petrograd would interest local visitors and quite rightly assumed that it would prove far easier to acquire than exhibits relating to other Russian or foreign cities. Moreover, the presence of veteran preservationists on the museum's board including, most notably Vladimir Kurbatov himself, ensured that the eighteenth- and early-nineteenth-century heritage of the capital received plenty of attention. The permanent display assembled by the Park and Garden Section culminated in an ecstatic description of the grounds at Pavlovsk, Peterhof, and Tsarskoe Selo. Six rooms in the exhibit of the Section of Urban Planning and Construction were devoted solely to Petrograd.[29] In addition, several separate permanent exhibits at the Museum of the City focused exclusively on the magnificent past of the northern capital. First and foremost these included the Museum of Old Petersburg itself.

Housed in cramped, expensive quarters on Isaakievskaia Square since the spring of 1917, the Museum of Old Petersburg had been desperately trying to relocate for months and was on the brink of bankruptcy by the time the Museum of the City came into being. With more space than it could conceivably fill on its own in the immediate future, the board of the new repository approached the administration of the Museum of Old Petersburg and proposed a merger.[30] The compact that the two institutions signed in November 1918 stipulated that the Museum of Old Petersburg's holdings would not be dispersed. It was incorporated into the Museum of the City as a separate department, retaining its old name, certain bylaws, traditions, and part of its staff. Petr Veiner served as the department's curator until his arrest in 1925.[31] Vladimir Kurbatov then stepped in to replace him.

In addition to the Museum of Old Petersburg, two other displays within the Museum of the City also worked primarily to illustrate the wonders of the imperial capital: the permanent exhibit of the Section of Interior Furnishings for Living Space and what was known as "the historical rooms." The first was housed in a mansion that, until the Revolution, had belonged to the Countess Karlova, the widow of Duke G. G. Meklenberg-Strelitsky.[32] When it was turned over to the Museum of the City in the spring of 1919, the building still contained most of the possessions left behind by Karlova after she fled into emigration, including furniture from various periods in a wide range of styles, the Duke's famous 12,000-volume library, and collections of paintings, lithographs, china, and silver. Using primarily this material, Lev Ilin transformed the mansion into an exhibit of interiors, rooms typical of the homes of the nobility, government officials, and the bourgeoisie of St. Petersburg at specific times in the city's history. The exhibit enjoyed popularity with museum visitors, and throughout the early 1920s its admission fees were seen as an important source of income for the museum.[33]

The section of the Museum of the City known as the "historical rooms" was even more popular with the public.[34] Located in the main building of the Anichkov Palace, this exhibit occupied about a quarter of the total floor space in the structure. It included the area of the palace that had been left undisturbed after the death of Tsar Alexander III as a memorial (known before the Revolution as the Personal Museum of Alexander III) and a series of rooms that had belonged to his wife Maria Fyodorovna. Although these late-nineteenth-century eclectic interiors, from the point of view of most early-twentieth-century art critics, were of little real aesthetic value, the board of the Museum of the City voted to preserve them, reasoning that they were "too characteristic of the era [in which they were created] to destroy."[35] As Vladimir Kurbatov noted in a report delivered in support of the decision to leave the Personal Museum of Alexander III intact, "It is not necessary to speak of that museum as a valuable artistic collection, but there are a series of valuable things in it, and the collection itself is characteristic of its epoch and will explain a great deal to historians in the future.... It is still questionable how future art historians will deal with the age of Tretiakov, the Vladimir Cathedral, and the emerging Abramtsevo group. That is why it would seem rational to preserve the museum in its present form."[36]

This kind of preservationist rhetoric was not uncommon at the Museum of the City. In the minutes of its board meetings, statements and opinions were often recorded that clearly reflect the values and ideas associated with the journal *Bygone Years*. Like many other cultural institutions, in the Civil War years and for most of the 1920s, the Museum of the City represented something of an uneasy compromise: preservationists and cultural workers who subscribed to new Soviet values served together on its board and jointly worked to set policy. As a rule, moderate views tended to prevail, with each group making some concessions to the other.[37] Hence, the museum ended up with both a substantial number of historical displays illustrating the way of life of the Russian nobility in the eighteenth and nineteenth centuries and a hygiene department that aggressively promoted the construction of new crematoria, bathhouses, playgrounds, and model apartment houses. Similarly, in terms of the practical contributions that it made to local planning and reconstruction efforts, the museum seems to have generally tried to find a middle ground between a desire for progress and a commitment to preservation work. When asked to participate in specific projects by the Leningrad Gubernia Department of Communal Management (*Leningradskii gubernskii otdel kommunal'nogo khoziaistva*, abbreviated Gubotkomkhoz) or other government structures, the board generally agreed with alacrity and dispatched appropriate representatives.[38] It helped select new names for city streets, drew up sanitation measures, gave advice on what colors should be used when old buildings were repainted, and monitored the condition of local cemeteries. In 1924, after the Commission on City Construction at Gubotkomkhoz was liquidated, the Museum of the City was asked to organize a temporary planning bureau to replace it, and for the next year assumed responsibility for all projects in the area.[39] Although, by and large, the stance of this organization must be characterized as pro-development, the museum did periodically use its influence to save historical monuments, speaking out against truly unfortunate projects. In 1924, when one of the city's communal management agencies proposed replacing the angel on top of the Alexander Column with a statue of Lenin or another Soviet symbol, the museum's board protested vigorously.[40]

The museum's ability to intercede in such situations diminished over time. Like other Soviet organizations, it faced new pressures as the relatively liberal period of the New Economic Policy (NEP) came to an end and the cultural revolution began. In many respects, 1927 marked the end of the uneasy truce that had allowed members of the old educated elite and Bolshevik officials to work together on pressing cultural tasks despite their ideological differences. With the economy and social structures significantly stabilized and new Soviet cadres emerging, the regime's attitude to old specialists grew increasingly ambivalent. Warnings about a possible bourgeois counterattack filled the press. In a series of widely publicized show trials, including the Shakhty case, engineers and other educated specialists were accused of wrecking. In this climate, the position of experts in the arts and humanities grew particularly tenuous: as the regime's priorities shifted and rapid industrialization emerged as a central preoccupation, they had less to offer and seemed increasingly expendable. Efforts to expand and preserve museum collections often came into direct conflict with official campaigns to locate valuables that might reasonably be sold for foreign currency, desperately needed in this period to finance the purchase of machinery and other key goods abroad. Appeals for the conservation of historical buildings and important cultural landscapes threatened to disrupt or delay key state-sponsored construction projects. Preservationists were easily labeled as obstructionists. Regardless of how much they moderated their stance and spoke publicly of the need for development as well as conservation, they inevitably seemed more focused on the past than the future. They were never ready to agree to modernization at all costs, in every situation set themselves the goal of preserving as much of Russia's cultural heritage as possible given political circumstances, and, as a result, always seemed, at best, reluctant partners in the regime's drive to make a great leap forward. If scholars like William G. Rosenberg are right to see Stalin's "revolution from above" as a response to a concrete problem of governance, the failure of NEP to produce "broad support, institutionally as well as culturally, for the 'modernizing' tasks at hand," then it is scarcely surprising that preservationist groups and institutions fell victim relatively dramatically.[41]

In 1928 the Leningrad Regional Workers' and Peasants' Inspectorate (Leningradskaia oblastnaia raboche-krest'ianskaia inspektsiia) subjected personnel at the Museum of the City to a vicious and protracted review procedure, eventually dismissing most. Interviewers attacked the museum for focusing too much on the past, questioned the class background of its employees, and leveled wild charges of corruption and theft. In one report, the inspectorate explicitly equated the actions of museum staff with the forms of industrial sabotage uncovered at the recent Shakhty trial.[42] Shortly before the review began, the museum had been forced to close its historical rooms.[43] Curators were given three days to dismantle the exhibit and told to turn over any articles of great historical or artistic value to the Central Scientific Administration (*Glavnyi komitet nauki*, abbreviated Glavnauka); virtually everything else was sent off to the warehouses of the Municipal Auction House (*Gorodskoi lombard*) and eventually sold for hard currency. The permanent exhibit of the Section of Interior Furnishings for Living Space soon met a similar fate.[44] In both cases, exhibits were undoubtedly sold as part of a national campaign to finance the industrialization projects of the First Five-Year Plan.

The Museum of the City never recovered from the losses it sustained during the first years of the cultural revolution. With its old personnel and many of its historical exhibits gone, it no longer had much to connect it to pre-Revolutionary preservationism and ceased to adhere in any direct way to the movement's values and traditions. All too aware of the charges leveled during the 1928 inspection, its administration shied away from anything that might be viewed as old-fashioned, un-Soviet, or even controversial. Although the Museum of the City remained in existence throughout the 1930s under a variety of names and administrative affiliations, it would never again show any real signs of independence or initiative.[45] It was finally liquidated in July 1941 as part of a broad campaign to eliminate nonessential institutions so that more resources could be directed at the war effort.

In terms of its history, the Society for the Study, Popularization, and Artistic Preservation of Old Petersburg and its Suburbs in many ways closely resembles the Museum of the City. Both organizations emerged in the first years after the Revolution and initially engaged in a broad spectrum of activities related to the study and preservation of the northern capital. Each, due in part to changes in the political climate, lost momentum later in the 1920s, and, by the early 1930s, had wasted into a shadow of its former self. In one important respect, however, the two organizations were fundamentally different: the society was a voluntary scholarly association rather than a public institution. Although this status did not keep it from experiencing a good deal of unpleasantness, it did mean that it was subject to different regulations and hence a slightly different set of pressures than the Museum of the City.

The Society for the Study, Popularization, and Artistic Preservation of Old Petersburg and its Suburbs was created in the fall of 1921. In the summer of that year, a number of reputable specialists, including veteran preservationists, established art historians, and disciples of the excursion theorist Ivan Grevs had gathered in Pavlovsk to study the palace and park complex for several weeks. The seminar proved such a success that, after participants returned to the capital in the fall, S. N. Zharnovsky, the head of the Art Department of the Second Municipal Region, began to look for ways to keep the project going. He suggested specifically that the group expand its efforts to include the study of Petrograd itself, thereby making it feasible to work together year-round. With the help of a number of fellow enthusiasts, he called an organizational meeting, inviting virtually everyone with any history of involvement in local preservation work or interest in the capital's past. The gathering took place on November 20. Those in attendance not only approved of Zharnovsky's proposal for a winter seminar in Petrograd, but also began to think in more ambitious terms, envisaging the creation of a scholarly society that would rekindle the enthusiasm of the intelligentsia for voluntary cultural work and resurrect all of the ambitious projects of the city's pre-Revolutionary preservation groups. It could mount the kind of retrospectivist exhibits that had in the past been sponsored by the journals *World of Art* and *Bygone Years;* defend, register, and document threatened monuments using the methods once employed by the Society of Architect-Artists' Commission for the Study and Description of Old Petersburg; and organize regular lectures on the history and architecture of the northern capital as the Museum of Old Petersburg always had. The new association, everyone quickly agreed, should be called the Society for the Study, Popularization, and Artistic Preservation of Old Petersburg and its Suburbs, or the Society of Old Petersburg for short. In either form, the name clearly represented an homage to pre-Revolutionary preservationism.

By the time Zharnovsky's organizational meeting came to a close, the first steps toward the creation of the new society had already been completed. Those in attendance had passed a basic set of statutes and elected a ten-person council to lead the new organization. The men selected included Alexander Benois, Sergei Troinitsky, Petr Veiner, Vladimir Kurbatov, Petr Stolpiansky, and several other important figures in the cultural life of the northern capital.[46] Although many of these specialists ultimately proved so busy with other commitments that they could devote only limited time to the society, the presence of their names on the first council lists probably made it easier for the organization to attract participants and negotiate with government structures.[47] In part thanks to them, the Society of Old Petersburg got off to an excellent start and managed to accomplish an enormous amount in 1922 and 1923. The group put hundreds of volunteers to work in central Petrograd photographing, measuring, and registering monuments; carried out a series of important restoration projects; and opened several museums.[48] It ran seminars in Petrograd during the academic year and at the suburban imperial residences during the summers.[49] In addition, it hosted concerts, regular lectures, and excursions; collected street signs, placards, and architectural details for the Museum of Old Petersburg; and mounted publicity campaigns designed to teach the public to appreciate the beauty of the northern capital.

All of these activities were accomplished without financial assistance from the government. Until 1924, the society was entirely privately supported. Its income came in part, of course, from membership dues, donations, admission fees, and ticket sales, but it also relied on a far more innovative fundraising scheme. In July 1922, the society organized an autonomous juridical entity called the Committee to Assist the Society (*Komitet pomoshchi*). The sole aim of this new organization was to generate income for the society through various business enterprises. It opened grocery stores, sold wood and various household goods, and even ran several small manufacturing concerns.[50] Because the committee was an autonomous organization with its own statutes and a fully independent board, the Society of Old Petersburg, in theory, only stood to gain from its activities; it could not be held responsible for any debts the committee incurred or be made liable for its actions.[51] Up until the spring of 1924 the committee regularly delivered profits to the society, encouraging the latter organization to launch a whole string of ambitious projects and to assume responsibility for the upkeep of a long list of local monuments. Then, due to various political and economic factors, both the society and the committee it had created fell into disarray.

When the Society of Old Petersburg was founded in 1921, it had adopted as one of its principal objectives "the care of certain monuments, places, buildings, and things . . . to which the guardianship of the government could not extend either because they were too small or because, given limited manpower and resources, it was not possible to preserve everything that should be preserved."[52] It assisted what it saw as underfunded and understaffed government structures by identifying for itself and completing worthwhile projects in building restoration and museum construction. In theory, of course, this was all "very well", the enthusiasm of dedicated volunteers meant that more could be accomplished. As the economic reforms of the NEP period took hold, however, many government agencies, particularly within Narkompros, began to feel intensely vulnerable. They faced budgetary cutbacks, constant criticism in the press, the threat of liquidation, and demands that they somehow suddenly become financially self-sufficient. In such circumstances, outside assistance all too often read as competition. Officials intent on proving that the structures they led were completing essential political, cultural, and economic tasks generally did not care to see other organizations duplicating their efforts in a given field. Agencies that were charging for lectures, excursions, and concerts or collecting museum admission fees as part of a self-financing drive had an incentive to bar would-be competitors from offering similar amusements even if they did not suspect their rivals of providing the masses with unhealthy or politically misleading cultural content. In the society's case, the issue of political reliability was never really off the table; the retrospective orientation of its programming made it an easy target for attack.

As a result of both political concerns and economic stresses, minor conflicts with government agencies and institutions began to occur almost as soon as the Society of Old Petersburg was founded, and gradually evolved into a substantial problem. By January 1923, the society was concerned enough about its strained relations with various public agencies that, with the aim of easing tension, it chose to abandon its independent status and affiliate itself with one of them: the Academic Center of Narkompros (*Akademicheskii tsentr*, abbreviated Aktsentr).⁵³ By placing itself under the jurisdiction of this organization, the society seems to have hoped to gain, in addition to protection against the complaints of other agencies, rent free office space and some budgetary allocations. As James T. Andrews notes in a recent study, in the early Soviet period voluntary associations often secured such benefits by affiliating themselves with government agencies.⁵⁴ In this instance, however, the arrangement proved something of a disappointment. The agreement the society made ultimately involved few obligations on either side, and, by the spring of 1924, the society found itself embroiled in a whole series of new conflicts. The Museum of the City and Gubotkomkhoz were sabotaging its efforts to participate in planning work. Politprosvet claimed to have a complete monopoly on adult excursion work, the right to grant or deny permission for most forms of public lectures, and, moreover, aspired to become the leading provider of summer seminars in the Petrograd area.⁵⁵ The Society of Old Petersburg desperately needed a powerful administrative entity to help it reach acceptable settlements in all of these disputes. With this in mind, in 1924 it began negotiating first with Aktsentr in Leningrad, then with the local Gubernia Executive Committee (*Gubernskii ispolnitel'nyi komitet*, abbreviated Gubispolkom), and finally with Glavnauka in Moscow. As the talks dragged on, failing to produce any real results, the society's problems multiplied. Its conflict with Politprosvet proved extraordinarily divisive and ultimately led to a wave of resignations from the society. The group had to cancel its summer seminars in Pavlovsk and Peterhof after it failed to find an affordable space to rent. Its attempts to organize a popular festival with traditional folk entertainment collapsed completely, leaving the organization with a mass of debts.⁵⁶ Because of changes in the economic climate in Leningrad, the stores opened by its committee began losing money. When the society, in response to all these negative developments, was forced to cancel events and projects—when it was unable to live up to its obligations and failed to maintain all of the monuments under its care—rumors started that it had "entirely abandoned its scholarly activities and was engaged exclusively in commercial affairs."⁵⁷

By the fall of 1924, the society's situation was desperate, and its rapidly shrinking active membership began to think in terms of increasingly radical compromises. At a September 18 meeting of the society's governing council, S. N. Zharnovsky delivered a long report in which he announced that he had come to the unshakable conclusion that "societies of this kind—cut off from the broad popular masses and not cultivating a new form of Soviet public spiritedness—are lifeless. Without the support of the Party (RKP) [Russian Communist Party] and the organs of government, societies like the Society of Old Petersburg . . . cannot exist."[58] Zharnovsky went on to propose that the society forge strong ties to the party, expand its membership base to include not just the intelligentsia but also the masses, and adopt a more contemporary focus. The reorganized society, he suggested, might be called the Society of Old Petersburg and New Leningrad. With this proposal on the table, the society held new elections in October 1924. Because so many of the society's members had quit, competition for posts was relatively light. Petr Nikolaevich Stolpiansky, a local historian with a notoriously splenetic temperament and, by 1924, a somewhat uneven reputation in preservationist circles, found himself, almost by default, installed as the new chairman of the society's governing council. Many activists doubtless read his selection as a sign that the society would take a more assertively pro-Soviet and pro-party line, as Zharnovsky had suggested.

Stolpiansky was the only well-known St. Petersburg preservationist with significant revolutionary credentials. A member of populist and Social Democratic organizations in his teens and twenties, following the Revolution of 1905, he had spent a year confined to the Orenburg fortress on charges relating to his work as editor of a local leftist paper before abandoning the cause for a career as a mainstream journalist.[59] By 1908 Stolpiansky had gained permission to move to the capital and begun submitting short occasional pieces to local periodicals on a variety of topics. A regular contributor to the journals *Bygone Years, Capital and Estate* (*Stolitsa i usad'ba*), and *Architect* (*Zodchii*) in the years leading up to the October Revolution, Stolpiansky made a name for himself in preservationist circles as an expert on old Petersburg. He wrote groundbreaking studies of early-eighteenth-century maps, fireworks displays, and imperial banquet tables and launched ambitious bibliographic and topographic projects. It seems likely that few of his associates in the world of preservationism in this period knew about his past involvement with revolutionary politics. Certainly, many reacted with shock in the early 1920s when Stolpiansky, probably in part with the aim of improving his family's material circumstances and protecting himself from official scrutiny, rediscovered his old convictions and began to publish hastily written guides to Revolutionary sites.[60] At meetings of the Society of Old Petersburg's Excursion Bureau in 1923, Stolpiansky stunned fellow members by demanding that "all excursions accepted as part of the program be revolutionary in their tendency" and by arguing against the confirmation of candidate members who had been convicted of crimes by Revolutionary tribunals in the past, directly challenging, in both instances, the "apolitical" stance that remained the norm in preservationist circles.[61]

Stolpiansky's election to the post of chairman did lead to changes in the way the society operated. In March 1925, members added the phrase *new Leningrad* to the society's name in accordance with Zharnovsky's suggestion and, about the same time, started revising its statutes to emphasize contemporary issues and cooperation with the organs of government.[62] To the disappointment of supporters, however, this shift in direction did not stem the organization's decline. Throughout 1925 membership and revenue continued to plummet as the society's negotiations with the Gubispolkom in Leningrad and Glavnauka in Moscow dragged on endlessly.[63] By the time a deal was finally brokered that transformed the society into an official affiliate of Glavnauka with limited subsidies, the organization was so deeply in debt and its members so demoralized that it took considerable time for even limited operations to resume.[64] The society was not able to revive the ambitious conservation projects that had been its hallmark from 1921 until the beginning of 1924. Its museums gradually closed or were taken away by the government, and its governing board lost contact with the experts it had relied upon for its restoration projects. After 1926, it largely confined itself to organizing lectures, excursions, and occasional concerts; drawing up lists of monuments that might merit preservation for various governmental structures; setting up memorial plaques; and delegating representatives to city-wide committees.[65] When it did find the energy to send petitions to state and local agencies, asking them to reconsider plans that seemed likely to damage the landscape of the city, its objections sounded like polite suggestions rather than impassioned calls to action. Even Stolpiansky seemed to find the society's loss of influence disheartening; although he remained its chairman until the end of the 1920s, he gradually distanced himself from its day-to-day operations.[66] In the final years of his tenure, he spent increasing amounts of time outside Leningrad, working as a traveling lecturer.

In the early 1930s, following Stolpiansky's departure, the society's situation became even more precarious. It lost its official subsidies and faced periodic, vitriolic criticism for its failure to attract the masses and coordinate its work with other organizations. As part of an effort to appease its critics, the society's governing board participated in the Stakhanovite movement and other national campaigns. Nonetheless, finding appropriate facilities for meetings and maintaining the society's official affiliation remained a constant struggle. In 1938, with the great purges in full gear, the society was finally closed. By this time the Soviet state had fully consolidated its power, and the fragmentary civil society that had emerged in Russia in the late-imperial period had been effectively crushed. Slowly consumed by predatory government agencies, progressively hamstrung by new regulations, and coerced into making one compromise after another until they lost both their identity and purpose, the voluntary associations that had played such a vibrant role in Soviet cultural life during the early 1920s had virtually disappeared.

The account provided here of the rise and fall of the Society of Old Petersburg in some respects recalls and in others seems at odds with the treatment of voluntary associations in James T. Andrews's monograph, *Science for the Masses*. Like Andrews, I show how, in the early Soviet era, veteran cultural workers relied on the state for funding and support. Nongovernmental societies affiliated themselves with government agencies in the hopes of securing privileges and protections that they desperately needed in order to continue their work. In the short run, in many cases, as Andrews suggests, such arrangements doubtless proved beneficial. Without having to change the essential nature of their programs, altering their rhetoric and focus only slightly, groups gained access to important resources and extricated themselves from potentially devastating conflicts with "rival" state structures. However, some agreements involved significant compromises from the very beginning. As early as 1924, voluntary associations such as the Society of Old Petersburg faced such significant pressure from potential "protectors" that their dealings with the state can scarcely be characterized as harmonious. In this respect, my research findings differ somewhat from Andrews's. I perceive relationships between state agencies such as Glavnauka and Aktsentr and the associations I study as less "symbiotic" and more "strained." I do not believe that the cultural workers I discuss here "skillfully kept the state from interfering with the direction of their public educational activities during the twenties."[67]

Andrews and I probably reach slightly different conclusions in part because we study different kinds of voluntary organizations. In his book, Andrews focuses on groups involved in popularizing the natural sciences. My work primarily considers cultural projects, including many efforts that examined Russia's imperial past. As many scholars have noted, the Soviet authorities began interfering regularly and dramatically with programs in the humanities and social sciences far earlier than they did in the case of the natural sciences.[68] By the mid-1920s, the state actively aspired to control Russian and Soviet historical narrative. It recognized that museum displays, public lectures, and the monologues delivered during guided tours could exercise a powerful influence on how the public understood both the recent past and current Soviet reality. An exhibit, lecture, or tour that showcased living conditions in the imperial period could potentially leave several different impressions. Viewers might leave condemning upper-class decadence or, alternately, could come away convinced that the Bolsheviks had done nothing but spread poverty and misery to new sectors of the population. Because both the material presented and the way in which it was exhibited and explained could significantly affect the message audiences absorbed, the state had a strong incentive to begin exerting significant pressure on organizations such as the Society of Old Petersburg fairly quickly. Protocols of meetings and reports from the period show that governmental structures were actively concerned about the "message" conveyed by exhibits and cultural events even in the very early 1920s.

Although work in the natural sciences also raised doctrinal issues, researchers were often shielded at first because their initiatives seemed to promote positivist values and a materialist worldview that were compatible with Bolshevism. Moreover, the state recognized that raising levels of scientific literacy could help to advance modernization and hence was inclined to view older science educators as a valuable human resource until quite late in the 1920s. Its attitude toward voluntary efforts in the arts and humanities was, in contrast, markedly negative even in 1923 and 1924; it tended to perceive independent undertakings in these areas as potential problems rather than assets and, as a result, exerted more pressure on them and provided less material support.

Unlike Daniel Peris in *Storming the Heavens*, I view the voluntary societies of the NEP period as reasonably diverse. Although all groups faced the same basic legal regulations and many received some funds or privileges from the state, these facts alone should not lead us to perceive them as "homogenized," "having the same agenda and in one voice proclaiming the social unity so long sought."[69] Voluntary associations varied in terms of their aims, the amount of support they received from the regime, and also their point of origin and membership base. Some, including the Soviet League of the Militant Godless, the subject of Peris's book, took shape at the behest of the party and remained, throughout their history, thoroughly "subordinate to the regime."[70] Others represented extensions of or attempts to revive pre-Revolutionary traditions.

Often dependent on the enthusiasm of the old cultural elite and hence steeped in its values, societies of this latter type faced growing pressure from state authorities as time passed. Until at least the mid-1920s, however, many groups managed to maintain something of an independent existence and identity. Their continued visibility and capacity for organized action during the NEP years suggests that civil society had not yet completely broken down in this period. Although Katerina Clark is doubtless right when she characterizes the second half of the NEP period as a time of "Sovietization" and the consolidation of state power, the trend took shape gradually, affecting some organizations and endeavors long before others, and did not reach its logical end point—the complete destruction of the public sphere—until after the cultural revolution had begun.[71]

For all the obstacles they encountered and despite their eventual sad demise, the preservationists of Petrograd made a significant contribution to early Soviet culture. In addition to aiding in the preservation of individual cultural monuments, creating museum displays, and hosting lectures, summer courses, and tours, organizations like the Society of Old Petersburg and the Museum of the City also helped, through their activities and by simply existing, to encourage a boom in the composition of new literature about the old capital of the Russian Empire. They represented key forums where experts on local history met, exchanged ideas, and worked together on projects. Kurbatov, Stolpiansky, Iatsevich—virtually all the great guidebook writers of the 1920s and 1930s whose work will be mentioned in these pages—had some dealings with the Museum of the City or the Society of Old Petersburg. Many collaborated with both. In this respect, these preservationist structures are very similar to the institutions that represent the subject of the next chapter, the early-twentieth-century excursion organizations with which Nikolai Antsiferov, the man commonly regarded as Russia's greatest guidebook writer, is so strongly associated. Both preservationist and excursion structures played an essential role in the evolution of the unique mode of expression that ultimately came to be so closely linked to modern *kraevedenie*.

4

The Excursion Movement and Excursion Methodology

With the exception, perhaps, of Alexander Benois, the most important and influential figure in early-twentieth-century St. Petersburg studies was almost certainly Nikolai Pavlovich Antsiferov. In the 1920s Antsiferov wrote a series of pioneering descriptions of the literary landscape of the Russian capital, including *Dostoevsky's Petersburg* (*Peterburg Dostoevskogo*) and *Petersburg in Reality and Myth* (*Byl' i mif Peterburga*).[1] Much admired when they first appeared, these books were not reissued in the Soviet Union until the *glasnost* period and quickly became bibliographic rarities, coveted by both professional scholars and ordinary Russian readers. When censorship restrictions lifted in the early 1990s, publishing houses in Leningrad and Moscow raced to put out new editions of Antsiferov's work.[2] His seventy-year-old books about the city emerged as legitimate bestsellers almost overnight.

Ecstatic explorations of both St. Petersburg and its literature that fuse long lyric descriptions of city landscapes, copious poetic citations, and philosophical discussions of the nature of art, Antsiferov's books enjoy enormous popularity in Russia today. Discussed on television programs, in newspaper articles, and in high school classrooms, their influence extends far beyond academic circles and, at least from the perspective of Western observers, seems to transcend established disciplinary boundaries. Russians refer to Antsiferov when talking about local history, literature, art and architecture, the origin and structure of cities, cultural theory, and even, on occasion, philosophy. In the West, where Antsiferov's books, for the most part, are known only to professors of Russian literature, they are usually perceived as having a far more narrow application: they are treated as scholarly explorations of specialized literary issues and texts. The works themselves, however, belie this categorization. Although Antsiferov's publications on Russia's northern capital contain many fine passages of textual analysis, as even passionate admirers will generally admit, they do not consistently conform to the norms of academic literary inquiry.[3] In his books, Antsiferov did not always prioritize factual accuracy; he sometimes seems at least as concerned with helping his readers achieve emotional catharsis as with promoting a clear understanding of texts; he often strays beyond the confines of literary studies.

Understanding the structure and purpose of Antsiferov's books, their enduring popularity, and the role they play in Russian culture today, entails returning to the early twentieth century and examining the origin and history of the Russian excursion movement. In some respects, perhaps the most important of the intellectual and social trends that ultimately came to be subsumed into the emerging discipline of *kraevedenie,* excursionism first appeared in Russia as a campaign for pedagogical reform. Shortly after the turn of the century, instructors at leading experimental educational institutions, including St. Petersburg's famous Tenishev School, began to use carefully structured trips and outings as a means of enlivening the curriculum. They described their efforts in popular magazines for teachers, promoting what they termed the excursion method as a viable approach at every level of the educational system and in every academic discipline. Endorsed by key factions within Narkompros after the October Revolution, in the 1920s the excursion method gave rise to academic research institutions, systematic programs for studying local areas, a popular performance tradition, and a new form of guidebook. At the Petrograd Excursion Institute (*Petrogradskii ekskursionnyi institut*) and other centers of methodological innovation, researchers crafted texts, referred to most commonly as *ekskursii* (excursion primers), that were intended to aid teachers and cultural workers in planning and conducting educational tours. Most of Antsiferov's famous descriptions of literary St. Petersburg adhere to the conventions of this descriptive form.

One of the most important figures in both the pre- and post-Revolutionary phases of the excursion movement was Ivan Mikhailovich Grevs, a professionally trained historian who, throughout much of his career, pursued a secondary interest in pedagogical theory. Grevs was among the first Russian educators to attempt to systematize excursions in the humanities and social sciences and one of the strongest advocates of their incorporation into educational curricula at all levels. A beloved mentor to an entire generation of excursionists, including, most notably, Antsiferov, he served on the faculty of St. Petersburg University and the Bestuzhev Women's Courses for many years and, during the early 1920s, headed the humanities division of the Petrograd Excursion Institute. Despite the fact that he wrote and published relatively little on the history and topography of Russia's imperial capital himself, Grevs is often hailed today as an expert in the field of St. Petersburg studies by virtue of the significant contributions he made to the methodology of local research.[4]

In the university-level seminars he ran in the first few decades of the twentieth century, Grevs trained several generations of students to investigate the culture of select topographic regions. Using a method of his own devising, he would first spend considerable time in the classroom, showing the young people how to work with histories, maps, guidebooks, and illustrations and then, if possible, take them on a long excursion to the area they had been studying. Armed with information gained from months of preparatory work, students could, upon arrival at the location under consideration, reasonably be expected to perceive traces of the past in contemporary structures, to understand cities as living organisms rather than just an assemblage of individual buildings and institutions. Although Grevs's classes generally focused on Western European cultural centers, his approach was easily adapted to areas closer to home. In dozens of articles on teaching methodology written both before and after the October Revolution, Grevs promoted his system for combining serious seminar work with excursions as both a cure-all for the ills of the educational system and a legitimate research tool. By the 1920s, thanks to Grevs's own agitation and to the efforts of his enthusiastic former students, many of whom went on to become professional pedagogues, the professor's technique had gained popularity in educational circles in St. Petersburg and to some extent throughout Soviet territory. It ultimately became fundamental to both excursion work and to the form of local research promoted by the Academy of Sciences' Central Bureau of *Kraevedenie*.

Because Grevs's influence was so immense, it seems worth looking in detail at the substance and the origin of his teaching methods before going on to examine the work of his disciples and the excursion movement of the 1920s. For a historian of his generation, Grevs's background and early professional biography are fairly typical: childhood spent on a provincial estate and attendance at a gymnasium in the capital, followed by enrollment in the Department of History and Philology at St. Petersburg University.[5] Grevs chose to specialize in medieval history, working under the guidance of V. G. Vasilievsky, the renowned scholar of Byzantine studies. He finished the program with honors and was immediately readmitted as a graduate student, simultaneously beginning to work as a teacher in the gymnasiums, military schools, and women's institutes of the capital. In 1890 Grevs began lecturing at the university and in 1892 first taught at the Bestuzhev Women's Courses. Soon thereafter Professor Vasilievsky fell ill, and Grevs was asked to assume responsibility for all of the general courses in medieval history. Twice he managed to escape these university teaching commitments and took long research trips to France and Italy to work on his master's thesis, *Sketches from the History of Roman Landownership (Principally in the Time of the Empire)* (*Ocherki iz istorii rimskogo zemlevladeniia [Preimushchestvenno vo vremia imperii]*). The work was published successfully, but soon after Grevs experienced a series of setbacks that temporarily led him away from his career as a history scholar, encouraging him to develop other interests, including experimental pedagogy.

Grevs had intended to make *Sketches* the first in a two-volume set, but before he could finish the second volume, he found that it had been partially anticipated by another historian.[6] Distraught, he abandoned the project, returning to it only many years later. Perhaps he would have found a solution to the conflict at the outset if he had not already been reeling from another disaster. In 1899 Grevs had lost his position at the university in a political purge following a series of student demonstrations.[7] Left with no means of supporting his wife and two small children, he returned to secondary school teaching, accepting a position at the innovative Tenishev School. While obviously not easy, the two years that Grevs spent in this academic exile before being reinstated at the university in 1902 were far from unproductive. The aspects of Grevs's work that most interest us, his pedagogical ideas and experimentation with excursions, can all be traced back to this period and to the heady idealism of the Tenishev School.[8]

Founded in 1898 by Prince Viacheslav Tenishev, a wealthy industrialist and noted philanthropist, the school was meant from the very first to serve as a laboratory demonstration of the advantages of progressive pedagogical methods and a spur to educational reform throughout the empire.[9] The program incorporated a whole series of ideas and slogans popular among theorists at the time. Some of the innovations reflected a desire to humanize the educational process and break down the rigid rules of order separating teachers and students: pupils needed to be treated with respect, taught independence, and instilled with a love of learning; parent-teacher conferences replaced grades and corporal punishment; physical education and proper nutrition were stressed as part of a campaign to meet the needs of the whole child. Other changes had more to do with the curriculum per se and can be seen as a continuation of the late-nineteenth-century "real" school movement. Classical programs, now labeled "book learning," gave way to subjects seen as less detached from "real life," most notably modern languages and the natural sciences. At the Tenishev School, this shift to non-bookish subjects was paralleled by a series of methodological innovations meant again to drag teachers and students away from their textbooks and into the real world. The key word in this case was *nagliadnost'* (visuality); textbooks wherever possible were entirely abandoned in favor of visual aids, science experiments, and excursions. Students had to be taught to learn through observation and independent work, to collect and correctly interpret information received from both the surrounding environment and from reference books.[10]

Within this general framework, excursions were viewed quite favorably because, even more than laboratory experiments and classwork with visual aids, they resembled immersion in the world at large. As Grevs noted in an article included in the school's 1900–1901 commemorative book (*pamiatnaia knizhka*), "excursions are the best available form of bringing students closer to the object of their study—to natural things and phenomena, to monuments, the environment, and the facts of human life; they intimately acquaint them with the authentic sources of those pieces of knowledge that have been communicated to them by the words of the teacher and reinforced by scholarly books."[11] Brought face to face with real phenomena, students, it was believed, would develop their powers of observation, sensitivity, and independence. They would learn to work as a group and would bond better with their instructors. In short, they would grow into exactly the sort of well-rounded, thoughtful young adults that progressive educators dreamed of producing. At the Tenishev School excursions were used in geography classes, the natural sciences, and, beginning in 1900–1901, were introduced into the brand-new history curriculum prepared by a committee of experts for the school's first fourth-grade class. All in all, eighteen separate trips were organized in the spring of 1901, including a three-day outing to Narva.[12]

Both the number of these tours and the inclusion of Grevs's theoretical article in the commemorative book for the year suggest a substantial commitment to the excursion technique. In 1901, the program at the Tenishev School was, however, still relatively new and remained experimental. Instructors had had little time to consider the methodological underpinnings of excursion work and probably had not established uniform guidelines for conducting tours. The article Grevs wrote for the 1901 commemorative book is in this respect quite revealing. In it, Grevs defers all discussion of methodological issues to a promised later article, not bothering even to offer a real definition of the term *excursion*. Based on a perusal of the article, one might reasonably presume that all treks beyond the confines of the schoolyard, including even spontaneous outings with no link to regular lesson plans, could qualify as excursions.[13] For the time, nonetheless, Grevs's statement on the importance of excursion work was cutting edge. In turn-of-the-century Russia, no one had progressed further than Grevs and his colleagues at Tenishev in the use of educational tours as a regular component of the school curriculum despite the fact that the notion that such outings might enhance student learning was far from new.

The idea that field trips and travel offer educational benefits has a long and respectable history in European pedagogical literature. Rousseau's *Emile* and the writings of the Czech educational reformer and religious leader John Comenius are often mentioned as early sources. In the late eighteenth century, Comenius's work was translated into Russian and persuaded Nikolai Novikov, F. I. Iankovich de Merievo, and V. F. Zuev to advocate the organization of strolls and nature trips for children. The Public School Code (*Ustav narodnykh uchilishch*) of 1786 mentions the usefulness of strolls, and the School code (*Shkol'nyi ustav*) of 1804 goes so far as to suggest, in addition to nature walks, visits to various manufacturing enterprises, workshops, and businesses. Similar ideas surfaced periodically in both pedagogical literature and official documents throughout the nineteenth century. In the 1880s some Russian schoolteachers began taking students on trips during weekend and vacation time on their own initiative. Instructors were usually uncompensated for the extra work, and the outings were almost always optional. To some extent, the government encouraged the trend, taking steps, for instance, to promote student travel to the Nizhni-Novgorod Fair in 1896 and issuing a circular in 1900 that suggested that, instead of giving summer homework assignments, teachers take students on "educational strolls or trips."[14] Following the publication of this last appeal, the numbers of school trips taking place in Russia did increase. Most of the tours organized in response to the circular were not, however, particularly well-integrated into the school curriculum and appear to have offered little of real educational value.

Eighteenth- and nineteenth-century reformers failed to make field trips an integral part of the school curriculum in Russia largely because they did not provide teachers with the specialized instruction and resources they would have needed to organize such outings effectively on a regular basis. The success of the trips depended entirely on the enthusiasm and methodological sophistication of individual teachers, and, as a result, tours varied widely in quality and could all too easily degenerate into poorly planned recreational activities. At the Tenishev School, excursions were made one of the focal points of the curriculum for the first time; they were viewed as essential educational tools in a variety of disciplines and assigned important functions. As an entire collective of teachers worked to meet these new expectations, the trips quite naturally became more systematized. It took a number of years, however, for a detailed excursion method to evolve.

Towards the Theory and Practice of Excursions as a Tool in the Scientific Study of History in Universities (*K teorii i praktike "ekskursii," kak orudiia nauchnogo izucheniia istorii v universitetakh*), Grevs's first serious attempt at a methodological statement on the excursion, appeared only in 1910, long after he had left the Tenishev School and returned to university teaching. In the book, Grevs argues that in order to fulfill their potential as teaching tools, excursions need to be carefully planned and connected to classroom work, and he offers a detailed description of a tour to Italy as a blueprint for future efforts. Grevs's "model," the account of his 1907 trip to Venice, Padua, Ravenna, Florence, Perugia, Assisi, and Rome with sixteen graduates of his history seminars, became a classic in the field of historical excursion work. In it, in at least embryonic form, we find many of the features that later became standard for pedagogical excursions in the humanities and social sciences: an interest in literary sites, the use of maps to trace the "biography" of cities, attempts to recreate the atmosphere of history by combining visits to actual sites with stirring narrative, a concern with group dynamics, and a conviction that weather and time of day needed to be factored in when considering how to present a site for the greatest emotional effect. Most significantly, Grevs makes a clear distinction in this pamphlet between excursions and tourism. The trip to Italy was not meant to be a mere vacation; its aim was to "continue with methodological consistency and rigorous effort the labor begun in the 'laboratory' setting of the seminar, transferring it to a new environment, acting with the help of new sources."[15] Students were expected to function as trained investigators, exploiting all of the background knowledge on Italian culture and history they had acquired before departure. They were supposed to explore and think independently, finding in the architecture and topography of each city traces of the past.

This emphasis on individual enterprise should not be interpreted to imply a lack of structure. While they may have superficially resembled an immersion experience, Grevs's excursions were in fact exquisitely constructed and almost entirely artificial learning environments. The professor, despite all his references to "natural phenomena," did not drop students into "the real world" to conduct research; he escorted them along a painstakingly planned route meant to illustrate and expand upon material covered in class. In their seminar work, students had studied the medieval Italian city and its role as cradle for the early Renaissance; when planning the trip to Italy, Grevs carefully chose sites that best demonstrated this central theme. Cities that retained few features from the Middle Ages were eliminated even if they were intrinsically interesting.[16] Aside from this, Grevs made sure to familiarize himself with the route in advance, deciding how best to present material to students. A passage from *Towards the Theory and Practice of Excursions* on the usefulness of special predeparture courses is indicative of the degree of preparation Grevs expected from group leaders:

> Aside from "general" preparation in the area of issues and phenomena toward the study of which the trip is supposed to serve, special preparation is also essential. This means that before going and working on site, one should, in a sense, realize the trip at home, theoretically: work through its plan and contents step by step, using books and snapshots, paintings, maps, plans, sketches and other aids. You need to know exactly what you will see and do, so that the realized excursion will be, in a sense, an incarnation of that which has already passed through the mind and imagination in any of a number of symbolic signs.[17]

Ideally the teacher would first familiarize himself with the material to be covered and then run a six-month-long seminar for students, where lectures, individual reports, trips to museums, and literary discussions would provide background on the specific objects. For the 1907 trip, Grevs was not able to implement this idea fully. He did not have a special predeparture course, relying instead on short lectures during the trip to fill in any holes in student knowledge. The most important features of the excursion method were, however, already in place: a purposefully constructed route and a profound sense of educational mission. A rigorous schedule of excursions, seminar-style discussions at meals, and evening meetings to recapitulate and contextualize what had been seen all helped to increase the trip's pedagogical impact.

In 1912 Grevs organized a second excursion to Italy, partly with the intention of correcting the methodological failings of the first trip. The route and the pedagogical approach remained essentially the same, but the level of student preparation and planning was significantly improved. Participants were drawn from Grevs's seminar on Dante, attended his seminar on Francis of Assisi, and took a special course on Florentine history. Nikolai Antsiferov, one of the students who took part in the trip, described the content of this third course years later in his memoirs: "Instead of Dante and the *Enciclopedia dantesca*, maps, plans, and numerous views of Italy appeared on his table. Ivan Mikhailovich acquainted us particularly thoroughly with the plan of Florence, which had grown from a Roman camp with its intersecting lines. . . . We became familiar with maps of Italy upon which I. M. Grevs showed us the route he had so carefully thought out."[18] In addition to this higher level of preparation, plans for the 1912 excursion show that Grevs was making significant progress toward the development of a unified approach to new cities. Daily schedules emphasize the importance of first encounters, noting repeatedly that the initial outing in each city must "without fail!" include a panoramic view from the central cathedral or another elevated spot. Other elements, which would later become standard, also begin to appear: cruises past the city by boat, entering the city on foot, literary strolls, and the use of dramatic readings to set an appropriate mood while touring a site.[19]

Grevs's Italian excursions were profoundly innovative and not at all representative of the average level of pre-Revolutionary excursion work. Although in the first decades of the twentieth century an unprecedented boom in student travel took place throughout the Russian Empire, most of the activity remained very unstructured and hardly merits comparison to the first efforts at the Tenishev School, let alone Grevs's later experiments. The teachers working out of the Tenishev School and other progressive establishments represented an educated vanguard, influential because they published books about their work and contributed widely to pedagogical journals, but statistically insignificant when viewed against an army of ordinary zemstvo teachers. As Scott Seregny movingly describes, teachers hired by the local assemblies charged with providing an elementary education to the lower classes often lived in extreme poverty and isolation, particularly before 1908; they had only limited access to reading materials and little opportunity for continuing pedagogical training.

Although in the years before World War I, salaries to some extent increased and the amount of methodological support available to zemstvo teachers improved, they remained underprivileged and, in most instances, poorly prepared in comparison to instructors in more elite institutions.[20]

Grevs, even in the rarefied context of the progressive pedagogical circles of the capital, cuts a rather striking figure: the mild-mannered scholar with his *Enciclopedia dantesca* and his lectures on stigmata. It is worth keeping in mind that university trips were unusual; almost all pre-Revolutionary excursion work remained confined to elementary and secondary schools. While tours of up to a month in duration did gradually become more common, they rarely included destinations outside the Russian Empire. Travel abroad, the exposure to foreign countries that Grevs believed conferred particular benefits, was too expensive and involved too many bureaucratic hurdles to be practical for most groups.[21] In addition to these differences in educational level and in range, Grevs's work is atypical for its subject matter. Modern prejudices lead us to associate excursions with tourism and assume that their content will most naturally fall within the broad confines of history and the humanities. In 1910, when Grevs was writing *Towards the Theory and Practice of Excursions,* however, nothing could have been further from the case. Most pioneers in the development of the pedagogical excursion were science teachers who took students out into nature's classroom to study botany, geology, and geography.[22] Pupils explored swamps and forests, took measurements, and collected samples for school museums. They traveled to factories to see how chemistry and physics lessons translated into applied science and engineering. Literary excursions as such did not exist; those covering historical material were universally acknowledged to be poorly developed methodologically, and trips to museums were often denied the label *excursion* entirely on the grounds that they did not expose students to "the real world."[23]

For a picture of average pre-Revolutionary excursion work, we need to turn away from both Grevs's scholarly pamphlets and the groundbreaking articles put out by the faculty at progressive academies like the Tenishev School and look instead to the popular excursion journals that began to appear in 1913: *School Excursions and the School Museum* (*Shkol'nye ekskursii i shkol'nyi muzei*), published in Odessa and later Bendery (1913–17); *The Russian Excursionist* (*Russkii ekskursant*), based in Yaroslavl (1914–17); and *The Excursion Herald* (*Ekskursionnyi vestnik*), the elegantly printed periodical supported by the Central Excursion Committee of the Moscow School District (1914–16).[24] That all three of these magazines started to come out in a single twelve-month period is in and of itself significant. Excursions, on the eve of World War I, suddenly went from pedagogical experiment to educational fad. Every school in the empire began to draw up an excursion plan and form a financing committee; teachers wrote letters demanding discount train tickets; zemstvos and school boards raced to organize reception centers for arriving groups, and whole armies of school children began to fan out across the country.

This boom was partly the result of years of publicity about the experiments at institutions like the Tenishev school, but it also drew energy from a number of other sources, both Russian and international. The one-hundredth anniversary of the War of 1812 and the three-hundredth anniversary of the installation of the Romanov dynasty in 1913 inspired huge commemorative ceremonies and provoked unprecedented interest in domestic tourism.[25] Patriotism and nationalism were on the rise all over Europe, leading to the growing importance of *Heimatkunde* (homeland studies) in the school curriculum, for instance, in Germany. By 1908 Prussian circulars recommended emphasizing local and national elements in all disciplines and suggested regular "educational strolls" to nearby sites remarkable in terms of their natural landscape, history, or culture.[26] The scouting movement in England articulated similar concerns. Russian teachers were exposed to these ideas through surveys of foreign literature and trends printed in pedagogical magazines and quickly moved to develop similar programs. The introduction of local material and tours, many instructors hoped, would enliven the school curriculum, making its seem less abstract and theoretical, and might simultaneously help to instill in the young a deep and abiding love of the motherland. As I noted earlier, spending on local education increased significantly in Russia between 1908 and 1914. With more resources available, even ordinary zemstvo teachers began to petition for funds to support innovative new programs such as excursions. The growth of railroads, a burgeoning middle class, and the evolution of museums and tourist destinations all also helped to encourage the trend. By the beginning of the twentieth century, group travel at modest or even minimal expense had at last become possible, making site-seeing and trips to even far-flung destinations accessible to a far-broader segment of the population. Just as the nineteenth-century "grand tour" had been touted as an important element in the upbringing of young gentlemen and ladies, early-twentieth-century excursions were advocated as broadening experiences for teachers and their charges. Both tourism and education now served a larger audience.

Each of the three Russian journals created to cater to this new enthusiasm for educational travel had a slightly different character and mission. *School*

Excursions and the School Museum focused overwhelmingly on science and regularly featured articles explaining how to prepare samples gathered during trips for display in school museums. *The Russian Excursionist* cast itself as a budget travel companion, including patterns for making backpacks, advice about nutrition and first-aid kits, and elaborate travel sketches under the heading *rodinovedenie* (homeland studies). *The Excursion Herald,* closely affiliated with the Central Excursion Committee of the Moscow School District, is predictably the most official in tone. While its inaugural issue did contain a call for submissions, most articles that appeared were penned by established educators and academics from Moscow and St. Petersburg. As a result, the quality of the magazine is much more even, with none of the clumsy homemade touches that characterize *The Russian Excursionist*. The first few issues contain an elaborate series of articles on the Moscow Kremlin, so lovingly illustrated that they could easily have appeared in *Bygone Years*. Such lavish treatment of central tourist destinations corresponded to an orientation on a better class of excursion-goer; most articles in *The Excursion Herald* describe the activities of relatively well-funded gymnasiums and "real" schools. While certainly not laboratories for educational progress like the Tenishev School, such institutions still stood far ahead of simple zemstvo affiliates in their ability to implement new methodological techniques accurately. The efforts of this last most primitive category of elementary school to conduct excursions in the humanities were far more fully reported in *The Russian Excursionist*.

The letters and articles submitted by provincial school teachers to this Yaroslavl magazine make it clear that, although well-intentioned and generous with their time, they lacked the resources to focus on niceties like advance reconnaissance and ideal group size. Planning and theory often ended up abandoned in the rush to resolve practical concerns. Perhaps the shoestring excursions that resulted offered little more than life experience to students, but, as D. Zolotarev noted in one article, mere exposure to something new could significantly benefit children from a limited background.

> It is true that excursions conducted in the vicinity of the educational institution often turn into strolls that bear little resemblance to scientific educational excursions. Long-distance excursions are a different matter all together. By exciting interest and inquisitiveness, providing an inexhaustible reserve of completely new impressions for the participants, and transporting them to a different environment, they are already very valuable in and of themselves. Even "roaming from churches to museums,

from historical monuments to electrical or telephone stations" . . . has its own justification. For provincial school children, who have never left their native towns and never seen even a large city, let alone the capital, the capital is important as a large city with all of its distinctive features.[27]

In other words, methodological dictates could be safely bent without completely nullifying the value of the trip.[28] Relaxed standards translated into support for individual initiative, heroic attempts to surmount bureaucratic obstacles, collect money, and set off *somewhere,* even if it meant sacrificing vacation time or involved personal expense. K. Studitsky, an instructor at an orphanage in the Yaroslavl area, sent *The Russian Excursionist* accounts of the walking expeditions he organized for his charges each summer. At the cost of thirty-eight kopecks per child per day, he would single-handedly take groups of fifty or sixty youngsters on month-long tours. Walking alongside the Volga at a rate of twenty versts a day, he found he could cover 500 versts in one trip comfortably, stopping to show his charges factories, see the sites in each town passed, and, when appropriate, spend several days helping local peasants with their summer field work.[29] Zemstvo schools in the Voronezh gubernia brought peasant children to the city for three or four days to introduce them to factories, movie theaters, and manufactured sweets, and similar programs brought city children to the countryside, or at least to the fields outside of town, to improve their understanding of agricultural imagery in literature.[30]

To the editors at *The Excursion Herald* such efforts no doubt seemed depressingly provincial.[31] Regardless of their methodological limitations, however, these primitive tours played an important role in the pre-Revolutionary excursion movement. Travel by large numbers of under-funded and poorly prepared groups encouraged zemstvos and other local administrative bodies to create procedures and structures to assist would-be excursionists. For outgoing parties, support included direct financial aid, the donation of supplies, and help in obtaining discount train tickets. Arriving groups were often directed to newly created excursion bureaus staffed by volunteer tour leaders and equipped with libraries of guidebooks. School and community buildings doubled as hostels, providing straw mattresses, bedding, and even tea. These administrative efforts to create a structural base for the excursion movement served as an important model for reformers in the years following the Revolution, proving that tours did not have to be the exclusive province of elite gymnasiums. Centers could be created to assist individual instructors with routes and logistics, allowing large numbers of students to be efficiently funneled through a single site and, prospectively at least, guaranteeing a certain measure of quality. If these bases could ever be brought up to standard, provided with facilities, and staffed on a par with the Tenishev School, then perhaps the dreams articulated by pre-Revolutionary reformers could at last expand to accommodate the masses.

In fact, as early as 1918 a number of structures within the Commissariat of Enlightenment began to express interest in reviving the pre-Revolutionary tradition of excursion work and specifically in organizing networks of stations. Compared with other progressive pedagogical devices, excursions had the advantage of being relatively well known and well respected. Cutting edge but not controversial, they appealed at once to veteran educators committed to the legacy of the zemstvo reform years and to the conservative faction at Narkompros, Bolsheviks like Lunacharsky and Ludmila Menzhinskaia who wanted the newly created "united labor school" to provide students with something more than a limited professional education.[32] Excursion theory, with all of its references to engaged, contextualized, active, hands-on learning, offered a convenient alternative definition for all the labor supposedly taking place in the new public schools, a way of keeping the children of the dictatorship of the proletariat studying science instead of wielding tools. Perhaps the most developed expression of this point of view appears in a 1922 book by the excursionist Boris Raikov. After first defining movement (*motornost*), the involvement of all of the body's muscles in the task of learning, as the chief characteristic of the excursion method, Raikov makes the easy leap from muscles to labor and announces, "the labor school is, first and foremost, an excursion school."[33] Such arguments tended implicitly to suggest that the schools should continue to pursue broad aims, offering students a humanistic curriculum reminiscent of the best experimental programs of the pre-Revolutionary period. As Ivan Grevs noted in a 1921 article for *Pedagogical Thought* (*Pedagogicheskaia mysl'*): "Without a doubt, school cannot be exclusively or predominantly 'bookish' . . . but must leave in the arrangement of things ample room for laboratory and excursion work as well as the organized, independent labor of the students: mental, artistic, and manual. But this labor should be the kind that, while providing practical experience valuable for working life, pursues an educational rather than a professional aim."[34]

Both the old specialists and the anti-trade-school block at Narkompros rejected narrow utilitarianism, the equation of human value with functionality, as antithetical to personal growth and the development of healthy individuals. They believed that the schools must "help a child become a human being, first and foremost—and only thereafter a citizen and a specialist"; that nothing less than a solid general education, including both the natural sciences and the humanities, could ensure social progress and guarantee a workforce literate and flexible enough to adapt to the changing needs of the economy.[35] They also recognized that limiting the kinds of subjects studied in Russia's schools just when a broad segment of the population was gaining access to all of the fruits of enlightenment raised real issues of fairness: didn't the masses deserve to learn about the full range of human cultural and scientific achievement?

Intent on upholding these essential pedagogical principles, Grevs, Raikov, and many other well-known figures from the pre-Revolutionary excursion movement ultimately consented, despite their reservations about the Bolshevik regime, to cooperate with Narkompros and lend their experience to new sections, stations, and publications. While they continued to complain bitterly about the destruction of civil society and constraints on private initiative, these veteran reformers could not conceive of abandoning educational work for very long, seeing in enlightenment and the growth of culture the only way to resolve the current social crisis.[36] By early 1919, staff lists at Narkompros affiliates in Petrograd bristle with familiar names: Boris Raikov, Dmitri Kaigorodov, N. Sokolov, I. I. Poliansky, and, of course, Grevs. Many had taught at the Tenishev School or at the Lesnoe Commercial School, another well-regarded progressive educational institution in the Petrograd area that promoted excursion work; others had organized summer teacher-training courses in the suburbs of Petrograd before the Revolution.[37] The contributions of these old specialists and institutions at least temporarily insured Petrograd's status as a leading educational center, despite the gradual erosion of resources and influence to Moscow.[38] In the narrow field of excursion work, it continued to dominate, consistently surpassing the new capital's efforts both practically and methodologically.[39] Three separate Narkompros divisions opened excursion sections in Petrograd during the Civil War: the Department of the United Labor School, the Museum Department, and the Sub-Department of Adult Education.[40] Obviously the existence of so many similar structures within one large organization made duplication and conflict over jurisdiction almost inevitable. As Sheila Fitzpatrick notes in her study of Bolshevik educational policy, such problems were endemic to Narkompros at the time and inspired a series of poorly implemented plans for reorganization and rationalization.[41] The constant turmoil and name changes that resulted make it very difficult to outline the limits of any department's responsibilities accurately at any given time. In principle, however, each of the three sections did have a different orientation.

The Excursion Section of the Collegium of the United Labor School was created in February 1919 to organize work in the primary and secondary schools of Petrograd and the surrounding area. Realizing that most teachers lacked the pedagogical training and the practical acumen to put together even day trips to the suburbs, the section immediately devoted the bulk of its efforts to creating a network of stations in and around the city.[42] By May the first six had opened, all of them oriented toward the natural sciences: in Pavlovsk, Detskoe Selo, Lakhta, Sestroretsk, Peterhof, and at the Kamennoostrovsky Agricultural Institute. Gradually, the section added new bases to this list, reaching a total of fifteen before financial cuts forced closures in 1922. Facilities eventually included two yachting clubs offering marine biology excursions and athletics and a center in Pskov that was meant to service both local groups and visitors from Petrograd. Science programs significantly outnumbered those in the humanities and largely set the standard in terms of the organization of bases. Stations generally had a laboratory, a small museum, classrooms for slides, lectures, and discussions, and a cafeteria. Some offered sleeping accommodations. Theoretically they operated year round, although more groups arrived during the summers. In the winter personnel worked on research projects, put together exhibits, ran tours for local schools, and developed excursion routes and plans for the next season. Stations were set up to receive one group of fifty students each day, relying on the central office of the Excursion Section to control reservations. While the facilities provided their own guides, they always suggested that teachers of appropriate subjects accompany groups, partly hoping that the trip would at least give instructors a taste of the new methodology, encouraging them to reinforce material covered in later lesson plans and perhaps even enroll in one of the teacher training courses offered at the Pavlovsk base each summer.[43] Unable to provide regular excursions to every schoolchild in the district single-handedly, the stations from the beginning defined themselves as showrooms for progressive methodology. This model, like so much else at Narkompros, radiated a blind optimism that was entirely incongruous with outside events: wartime Petrograd encircled by scholastic phalansteries. The work hummed along more or less productively despite shelling from Iudenich's troops, periodic arrests, and trains that either failed to run or, when they did, brought hungry, shoeless students.[44] Somehow the children were coaxed through programs, generally fed, and safely returned home.

For groups interested in history and the arts, the facilities created by the Excursion Section of the United Labor School offered a somewhat more specialized range of services. In January 1920 the section opened a base in the

Anichkov Palace alongside the Museum of the City. Called the Central Station for Excursions in the Humanities, it served as a reception point for out-of-town groups, providing dormitory beds for 200 and some cafeteria meals.[45] Unlike the science bases in the suburbs, this station did not have many permanent guides. Instead, employees took reservations for tours and then passed them on to other organizations, primarily the Excursion Section of the Museum Department. Aside from maintaining these booking lists, staff at the station organized a variety of pedagogical training programs, often attracting important specialists as lecturers. One two-week course in 1920 featured talks by Vladimir Kurbatov, Ivan Grevs, Petr Veiner, Sergei Troinitsky, and Lev Ilin.[46] In both formal lectures and excursions, they tried to provide Petrograd teachers with a basic background in city and art history, while simultaneously offering an introduction to local museums and cultural resources. Another program at the station regularly ran demonstration excursions and other educational experiments for groups of schoolchildren and their teachers. These events gave the staff at the station a chance to test innovative ideas and offered audiences new and vivid educational experiences. In 1921, for instance, three hundred high school pupils came to the Anichkov Palace one morning to hear Anatoly Koni reminisce about Dostoevsky and Nikolai Antsiferov discuss depictions of St. Petersburg in the author's novels.

In addition to the star-powered central station, the Excursion Section of the Collegium of the United Labor School set up far more modest bases to service humanities classes at the palace-park complexes in Detskoe Selo, Peterhof, and Pavlovsk. Initially equipped with little more than registered lists of tested leaders, these points of support eventually added cafeterias. In Pskov the section's excursion facility ran multiday programs in medieval history and culture.[47] Because its outlying location eliminated the possibility of assistance from comparable organizations, this last station, like the science bases, was designed to function as a virtual oasis, offering a full range of services to groups: housing, meals, classroom facilities, and trained leaders. If the Collegium of the United Labor School never felt obliged to put together similarly packaged programs for the humanities in the Petrograd suburbs and the city proper, it was probably because organizers planned from the first to coordinate all efforts with the Excursion Section of the Museum Department.

Created in 1918, the Excursion Section of the Museum Department theoretically worked with groups of all ages, but tended to focus on the needs of the schools. Packed with young associates and disciples of Ivan Grevs and clearly oriented toward the humanities, it consciously aligned itself with the traditions of the Tenishev School and set as its primary goal the composition of a single multiyear excursion plan for the Petrograd schools, an orderly sequence of methodologically formulated tours tied to specific segments of the curriculum. Obviously this was a complex task involving the coordination of many individual projects at sites throughout the city. Each route and topic had to be developed, tested, and approved before being fitted into any larger framework. From 1918 to 1921, leaders at the Museum Department conducted 3,403 tours to sixteen different museums and through the city, serving 101,347 individuals.[48] Many of these institutions were brand-new, such as palaces and mansions opened to the public for the first time. Others had been extensively reorganized after the Revolution. None had ever attempted to provide a mass audience with guided tours or even thought much about how the arrangement and display of exhibits might be used to educational effect.[49] Stage one of the Museum Department's project involved creating rudimentary educational programs for the city's most significant cultural repositories: the Hermitage; the Russian Museum; the Ethnographic Museum; the Stroganov, Iusupov, and Shuvalov mansions; and Peterhof, Pavlovsk, and Detskoe Selo. A working group was assigned to each site which, using seminar style methods, gathered material and selected thematic focal points. Large museums like the Hermitage were broken down into multiple topics that could be introduced at various stages of a child's academic career: "Daily Life in Dutch Painting," "Antiquity in French Painting of the Seventeenth and Eighteenth Centuries," "Beauty and the Characteristic."[50] Once adequately polished and practically tested, the tours were often written up and submitted to pedagogical magazines and collections. By 1921, the Excursion Section had accumulated enough material to stitch together a preliminary excursion plan for the schools. A first draft appeared in the second edition of Boris Raikov's fundamental collection, *School Excursions: Their Significance and Organization* (*Shkol'nye ekskursii, ikh znachenie i organizatsiia*).[51] A second version made its way into *Excursion Matters* (*Ekskursionnoe delo*) later that same year.[52] Bare lists of topics organized by school year and suggestions for which central themes they might best illustrate, these primitive plans are of interest mostly as the first examples of what later became a popular tradition in excursion work: the development of a unified curriculum.

For nonschool groups, Narkompros set up an excursion section at the Subdepartment of Adult Education at the Petrograd Education Department. Renamed the Excursion Subdepartment of Politprosvet after one of Narkompros's periodic efforts at reorganization, this last entity had enormous problems gaining control both methodologically and administratively of its allotted territory. In the pre-Revolutionary era, excursion activists had operated almost exclusively through educational institutions and hence paid little attention to the special needs of working adults. Now, as part of Politprosvet's larger efforts to spread enlightenment and outright propaganda to the masses, excursions had to adapt to both a new audience and different aims. Organizers quickly found that adult groups generally did not have a uniform level of preparation; they could not easily be corralled into regularly attending cycles of events, and they resented any activity that absorbed free time without delivering a certain amount of fun and relaxation. Given such basic limitations and abysmal literacy levels, adult tours almost inevitably sank into superficiality and sensationalism, degenerating until they became little more than standard elements in Sunday afternoon cultural programs, alternatives to drink and church services that at best conveyed simple political messages. If this was all an excursion signified, then anyone could run one. Trade unions, factories, clubs, the Union of Militant Atheists, and countless other organizations put together their own excursion programs in the 1920s. While some groups like the Society of Old Petersburg tried to hire experienced excursionists and experts on the city, on average standards were undeniably low. Both the pedagogical and the political credentials of leaders were a constant cause for concern. One 1923 report, for instance, lodged the following complaints against employees giving makeshift tours at the Winter Palace:

> The latter, aiming solely to increase their personal income, try to interest their audience with all sorts of fables, authenticating them by saying in most cases that they themselves, supposedly, were present, being as they have been in service at the palace for a long time. Moreover, after such a tour, the listener remembers only isolated details, facts that are in no way connected; he does not bring away anything complete, any idea. After an excursion with a leader, he leaves with definite impressions of the palace and its inhabitants, of their attitude to the people and so forth.[53]

In part the problem was economic. With inflation, unemployment, and constant budgetary cuts at cultural institutions, excursions had become a convenient way to make extra income. Museum employees, writers, and teachers eagerly snapped up such assignments, often taking on far more than they could reasonably manage. In an age when cultural workers commonly juggled many commitments, even experts on the city could easily slip into frustrated cynicism; rank amateurs had no chance of living up to the excursion method's rigorous standards for preparation and execution.[54]

Diverse providers and uneven quality did not bode well for the Excursion Subdepartment at Politprosvet, which had a vested interest in maintaining the perception of its own usefulness. In 1920 it launched a protracted administrative struggle against the competition, lobbying to force the trade unions, the military, the Museum Department, and everyone else to stop arranging tours for adult groups. Like the Excursion Section of the United Labor School, Politprosvet argued, it should have a monopoly: all nonschool orders could be turned in to its central office and then filtered out to a network of stations and trained guides. Efficiency and quality would rise as groups of adults set out to tour specific sites according to a neat schedule. Perhaps to back up the claim that it represented the equivalent of the Excursion Section of the United Labor School and hence deserved similar privileges, Politprosvet began to imitate the structure of the successful children's program. It quickly opened eight suburban bases with offerings in both the humanities and sciences and one central House of the Excursionist to receive incoming groups.[55]

The decree Politprosvet longed for was eventually signed, and the organization was formally granted a monopoly in adult excursion work. Its Excursion Subdepartment continued, however, to struggle as an organization. It had trouble attracting participants to its programs and could not effectively enforce its new prerogatives.[56] At least the former problem seems in part to have been the result of poor strategy. When it opted to slavishly imitate the programs of the Excursion Section of the United Labor School, Politprosvet chose to ignore the needs of its own clientele, pigeonholing diverse adult groups within a framework meant to complement a specific educational process. Shipping workers out to collect botany samples and measure sediment made little sense; outside the context of a general science course such outings lost their pedagogical relevance and as a form of mass recreation or political instruction offered few advantages. If excursions were ever to play a meaningful role outside the schools, they needed to move away from the living classroom, free themselves from the legacy of lesson plans, and find new objectives. No doubt as a result of this realization, the Excursion Subdepartment at Politprosvet launched a second and at least initially more productive campaign to cement its position within the world of cultural work.

At the end of 1921 and the beginning of 1922, budget cuts forced changes in the programs of all three Excursion sections. The groups at the Department of the United Labor School (now renamed the Sector of Social Education) and at Politprosvet had to shut down about half their stations. The Excursion Section at the Museum Department closed altogether. As often happened at

Narkompros, the financial savings and structural efficiency expected from this last cut decreased as related departments absorbed both laid-off employees and canceled programs. The practical work of leading tours largely shifted to the Central Excursion Station for the Humanities at the Sector of Social Education. Methodological projects, including the attempt to write a unified curriculum for the schools, eventually ended up in the sphere of influence of Politprosvet. The head of its Excursion Subdepartment, Emma Krasnukha, had acknowledged the need for methodological help by November 1920 and had recruited a group of experts to redesign the section's programs. Largely borrowed from other Narkompros divisions, these paid consultants quickly moved from discussing Politprosvet's preexisting projects to recommending the creation of an excursion institute, a teaching and research facility that would graduate professional tour leaders and further the development of the pedagogical method. Krasnukha herself leapt on board enthusiastically. She found the idea of serving as director flattering and hoped the project would draw greater attention to the problems of adult work. An expanded committee, which included Grevs and his disciples as well as prominent figures in the sciences and technology, met throughout 1921 to discuss concrete proposals.[57] Ultimately, the group agreed that the institute should offer a two-year course geared toward the graduates of pedagogical institutes. Less expensive to assemble than a full four-year post-secondary-school curriculum, such a program seemed more likely to make it through the approval process at the State Academic Council (*Gosudarstvennyi uchenyi sovet* [GUS]). Structurally, the committee proposed that the institute be divided into three departments: the humanities, the natural sciences, and economics and technology. Each would offer advanced courses in its subject disciplines, lectures on pedagogy, elaborate seminars, and practical work. Both short- and long-distance field trips figured prominently in plans.

Aside from training a new generation of excursionists, organizers always suggested that the institute would conduct some form of research. Initially accorded little attention, this aspect of the program grew increasingly important after July 1921 when, in the hopes of finally securing funding, the committee transferred its application from Podguch to the Academic Center. The new affiliation required a greater emphasis on research, pushing the group to define the proposed subject of investigation clearly.[58] In as much as methodology remained a prominent issue, the framers foresaw continued work on programs and guidelines. The drafting of routes replaced term papers in the curriculum; those enrolled in the institute, it was decided, would turn in written outlines of tours and give demonstrations of their skill as leaders. In addition to these clear-cut tasks, however, another kind of research helped to fill out the new proposals: the interdisciplinary study of Russian territory. Even in the pre-Revolutionary era, excursion work had always blended rather well with appeals for the exploration of native traditions and phenomena. The editors of *The Russian Excursionist,* for instance, had devoted nearly half of each issue to promoting homeland studies (*rodinovedenie*), a loosely defined educational program that was modeled on German *Heimatkunde.* According to one article, the principal aims of *rodinovedenie* included "opening the eyes of rising generations to this wondrous picture of our motherland, letting them feel all the charm of Russian nature, drawing them toward the endlessly interesting sides of the daily lives of her many tribes."[59] Contributors wanted the magazine to serve as "an interpreter of this beauty, a sensitive guide to the living museum of Russian art, ancient and new, awakening in young hearts the best feelings, those that the contemplation of beauty can give to a person."[60]

While sentimental nationalism flavored much public speech on the eve of World War I, the effusive appeals for a patriotic academic agenda made by the leadership of the excursion movement at least in part reflected the specific nature of their project. Properly planning trips required access to scholarly descriptions of each site; any shortage of such information would naturally inspire dedicated pedagogues to turn into investigators themselves and to publish relevant findings for the benefit of later groups. In addition, excursions themselves offered opportunities for observation and for collecting material, some of which might arguably have real scholarly value. Both of these factors tended to draw tour organizers closer to provincial collectors, amateur historians, and other "experts" on Russian territory, leading if not to a unified constituency, then at least to broadly overlapping interests. In 1921, when drafting plans for the institute, excursionists quite naturally remembered their old affection for area studies, inserting it in programs in an updated and more academically sophisticated form: the increasingly fashionable word *kraevedenie* (local or regional studies) had largely replaced *rodinovedenie* as the term of choice. This substitution suggested a greater emphasis on the idea of examining discrete regions as holistic units. Both amateur and professional researchers, it was hoped, would begin to look at their immediate surroundings, descending from theory and sweeping overviews to examine the concrete phenomena specific to a given place. Aside from this, and a slightly greater emphasis on solving concrete social and economic problems, the rhetoric remained unchanged. Life itself again demanded the immediate investigation of Russia, "as fully, broadly, and from as many sides as possible, in the shortest possible time," and, in this context, research excursions represented an essential tool.[61]

Nods to contemporary issues aside, the elaborate portfolio of documentation put together by the institute's organizing committee had trouble winning approval when Grevs and Krasnukha finally presented it to the State Academic Council in October 1921. Petrograd already had teachers' colleges, and in a period of fiscal restraint anything new required clear justification. The idea of specializing in excursions found advocates on the committee, including a cautious Krupskaia, but other sections of the proposal raised eyebrows. Mikhail Pokrovsky in particular considered the expansive research agenda unacceptable, arguing that a teaching college's forays into *kraevedenie* would only duplicate work already included in the state plan and assigned to appropriate agencies.[62] In the end, the council voted to confine the institute's research to methodology, allowing other studies only when directly useful for excursion work. Pedagogy, members said, should remain central to all activities, and the council sent the delegates from Petrograd off to redo the proposal. A week later the council met to check the revisions, but by this time a new law had passed placing all higher educational institutes under the control of Glavprofobr (the Central Administration for Professional Education). Desperate to avoid new bureaucratic hurdles, Krasnukha and Grevs renounced all interest in instruction and begged to have the institute approved as a research facility. Surprisingly enough, the council agreed, placing the Petrograd Excursion Institute under the jurisdiction of the Academic Center and assigning it to study methodology. A facility conceived as a teachers' college had suddenly veered into pure theory.

Returning to Petrograd in the wake of this odd resolution, Krasnukha and Grevs faced assembling a program that no one had really foreseen. Bureaucratic chance, vested interests, and spending cuts had stripped the institute of many of its anticipated activities, eliminating regular classes, practical excursion work, and all but the most modest involvement in *kraevedenie*. At informational meetings prospective staff quickly regrouped, tossing aside months of work and fifty applications from would-be students. The institute would, for now, confine itself to drafting programs and describing routes. Employees joining the three departments drew up individual plans for the coming year, selecting specific sites, historic periods, or problems to tackle. Whenever possible, they chose to work in groups, using seminar tactics to enrich research. Material collected served as the foundation for papers and excursions that were presented at general meetings and, ideally, published. The institute regularly organized open lectures and demonstration tours; it put on four conferences, published several collections of articles, and, in March 1922, printed one issue of an in-house journal, *The Excursion Herald* (*Ekskursionnyi vestnik*).[63] In addition, members often made independent arrangements for publishing their work; they contributed to pedagogical magazines and anthologies and, in certain cases, released longer pieces of writing as books. Finances made travel almost impossible, so projects centered on Petrograd and its immediate surroundings. Aside from one expedition to the Russian North in the summer of 1922, employees stayed home, devoting the bulk of their attention to designing tours of local sites and creating tools to help others do the same: methodological treatises, bibliographies, guidebooks, and excursion primers.[64]

In the humanities and science departments, personnel made every effort to involve outsiders in institute projects, opening some seminars to the public so that groups, primarily made up of veteran educators, could experience the process of writing an excursion. Grevs ran a multiyear seminar on the Fontanka region; a group run by the talented young excursionist Georgy Petri developed city tours; and Antsiferov chaired sessions on literary St. Petersburg. Other groups worked in major museums and palace-park complexes or assembled anthologies of literary and historical sources on the city.[65] While no replacement for a two-year curriculum, these study circles did allow institute staff some opportunity to continue pedagogical work, preparing qualified guides for the schools and other organizations. In principle, such courses were nothing new: pre-Revolutionary organizations, Narkompros excursion sections, and the Society of Old Petersburg had all run seminars to train leaders. Important specialists had always generously volunteered their time, and standards often reached surprising highs. With the creation of the Excursion Institute, however, the atmosphere surrounding such projects noticeably changed, particularly in regard to the humanities. Whether due to natural progress in the field or as a result of the new research orientation, institute faculty began to see their profession in a different light. The term excursionist no longer merely identified a pedagogue with specialized training. It implied an expert scholar with the creativity necessary to weave the results of years of study into affecting emotional and intellectual events. Transforming raw information into a polished monologue, this new master guide completed tasks analogous to a performance artist's: scripting, blocking, and staging his presentation. More than ever, he was inclined to write up the results of all this effort, hoping to capture at least the shadow of a fundamentally ephemeral event for the benefit of colleagues and perhaps posterity.

The foremost faculty of the humanities department preached this expansive vision both in their activities at the institute and while on assignment with other organizations. Antsiferov, Georgy Petri, Ia. A. Vliadikh, O. M. Ryndina, V. G. Konradi, and Kseniia Polzikova-Rubets all took their methodology from Grevs. As veterans of the Museum Department or of his university seminars, most defined themselves as his students long before 1921. The realization that they as a group constituted a distinct school within a larger excursion movement, however, may have come to them only after the institute opened. United by a common structure and expected to issue responses on disputed topics, they saw not only what they shared, but also how they were perceived. At conferences and in publications they stood out: the Petrograd group led by Ivan Grevs. As everyone immediately recognized, all of their routes and papers grew organically out of the professor's pedagogical ideas, an understanding of tour work that, in the hothouse environment of the institute, grew progressively more refined.

Grevs himself returned to fundamental concepts in these years, reexamining the excursion movement's prewar heritage. He cataloged all the old definitions for the term "excursion" and then improved them with forays into etymology and semantics.[66] Most important, he looked back at his Italian notes, extracting from them a general technique for learning about prominent municipalities. Grevs outlined his ideas in his 1921 article "The Monumental City and Historical Excursions" (*Monumental'nyi gorod i istoricheskie ekskursii*), providing a blueprint for instructors that could, with a little work, be adapted to fit almost any large city and a variety of educational settings. In it Grevs broke down the investigative process into separate stages and tasks. He suggested that teachers interested in exploring a municipality with their students begin by providing their charges with an introduction to the geography and the prehistory of the area under consideration. This background would help pupils understand the circumstances surrounding the city's birth and would prepare them for the next task: an "anatomical" investigation of the municipality, charting its growth, transportation arteries, and economic cells, first with the help of historic maps and then through carefully designed excursions. On an initial outing, Grevs suggested, groups might take in a bird's eye view and perhaps a panorama from an outlying riverbank or hill.[67] Considered from such vantage points, the layout of streets and squares would offer clues to the location of the original nucleus of settlement and reveal the extent to which conscious design influenced the city's final form. After students had grasped these basic issues, Grevs suggested that instructors move on to one of several systems for organizing the remainder of the project. They could trace the lives of famous individuals connected with the locality, examine eras in its history, or break the territory down into smaller component parts. Architecture, the literary landscape, living conditions among various social groups, trade, and the economy all merited exploration; ideally, "the biography of the city should be studied from as many sides . . . as possible."[68]

Not all cities provided enough material for such an elaborate course of study. Ignoring peasant settlements entirely, Grevs acknowledged that even in many towns, excursion leaders would have to supplement the program with forays to a regional capital in order to provide students with a full picture of municipal life. The blueprint worked best in areas with a developed historical tradition like Novgorod, Pskov, Vladimir, or Smolensk. Concentrating research on such towns or, better yet, on the nation's two capitals offered enormous advantages to social scientists. Grevs explained:

> Cities are both laboratories and reception points, cultural repositories and the supreme indices of civilization. In them cultural processes are condensed, their results saturated; they are the largest form in which the elements of civilization are combined, the confluence and balanced interaction of its various constituents and trends. A city is simultaneously a center of cultural attraction and of radiation, the brightest and most visible measure of the level of culture; the history of the city is a wonderful guide to determining [the culture's] course and fate.[69]

In other words, urban centers rise and fall along with a country's overall level of development. By investigating them, social scientists can determine the true direction and nature of ongoing historical processes affecting a civilization as a whole. They are, despite social problems, engines for progress, and any sign of stoppage represents a serious setback. "The tragedy of a city," Grevs asserted, "always serves as a symptom of the tragedy of a whole culture."[70]

Applied to Petrograd, the municipality Grevs used most consistently as an example in "The Monumental City," this assertion inevitably raised questions. The old capital had suffered greatly during the Civil War and, in 1921, seemed dead or dying to many observers. Contemplating present conditions in the city, Grevs himself noted: "For now, in one's mind, one still anxiously asks—if this is dying or an illness before rebirth and new magnificence. One dearly hopes that the latter is correct." Grevs remained so uncertain about Petrograd's fate that in "The Monumental City" he refused to endorse attempts to study the old capital's present, noting sadly: "Perhaps even contemporary Petrograd with its changed face is the subject for a special sketch, but this ends on a question mark."[71] In Grevs's view, cities, like any living organism, move inevitably along a trajectory from birth to death. Therefore, logically, for any scholar who wants to study decisive moments and productive cultural periods, the endpoint to this process will determine the rational limits of research. Grevs refused to encourage studies of contemporary St. Petersburg in "The Monumental City," because, in his view, if the city was moribund, then its present represented nothing more than a vestige of a vibrant past.

The complex of ideas Grevs expressed in "The Monumental City" later came to be known as *urbanizm* (urban studies) or *gradovedenie* (city studies). Although synonyms, more or less, the terms tended to be used in slightly different contexts. When writers talked about the role of cities in history, the connection between their rise and fall and the fate of larger units of civilization, they generally used the term *urbanizm*. If they were more concerned with mapping the various parts of a city, identifying its main arteries of transportation, its banking center, and its shopping district, they usually emphasized the word *gradovedenie*. Coined, no doubt, by analogy with *rodinovedenie* and *kraevedenie*, this second term appeared most frequently in literature during the brief boom in local studies in the mid-1920s.

Under both names and in each of these variant forms, Grevs's science of cities seeped into the fabric of the Petrograd excursion movement, influencing everything from terminology to the arrangement of materials. "The Monumental City" offered followers basic guidelines that, unlike the collective programs of the Museum Department, were profoundly flexible. Instead of paying attention to specific school curricula and monuments, it paired a general approach with a developed conceptual framework. Effectively, the reader received a basic grid dotted by empty spaces, each of which marked a topic for future work. By reaching in and choosing a specific research project, the individual automatically participated in something larger, a survey of urban areas that potentially at least roamed freely past national borders and through every era of history. In St. Petersburg, where most efforts actually centered, the project produced measurable results. Between 1921 and 1926, Grevs's disciples published excursion primers in which most of the suggestions made in "The Monumental City" were realized. These written texts, in many respects, represent the most significant legacy of the Excursion Institute. They offer us a tantalizing glimpse of how Grevs's theories translated into practice, of what the finest educational strolls were really like in the 1920s.

5

Excursion Primers and Literary Tours

The excursion primer is undoubtedly the most exotic and poorly understood of the subgenres of the Russian guidebook. Because, when fully fleshed out, such works closely resemble ordinary guides, even meticulous Russian bibliographers often fail to mark their special characteristics. In catalog copy and in lists, the best excursion primers almost always appear under the general heading of *opisaniia* (descriptions) or *putevoditeli* (guidebooks). Their more sketchy brethren, outlines so bare that the distinctive structure and concerns of the excursion as a written genre become unmistakable, are all too frequently forgotten, tossed aside as mere technical literature. To some extent this problem with terminology is understandable: the excursionists who elevated and perfected the primer as a form of literature in the 1920s never really settled on a label themselves. In titles and in introductions writers usually referred to such works as *ekskursii*, but the terms *progulka* (stroll) and *putevoditel'* also appeared. Regardless of the designation used, excursion primers are distinguished from other kinds of guidebooks by both their explicit function and their target audience. At least superficially, they act as professional manuals offering instruction to would-be tour leaders. They typically contain suggestions on how best to present material, references to group dynamics, attention span and participatory activities, and general discussions of the pedagogical advantages of the excursion method. All of this instruction in professional skills might suggest that written excursions do belong in the category of "technical literature": that they represent books of interest to a narrow circle of specialists. In the best excursion primers, however, methodological suggestions are encapsulated within a full and often very lyrical description of a site or route, complete with historical background, anecdotes, a discussion of artistic styles, and snatches of poetry. Eminently readable, they can attract a general as well as professional audience.

One of the best examples of this kind of polished excursion primer is Nikolai Antsiferov's 1924 *Petersburg in Reality and Myth* (*Byl' i mif Peterburga*). A study of the city's origin and rumination on its fate, the book is organized into a series of four excursions. Three roughly fall into the category of the geographical or historical, using popular tales and literary citations primarily for contrast with standard factual sources. The last examines Pushkin's *Bronze Horseman*, pointing out mythic elements in the poem and connecting them with popular attitudes to Peter I. In his work with literature, Antsiferov was a great pioneer, so far ahead of all his colleagues that talk of influences seems almost misleading. The legacy he received from his mentor Ivan Grevs comes across most clearly in tours that focus on the social sciences. In this respect, the first three routes in *Petersburg in Reality and Myth* offer particularly good examples, in part because they cover topics that correspond to the initial and most extensively described section of the program Grevs outlined in "The Monumental City." They "characterize the conditions of Petersburg's birth, its nucleus and original settlement," comparing the capital's development with the pattern of growth in ancient Russian towns.[1] As Grevs suggested in "The Monumental City," Antsiferov organizes this series of excursions so that the focus gradually shifts from geography and prehistory to street plans documenting the colony's growth from a central point.

More significant than this general similarity, however, is Antsiferov's description of the tours themselves. Borrowing a device straight from Grevs, he suggests that the first excursion take place on the observation deck at St. Isaac's Cathedral. Antsiferov notes that he generally begins by having the group imagine how the river delta spread beneath its feet might have looked in the Cambrian period when waves washed through the entire valley. He next calls attention to the natural transportation routes that attracted both the Russians and the

Swedes to the area, leading them to disregard its notoriously harsh climate and swampy soil. Describing St. Petersburg's foundation and early history, he then points out the traces of various plans for ordering and improving the city. He acknowledges that, particularly in periods of rapid development, spontaneous growth often won out over planning, and many well-publicized imperial projects failed, but he also notes that even unsuccessful proposals sometimes left a lasting imprint on St. Petersburg. "The lines and prospects of Vasilievsky Island," for instance, Antsiferov points out, recall Le Blond's scheme to dig a network of canals and transform the area into "something similar to Venice."[2]

Effectively, in this first route, Antsiferov treats the body of the capital as a primary documentary source and, based on an examination of its contours, poses answers to the questions suggested by Grevs in the first section of "The Monumental City." What factors led to the city's growth? Was its development largely planned or spontaneous? What traces of its early history remain today? In the next two excursions described in *Petersburg in Reality and Myth,* Antsiferov works to answer the same questions and employs similar strategies. The second walk opens with another panoramic view of the city, this time from the Trinity Bridge. In "The Monumental City," Grevs had recommended introducing such profile vistas, noting that they complemented the more standard panoramas from above.[3] After calling attention to locations associated with the events of 1703, Antsiferov moves on to explore the Peter and Paul Fortress, the nucleus from which the city St. Petersburg grew. There he sketches an elaborate comparison to more traditional Russian fortifications, noting, in particular, ways in which the early-eighteenth-century construction differed from and seemed designed to replace the great kremlin in Moscow. Always aware of where he wants his group to look, Antsiferov often gives detailed instructions concerning lines of sight and approaches.[4] He shows how he controls the gaze of his audiences so as to ensure that they receive visual impressions that ideally illustrate the points made in his monologue.

The third tour described in *Petersburg in Reality and Myth* moves from the Peter and Paul Fortress through the adjacent Trinity Square section of the Petrograd Side. The city center during the first few years of St. Petersburg's existence, this district fell into decline once construction expanded to the other side of the Neva River. Almost entirely rebuilt in the late nineteenth and early twentieth centuries, by the 1920s it contained few traces of the earliest phase of its development. For this reason, during much of the walk, Antsiferov relies on information drawn from old engravings and clues provided by original place names in his efforts to reconstruct the initial contours of the region. He notes the location of old streets, market places, pie shops, and inns; describes the architectural forms employed during the Petrine period; and characterizes the district's first settlers. The tour concludes with a visit to the only extant early-eighteenth-century structure in the vicinity of Trinity Square (aside from the Peter and Paul Fortress): the small wooden cabin (*domik Petra*) in which Peter I resided during the first phase of the construction of St. Petersburg.

This final stop signals something of a shift in direction. Encased in a protective structure since relatively early in the eighteenth century and boasting a small chapel with a wonder-working icon, the cabin functions as a monument and religious shrine honoring the memory of the city's founder. As Antsiferov tacitly acknowledges following a detailed description of the small house's façade and interior, for all its "authenticity," it is perhaps more relevant to the contemplation of the city's myth than to a conversation about its historical development.

> Petersburg . . . made an ineffaceable impression on the witnesses of its fantastically rapid growth. This amazement created advantageous soil for the birth of legends.
>
> Peter . . . turned into a titan, a demigod who created the city out of nothingness. . . . Just as kites hovered over Romulus at the moment the eternal city was founded, an eagle hovered over Peter as the first stone was laid for the Peter and Paul Fortress. The house of the founder of Petersburg with its icon of the Savior had a strong effect on the imagination of the population and turned into a particularly revered sacred site. In the same way in Rome throughout the centuries the *domus Romuli* was maintained. Later fortune developed this mythic element, which was expressed in its most classical form in Pushkin's *Bronze Horseman*.[5]

In this brief passage, Antsiferov shifts from analyzing the physical structure of the old imperial capital to commenting on the links between its popular image, myth, and most famous artistic representations. In the process, he takes the pedagogical excursion into territory that at the beginning of the 1920s remained relatively unexplored: he moves toward using tours as a means of studying cultural constructs and literary texts.

Before Antsiferov began to publish his primers, attempts to tour writers' homes and other literary sites, when they took place at all, were generally primitive. The few accounts of such events published in Russia's pre-Revolutionary excursion journals focus, by and large, on biographical or historical issues as opposed to literary texts per se and, as often as not, contain no references whatsoever to the presence of a group, leaving the impression that they record private pilgrimages as opposed to true pedagogical outings.[6] The influential first edition of *School Excursions: Their Significance and Organization,* the collection of articles published by instructors at the Lesnoe school in 1910, contains two submissions on literary tours: a general methodological statement by N. M. Sokolov entitled "Literary Excursions" (*Literaturnye ekskursii*) and G. Tumim's outline of a sample tour "In the Footsteps of Peter the Great" (*Po sledam Petra Velikogo*). Sokolov's statement is historically important because it provides the first convincing explanation of the function of literary excursions. Such events, the author argues, provide pupils with the visual cues necessary to picture fictional events more fully and, as a result, make it possible for them to become more "creative" readers.[7] A trail of citations throughout the excursion primers of the 1920s testifies to the relevance of this idea to later scholars, including Antsiferov. Many of the kinds of tours Sokolov lists as examples in his article, however, appear on balance more historical than literary: they travel to sites only tangentially connected to literature (places associated with the lives of historical figures such as Peter the Great, typical noble estates . . .) and appear not to make use of classic literary texts, relying instead on letters, chronicles, diaries, and official acts as sources. G. Tumim's sample excursion, which reads as an effort to put Sokolov's ideas into effect, predictably suffers from similar limitations.

Pre-Revolutionary excursionists had difficulty applying their formula to literary texts because of a fundamental methodological problem. An excursion had always meant a pedagogical device designed to move students out of the classroom and into the real world; it was a journey that would bring them face to face with the object of study, so that they could observe it in its natural context. Pupils learned chemistry in factories, studied economics at the farmers' market, and absorbed history by visiting monuments and ruins. In the case of each of these disciplines, the term *excursion* translated into a trip to one or several locations and visual contact with a specific object. It suggested physical movement, active learning, and an escape from books. How, given this definition, could a literary excursion even be imagined? In what sense could the constituent matter of literature—the word—become a source of visual impressions? In what way could it be visited? In a series of publications culminating in the 1926 *Theory and Practice of Literary Excursions* (*Teoriia i praktika literaturnykh ekskursii*), Antsiferov identified this stumbling block and suggested a way around it. While indeed, he pointed out, words could not directly serve as the object of examination during an excursion, tours could approach literary texts indirectly, offering valuable illustrations, commentary, and perhaps even interpretations. They could bring the text to life for the reader, inspiring him to go home, "open up the book and reread the excerpts that excited" him, which now "appear" before him "in a new light."[8] In this respect, they functioned much like theatrical productions, which often helped to satisfy the need of the broad masses for illustration and sometimes significantly altered attitudes to classic texts. In fact, Antsiferov notes in *The Theory and Practice*, excursions resemble theatrical productions in all but a few key respects: "The theater is a spectacle. Something is shown; we receive rich, concrete, visual impressions. Of course, there is no excursion inasmuch as there is no route, no analysis of visual material . . . , but there are certain elements of an excursion: departure (*excurs*) to a new place and rich, concrete, visual impressions" (5). This comparison allows Antsiferov to sidestep his own central methodological concern: excursions become a form of creative self-expression and as such no longer need to demonstrate anything directly. They can reveal words and images from books figuratively, coaxing listeners into projecting scenes onto a real-life landscape. In this way, the text becomes as easy to display or visit as a forest habitat; both the leader and the group enter a special space created through a creative act, a window that tangibly connects the physical world and a particular literary work.

In *The Theory and Practice*, Antsiferov lists five ways of incorporating literature into excursion work. Only a couple of the techniques result in trips with a true literary focus; in other cases, the leader concentrates on something else, but supplements material with references to classic texts or expects the excursion to fulfill some secondary literary purpose. Antsiferov's first category, excursions with literary illustrations, consists of field trips that focus on a nonliterary subject but use occasional quotations to emphasize a point, synthesize material, or elicit an appropriate emotional response from the group. An excursion to a large city street might conclude with a citation from Mayakovsky that emphasizes key elements of urban life: "the movement of the crowd, fragments of conversation and phrases, the bells of the trams, car horns and the hum of wheels, the cries of newspaper boys, as short and garish as posters" (18). Excerpts from Gorky ideally complement tours of factory slums; Esenin might help illustrate an excursion to a village.

Auxiliary excursions (*vspomogatel'nye ekskursii*), the second type of literary tour Antsiferov identifies, are also primarily extraliterary in focus, including potentially even some events during which leaders never mention literature explicitly. Such excursions provide participants with background information useful for understanding classic texts. A trip to the Ukrainian culture exhibit at the Ethnographic Museum, for instance, might acquaint students with the kind of everyday objects that appear in Gogol's *Evenings on a Farm Near Dikanka* (*Vechera na khutore bliz Dikan'ki*), specific tools and items of clothing that Russian children generally cannot identify. Antsiferov explains that in such tours artistic representations of objects and processes can sometimes replace authentic relics, provided the excursionist takes "into account the peculiarities of the artistic style of the epoch and the individuality of the master" when developing the route (30). Just as old engravings and images stamped on coins can give us an idea of how ruined temples once looked, the paintings at the Russian Museum can help us visualize the world Derzhavin described in his verses. Aside from providing a general impression of the bonnets, chairs, and military regalia characteristic of the period, they also give us a sense of society's standards of beauty, its attitudes to color and decoration, and its preference for particular mythological references or symbols.

The third category of literary tour identified by Antsiferov in *The Theory and Practice,* and the first to focus primarily on literary material, consists of the old standby: excursions illustrating an author's biography. Antsiferov opens his discussion by acknowledging the popularity of the form and connecting it to the tradition of the pilgrimage: "The words 'in that very place' have some special power over our consciousness. It is as if the place marked by the memorable event conquers time. When you stand in it, . . . the experience of days gone by bursts back to life." Such "historical and topographic sentiment," the hope of "preserving and deepening a connection" to an event or person," Antsiferov notes, draws visitors to specific sites, giving rise, over the course of time, to a "particular kind of cult" (43–44). Just as religious believers aspire to see the places in which key Biblical events transpired and history buffs dream of surveying battlefields, many readers of modern poetry and fiction long to see sites associated with a favorite author. Because people often implicitly believe that old haunts and personal artifacts can reveal important facts about an individual's tastes and habits, Antsiferov points out, even insignificant articles, like ticket stubs and matchboxes, if once owned by a famous writer, can attract public interest: mankind still subconsciously remains under the sway of the primitive belief that "an invisible part of the owner lies preserved in his belongings" (48). How should educators respond to this sentimental relationship to things? Although he acknowledges that such superstitions represent "survivals" and no longer correspond to the ideology of the day,

Antsiferov argues for tolerance. Excursionists, he suggests, can use such old-fashioned beliefs to build interest in more serious investigative work.

In *The Theory and Practice* Antsiferov also discusses utilizing literary tours in the context of local studies. By "excursions in *kraevedenie*" he seems to mean forays to collect material in accordance with a preset plan. Such expeditions, he argues, "give free rein to the initiative of each member of the group. The work acquires the character of an investigation or sometimes even research" (90). In the next two chapters I will discuss the definitions applied to the word *kraevedenie* in the 1920s and will comment on the history of the Academy of Sciences' Central Bureau of *Kraevedenie* and its affiliates. For now, suffice it to say that in his treatment of literary *kraevedenie* Antsiferov relies heavily on the ideas of Nikolai Piksanov, a researcher who in the 1920s tried to redress what he saw as the pervasive centrist biases in Russian literary scholarship by calling for the study of provincial cultural centers. While critical of some of Piksanov's more extreme regionalist ideas, Antsiferov encourages excursionists to gather information on the literary heritage of the regions in which they live, focusing either on prominent writer-residents or else on the conventions employed in the description of local sites.

The last kind of tour described in *The Theory and Practice*, "literary excursions in the narrow sense of the word," were, Antsiferov admitted, by far the most difficult to conduct and "in view of their peculiarities," might well "never be broadly practiced" (89). They required artistry as well as erudition; leaders had to capture the imagination of their listeners while guiding them past landmarks evoking scenes or images from a text. Dramatic nuances, a concern for audience response, staging, lighting, and blocking became particularly important. In such tours, Antsiferov noted, he generally chose to focus on a single work or several short related pieces, but sometimes, as a variation, he might take a group to a popular setting like the Catherine Park in Tsarskoe Selo and examine its reflection in Russian literature. In either case Antsiferov fully acknowledged the "independent significance of the artistic work." In *The Theory and Practice,* he writes:

> Of course the "Three Pine Trees" [*Tri sosny*], the inn of "The Unknown Woman" [*Neznakomka*], and "The Statue in Tsarskoe Selo" [*Tsarskosel'skaia statuia*] exist "outside of space," that is, outside of any connection with concrete places . . . they exist in the special world of art. Their value does not depend at all on whether or not there is a sweet girl with a pitcher in the Catherine Park or whether there are three old pine trees on the road

to Trigorsk or whether, finally, on the outskirts of the northern capital there really is an inn frequented by a pensive poet and reflected in one of his best creations. (79)

But "does it necessarily follow from this that in order to comprehend a work of art we must forget about the material the artist took from life?" (10–11). In *The Theory and Practice,* Antsiferov explicitly argues for the value of studying the model. He suggests that by considering what a writer borrows from the real world and what he changes or abandons, we can learn about the peculiarities of his individual style and about the creative process in general.

Antsiferov developed a number of pure literary excursions in the early 1920s, but he expended particular effort on two themes: Pushkin's *The Bronze Horseman* and Dostoevsky's novels. In each case, he constructed detailed routes, which he described repeatedly in magazine articles and conference papers. Full, refined versions appeared in the book-length publications *Petersburg in Reality and Myth* and *Dostoevsky's Petersburg.* While primers can no more duplicate the experience of participating in a stroll than reading scripts can substitute for watching films, these two exceptionally thorough accounts give at least an idea of what Antsiferov's textual excursions looked like in practice. Revolutionary when first published, the books exerted an enormous influence over all later efforts to design literary strolls. Even now, most Dostoevsky walks in St. Petersburg use modified versions of Antsiferov's routes, and most Pushkin tours borrow significant moments from his *Bronze Horseman* work. Moreover, Antsiferov's basic approach to the study of literary topography and urban myth, as well as his language and concepts, have influenced later Russian academic discourse in a number of important respects. Since the 1980s, members of the Tartu school of semiotics have repeatedly acknowledged a substantial debt to Antsiferov's work in papers on Russia's two capitals.[9] Lotman and Uspensky's famous articles "Echoes of the Conception 'Moscow—the Third Rome' in the Ideology of Peter I" and "The Symbolism of Petersburg and the Problems of a Semiotics of the City" both reprise Antsiferov on many points, even falling back on his citations.

The second, literary half of *Petersburg in Reality and Myth* begins with a substantial introductory statement connecting the St. Petersburg myth with Middle Eastern and classical traditions. Citing Viacheslav Ivanov, Antsiferov notes that long-dormant mythological structures often reappear during violent social upheavals. Desperate for some explanation of the cataclysmic changes taking place, the populace begins to measure events against the pattern set by ancient sagas, epic accounts of battles between opposing forces that commemorate a cosmic mystery: creation, flood, or apocalypse. Thus, Antsiferov explains, early-eighteenth-century traditionalists, and particularly Old Believers, consistently identified the Westernizing tsar Peter I as the antichrist and connected his policies to Biblical prophesies regarding the end time.

Not everyone, however, accepted this apocalyptic reading of events. In *Petersburg in Reality and Myth* Antsiferov points out that Peter I had passionate apologists who refuted the negative images circulated by conservatives with two important mythological constructs of their own. According to the first, Peter I was a kind of modern-day Romulus who, heralded by signs of celestial favor, personally selected the site for the construction of a major metropolis. The reverence accorded the tsar as the capital's founder, his popular acceptance as a kind of "civic god," complemented, Antsiferov suggests, the second positive mythological construct found in early accounts of his reign. Eighteenth-century writers, Antsiferov argues, often depict the tsar organizing chaos: they show him, like the god of Genesis, calling forth land from formless, watery space and creating gardens and palaces where once there was only wilderness. Because Peter I's modern capital regularly faced the threat of floods, a natural dichotomy between creative and destructive forces emerged, which, Antsiferov notes, calls to mind creation and inundation narratives from a host of ancient traditions. In Chaldean myth, Marduk vanquishes Tiamat, the goddess of the oceanic abyss, and splits her body into pieces to create the heavens and the earth. Surviving visual representations of this legend depict Marduk as "a mighty warrior" and Tiamat as "a winged dragon or other snake-like creature."[10] Similar stories appear in Old and New Testament books as well as in hagiographic works and popular literature. The section of the book of *Revelation* in which the Archangel Michael leads a host of angels against a dragon, the legend of St. George, and the traditional account of St. Petersburg's creation, all, Antsiferov contends, represent incarnations of the same mythic archetype (60).

In *Petersburg in Reality and Myth* Antsiferov argues that Pushkin, on balance, sided with Peter I's apologists. Despite all the poet's qualms about the tsar as "a human being," despite his awareness that the reformer had "despised humanity perhaps more than Napoleon," Pushkin found in Peter I "the creative spirit, merciless and terrible," and deemed him worthy of "apotheosis" (63). In *The Bronze Horseman* Pushkin, according to Antsiferov, gave narrative form to the positive mythic elements long present in the popular consciousness, successfully combining the legend of the civic god and the chaos fable; Pushkin wrote an epic poem, updating Virgil's genre to accommodate post-Renaissance sensibilities, including faith in the dignity and power of mankind. *The Bronze Horseman*, Antsiferov argues in *Petersburg in Reality and Myth*, represents a "Petersburg mystery play" with four characters:

> Peter, replaced later by the Bronze Horseman, the creative and protecting spirit, the Cosmocrator; the Neva, the water element, faceless chaos; Petersburg, the created world. All the characters of the old myth. Alongside them a new person is brought out, created by the problem of man as an end in himself—Evgenii—the sacrifice constantly brought by history in the name of ends it does not know itself, those of the collective super-individual source. (65)

Each character, Antsiferov notes, is sketched in "abstract, spectral" brushstrokes, stripped of all personal features as dictated by the conventions of myth. Peter I, for instance, to the discomfiture of nineteenth-century censors, appeared not as a real autocrat, but rather deified: "transformed into an idol around which the mystery play takes place" (62–63).

This reading of Pushkin's poem, its relationship to myth and history, perhaps seems a little content heavy for educational travel, and indeed Antsiferov does simplify concepts somewhat when he passes from his long introductory statement on the meaning of Pushkin's text and begins to describe the excursion itself. On the whole, however, he retains a surprising amount of analysis. The route he proposes includes four stops, one for each of the poem's characters. The first is once again the gallery of St. Isaac's Cathedral and focuses on St. Petersburg itself. Reciting passages from the introduction to Pushkin's poem, Antsiferov stresses the dark, chaotic images used to describe the initial wilderness and then the sudden change in tone that accompanies the creator's appearance: "harmony, splendor, and brightness" suddenly fill the landscape (67). After carefully comparing Pushkin's setting with the actual panorama visible to the group, Antsiferov moves on to note those aspects of the vista that suggest that St. Petersburg's growth was planned, as opposed to spontaneous, and hence provide support for the myth of the "miracle working builder" who personally guided the creation of the metropolis (68). He notes that, although by no means irrational, Peter I's decision to build at the mouth of the river Neva was, in a sense, made in "defiance of the elements." St. Petersburg, Antsiferov tells us, "was built as an antithesis to surrounding nature, as a challenge to it. Even though under its squares, streets, and canals 'chaos stirs,' it itself is all calm, straight lines, of hard, stable stone, precise, severe, and regal" (68–69).

Antsiferov's second stop is on the granite embankment by the Admiralty and focuses on the river. Floods, he notes, plagued the city from the moment of its creation. With each successive inundation, the population grew more inclined to regard water as the city's natural enemy, responsible for any number of ills, including Peter I's own sudden death: the tsar reportedly caught cold trying to save others from drowning in a storm. Such popular attitudes, Antsiferov argues, form part of the background of Pushkin's poem. Using citations from the epic, he reconstructs the poet's vision of the hostile river, focusing on meter and sound effects. The Winter Palace, itself caught up "in the restless movement of the baroque," rises out of Pushkin's verses, an island buffeted by stormy water (72–73). Alexander I stands on a balcony, observing natural havoc—a modern, human tsar capitulating to the elements. His presence contrasts with Peter I's superhuman stature.

Antsiferov introduces Evgenii, the third character, as the group approaches the house of the Lobanov-Rostovskys. Shifting back and forth between the textual and physical landscapes, Antsiferov describes the area at the time of the great flood of 1824: St. Isaac's still in scaffolding; the Senate and Synod not yet built; and Evgenii, seated on his lion, looking frantically out at Vasilievsky Island:

> Between two struggling powers: the faceless chaos of the watery deep—the source of destruction—and the superhuman genius, who determines the fate of peoples—the source of creativity—an individual man with his dream of personal happiness loses all historical reality.
>
> To us, standing here on the steps of the portico of what was once a "new house," between the "lion sentries," Evgenii also seems a far-off specter. But his tragic fate and the problem common to all mankind that is connected with it have not only not lost their significance but have gained, amidst the great events of our terrible time, unprecedented acuteness. (77)

Much has changed since Pushkin's time. Traffic crowds the streets and the trees have all filled in, blocking our view of the square; but if one walks back down the stairs, the Bronze Horseman comes into view. Antsiferov suggests groups walk slowly around the monument so as to see it from all sides. Movement, he points out, spirals up from the rock, through the coils of the snake, and into the statue itself, only to freeze in the front legs of the horse. "Frozen stormy motion," the main impression created by the sculpture, finds reflection in

Pushkin's descriptions as well (83). Citing the passage where Evgenii first notices the horseman, Antsiferov writes: "In this description the twofold motion of Falconet's statue is wonderfully emphasized. On the one hand, the fiery horse rushing toward unknown and terrifying distant lands, on the other, the terrible rider with great thoughts on his brow . . . stops his horse on the very edge of the abyss with a powerful motion" (82). In both Falconet's monument and Pushkin's poem, Antsiferov suggests, Peter is ultimately triumphant: "on a fiery steed, reducing the snake to dust! Flouting the elements, flouting the fate of little men, he draws a great country on into an unknown future" (85). Pushkin, Antsiferov notes, concludes his poem on an optimistic note. Daybreak has wiped away all traces of the flood, leaving St. Petersburg beautiful and regal once more.

In four stops Antsiferov successfully incorporates most of the ideas outlined in the introductory remarks that precede this tour. He connects Pushkin's poem to ancient myth and popular superstition, identifying as the central conflict the battle between a creative spirit and a destructive force. The landscape of the city, including specific monuments, not only illustrates Pushkin's poem, but also helps underscore Antsiferov's own interpretive ideas. Properly approached and introduced, Falconet's monument reinforces all preceding references to chaos myths: we recognize Marduk, Michael, and St. George in the rider and connect the snake to the dragon Tiamat.

In *Petersburg in Reality and Myth* Antsiferov uses an excursion to demonstrate a thesis; he proposes that Pushkin, when composing *The Bronze Horseman,* gave epic form to mythic elements long present in the popular imagination, producing a new incarnation of a very old tradition: once again a creative, ordering force confronts watery chaos in a cataclysmic struggle. This "myth of the miracle-working builder," as Antsiferov calls it, also figures in the first of the two excursions outlined in *Dostoevsky's Petersburg*. Against the backdrop of the Mokrushi region of the city, Antsiferov explores Dostoevsky's complex attitude to the capital, showing how the novelist reworked the archetype that lies at the heart of Pushkin's poem using darker tones. "The myth of the Bronze Horseman lives on in the soul of the author of *Crime and Punishment,*" Antsiferov asserts at the beginning of the tour, but then quickly adds that, unlike Pushkin, "Dostoevsky does not believe in the triumph of the city and doubts its truth."[11] To Dostoevsky, Antsiferov explains, the city's grand palaces and ministries represented a shimmering mirage, the product of a spell laid on the Finnish swamps by the "miracle-working builder," and hence might at any moment disappear. The water element, the primeval destructive force that so often threatened imperial St. Petersburg, Antsiferov notes, pervades

Dostoevsky's descriptions of the city and, in the form of canals, rivers, foul weather, and wet snow, plays a negative role in the lives of many of the author's most famous characters.

Water, for instance, Antsiferov reminds us, figures prominently in the story of *Crime and Punishment*'s Svidrigailov. The debauched landowner committed his most appalling crime "on a dark night, in the gloom, in the cold, in the damp thaw, when the wind howled" and then ever afterwards disliked natural elements that reminded him of his offense, including "the noise of the trees in the storm" and "water, even in landscapes."[12] Drawn back to the scene of the crime at the end of the novel, he roams through the low-lying neighborhoods on the Petersburg Side. There, in a hotel room in the middle of a driving storm, he fitfully dreams of a girl displayed in her coffin, her face framed by long wet hair. Cannon shots warning of floods call him back out into the rain: "What am I waiting for? I will go out now, I will head out straight for Petrovsky Island: somewhere there I will choose a big shrub all dripping with rain against which I can lean my shoulder a bit and blow my head to a million smithereens."[13] "Ancient chaos," the inherently destructive water element that figures so prominently in the St. Petersburg myth, Antsiferov argues, plays a role in luring Svidrigailov to both his moral downfall and his eventual death. By retracing the movements of Dostoevsky's character on the last night of his life, Antsiferov suggests, we too will sense "the terrible pull of water that led all of Dostoevsky's wanderers to linger for long periods of time on bridges, looking into the water."[14] Suitably miserable weather, a late hour, and sensitive commentary will intensify the experience even further.

The Svidrigailov tour that Antsiferov outlines in *Dostoevsky's Petersburg* takes place in a section of the Petrograd Side that, like the Trinity Square area surveyed in the third excursion included in *Petersburg in Reality and Myth*, had changed dramatically in the late nineteenth and early twentieth centuries. Because of this, organizing an effective excursion to the sites associated with Dostoevsky's 1866 novel presented certain challenges. Beyond Tuchkov Bridge and basic geographic features like rivers, Antsiferov had few landmarks to show his audience. Most of the streets mentioned in connection with Svidrigailov's final walk had, by the 1920s, lost their old character entirely; if Dostoevsky had a real edifice in mind when he described the Hotel Adrianople, the place Svidrigailov stops to spend his last night, it did not survive; the structure that, most likely, served as the model for the building in front of which Svidrigailov killed himself was still standing, but the watchtower once attached to it had been replaced, significantly changing the look of the site.

The altered landscape of the Petrograd Side made it impractical for Antsiferov to adhere perfectly to the route suggested for Svidrigailov's walk by the text of Dostoevsky's novel. At several points in the tour, Antsiferov takes detours, doubling back or zigzagging through neighborhoods to avoid obtrusive new construction or to incorporate a vista that recalls the look of "Dostoevsky's Petersburg" especially effectively. At the approximate site of the Adrianople hotel, Antsiferov pauses in front of an ordinary two-story wooden house. He recommends standing with it suggestively in view while retelling Svidrigailov's dreams to the group and allowing it to serve as a kind of visual substitute for the missing structure. Such effects call attention to the fact that in his excursions Antsiferov does more than follow textual clues: he selects appropriately atmospheric locations for talking about books and characters at least as often as he reveals authentic models.

The second route included in *Dostoevsky's Petersburg* runs through the Haymarket district, an area that in the 1920s offered better examples of genuine literary sites. Copiously described in *Crime and Punishment,* it had stood largely untouched since the mid-nineteenth century. The market itself, the Iusupov Garden, and many of the buildings Raskolnikov would have passed as he counted out his infamous 730 steps all remained intact. Even when describing this region, Antsiferov, however, often seems more interested in discussing Dostoevsky's creative method than in pointing out specific landmarks. How, he asks in *Dostoevsky's Petersburg,* did the author depict Russia's northern capital, and what reaction do his descriptions provoke in us? Dostoevsky, Antsiferov points out, constantly "measures, numbers, and strives to create an exact frame for the action" in his books, almost as if "his characters, stepping out of the Petersburg fog, need this concrete map in which they find a link to a real, stable environment" (221). After reading one of his books, "one wants to go to the place that has been indicated so exactly and check Dostoevsky's description against that corner of Petersburg" (222). Excursions can try to fulfill this desire by taking us out to find Raskolnikov's garret or the pawnbroker's apartment, Antsiferov notes in *Dostoevsky's Petersburg,* but their value extends far beyond this limited task. "Perhaps," Antsiferov suggests toward the end of the book, "a series of mistakes have been made here, perhaps even the supposition itself that this house, which Dostoevsky considered the house of Raskolnikov, existed in reality is flawed. Nonetheless, our work does not lose its meaning. The house we have found can serve as an excellent illustration to the novel and . . . will excite our topographical sense with memories of the characters and events of *Crime and Punishment*" (251).

For Antsiferov, buildings are primarily valuable as tools; they are visual aids useful for developing the imaginative skills of groups. He conscientiously follows clues, but accuracy as such remains so secondary to his purpose that he can easily imagine the identification of landmarks as a participatory exercise. Why not, he suggests at one point in *Dostoevsky's Petersburg*, let the group pick out Sonia's house? Listening as the leader reads relevant passages from the novel, the excursion-goers could themselves choose where to turn, wandering through the stifling city until they came upon a building that resembled Dostoevsky's fictional description (255–56).

Accurately recreating the atmosphere associated with a particular setting represents Antsiferov's primary concern in both his Dostoevsky presentations. For the Mokrushi tour this meant a stormy night, dilapidated wooden buildings, and approaching chaos. In the Haymarket excursion the city projects an entirely different image: it is "scorched by the summer heat, dusty, dirty, fetid" and such a potential source of fever and corruption, that it seems almost culpable for Raskolnikov's crime (241). "The character's guilt, Antsiferov notes, "is the product of an inflamed mind, and the city itself, in this way, serves as the inspiration for the character" (241). At the heart of Antsiferov's work lies the discovery that the setting plays a major role in Dostoevsky's writing, alternately influencing and mimicking the behavior of the author's heroes. Antsiferov argues that studying the real-life environment depicted in a particular book can help us to understand the literary work itself. However, he also posits the opposite: that books provide the key to understanding the physical world. "A real connection exists between a work of art and the monument or simply the locality that inspired it. By visiting the places that have been described, the connection can be revealed, and it can lead us to a better understanding of both *the one and the other* [italics mine]" (178). Cities such as St. Petersburg reveal their essential nature to perceptive writers and, for this reason, in great literature the attentive reader can find, despite the fact that every author introduces something subjective into his or her descriptions, an accurate representation of these places of human settlement.

In Antsiferov's textual tours, the pedagogical excursion reached its highest stage of development, emerging as a kind of performance art. Aside from Antsiferov's own primers, few records now exist of either these events or their reception. Occasionally comments appear in the introductions to other people's books or in the memoirs of students and associates, but most descriptions of Antsiferov in action are frustratingly vague. The source that comes the closest to providing us with a glimpse of how live audiences perceived

Antsiferov focuses on a lecture rather than a full excursion. In 1923 Antsiferov gave a paper based upon his *Bronze Horseman* work at the Petrograd excursion conference. The ensuing discussion, which was published along with the event proceedings, includes about a dozen largely positive evaluations. The only criticism relates to the difficulty of replicating the experiment. A. Ia. Dzeiver, for instance, noted: "That was not a paper, a lecture, it was a work of art; in terms of the clarity and the symmetry of its construction, it was pure Pushkin. . . . However, alongside this sense of admiration, practical considerations arise. . . . Is such an excursion . . . feasible for the ordinary practical worker, the teacher of literature . . . ? Isn't this excursion viable only for N. P. himself and for other deeply emotional kindred natures; something at which only he can succeed?"[15] While Antsiferov quickly countered that the plan did not need to be followed exactly, the problem lay in the approach rather than in the specifics of any given route. Antsiferov's method demanded such a high level of skill, such comprehensive knowledge of literature, history, and art, that his textual tours did prove difficult to duplicate.

Simpler, nonliterary models dominated excursion work. One approach worked out by Grevs's disciples and frequently described in conference papers and articles involved taking an individual street or square and then identifying its "characteristic function." Sadovaia became "the street of markets."[16] Kamennoostrovsky Prospect, which, like the Champs-Elysées in Paris, led out to a fashionable suburban recreational district, was identified as a "parade ground" for the very wealthy.[17] One particularly successful example of this kind of functional analysis, Vladimir Fedorov's "An Excursion to the Domain of Financial Capitalism," redefines Nevsky Prospect as a "street of banks." Fedorov looks back at the history of the thoroughfare, tying each phase in its development to a dominant economic activity and a typical architectural form. He notes that in the late nineteenth century banks began to replace fashionable shops as tenants. These new arrivals commissioned grand offices that architecturally expressed the triumph of capital by borrowing forms and devices associated with older dominant social groups: from the street most bank buildings looked like "palaces."[18]

Many tours focused on individual sites: former imperial residences, churches, and museums. Antsiferov and Georgy Petri, for instance, issued a two-route primer on the Hermitage, which used the Spanish, Dutch, and French painting collections as material for historical reflection. In the first route, Petri compares the work of artists from "aristocratic" Spain and "bourgeois" Holland, drawing generalizations about the concerns of each society based on the approaches and subjects that predominated in its art. Looking at the Hermitage's Spanish exhibit with its huge religious canvases and formal portraits, he notes: "Not a single thing in the entire hall speaks of the home and hearth, about the joy of labor, about interest in the real conditions of life."[19] The very opposite characterizes Dutch paintings: "full of warmth and light, meant to decorate family living quarters," they continuously depict "the energetic labors of man."[20]

In the second half of the book, Antsiferov uses a similar technique to comment on some of the Hermitage's French paintings. Early in his tour, he analyzes Largilliere's painting of *The Paris Municipal Magistrates* in some detail, finding in the canvas a powerful visual representation of absolutist ideology. After noting the magnificent clothing worn by the magistrates, the splendor of the meeting room, the sun imagery used to decorate individual pieces of furniture, and the repeated depiction of the French king in sculptures and paintings shown within the frame, Antsiferov writes: "All of this splendor, all of this magnificence and pomp are only the reflection of the sun king. The grandeur of the fathers of the city does not come from within. They are only elevated in relationship to mere mortals; before the head of the absolute monarchy, they are nothing. He is the state. Their power is his power."[21] Moving on to describe other canvases from the Hermitage collection, Antsiferov notes that when the French monarchy began to weaken, the image of the king that had "ruled" in French art for so long gave way and other themes appeared: intimate, dreamy scenes, particularly pastorals.[22]

Sophisticated analysis of visual information and imaginative interdisciplinary approaches characterized work at industrial sites as well. Aside from acquainting students with the manufacturing process, such excursions often asked them to consider the factory as a social environment. What services and salaries did workers receive; what activities did they participate in; how could the sights and sounds that filled their lives be reflected in art? In perhaps the finest primer describing a tour of an industrial site, *Excursion to the State Porcelain Factory* (*Ekskursiia na gosudarstvennyi farforovyi zavod*), V. G. Konradi outlined a plan for an excursion so elaborate that, as the author confessed, it required two leaders: one with training in the humanities to give a historical introduction and discuss the artistic merit of the production, and another with technical qualifications to explain the science underlying activities in the various workshops.[23] Konradi's excursion plan called for the inclusion of information on European efforts to discover the secret of Chinese porcelain, eighteenth- and nineteenth-century stylistic trends, and changes in the factory's management and aims over time.

Problems of everyday life attracted a great deal of attention from Petrograd excursionists. Many primers give an account of trips to apartment buildings, stores, cafeterias, markets, or other ordinary sites. By and large such tours were meant to supplement specific aspects of the school curriculum, and, as a result, primers describing them often include suggestions for pre- and post-excursion lesson plans as well as ideas for group activities that could be conducted as part of the tour itself. At a farmer's market, for instance, students might be broken up into small groups and sent to roam through the stalls, using their own senses to gather information and addressing set questions to passersby. Although sometimes primer writers working on this kind of topic chose a famous central site as their model, describing one of the city's leading stores or a particularly famous apartment house, they almost always suggested ways in which their plan could be adapted to more modest facilities. In primers that explored everyday life, teachers were generally encouraged to organize tours to sites near the schools in which they taught.[24] Aside from its obvious logistical advantages, this neighborhood approach neatly complemented a pedagogical theory popular at the time: localization. Students, it was argued, focused best on objects closest to their own experience. Hence school programs should begin with topics like "my family," "my apartment house," and "my school" and then gradually expand outward to themes at a further physical or temporal remove.[25] Of course, the trick to this whole approach lay in making the child's immediate surroundings seem worthy of attention. Children had to be taught "to look with care around themselves, to quickly orient themselves in what is spread out before their eyes." These skills would in turn "enrich" the individual's "internal world." "A boring, everyday, commonplace environment in the process of such work" would fill with "interest and content."[26]

As the sampling of topics given above probably suggests, excursionists gradually came under increasing pressure to develop tours that focused on issues that the Bolshevik regime deemed important and that conveyed clear political and economic messages. In this they shared the fate of other Soviet cultural and educational workers. As Peter Kenez notes, although often described as a time of tolerance, moderation, and relative freedom, the NEP era represents the point of origin for many institutions and trends associated with the Soviet propaganda state. Fears that the reintroduction of limited forms of private enterprise might allow the enemies of socialism to fight back led Soviet leaders to view political education work as increasingly important.[27] Although, in the first difficult years following the end of the Civil War, the need to impose fiscal discipline, restart the economy and stabilize key social structures took precedence, as soon as these objectives seemed at least partly achieved, efforts to promote pro-Soviet attitudes and the basic elements of a socialist world view intensified. In the mid-1920s state and party officials grew increasingly assertive in their use of both financial leverage and administrative prerogatives to coerce public institutions and voluntary associations into doing a better job of tailoring their efforts to the regime's priorities. Applied unevenly, these tactics, as I indicated in Chapter 3, affected some endeavors and spheres of activity far more quickly than others. In excursion work their influence is clearly discernable by 1924. Primers published in that year frequently contain discussions of class, production relations, and the labor struggle. In addition, they tend increasingly to focus on contemporary, as opposed to historical, concerns. Tours of workers' settlements, collective farms, and factory cafeterias begin to replace accounts of the extravagant lifestyles of the nobility in the eighteenth and nineteenth centuries. Writers often take pains to emphasize the enormous strides made by Soviet society since the October Revolution and speak enthusiastically about plans for the future.

Despite this shift in content, however, excursion work remained, at least for a time, a vital, creative field of endeavor. In the mid-1920s, many primers appeared that responded to the new requirements without obviously pandering. Antsiferov's piece on French painting represents a good example. In it the themes of class and revolution emerge organically out of the images under consideration. Their introduction lends necessary social context and in no way signals a relaxation of the author's usual investigative standards. The pedagogical excursionists of the mid-1920s seem, in many instances, to have taken new dictates as challenges; convinced that, if properly thought out, almost any subject or idea could give rise to an effective and provocative excursion, they worked hard to find innovative approaches to every topic they undertook to illustrate.

Throughout the mid-1920s Grevs's followers consistently rejected standardization in favor of variety and creative enterprise. Primers almost always carried notes reminding teachers to trust their own judgment and adapt the model routes wherever needed. Antsiferov's remarks in the introduction to *Petersburg in Reality and Myth* are typical in this respect:

> Not being a proponent of conducting excursions according to one plan that has been worked out in detail in advance, I, nonetheless, have tried to give my outline the character of an excursion plan. It should be understood as one of the ways to conduct an excursion on the given topic. However,

this plan is not a simple account of the excursion. There is far more material in it than ought to be used in one effort at implementation. If placed within the framework of one stroll an overload will occur. I have done this with the aim of broadly opening the topic, which should then be correspondingly narrowed and modified, depending on the group of excursion-goers or other external factors.[28]

The primer was a stepping-off place, an invitation to the reader to explore the city further on his own. While presumably the audience for such literature consisted primarily of potential excursionists, educators who would eventually begin leading tours themselves, writers openly acknowledged that the manuals could also serve as a useful tool for self-education. As Antsiferov wrote: "Alongside excursions, one should not forget solitary strolls, and I appeal to my readers, once they have familiarized themselves with the topic, to choose an appropriate hour and take a walk by themselves through the corners of Petersburg investigated here."[29]

This atmosphere of tolerance, this conviction that instructors could be trusted to develop their own approaches, that private individuals would understand what they saw on strolls with only a pamphlet for assistance, faded from the scene only gradually and as a result of a complicated confluence of factors. In addition to growing ideological pressure, new budgetary cuts at the Commissariat of Enlightenment, changes in pedagogical fashion, interagency conflicts, and personal rivalries all played a role in bringing the golden age of excursion work to a close. Because of the way in which the decline took place, identifying an exact starting point and constructing a convincing narrative account of the movement's collapse is difficult. At least in hindsight, however, the problems seem to have begun in the spring of 1924. At that time, Politprosvet decided to launch a major offensive against its "illicit" competitors in the field of adult excursion work, targeting in this case primarily the Society of Old Petersburg.

The society had played an important role in excursion work since it was first created. As was mentioned in Chapter 3, it had, in a sense, grown out of a summer seminar that was held in Pavlovsk in 1921 with the participation of many of Petrograd's leading excursionists. From the very first, the society's founders had planned to continue to work on similar projects. During the early 1920s, the organization had run a whole series of training seminars for guides in both Petrograd and the surrounding suburbs. Led by Antsiferov,

Georgy Petri, Tatiana Sapozhnikova, and a number of other important figures from the humanities division of the Excursion Institute, the programs provided participants with a comprehensive introduction to excursion work. Those who took part attended lectures and discussion sections, learned to develop new routes and monologues, and then finally tested their skills by offering tours to the public. During the summers, in particular, a great deal of emphasis was placed on acquiring practical experience: seminar participants led thousands of excursions for both adult groups and schoolchildren in the early 1920s in Pavlovsk, Peterhof, and Oranienbaum. In addition, in 1923 Antsiferov, Petri, and Sapozhnikova moved to expand the society's involvement in practical work by opening a full-scale excursion bureau in the Stroganov Palace.[30] Restricted to "research projects" at the Excursion Institute, they needed a place where they could test out new routes and also seem to have seen the new bureau as a potential source of much needed personal income.

In her capacity as head of the Excursion Subdepartment at Politprosvet, Emma Krasnukha, however, strenuously objected as soon as she heard of the plan. She renewed her efforts to enforce Politprosvet's monopoly on practical excursion work with adult groups and, for good measure, started to question the society's right to lead training seminars for guides. In an effort to resolve the dispute, negotiations were organized which, at least theoretically, involved three separate entities: the Society of Old Petersburg, Politprosvet, and the Excursion Institute. Overlapping affiliations, however, led to confusion about which person represented what organization and ultimately created a perception of impropriety. Egged on by Petr Stolpiansky, the board of the Society of Old Petersburg formally complained that its interests had not been adequately represented at the negotiations.[31] Antsiferov, Sapozhnikova, Petri, and other members of the Excursion Institute all quit the society amidst the ensuing furor. Left alone in charge of the society's excursion programs, Stolpiansky proved unable to continue most projects.[32] For all intents and purposes, the society ceased conducting excursions almost entirely until fairly late in the 1920s.

The Excursion Institute had never enjoyed a secure funding line. Six months after its official opening, the government threatened to shut it down, and the school's administration had to accept a reduced allocation, which left employees on half and quarter salaries.[33] The situation worsened with each passing year, and out of desperation the administration even turned to opening printing facilities, bookstores, and movie theaters in the hope of making a profit. In June 1924 the facility was ordered to merge with the Institute of

Scientific Pedagogy and the Pedagogical Museum and vanished as an organized entity in the ensuing battle over allocations.[34] Former employees scrambled to find jobs in other organizations. The Excursion Sections at Politprosvet and the Sector of Social Education hung on a little longer, but their influence soon also began to wane. As specialized excursion structures first weakened and then disappeared, the task of leading and supervising tours fragmented, becoming the affair of individual museums and cultural organizations. In the shift, the methodological school that had emerged under the careful tutelage of men like Grevs and Boris Raikov lost its position of dominance. New priorities, new pressures, and new cadres rapidly began to change the nature of excursion work.

One of the trends that emerges most clearly in the late 1920s and early 1930s was an increased emphasis on the excursion's recreational value. Left to their own devices, with little methodological guidance concerning the organization of tours, factories and workers' clubs felt free to organize unambitious day trips that gave participants an opportunity to see something new, relax in a pleasant setting, and bond with a social group. While such tours often included simple agitational messages, they were primarily meant to entertain: organizers hoped to draw workers away from less desirable leisure-time activities like drinking and religious observances. In many cases variety shows, amusement rides, and competitions represented part of the outing. Organizations could rely on their own cadres to put together programs or hire outside guides. Petr Stolpiansky regularly arranged trips for factories, trade unions, and clubs during this period. Programs for several of these events are preserved in his personal archive at the Russian National Library in St. Petersburg. One in particular, a wry description of a boat tour for the Union of Metalworkers, may help to illustrate the new spirit taking hold in excursion work. I include an abridged version here:

> 1. Time of the excursion—July 10; assembly at 9 a.m. Place of assembly—the pier at Birzhevoi Bridge. 2. Each participant in the excursion receives a ticket listing the number of the boat in which he will sail. 3. The passengers in each boat will elect from amongst themselves a senior person who will be responsible for the condition of the boat and maintaining order in it. . . . 4. Drinking alcoholic beverages in the boat is forbidden; anyone caught doing so will be put ashore. . . . 5. If, during the excursion, it starts to rain or the wind picks up, the excursion comes to a halt. . . . 6. . . . The participants in the excursion are responsible for following and carrying out all of the instructions of the regional admiral;

failure to fulfill these instructions will result in punishment: being put ashore and the end of the excursion. 7. After assembling and listening to the first talk "What is the Neva?" ... the excursion-goers will board their boats. 8. Following behind the motor boat of the Red admiral, the boats set sail to the tune of "Downstream along the Volga, our beloved mother" [*Vniz po matushke po Volge*]. 9. ... The boats turn in to shore by the Peter and Paul Fortress to the tune of "They victim fell" [*V zhertvoiu pali*] ... the excursion-goers do not get out of the boats. Here the second talk is given—"Peter and Paul Fortress—Bastion of Autocracy." 10. ... the Bolshaia Nevka. 11. ... Aptekarsky Island ... 12. ... the Stroganov Embankment ... 13. ... Kamenny Island ... 14. ... Musical and dramatic entertainment. Games. Swimming. Singling out and exclusion from the excursion of violators of point four ... 15. ... End of the excursion. Participants depart for their respective homes singing.[35]

It is hard to know how to read this colorful document: does it satirize or just epitomize a contemporary trend? The text shares a host of features with other excursion programs from the late 1920s and early 1930s: information about sites has been cut down to illustrate simple political points and then packaged in a recreational format. Instead of actively observing, imagining, or discovering, participants here are passive creatures who, it is hoped, will respond in accordance to the dictates of the program. Small prepared groups and caring pedagogues have disappeared, replaced by the masses and beleaguered activists.

By the late 1920s, the word "tourism" had begun to appear more frequently in reference to excursion work. In part this change in usage reflected the increased emphasis on recreation as opposed to educational aims. It also coincided, however, with the emergence of a second, almost contradictory trend: the concept of the productive use of leisure time. In the age of crash industrialization campaigns and Five Year Plans, even excursions were expected to contribute to the common cause. In March 1930 the Society of Proletarian Tourism and Excursions (*Obshchestvo proletarskogo turizma i ekskursii*, or OPTE) was created with the express aim of making tourism more responsive to socialist goals.[36] This new organization went into production sites and set up voluntary "cells," gave talks on possible travel destinations, and tried to interest workers in various options for spending leisure time productively. The tours it advertised always offered some measurable benefit: factory excursions acquainted workers with new production techniques and gave them an opportunity to share experience; military outings taught basic soldiering skills; city tours illustrated revolutionary themes or provided information about socialist construction. Often tourists were encouraged to donate labor to the sites they visited, helping crews that had fallen behind "meet the plan" or sprucing up a drab local holiday celebration. Sometimes the entire trip revolved around collecting geological samples or taking topographic photographs.[37] The most extreme examples of this kind of cultural work hardly resemble tours at all: they seem more like *subbotniki*—campaigns in which workers, at the urging of party and government officials, "voluntarily" performed extra labor, usually on a Saturday, in order to help the economy. Such outings predictably did not enjoy much success with the general population and remained little more than oddities. The concept that excursions represented productive labor, however, did have one lasting effect: it reinforced the idea that tourism should be taken seriously.

The most important trend to emerge during the late 1920s and early 1930s in excursion work predictably concerned content. All tours were now expected to contain a clear political message. Manuals for cultural workers from the period abound in helpful suggestions for how to pack a moral into an otherwise bland route. An excursion through the primitive man section of the Ethnographic Museum, if done properly, might prove that religion was a product of human invention. St. Isaac's Cathedral provided an excellent opportunity to discuss church construction, the imperial court, and graft.[38] The inclusion of such positive messages, however, now represented only one aspect of a larger issue: control over information. Cultural organizations wanted to regulate both what guides said and, even more important, what tourists perceived. By the mid-1920s writers of travel literature regularly voiced concerns that groups were not properly interpreting relics from the past. They feared that while visiting an exhibit of "historical rooms" in one of the former imperial palaces, tourists might react positively to the way of life of the last Romanovs, admiring all the pomp that had now slipped into the past. As the capital of the old tsarist state, St. Petersburg presented specific problems in this respect. Aside from all its former palaces and mansions, the city abounded in tsarist monuments. How was a visitor to interpret all the equestrian statues, the angel on the top of the Alexander Column in the middle of Palace Square, the many architecturally significant churches? Some could be taken down, but the others had to be explained. Finding new ways to understand old imperial monuments and symbols represented one of the major preoccupations of

Soviet cultural workers in the 1920s. In order to be safe for the men and women of the new age, totems had to be somehow contextualized, cleansed of dangerous associations, and invested with new Revolutionary significance. Russian history and, by extension, the landscape of the old imperial capital, had to be reimagined, made at least to some extent compatible with the new Soviet forms of identity that the Bolshevik regime was working to promote.

A children's book from 1925 entitled *In Lenin's City* (*V gorode Lenina*) illustrates this problem neatly. It describes in fictional form one Young Pioneer's trip to the northern capital. Hearing that his father will be going on a business trip, Petka begs to go along to see the "city of the proletarian revolution, red Leningrad."[39] When, upon arrival in the old capital, he exits from Moscow Station and immediately stumbles on Trubetskoi's equestrian monument to Alexander III, he is hopelessly confused: what is such a statue doing on display in Lenin's city? Petka's father saves the situation by making the following wry comment: "Do you see that monstrosity? That is Tsar Alexander, the daddy of the last Nicholas." Petka laughs and thinks to himself: "There's a daddy for you! He and the horse have the same build. If you put the daddy on all fours and sat the horse up on top, it would be all the same."[40] Then he goes up to look at the Demian Bedny citation that has been added to the tablet under the horse:

> *My son and my father were put to death in life,*
> *But I reaped the lot of posthumous infamy;*
> *I stand here as a cast iron scarecrow for a country*
> *That has forever cast off the yoke of autocracy.*[41]

As Petka proceeds through Leningrad, he repeatedly encounters similar vestiges of the past, but someone always steps in to put things in perspective: his father, a local Young Pioneer detachment that takes him under its wing, or a worker. Often the explanations reflect substantial efforts to invest a familiar monument with entirely new significance. At the Bronze Horseman, for instance, one of the Young Pioneers explains to Petka: "The horse is the revolution, and the tsar wants to hold it in check." Another boy adds: "They held on for 300 years, but still they couldn't keep holding it back. The horse broke free."[42] A monument that had long been understood as a tribute to imperial might, here receives a new Revolutionary interpretation.

In real life, of course, ideologically correct commentary was probably a little harder to come by. You couldn't bank on having a brigade of Young Pioneers or a conscious worker on hand to help every visitor. Hence the need for books like *In Lenin's City* that targeted the individual tourist. Those who could not or did not want to participate in group excursions could at least be given a publication. "Self-educational excursions" emerged as an important niche product in the 1920s and 1930s. They usually combined factual information and interpretations of sites with practical advice on transportation routes, cafeterias, and recreational options.⁴³ In general, however, activists seem to have continued to view individual tourism with some trepidation. Publications from the period often note that workers should be encouraged to take organized excursions rather than to sightsee on their own.

> Our museums have not become completely "unrecognizable." Many old museum skills and traditions, many stagnant things, many awkward ones, slavery to routine, many old exhibits and departments that remain almost untouched from pre-Revolutionary times are still preserved in them. This circumstance frequently makes interpreting the material harder for the viewer with little preparation. The methodology of the exhibit, which is foreign to us, will not allow it to be properly illuminated. Because of this, poorly prepared visitors must try to visit museums with a leader, without fail. He can use his living word to fill in any gaps or unintelligible spots in the exposition, to establish the basis for the correct interpretation of the material.⁴⁴

With vestiges of a hostile culture all around, it just seemed simpler and safer to chaperone visitors to most landmarks.

Within museums, tours generally became the responsibility of internal education departments. They hired and trained their own guides, giving them permanent positions on the staff and regular benefits. By 1936, the Commissariat of Enlightenment had issued formal regulations dividing excursion leaders into three categories, according to training and experience, and setting specific norms limiting the number of tours that a guide could be required to give in a day. Now defined as "academic staff" (*nauchnye sotrudniki*), guides received time off for methodological preparation, courses, and in-house research.⁴⁵ Depending on the size of the collection, they either worked to refine a single standard tour or developed specialized routes for specific age groups or topics. Once outlined, tested, and written out as narrative text, these excursions were submitted to approval committees. "Primers" played no role in this process; museums now bore full responsibility for tours and had no incentive to issue brochures soliciting the help of imaginative amateurs. Instead the primary form of description became the five-columned excursion plan; a neat chart for internal use listing route, place of stop, content conveyed, method of elaboration (narrative or question and answer), and time spent. The last item was generally calculated to the nearest minute, in effect proving that an exact text for each section had already been written and timed.[46] Excursion and tourist bases, although less academic in their approach to the material, used a very similar procedure for developing new routes. Enforced for sixty years, this system only began to disappear in the *glasnost* era. It continues, to some extent, to exert an influence on Russian excursion work even today. Courses for guides in Russia still generally teach students to use and write plans. Until quite recently, trainees were given blocks of text to memorize and then expected during practice tours to recite each monologue within the number of minutes allocated according to the plan. A sentence missed or added meant deducted points.[47]

All these regulations conspired to turn excursions into cheap mechanisms of control, stripping them of all external resemblance to their more imaginative predecessors. In each city, a fixed list of routes represented a standard element of the school curriculum from the beginning of the 1930s to the end of the Soviet period. The same tours were, with minor modifications, offered to domestic and, in some cases, foreign tourist groups. Like school textbooks and popular films, these excursions played an important role in the dissemination of official historical narrative and hence in strengthening Soviet conceptions of identity. Given this fact, one might reasonably have anticipated an enormous backlash against organized excursions in the early 1990s, their immediate rejection, along with work details and the Young Communists' League (*Kommunisticheskii soiuz molodezhi*, or Komsomol), as hateful relics of the old forms of social organization. Nothing of the kind, however, really took place. If Russians opt out of excursions at museums today, it is often because they cannot afford them; many continue to view guided tours as both valuable educational experiences and a pleasant recreational activity.

In some respects, in fact, excursions have flourished in the post-Soviet era. The republication of important works by Grevs and Antsiferov in the early 1990s reacquainted Russian cultural workers with the ideas and high standards once propagandized at the Petrograd Excursion Institute and encouraged many to develop innovative routes and monologues. In doing so, they inevitably had to grapple with the legacy of the Soviet era and the problem of national and regional identity. They had to decide which aspects of recent history to foreground and which to forget; rework established historical narratives; and negotiate new spatial, temporal, and conceptual boundaries. To what extent might Leningrad and St. Petersburg be said to represent separate mythic, historical, or even geographical realities? Did the artifacts of Kievan Rus constitute the heritage of one or all of the contemporary East Slavic states? How were Russianness and Sovietness related? Much like the cultural workers of the early 1920s, post-Soviet excursionists set themselves the task of exploring what for all intents and purposes represented uncharted space: they aimed to describe and conceptualize new territorial entities, to establish the relationship of these geographic units to both their most obvious precursors and their immediate neighbors.

Today leading Russian excursionists often view themselves as part of a larger community of educators and researchers, all of whose work involves the exploration of a similar range of issues. They tend, at least insofar as the tours they write and lead focus on institutions, sites, and materials located within the areas in which they live, to self-identify as *kraevedy*, to see themselves as heirs not just to the traditions of early-twentieth-century excursion agencies, bureaus, and institutes, but also of the entire sprawling and diverse network of local cultural and scholarly organizations that came to be affiliated with the Academy of Sciences' Central Bureau of *Kraevedenie* at the beginning of the 1920s. The next chapter explores this second identity. It looks at how the interest that even very early groups of excursionists often evinced in regional research (*rodinovedenie* or *kraevedenie*) gradually evolved into a deeper and more profound pattern of identification. It charts the way in which the meanings assigned to the term *kraevedenie* shifted and changed over the course of the 1920s, how this in many respects new word ultimately came to be perceived by most Russian speakers as encompassing a broad spectrum of local investigative techniques and traditions.

Based in Petersburg and/or Moscow throughout its brief and tumultuous existence, the Central Bureau was an administrative entity and did not directly engage in on-site research itself. As a result, the exploration of its history and significance will take us temporarily away from the discussion of concrete efforts to study and describe the landscape of Russia's northern capital. The next chapter will instead focus on how the regional research was organized on a national level during the 1920s. It will also include an account of the devastating purge of Russia's *kraevedenie* organizations, which began in 1929. This wave of arrests, as I noted in the introduction to this monograph, in important ways continues today to shape the self-conception and worldview of Russia's local reearchers.

6

Kraevedenie in St. Petersburg

Despite their long-standing interest in local studies, excursionists did not immediately identify themselves with the network of regional cultural organizations that banded together under the leadership of the Central Bureau of *Kraevedenie* in the early 1920s. Establishments like the Excursion Institute occasionally included the term *kraevedenie* in a research plan, noting that they would be studying the past and present of certain sections of the country, but most members had no interest in formally allying themselves with the new associations of enthusiasts known as *kraevedy*. In fact, when Ivan Grevs began making announcements to the board of the Excursion Institute about the Academy of Sciences' recently created Central Bureau of *Kraevedenie* in the spring of 1922, colleagues reacted extremely coolly, changing the subject each time he suggested greater involvement on the part of the Institute.[1] Eventually they did give Grevs some kind of mandate to sit in on meetings, allowing him to function as a semiofficial liaison between the two organizations, but the response to suggestions for joint events remained more reluctant than enthusiastic. Judging by the protocols of organizational committee meetings,

Grevs deserves sole credit for the Institute's decision to devote substantial time to the issue of *kraevedenie* at the 1923 Petrograd Excursion Conference.[2] He opened the three-day event himself with a paper entitled "*Kraevedenie* and Excursion Matters" (*Kraevedenie i ekskursionnoe delo*), which essentially argued for greater cooperation between the two movements, pointing out that their interests and their research methods often overlapped:

> *Kraevedenie* and excursion studies are brothers. *Kraevedenie* is more settled than excursion studies; excursion studies is more of a traveler than *kraevedenie*. In *kraevedenie* research is more prominent (long-term, permanent, active scientific expeditions), with an aspiration toward synthetic completeness. In excursion studies the educational aim predominates (the one-time, more rapid study of individual aspects), with the alternation of individual topics. But certain features that draw the two movements closer together can also be noted: the excursion method is used in *kraevedenie*, and the investigative approach also needs to be practiced by excursionists.[3]

While Grevs meant to emphasize the existence of common ground, his essay, as the passage above indicates, also called attention to a significant difference. By the early 1920s, excursionists had clearly defined themselves as educational activists advocating the adoption of a single pedagogical trope. All of their activities, even those that seemed furthest from the practical work of teaching, were meant in the long run to assist the efforts of individual instructors. Library research, fieldwork, and the composition of guidebooks all represented tools employed to achieve a single aim: the development of effective tours. *Kraevedenie,* on the other hand, remained fuzzily defined, uniting individuals who often seemed to share little more than an interest in learning about the regions in which they respectively lived. Self-proclaimed practitioners argued incessantly about everything from aims and spheres of activity to basic terminology. They could not even agree about how to categorize the phenomenon in which they participated: some claimed that *kraevedenie* represented a whole new science; others more modestly called it a method; and a third group emphasized its status as a popular movement.[4] Understood most broadly, the term embraced almost any interdisciplinary investigation of Russian territory. It was the desire "to know the motherland, to understand it and to serve it," generally by studying one's own native region, the *krai* in which one lived.[5] If this was what it meant, the Excursion Institute, the Society of Old Petersburg, and the Museum of the City all regularly practiced *kraevedenie*. Other definitions, however, set considerably narrower boundaries, describing the phenomenon in terms that either patently excluded or marginalized scholars of the northern capital.

Contemporary researchers used to understanding *kraevedenie* in the broadest possible sense can all too easily forget that in the early 1920s the word chiefly called to mind a concrete network of provincial organizations that had, for all intents and purposes, come into being only at the end of 1921. At that time, recovery from the turbulent Civil War period was just beginning. Devastation remained widespread, particularly in the provinces: factories had shut their doors, key transportation and communication structures had suffered damage, unemployment was high, many people subsisted on what they could scrounge by stripping parts and materials from idle institutions and concerns. Overworked local officials who often had little education and no specialized training in the arts distributed property confiscated from wealthy families, organized brigades that collected old paper and metal for recycling, and played a key role in deciding the fate of cultural institutions.

In Moscow, the Commissariat of Enlightenment recognized that in this situation, provincial museums, archives, and collections were inherently vulnerable. It wanted to do what it could to save them and also to assist local researchers and cultural workers. Short on both funding and personnel, it could not, however, reasonably dispatch an army of representatives to coordinate research and preservation work on-site. As a result, it often had to rely on voluntary associations for assistance. In many areas of Soviet Russia old historical and geographic clubs, societies of nature-lovers and preservationists, and even tsarist-era archival commissions had continued to function after the Revolution. Unpaid and often at considerable personal risk, individuals associated with such organizations spoke out against the destruction of documents and artifacts during the Civil War years. They knew the value of zemstvo records, private ethnographic collections, and the data compiled by local geographic societies. In a country short on specialists, they represented a tremendous resource, provincial manpower that could be used to accomplish all sorts of labor-intensive projects.

With this in mind in December 1921 the Academic Center of Narkompros invited representatives of a diverse array of provincial voluntary cultural and scholarly associations to Moscow for a ten-day convention, which it dubbed the First Conference of Scientific Societies for the Study of Local Regions (*krai*). Encouraged to compare notes on current problems, delegates quickly discovered that, despite all their apparent differences, the organizations they represented shared certain basic interests and needs. All local scholarly and cultural societies wanted academic ration cards, financial help for regional museums, and some means of communicating effectively with various agencies in Moscow and Petrograd. They also all recognized that they could accomplish more by coordinating their activities and programs. By the end of the conference, delegates had decided that they needed a permanent administrative entity to link them all together and also to represent their interests in the center. Perhaps at the suggestion of Narkompros officials, they voted to petition the Academy of Sciences for help in this matter, asking it to assume responsibility for directing the board they began to call "the Central Bureau of *Kraevedenie*."

This name is tremendously significant. In 1921 the word *kraevedenie* would have sounded unfamiliar to many Russian speakers. A relatively recent coinage, it, as I explained in the Introduction, had entered the language shortly after the turn of the century as one of several calques for the German term *Heimatkunde*. Less common than the rival forms *stranovedenie* and certainly *rodinovedenie*, it appeared in print only occasionally during the pre-Revolutionary period, usually in pedagogical publications. Usage patterns suggest that during these early years the terms *rodinovedenie, stranovedenie,* and *kraevedenie* for the most part functioned as undifferentiated synonyms: they all referred to a single program of educational reform with the rare appearances of the word *kraevedenie* in no way signifying a narrower geographic focus than usual. Advocates felt the schools spent too much time on abstract and classical material; they wanted them to focus more on the motherland, either by instituting a entirely new course or by encouraging the introduction of local examples throughout the curriculum.[6] Museums and preservation campaigns, excursions and expeditions figured into work, but they usually served as convenient tools for achieving larger pedagogical goals rather than as ends in and of themselves.

By choosing to embrace the relatively obscure term *kraevedenie* instead of its more familiar synonym *rodinovedenie,* delegates at the First Conference of Scientific Societies for the Study of Local Regions in 1921 at once paid homage to and separated themselves from this pre-Revolutionary legacy. Many of those who participated in the meetings were by profession teachers and clearly hoped to revive the issue of localization in the school curriculum. Others, however, saw themselves as researchers rather than educators; they wanted to collect information on Russia's national resources and climate, study regional folklore, or identify and preserve local historical monuments. Because it had so little history, the term *kraevedenie* represented a convenient umbrella for them all. It seemed at once reminiscent of *rodinovedenie* and yet also potentially suggestive of something larger. The term bound together organizations and individuals that had never before perceived themselves as a community. By the end of the First Conference, delegates had embraced a new collective identity: they had begun to see themselves not just as amateur ethnographers, historians, preservationists, and nature lovers, but also as *kraevedy*. It seems worth noting that the pre-Revolutionary *rodinovedenie* movement had never given birth to this kind of an agent noun. It was a pedagogical approach, an argument for studying the homeland that could be outlined in an impassioned editorial, but it had never been identified with a concrete network of organizations. In 1921 *kraevedenie* evolved into something that enthusiasts could join.[7]

Delegates to the First Conference had a clear sense of how they wanted the Central Bureau of *Kraevedenie* to be structured and what they wanted it to do. Anticipating that the Academy of Sciences would approve their petition, they elected twenty-nine scholars to the proposed organization before disbanding: nine from Moscow, eight from Petrograd, and twelve from the provinces. Resolutions stipulated that the bureau would engage in four lines of work: "1. carry out a survey of the *kraevedenie* movement in Russia; 2. take measures to aid the activities of provincial societies and individuals in every possible way; 3. establish a regular link between the bureau and the societies with the aim of coordinating the work of *kraevedenie* on site and inform the societies of the state of *kraevedenie* in Russia; and 4. propagandize the ideas of *kraevedenie* in Russia."[8] Hands-on research, scientific expeditions, and all other forms of active participation in local work remained quite pointedly off the list. The delegates at the Moscow Conference did not conceive of the Central Bureau as a society of *kraevedy*; rather, they saw it as an outside board brought in to organize, oversee, and assist a spontaneously developing provincial movement. This distinction between center and periphery grew even clearer when the project reached the implementation stage.

In January 1922, the Russian Academy of Sciences approved the Moscow Conference's suggestions with one significant amendment: it initially did away with all the provincial emissaries, convening only the representatives from Moscow and Petrograd. Two semiautonomous divisions took shape, each filled with academic luminaries; the Orientalist Sergei Oldenburg, the historian Sergei Platonov, the geochemist Alexander Fersman, and the father of the Russian school of anthropology Dmitrii Anuchin all took part. When these academicians, presidents, and permanent secretaries of the Academy of Sciences addressed an audience of provincial hobbyists, they could not help but articulate methodological standards and intellectual priorities that instantly eclipsed much of the work taking place on-site. At any forum they stood out, extrinsic to the movement they sought to lead. Although provincial representatives joined the bureau in October 1922, they did not succeed in drawing it any closer to its constituency. In the publications that it issued in the 1920s, particularly the magazines *Kraevedenie* and *News of the Central Bureau of Kraevedenie* (*Izvestiia TsBK*), writers constantly spoke the language of division, approaching every issue in terms of "us" and "you." "We" were the esteemed editors and writers who sent out surveys, issued instructions, and lobbied the authorities. "You" meant the local organizations that needed "our" guidance and assistance. The professional scholars of the academy might give the *kraevedy* an assignment, asking them, for instance, to locate and save the archives of regional draft boards, but they also kept in mind their helpers' limitations. As B. N. Vishnevsky wrote in a 1923 article: "the *kraeved* is an amateur scholar." He can be expected to track down documents and perhaps, with adequate instruction, copy them, but he should not try to engage in science himself. "In terms of the scientific processing of these materials," Vishnevsky bluntly explained, "that demands a certain amount of specialized knowledge and can be carried out more successfully in the center where all the materials should be sent."[9]

Although unique in terms of its tactlessness, Vishnevky's article articulates a basic idea that was quite common during the early 1920s. Most contributors to the journals issued by the Central Bureau in this period considered *kraevedenie* inherently "provincial" in respect to both its geographic range and its character. The editorial statement introducing the first issue of *News of the Central Bureau of Kraevedenie* in 1925, for instance, notes that "*kraevedy* are first and foremost, 'people in the provinces,' who stand facing directly towards the village."[10] Members volunteered their time. They came from different backgrounds, could not be assumed to possess a complete education, and operated somewhat unpredictably. As one writer explained: "All of these provincial workers are snowed in under compulsory, controlled, and sometimes forced labor, which at times is heaped up over their heads. They passionately want to work on studying the life around them by *their own choice,* as free initiative, voluntarily, on a non-compulsory basis, 'for their souls,' in the true sense of community work, as the free, organized, spontaneous action of local people."[11] Enthusiasm and close ties to the community represented their real contributions, making up for any deficiencies in scientific preparation, a style of work that did not always conform to the "professional" academic standards of the capitals. As one contributor writing in to the journal *Kraevedenie* from "a provincial perspective" put it, researchers in the center,

> long since torn away from their native place, used to operating solely with bare facts and abstract schemes, are either entirely indifferent to *kraevedenie,* or understand it as a kind of geographic discipline, as a mere part of their general scheme, a source of statistical material registering facts. The provincial workers who carry out the work on site are an entirely different matter altogether: for them the business of *kraevedenie* is something much larger, they are somehow indissolubly merged with it, gaining from it joy, significance and justification for their personal lives.[12]

In short, a split ran through the entire movement, dividing *kraevedy* into two camps: active provinces and administrative heart. The former engaged in on-site research; the latter, despite all its impressive credentials, played an ancillary part within the context of the movement as a whole.

Given this initial division of labor, organized *kraevedenie* really had very little to offer anyone interested in actively investigating Petrograd in the early 1920s. Helping out at the Central Bureau of *Kraevedenie,* while no doubt noble, advanced provincial efforts rather than work in the northern capital, and the other obvious option for participation—establishing an active affiliate patterned after other groups of *kraevedy*—must have seemed patently absurd. University-educated intellectuals, published art historians, and professors living in what had until recently been the capital did not see themselves as either "amateur" or "provincial." Why would they identify themselves as *kraevedy,* choosing willingly to accept a label born in areas with less elevated scholarly traditions? Moreover, indigenous institutions for the study and preservation of the city of St. Petersburg already existed when the First Conference of Scientific Societies for the Study of Local Regions (*krai*) took place; the Museum of the City, the Society of Old Petersburg, and the Excursion Institute had effectively absorbed most of the energy and enthusiasm that in other places fed *kraevedenie*. Each of these three institutions had its own methodology, organizational procedures, and priorities. Inertia and territoriality alone would have made it unlikely for any of them to merge with a large and nebulously defined association.

Only a few small groups of active, self-identified *kraevedy* sprang up in the Petrograd area before 1925. Most, interestingly enough, did not focus attention on the metropolitan center and the primary imperial summer residences; they worked in places largely ignored by established research institutions, semi-rural environments that were arguably more than a little "provincial" in character. One group, for instance, investigated the area to the north of the capital. Started as a study circle at the old Lesnoe Commercial Academy in 1916, it joined the Society of Old Petersburg in 1923 as a semiautonomous affiliate, becoming its Division of the Northern Environs (*Otdelenie Obshchestva Starogo Peterburga v severnykh okrestnostiakh*). The only permanent section of the organization to focus on a geographic area outside the city center, it alone regularly described its work in terms of *kraevedenie*.[13] Most other early groups of self-proclaimed *kraevedy* in the northern capital emerged out of the University or other institutions of higher learning. While they did conduct some studies of the Petrograd region, they also set themselves a broader educational goal: they wanted to attract young people arriving from other areas, students who aimed "to use the period of their stay in Petrograd to prepare themselves for practical work in the provinces."[14] Hence organizers stressed basic techniques that could be adapted to any region and encouraged members to maintain ties with their provincial homes. *Kraevedenie* as such, rather than St. Petersburg, dominated the agenda.

The first broad-based organization specifically created to conduct *kraevedenie* in the old capital was The Leningrad Society for the Study of the Local Region (*Leningradskoe obshchestvo izucheniia mestnogo kraia*, or LOIMK). It appeared in May 1925. At the time, the Central Bureau's network of affiliates was growing rapidly and its rhetoric becoming progressively expansive. Many bureau members had begun to perceive *kraevedenie*'s exclusively provincial orientation as a liability that might ultimately hamper efforts to gain further recognition and resources. They viewed the creation of strong local clubs in Moscow and Leningrad as essential to the movement's continued development. Early in 1925, in deference to this opinion, the Central Bureau empowered a special commission to promote *kraevedenie* in the capitals.[15]

LOIMK, the primary result of the bureau's efforts in the North, at least initially attracted a number of prominent members.[16] The excursion movement was gradually collapsing and the Society of Old Petersburg teetered on the edge of bankruptcy at the time, leaving scores of veteran researchers looking for new homes. Many opted to affiliate themselves with the *kraevedenie* movement, by either accepting posts with the Central Bureau itself or joining LOIMK. Hence, the original membership lists for the new city organization included luminaries like I. I. Poliansky, the former editor of *Excursion Matters;* G. G. Shenberg, the author of the standard text on geographic excursions; and Ivan Grevs.[17] In an initial burst of energy, the group raced to open up divisions in surrounding towns like Trotsk, Peterhof, and Luga. It also created a commission for the preservation of natural and cultural landmarks, which reached out to coordinate its activities with the Museum of the City, and launched all sorts of research and mapmaking projects. Most efforts, though, focused on the sciences and technology. In response to growing demands that *kraevedy* contribute more substantially to national reconstruction, groups concentrated on work with immediate practical applications; historical approaches now had to be justified.[18] The great age of independent initiative in the arts and social sciences had already passed. Museum and educational work, efforts to preserve the nation's cultural heritage, were gradually becoming the exclusive prerogative of governmental agencies; they consumed or rebuffed at will the tentative overtures of "voluntary" organizations, progressively limiting their freedom of action. Hence, perhaps it is not surprising that LOIMK contributed little to the development of new literature about the northern capital. The few publications that tried to analyze Leningrad from the *kraevedenie* movement's perspective, like the 1928 volume *Leningrad: An Anthology of Kraevedenie* (*Leningrad: Kraevednyi sbornik*), discussed almost nothing except construction projects, city planning, and industry.[19]

If active *kraevedenie* contributed so little to the study of northern capital, if LOIMK and the other local organizations really do pale in comparison to the Society of Old Petersburg or the Excursion Institute, what explains the stellar reputation of the St. Petersburg school of *kraevedenie* among contemporary specialists? When did the broadest possible definition of *kraevedenie* take hold, pushing aside narrower patterns of usage until every scholar of the city became a *kraeved*? Why is it that Russian scholars now associate almost all the books and institutions discussed in this study with the term *kraevedenie*? In part the answer lies again in the policies and rhetoric of the TSBK and its affiliates during the 1920s and 1930s. As I have already noted, many activists associated with these organizations believed that *kraevedenie* represented something more than just a contemporary voluntary movement. They saw it as a distinct discipline, which had emerged organically out of efforts to explore problems left unaddressed by other sciences and, for all its seeming novelty, had deep roots on Russian soil. In a series of articles that appeared in the journals of the TSBK in the mid-1920s, proponents of this view identified as part of *kraevedenie*'s history not only obvious precursors like pre-Revolutionary *rodinovedenie* but also a host of more distant phenomena, including the literary-ethnographic expedition authorized by Grand Prince Konstantin Nikolaevich in 1856 and Lomonosov's first attempt to send out survey questionnaires.[20] Neither the term *kraevedenie* nor the Central Bureau and its affiliates had existed when these studies took place, so clearly their inclusion in historical accounts of the rise of local studies signified that something other than self-identification was believed to mark *kraevedenie*'s outer boundaries. Writers noted that all of the expeditions, quests, and studies that they identified as examples of *kraevedenie* stemmed from a common impulse: a yearning for a clear sense of regional or national identity, which unquestionably represented a dominant theme in Russian cultural history. All represented or had yielded efforts to describe specific segments of the Empire, to show both the peculiarities that distinguished particular cities, regions, and population groups and the commonalities that all of Russia and all Russians shared.

Obviously this line of reasoning had some practical ramifications. First, disciplinary status necessarily implied a need for increased funding. More than movements, disciplines require a developed infrastructure: professorships, departments, research and teaching institutes. Second, by defining *kraevedenie* in the broadest possible terms, activists made it easy for the Central Bureau's network of affiliates to grow—both on paper and in reality. If *kraevedenie* meant nothing more than the study of some part of Soviet territory, then any number of regional societies were engaging in it. In 1923, the Central Bureau counted 230 local organizations specifically dedicated to *kraevedenie;* three years later the total had grown to 1,405.[21] As the Central Bureau itself sometimes seemed almost tacitly to acknowledge, the latter figure doubtless included some groups with which it had little contact.[22] Much of the growth, however, does appear on balance legitimate: during these years hundreds of new regional societies appeared with the words *krai* or *kraevedenie* in their names; some pre-Revolutionary associations accepted the bureau's protection. By the late 1920s, scholars generally estimate that the *kraevedenie* movement included 2,000 separate groups and had a total membership of around 50,000.[23]

The existence of a huge semi-independent association with outposts throughout Russian territory might well have inspired ambivalent feelings in the young Soviet government.[24] In many respects the situation was all too reminiscent of the Proletkult debacle of 1920. Narkompros had once again gotten itself into a complicated relationship with an army of volunteers that did not always seem willing to take direction from government authorities.[25] As an affiliate first of the Academy of Sciences and then, after 1924, of Glavnauka, the Central Bureau of *Kraevedenie* represented a Narkompros operation. It received funding through the Commissariat and at least theoretically existed within its chain of command. For most of the 1920s, the regional societies of *kraevedy*, however, remained formally independent, outside the control of any particular government department. The Central Bureau could advise them, but it was not set up to command. It was a coordinating board that used periodicals, circulars, and conferences to link together geographically dispersed organizations. Drawn out of their relative isolation, transformed into a real community, local *kraevedy* became more effective cultural workers, but they also might have started to resemble an independent power base. As the number of societies multiplied and spread, as the movement's rhetoric became more expansive, it is scarcely surprising that the *kraevedy* started to attract the attention of the party and state officials.

It would be a mistake to echo the invective of the purges and paint the *kraevedy* of the 1920s as oppositionists, regularly interested in politics. It is worth noting, however, that they sometimes showed a disconcerting propensity for both independent thought and coordinated action. In a period of growing centralization, the *kraevedy* often spoke out in favor of diversity and modest regional independence. Many wanted to believe that the Revolution had freed the provinces from thralldom to the hungry capitals, so that they could finally develop cultures of their own. Nikolai Antsiferov, who went to work for the Central Bureau after the Excursion Institute closed, expressed this view succinctly in a 1927 article:

> The Revolution, crushing the centralist empire, created the Union of Republics, in which a clear pull towards the decentralization of culture is visible. The rebirth of national cultures, even the most primitive, is an interesting feature of our epoch. And the Russian provinces could not, of course, remain untouched by this general movement, and, here too, interest has risen in our provincial cultures. The great territory of the former Russian Empire has come to life in all its constituent parts. It is possible to believe that the new culture, in the conditions of existence created by the revolution of the Union, will take shape in accordance with the federalist model. A whole will be born that can develop alongside the harmonious development of its parts. In the process outlined a great role should be played by the *kraevedenie* movement.[26]

In principle, Antsiferov is not saying anything all that shocking or original here: the rhetoric of regional and ethnic independence surfaced regularly throughout the Soviet period. In the 1920s, Russian *kraevedy*, however, often seemed poised to make the leap from words to action, resisting when Moscow moved to claim a new prerogative. In 1925, for instance, when provincial organizations were ordered to transfer to Tsentrarkhiv all their archival materials including, in some cases, files necessary for day-to-day work, the *kraevedenie* journals protested vociferously, and many enthusiasts were arrested for noncompliance.[27] Even more significantly, *kraevedenie*'s Central Bureau proved a surprisingly stubborn bulwark of resistance to centralism. Until relatively late in the 1920s, despite mounting pressure from state, party, and planning authorities, many members stubbornly continued to defend the right of local *kraevedy* to choose projects on the basis of their personal research interests rather than the needs of the state. As a result, the bureau gradually found itself engulfed in a conflict that, at least to some extent, played out according to a familiar cultural pattern: as a jousting match between Russia's rival capitals.

When first created as an affiliate of the Academy of Sciences in January 1922, the Central Bureau of *Kraevedenie* was divided into two branches, Moscow and Petrograd, each of which theoretically wielded equal power. All important issues were discussed at each section's separate meetings, and then, in the case of a major disagreement, a joint session was called.[28] In December 1924, however, delegates at the Second All-Union Conference on *Kraevedenie* made a series of important organizational changes. They broke ties with the Academy of Sciences, placing themselves instead directly under the jurisdiction of Glavnauka, apparently in the hope that administrative independence would bring greater prestige, closer ties with other organizations, and a secure line of funding.[29] They also elected a new slate of members to the bureau from the capitals, ten from Moscow and fourteen from Leningrad.[30] Representatives from the provinces were supposed to be designated at later regional gatherings.[31] In the meantime, however, the group from the capitals started to work, deciding almost immediately after the conference to end the tedious system of dual power in effect up to that point by eliminating the Moscow branch as a separate entity. They had all the bureau's property shipped to Leningrad where they proclaimed the existence of a new "unified" office. Day-to-day operations and most meetings from this moment on would take place in the North. Occasionally a special forum would be called in Moscow, but generally, if the city's delegates wanted to participate in the bureau's affairs, they would have to travel to Leningrad.

Consolidating operations in a single city, no doubt, offered real benefits: it streamlined many procedures and presumably cut costs.[32] The decision to choose Leningrad, as opposed to Moscow, as the site for the new unified office is, however, striking in the context of the times. In part, it probably reflected the geographic biases of the TSBK's membership. In 1924 Leningraders outnumbered Muscovites on the bureau; many members had strong ties with academic institutions that remained in the North, including the Academy of Sciences. Another factor may also, however, have come into play. By this time, as I have already mentioned, both members of the Central Bureau and local *kraevedy* faced mounting pressure from state, party, and planning authorities. Officials wanted volunteers to do more to aid in the reconstruction of the national economy, to spend a greater percentage of their time searching for deposits of natural resources, pitching in at emergency drives, and helping to rationalize production. Some bureau members may have naively hoped that in the old capital they would attract less attention and might be able to act with greater independence.

If anxiety about official interference did not provoke the decision to shift day-to-day operations to Leningrad, concerns must have grown considerably shortly after the move. By January 1926, when the bureau returned to Moscow to hold the Sixth Session, its first major out-of-town event after the Second Conference, external pressure was starting to produce fissures within the organization. The bureau's Moscow delegates, no doubt partly at the instigation of outside forces, began to function as a distinct power block and to pit themselves against "the academics" from the North. While it would be a mistake to oversimplify a complex moment of transition in the movement's history and to paint the issue in black and white terms, in general, the Moscow faction took what might be termed a pro-government stance. In discussions at the Sixth Session, Muscovite delegates repeatedly called for closer ties with party, government, and planning structures. They also questioned the bureau's decision to relocate to the North, noting that the move had made collaborative efforts extremely difficult and had deprived provincial *kraevedy* who visited the capital of a necessary base of support.[33] The Leningraders argued that the *kraevedenie* movement must retain its independence and that individual enthusiasts should not be pressed to choose research projects based on perceptions of immediate utility.

The most significant altercation between the two groups was prompted by Albert Pinkevich, a delegate from Moscow. On the first day of the Sixth Session, he gave a paper on the meaning of the word *kraevedenie* in which he declared:

> *Kraevedenie* is not some kind of new discipline, but is a method for the synthetic scientific study of a certain defined, comparatively small territory that is distinguished by an administrative-political,

national, or economic feature; a study that is subordinated to the life or death, cultural or economic needs of the territory and that has as its starting point the production forces of the region (*krai*). This study is conducted by collectives or separate individuals according to the directives of some organization.[34]

Two aspects of this definition proved instantly inflammatory: the assertion that research should invariably target practical problems, particularly those connected to the economic infrastructure, and the claim that *kraevedy* ought to follow the directives of unnamed outside organizations. According to printed summaries of the discussion that followed Pinkevich's paper, a whole list of delegates from Leningrad immediately protested. N. N. Pavlov-Silvansky, for instance, noted that "it is not necessary to allow explicit aims to narrow the tasks of *kraevedenie,* which is what the person giving the report is doing. Even without an explicit aim, *kraevedenie* remains *kraevedenie*. Science itself does not require an explicit aim in order to be recognized as science."[35] V. B. Tomashevsky later added: "The definition of the concept should proceed from the voluntary aspect of the question. *Kraevedenie* differs from other forms of investigation in as much as the masses take part in the work of *kraevedenie*. You can't look at *kraevedenie* as an approach that is contained within certain compulsory boundaries."[36] If published summaries are accurate, the delegates from Moscow who contributed to this particular discussion all defended Pinkevich's remarks; provincial reactions to the paper were mixed.

The debate on Pinkevich's paper was impassioned on all sides, but it apparently remained within the bounds of polite discourse. At the Sixth Session delegates still could find enough common ground to move beyond their differences occasionally and, on the last day of meetings, held a relatively open discussion of current problems. Delegates from Leningrad admitted that the Central Bureau had many failings: it had not provided proper leadership in the provinces, many members remained inactive for one reason or another, and its meetings were poorly attended. Muscovites like Boris Sokolov and Mikhail Fenomenov, who apparently had not participated in the Pinkevich debate, spoke up to note the positive aspects of the Central Bureau's recent record.[37] The resolutions from the Session include the following point on the split between Moscow and Leningrad: "Taking into account the work that the TSBK (Central Bureau of Kraevedenie) can reasonably accomplish, nonetheless it is necessary to note that the organizational connection between members of the TSBK in Moscow and Leningrad has been inadequate. In the future it is necessary to find and create better conditions for joint work, more frequent visits to each other, a more equal distribution of the work as a whole between Moscow and Leningrad."[38]

Pleasantly conciliatory in tone, this statement helped bring the Sixth Session to an amicable conclusion. In the long run, however, it did not result in any significant practical change. As 1926 and 1927 passed, polarization represented a growing problem in the Central Bureau. Judging by the regular reports printed in the movement's press, the uncertain status of the Moscow Branch remained the primary bone of contention. In December 1927, the Bulletin for the Third All-Russian Conference on *Kraevedenie* included an article by Albert Pinkevich detailing the grievances of the Moscow party. Pinkevich noted that the Muscovite delegates, "doomed to inactivity" by the Second Conference, had eventually decided to reopen the Moscow Branch on their own initiative, hoping by this means to address a series of organizational "inconveniences." They wanted to provide provincial *kraevedy* who visited Moscow on business with access to the bureau, and they hoped to insure the even development of the movement in each of the nation's capitals.[39] Although "the majority of the Muscovite members on hand" had participated enthusiastically, the "general conditions" in which the branch had to operate, according to Pinkevich, remained "unfavorable." Because the spontaneously reconstituted outpost lacked any legal mandate, the central organs could not negotiate with it and forwarded all inquiries on to Leningrad automatically. The Moscow Branch had no say in the distribution of the budget and could not send representatives to other regions to make connections or participate in conferences because of a lack of financial resources. It had only one paid staff member to handle all its correspondence and record-keeping. Most important, all the "joint work" and the "visits" promised at the Sixth Session had never really materialized: the Presidium of the Central Bureau had traveled to Moscow only twice; on two other occasions one member of the Moscow group had managed to appear at a Leningrad meeting.[40]

Pinkevich's report functioned as a rallying cry, mustering the troops before a decisive battle. The Third All-Russian Conference on *Kraevedenie* opened on December 11, 1927, in the middle of the XV Party Congress. Delegates at the larger forum were in the process of passing directives for the creation of the First Five-Year Plan; all of Moscow echoed with calls for "victory on the cultural front as a necessary condition insuring the realization of the latest tasks of industrialization, rationalization, and the continued involvement of the masses in the matter of socialist construction."[41] Little surprise then that the *kraevedy* found themselves facing a complementary agenda. Kalinin, Rykov, Stalin, Lunacharsky, Krupskaia, and Pokrovsky were appointed to the Third Conference's honorary presidium. Krupskaia appeared before its delegates to read a rousing speech.[42] The Chairman of the Central Bureau, Sergei Oldenburg, suspiciously pleaded illness and opted to stay at home in Leningrad, sending in his stead a lengthy telegram containing an impassioned defense of the primacy of academic values in the face of reductionist demands for greater focus on problems of production.[43] At the same time, he apparently submitted a formal letter of resignation; Oldenburg claimed that his duties as Permanent Secretary for the Academy of Sciences left him with no time for a second post.[44]

The decision was a timely one: the tide had sharply turned against the Leningrad faction in the Central Bureau and against "academic" values. The Third Conference of 1927 effectively reversed all of the organizational changes made three years before. A new slate of members was elected to the Central Bureau. It included 42 representatives from Moscow, 26 from Leningrad, and 128 from the provinces, regions, and autonomous republics.[45] With tables turned and Muscovites in the majority, delegates quickly moved to re-empower the Moscow Branch legally, giving it a full mandate and assigning it a real role in bureau activities. From now on, Moscow would take charge of all administrative and organizational issues while Leningrad focused attention on scientific and methodological work. The Seventh Session of the TSBK, which was convened on December 15, immediately after the Third Conference closed, used this broad decree to carve up bureau activities, responsibilities, and property into two exclusive spheres of influence. Moscow assumed control of *kraevedenie* in the schools, among national minorities, and among post-secondary students. It claimed responsibility for museum work; for the preservation of monuments of art, antiquity, and nature; coordination with outside excursion organizations; and for maintaining contact with central agencies, voluntary organizations, central scientific institutions, party organizations, and the Komsomol. Leningrad was left to play a clearly secondary role: it was charged with developing methodological guidelines, directing work in the Leningrad area, and facilitating contact with Leningrad institutions. It could correspond with regional organizations, offering advice of a specifically methodological nature, and could provide consultations to visitors from the provinces, but it had to get permission from the Presidium to send emissaries out for on-site visits. The Seventh Session also divided up bureau publications, assigning Moscow the task of printing *News of the TSBK* (*Izvestiia TSBK*), all leaflets, brochures, and programs. The Leningrad Branch retained control over the bureau's more scholarly publication, *Kraevedenie*, and was allowed to issue methodological guides.⁴⁶

The shift of the balance of power from Leningrad to Moscow followed close upon the heels of another significant change affecting the status of the *kraevedenie* network as a whole. As mentioned earlier, the Central Bureau of *Kraevedenie* had always functioned as a state agency, first under the control of the Academy of Sciences and then later affiliated directly with Glavnauka. The local societies that it oversaw, however, remained fundamentally independent until August 11, 1927. On that date the Council of People's Commissars of the RSFSR passed a resolution placing all institutions and organizations on Russian territory that specialized in *kraevedenie* under the direct jurisdiction of the Commissariat of Enlightenment. Henceforth, anyone wanting to open a new society of this kind would have to work directly with the Commissariat. "In addition," the decree specifically noted, "all work related to *kraevedenie*, conducted on the territory of the RSFSR by scientific institutions affiliated with organs of the Union of Soviet Socialist Republics, is now subject to the approval of the People's Commissariat of Enlightenment of the RSFSR."⁴⁷ In its publications, the Central Bureau tried to assuage fears that this sudden change in status would deprive local groups of their independence, that they would cease to be "voluntary social organizations." A soothing article penned by Pavlov-Silvansky argued that the decree, on the contrary, signified the official recognition of the importance of *kraevedenie*. This would naturally translate into more money for regional organizations and also, in all likelihood, into more power. In the past any agency could carry out work in the field, conducting important studies without the knowledge or input of local *kraevedy*. Now that Narkompros had acquired ultimate authority over all projects classifiable as *kraevedenie*, the regional societies it had recently annexed were far more likely to have some say in the work being done in their own backyards. In fact, Pavlov-Silvansky declared: "Organizations of *kraevedy* on site, in close contact with the organs of Narkompros, ought to do their utmost to insure that this resolution of Sovnarkom, which is so favorable to them, is not ignored in the provinces and is realized with full efficacy." "On its end," Pavlov-Silvansky went on to assure his readers, the TSBK would "take all necessary measures to support those organizations and institutions of *kraevedenie* that cannot on their own gain the recognition of their right to participate in the broadest sense in the resolution of those tasks involving *kraevedenie* now facing agencies."⁴⁸

By making reference to the views and plans of the TSBK in his statement, Pavlov-Silvansky effectively implied that he spoke for the organization as a whole. He may well have been supported by most fellow bureau members, but his article should not be taken as a unanimously accepted position piece. The November 1927 issue of *News of the TSBK* carried a long editorial by Boris Raikov, the veteran Leningrad excursionist and member of the Central Bureau, opposing Pavlov-Silvansky's views. Raikov wrote:

> The *kraeved* is not a bureaucrat; he is not a Soviet employee in as much as he works voluntarily: as much as gives him personal satisfaction. Try to put him under someone's orders, to make his work involuntary, and he will abandon his work, and you won't be able to do anything about it. The form will remain, but there will be no life behind that form. As soon as the volunteer *kraevedy* begin to receive mandatory assignments—"do this and don't do that," as soon as they begin to be "planned" and "coordinated" against their will, even with the best intentions and in the best way, they will slowly begin to leave their work. . . .
>
> Profess "the state significance" of the work of *kraevedenie* as much as you like, help it as much as you can, but leave its independent *voluntary public* character alone. I think that many, many thousands of *kraevedy* would sign their names to this plea. But things are turning out in the opposite way. There is no material help whatsoever, but in terms of orders, as many as you like.[49]

The new decree accomplished everything that detractors like Raikov feared; it effectively nationalized societies of local "volunteers," ultimately leading to orders from above and compulsory participation in national economic drives. In addition, the resolution was probably meant to achieve an important short-term goal: to ensure the presence of a more docile slate of delegates at the Third Conference, provincial representatives who could be counted on to support the center.[50] Once Narkompros had brought the regional societies into the fold, once the Moscow Branch had reclaimed its legal mandate, the fate of the Leningrad group was largely sealed.

Over the next two years the Central Bureau's outpost in the northern capital was slowly forced to scale back its operations. First its school commission collapsed, stymied by the need to coordinate all efforts with a similar body that had opened up in the South. Then the bibliographic commission was forced to cede most of its current projects to Moscow; members publicly complained at the time that their rivals had decided "to approach the publication of lists of *kraevedenie* literature on the USSR on a different scale and according to another plan."⁵¹ As late as March 1928, the Leningrad Branch tried to carry on with business as usual, insisting in the press that: "Ordinary contact with the provinces has not decreased and is being maintained both through correspondence and through the visits of local workers despite the transfer of the center of the TSBK to Moscow."⁵² By February 1929 they had grown more cautious, swearing at every opportunity that all projects and contacts with provincial groups directly related to their official sphere of influence: academic issues and methodology. At weekly meetings members claimed to focus on three basic tasks:

> (a) listening to and discussing reports from the provinces concerning *methodology;* this gives us the opportunity to take into account the *methodological* needs of the *kraevedenie* movement; (b) listening to and discussing reports of members of the TSBK and scientific workers in connection with their *methodological* missions to the provinces. During discussion of both kinds of reports, the activity of *kraevedenie* organizations is evaluated, and a resolution of an *academic* and *methodological* nature is reached: whether or not some kind of *methodological* article should be placed in the periodical organs of the TSBK, the *kraevedenie* organization in question brought into contact with some academic institution, and so forth; (c) at the Saturday meetings, projects for various undertakings are also considered, like, for instance, the plan for a course in *kraevedenie,* worked out by the Institute of Belorussian Culture and sent to the TSBK for evaluation.⁵³

Even this newfound public modesty failed to satisfy; by the beginning of 1930 a full-scale purge was under way.⁵⁴

Arrests took place throughout the country between 1930 and 1931, affecting even the smallest links in the *kraevedenie* network. However, the organs had clearly singled out Leningrad for special attention. The very real division that had arisen in the Central Bureau during the second half of the 1920s provided a perfect justification for a purge. As the campaign commenced, official polemicists released an endless stream of articles to the press, each one of which charged that "the most reactionary, Black Hundred-like elements in *kraevedenie* group" resided in Leningrad, promoting "an archival-archeological and imperialist" agenda that ran counter to the aims of socialist construction.⁵⁵

Much of the leadership of the city's bureau branch was immediately thrown in prison, including D. O. Sviatsky and Ivan Grevs.⁵⁶ Nikolai Antsiferov, who had been arrested in April 1929 and sentenced to three years in the notorious Solovetsky labor camp for his participation in a weekly discussion circle led by the philosopher Alexander Meier, was brought back to Leningrad in the summer of 1930 and repeatedly questioned about his involvement with the Central Bureau of *Kraevedenie*.⁵⁷ In his memoirs he later recalled that investigators had given him sheets of paper and told him to write out "a description of the activities of the TSBK." Vowing to confine himself to the truth, Antsiferov returned to his cell and sat down at the table:

> I wrote conscientiously, just as if it was an annual report; I wrote for a long time. All the same, I thought, something will get through to Stromin. After all, we had believed so firmly in the necessity of our cause, in its patriotic significance; we had loved our cause so much! We fought with the Moscow TSBK, which wanted to reduce *kraevedenie,* with its broad tasks, to "production *kraevedenie*" alone, discarding from its program the study of the past of the *krai*. We, the Leningraders, advanced the thesis: the *krai* must be studied not just around the edges (*kraeshkom*) but holistically; only then can *kraevédenie* become *kraevedénie*.⁵⁸

The first few essays Antsiferov turned in were rejected entirely as worthless. Finally, after several months in solitary confinement, an investigator visiting from Moscow managed to shake the following lackluster confession from him: "I confess that I am guilty: wherever the TSBK sent me, I insisted on the necessity of studying the past of the *krai* and in that diverged from the propaganda of production *kraevedenie*."⁵⁹

The notion that Leningrad represented some sort of base of operations for bourgeois *kraevedy,* a geographic hub of opposition to Moscow and its policies, surfaced frequently in interrogation sessions in part because investigators hoped to tie the *kraevedy* in with another group of suspect intellectuals from the North. In 1929 a number of academicians and many employees of the Academy of Sciences had been arrested, victims of a campaign that, like the assault on "historical" *kraevedenie,* sought to subjugate a relatively independent organization. The Academy of Sciences had stubbornly decided to remain in Petrograd long after the government moved to Moscow.⁶⁰ Although it had agreed to cooperate with the authorities by providing scientific support for national economic drives, it had, as Vera Tolz has shown, repeatedly resisted official interference in internal affairs like hiring and elections during the 1920s.[61] There was no party organization whatsoever within the academy until 1927, and even in March 1928 only seven of its more than one thousand employees were listed as full party members, these primarily filling low-level, nonacademic posts.[62] As the pace of cultural revolution accelerated, the academy came under increasing pressure to rectify this situation. In private conversations with its leadership, government officials finally suggested a specific list of candidates for the rank of academician. Throughout 1928, the academy's permanent secretary Sergei Oldenburg and a number of other moderates sat in formal and informal meetings, trying to negotiate a compromise. Ultimately the state's representatives agreed to let the academy install a new slate of nonparty scholars, provided it voted in an amended list of communists as well. This hard-won agreement provoked furious debate within the walls of the academy itself, with many individual scholars still opposing any compromise at all on the issue of appointments.[63] When elections took place in January 1929, there were so many protest votes that three of the communists initially failed to pass. In a panic, the presidium of the academy immediately called a second meeting of the general assembly and pushed through a petition begging the Sovnarkom for permission to hold a second vote. Eventually new elections were held in violation of all established procedural norms, and the three nominees in question did pass, but such a belated victory could hardly appease the authorities. The Academy of Sciences had proved itself capable of real defiance; calls to close the organization entirely or at least fundamentally overhaul it predictably multiplied.

By summer a special government commission had assembled to weed out "alien and harmful elements" from among the academy's employees, particularly those working in its library and the Pushkin House. Background checks and the discovery of "suspicious" activity inevitably led to arrests; Sergei Platonov, Evgenii Tarle, and a whole slate of other prominent scholars were imprisoned in the fall. Inspired by the Shakhty case, the prosecution of the Industrial Party (*Prompartiia*), and other important trials taking place in Moscow, Leningrad investigators quickly concocted an equally elaborate scenario. The academicians, they announced, had led "a monarchist counter-revolutionary organization" called "the Popular Union of Struggle for the Rebirth of Free Russia." Hoping to establish outposts in the provinces, they had recruited colleagues at Leningrad's Central Bureau of *Kraevedenie*, gradually transforming the whole organization into "an informational and organizational center" for the counterrevolutionary conspiracy. The bureau's activities, its conferences, and its members' business trips, had offered ample opportunity for anti-Soviet agitation; all 2,000 local *kraevedenie* societies would have to be investigated as possible "affiliates" of the monarchist union.[64]

The academic purge of 1929 to 1931 lashed out at two potential sources of opposition to centralization and the hegemony of Moscow: the Leningrad intelligentsia and the movement for regional cultural autonomy. For the Academy of Sciences, the campaign meant temporary disgrace and a permanent loss of independence. For *kraevedenie* it brought almost total destruction. Waves of arrests alternated with hopelessly ill-conceived reorganization schemes. The Leningrad Bureau Branch was liquidated in the spring of 1930, leaving Moscow free to experiment in the provinces. It opted to replace the old system of loosely connected societies with an orderly hierarchy of regional bureaus and local cells, all of which would now follow central planning directives. Writers in the movement's press eagerly condemned the voluntary nature of *kraevedenie,* its "amateurishness and lack of professionalism" (*liubitel'shchina i kustarnichestvo*) as relics of the past.[65] As P. Smidovich noted: "In the Soviet state, the boundary between voluntary work and state service is disappearing more and more all the time, and *kraevedenie* organizations, right up to the TSBK, occupy a new place in the State."[66] According to one estimate, 94 to 95 percent of all *kraevedenie* work focused on the study of valuable minerals by 1934.[67] This rigidity, this single-minded focus on the objectives of the Five-Year Plan, by most accounts combined with the purges themselves to produce a significant drop in the movement's membership nationwide. The old *kraevedy* disappeared, and no one replaced them.[68] Desperate to make contact with the masses, organizers moved on to new reforms, shifting constantly from one unsuccessful program to another. By the mid-1930s the movement had slipped into relative obscurity. A brief flurry of renewed activity during World War II led to some expeditions in search of new mineral deposits and natural substitutes, but for the most part *kraevedenie* remained a sleepy field.[69] Most work revolved around provincial museums and the creation of modest programs in local studies for the schools.[70]

Kraevedenie emerged from this state of slumber only during the Khrushchev Thaw. Like many other cultural traditions that were wholly or partly suppressed during the Stalin years, it acquired new vitality as restrictions on public life began to lift following the great leader's death in 1953. Never entirely forgotten, forms of activism, creative self-expression, and academic inquiry that had flourished in the 1920s proved important latent models as Soviet Union entered a period of comparative liberalization, and civil society showed some tentative signs of reemerging. In the case of *kraevedenie*, as in that of many other forms of endeavor, historical publications played an important role in generating renewed public interest. Articles describing the regional studies movement's past began to appear in specialized journals in 1957, one year after Khrushchev delivered the famous "Secret Speech" denouncing the Stalinist cult of personality at the Twentieth Party Congress.[71] While writers could not objectively relate the events of the late 1920s and the early 1930s, they could remind readers that *kraevedenie* had once enjoyed considerable popularity and prestige. It was a heritage and a name worth reclaiming, an activity that offered enthusiasts real opportunities for self-fulfillment. Across the country, involvement in all sorts of local projects, including ecology, preservation work, and the study of regional history, soared. All such efforts in the post-Stalin years tended to be viewed as forms of *kraevedenie*. After the purges and the collapse of the cultural institutions of the 1920s, the divisions and differences that had once separated preservationists, excursionists, *kraevedy*, and other regional activists had ceased to seem at all relevant. During *kraevedenie*'s long dormancy, the broad definitions once advanced by certain factions within the TSBK had won essentially universal acceptance; the term now clearly encompassed a wide array of scholarly approaches and cultural activities.

To the authorities in the post-Stalin years, *kraevedenie* generally seemed a harmless or perhaps even positive way for Soviet citizens to spend their leisure time, a hobby that might even reflect or instill feelings of patriotism. Hence, as Lev Lure and Alexander Kobak have pointed out in recent articles, the controls placed on researchers tended to be less restrictive than in fields like Soviet history. For young scholars in the 1960s and 1970s, local studies served as a kind of escape hatch, a haven from ideological pressures where "more was allowed."[72] While others wrote about military and industrial victories, *kraevedy* contemplated vast swathes of trampled wilderness and the overgrown foundations of medieval churches, in many cases developing a fanatical commitment to preservation work and a nostalgic attachment to the pre-Revolutionary past that meshed poorly with accepted Soviet values and state priorities. Just as it had in the 1920s, *kraevedenie* in the Thaw and post-Thaw years carried a hidden threat; although often perceived as an innocuous expression of love for the motherland, it had the potential to give rise to protests against the authorities and the system of centralized planning. Why had the state decided to destroy a certain monument? How could it ruthlessly despoil the environment in a particular area? In each case, if the local *kraeved* raised his voice, he inevitably attacked the very nexus of power. The directives all radiated from the Kremlin. Grassroots criticism of any aspect of the plan implied doubt in the system's fundamental assumption: that the center always knew best.

Even in Moscow interest in *kraevedenie* resurged after Stalin's death in accordance with this general pattern. Residents who began to study local history quickly learned of monuments lost to Stalinist construction projects in the 1930s, senseless acts of "vandalism" perpetrated by various state agencies, and unique regional traditions abandoned in the drive to create a single national "Soviet" culture. Many came to view the central state government as a kind of hostile occupying force engaged in the wanton destruction of the city that they loved. Paradoxical though it may seem, even in the capital itself resentment against the center grew. To many citizens, power had come to seem so perfectly concentrated, the ruling oligarchs so alien and inscrutable, that everything outside the Kremlin walls appeared almost equally a part of the periphery.

During the 1960s and 1970s Leningrad once again emerged as a leading center of *kraevedenie*. Stripped of its status as imperial capital by the Bolsheviks; slowly strangled, in the opinion of many local inhabitants, economically and culturally from the 1920s on; and repeatedly purged—"sacrificed," according to some accounts—to save Moscow in the war, the city had plenty of grievances and former glory to remember. It remained Russia's great historical alternative, the other capital, where residents lived amid the trappings of a vanished age: palaces with peeling paint, equestrian monuments to the tsars, triumphal arches, and decaying decorative flourishes. The city's "look" and its "soul" had been used throughout the 900-day German blockade to inspire the local populace to new feats of resistance. Both over the radio and in a variety of auditoriums, museum curators had delivered lectures on local history. As one of them later remembered: "Everyone wanted to know everything about Leningrad. . . . For that reason, talks about the city, lectures on the history of Leningrad . . . attracted particular attention and were truly necessary. . . . These lectures were given at factories, in institutions, schools, and particularly frequently in military brigades and hospitals."[73]

The war left the city rubble-strewn and its elegant suburbs totally demolished. With almost half the prewar population dead in battle or of famine, the remaining locals desperately wanted to feel that life was finally returning to normal, that the damage could somehow be repaired, that victory really would bring an end to desperate privation. In an effort to meet this need and create a physical symbol of the country's triumphant recovery, the government sent an army of restoration experts out to repair or rebuild a carefully chosen list of monuments. As the walls of Peterhof and the Catherine Palace rose again in a blaze of media coverage, Leningrad acquired a new identity and purpose: it was the hero city that had endured and now emerged from the ashes as beautiful as ever. Loveliness for Leningrad developed into a kind of civic mission in the postwar years. Each replanted park, every exquisite inlaid floor, testified, depending upon one's point of view, to either the triumph of Soviet socialism or the immortality of art.

The excitement of the great reconstruction projects of the 1950s, the ties forged between the city and its populace in the crucible of war, the presence of so many physical reminders of the glory of the imperial age, all helped, in the case of Leningrad, to foster renewed interest in local studies during the post-Thaw years.[74] Crowds flocked to specialized lectures on little-known architects, prices soared on pre-Revolutionary books about the city, and working as a tour guide became surprisingly fashionable.[75] A new generation of self-proclaimed *kraevedy* headed out into the streets to catalog iron grates, bridges, and lampposts; they dug through private and public archives in search of information on places, historical figures, and events. Enchanted by a past that they saw in idealized terms, appalled by the city's obvious decline, the young *kraevedy* of the 1960s and 1970s quite naturally began to see themselves as part of something that stood in opposition to official culture.[76] By the time *perestroika* started in the mid-1980s, these would-be preservationists had begun to band together into formal societies and organize mass demonstrations. Most notably in early 1987, a group known as Rescue (*Spasenie*) orchestrated a huge protest against the demolition of the Hotel Angleterre. Hundreds of citizens of all ages and professions occupied St. Isaac's Square and refused to leave, despite the presence of large numbers of militia. Although the authorities finally did manage to cordon off enough of the area to tear down the building, the demonstration provided an important impetus for future efforts: protesters had seen the government flinch. No one had been arrested for their actions, and a few sympathetic articles had even appeared in the press. The legalization of the preservation movement, the creation of a climate where the city's history and fate could be openly discussed, followed shortly afterward.

Leningrad's post-Thaw *kraevedy* were inspired partly by example. Sifting through card-indexes, old journal issues, and guidebooks at the Public Library, they had discovered the legacy left by their early-twentieth-century predecessors, scholars of the city associated with the Society for the Preservation of Old Petersburg, the Museum of the City, the Excursion Institute, and, to a lesser extent, with the Central Bureau of *Kraevedenie* itself. Alexander Benois, Petr Stolpiansky, Vladimir Kurbatov, and Nikolai Antsiferov each had written thousands of pages on the city and played an important role in preservation or educational work. To the young *kraevedy* of the sixties and seventies, they were heroes, individuals who had fought to save the city's landscape and capture its history despite tremendous difficulties and occasional opposition from above. Assessments of the relative importance of each figure varied. One name in particular, however, stood out, becoming somehow representative of everything that scholars of St. Petersburg had accomplished and had suffered in the decades after the Revolution: Nikolai Antsiferov.

A number of factors no doubt contributed to Antsiferov's posthumous installation as the city's quintessential *kraeved*. In his years at the Excursion Section of the Museum Department and at the Excursion Institute, Antsiferov had produced a corpus of undeniably significant and innovative work. He had developed a distinctive style and established himself as the foremost authority on an identifiable topic: literary St. Petersburg. The writer's value as a model for the younger generation, however, stemmed not just from his professional accomplishments, but from his character and his biography as well. Antsiferov emerged from the 1920s and the 1930s morally uncompromised: he had not participated in political attacks, curried favor, or chased awards. Moreover, multiple arrests had left him a strong patina of martyrdom. The only first-rank figure in St. Petersburg scholarship to associate himself closely with the *kraevedenie* movement per se in the 1920s, Antsiferov had endured a fate that in some way exemplified the suffering of an entire generation. Solovki, the White Sea Canal, the Butyrskaia prison in 1937—Antsiferov had been in every single place.[77] If, in the post-Thaw years, young investigators of Leningrad wanted to lay claim to the word *kraevedenie,* grasping at specific as well as broad definitions from the past; if they wished to pay at least a measure of homage to the old Central Bureau and its affiliates, to a spirit of independent thought and social activism that had been swept away in an early purge, then Antsiferov represented the ideal standard bearer. *Kraevedenie*'s great survivor, he had somehow managed to return to public life after all the purges. Released from the camps for the last time in 1939, he had gone home to his second wife in Moscow.[78] For the next seventeen years, he worked at the State Literary Museum, serving as the head of the Department of Nineteenth-Century Literature from 1944 to 1949. He was accepted into the Union of Writers; he defended a dissertation at the Institute of World Literature; and he began publishing again. In his spare time, he worked on his memoirs. Although excerpts from this account of his life only began to appear in print in 1981, certain sections, particularly those on the academic purge of 1930, Solovki, and the White Sea Canal, circulated widely in manuscript after the writer's death in 1958.[79] Since the collapse of the old censorship system, they have become one of the most frequently cited sources on this aspect of Soviet history, a rare firsthand account of the campaign against the *kraevedy* of the 1920s.

In light of Antsiferov's reputation as a *kraeved*, it seems worth examining the years he spent working for the Central Bureau. Did his move to a new base of operations after the Excursion Institute closed in 1924 lead to substantive changes in his approach to the study of the city? For the most part the answer seems to be no. Almost all of the books and articles on methodology that Antsiferov published in the second half of the 1920s represented refinements of the basic principles of *urbanizm/gradovedenie*, first laid out in Grevs's classic "The Monumental City and Historical Excursions." In the most famous of these, *Ways of Studying the City as a Social Organism* (*Puti izucheniia goroda kak sotsial'nogo organizma*), Antsiferov reiterated the idea that each urban center represented a kind of collective living being that could be analyzed in terms of its basic anatomy (its nucleus, arteries, squares, and sites), its physiology (functions like transportation, trade, industry, and medicine), and its psychology or soul.[80] Although remarkable for the clarity and thoroughness of its explanations, the book offered little in the way of new ideas. Another project from the same period, the three-volume set *A Book about the City* (*Kniga o gorode*), represented a vast compilation of famous literary quotations on the cities of the world. Intended, in part, as a teaching aid for middle-school social studies instructors, the series was put together by Antsiferov and his first wife, Tatiana.[81] Aside from these large-scale publications, Antsiferov continued to work as a journalist, contributing regular book reviews and topical articles to the *kraevedenie* press. He held a post at the Excursion and Information Bureau of the TSBK, represented the Central Bureau at provincial conferences, and collected statistical data on the movement's growth and activities.[82]

One aspect of Antsiferov's work during the late 1920s does merit substantial independent treatment: the role he played in the emergence of literary *kraevedenie*. The subject of the next chapter, this form of local research is important in the context of this book for two reasons. First, the story of its development neatly mirrors that of *kraevedenie* as a whole. Identified as a distinct investigative subfield and aggressively promoted by Central Bureau staff members in the mid-1920s, literary *kraevedenie* from the very first represented an amalgam of preexisting methods and traditions. Its early history offers a concrete example of the way in which the gradual expansion of the definition of the term *kraevedenie* brought together diverse and often seemingly incongruous programs, groups, and methods, allowing them at last to be perceived as part of a single scholarly trend. Second, a number of works standardly classified as great classics of literary kraevedenie, including, most obviously, Nikolai Antsiferov's *The Soul of Petersburg,* occupy a particularly important place in Russian culture today. Richly textured, beautifully crafted, and ambitious, they offer an excellent illustration of the heights to which *kraevedenie* aspires and, by the very fact of their existence, help to explain how this disciplinary tradition, despite its historical associations with volunteerism and amateurishness has on various occasions in the last half century intersected with and influenced better established academic fields.

7

Literary
Kraevedenie

When Nikolai Antsiferov joined the staff of the TSBK in the middle of the 1920s, literary *kraevedenie* basically did not exist. Despite all their public statements on the need to study Russian territory "holistically" and "from every possible angle," for the most part, *kraevedy* had never tried to expand their investigations to include literary materials and issues.[1] Certainly, there were isolated reports of societies out in the provinces that had helped to save a famous writer's estate from destruction, purchased important literary manuscripts for a local archive, or even set up a small museum display in honor of a given author.[2] These efforts, however, had been largely spontaneous: the response of individual local groups to singular opportunities and pressing circumstances. They had not been coordinated or even anticipated by the center, and they did not reflect the existence of a broad-based campaign to preserve monuments relating to the history of Russian literature or to conduct literary research on a local level. Until the mid-1920s, the Soviet *kraevedenie* movement, as a whole, showed little interest in these issues. Reports from the First Conference of Scientific Societies for the Study of Local Regions do not mention literature at all; during the first three years of its existence, from 1923 to 1925, the journal *Kraevedenie* did not publish a single substantial article on the subject of literary programs or research. In fact, surviving documents suggest that the first significant public statement on literature and *kraevedenie*, the first appeal for the movement to launch a nationwide campaign of literary research, was made in December 1924. Nikolai Piksanov, a professor from Moscow State University who apparently had never played a major role in the organized regional studies movement before, gave a paper at the Second All-Union Conference on *Kraevedenie* in Moscow entitled "Cultural Nests in the Provinces."³

Judging by the abstract included in the conference journal and by later published versions of the paper, Piksanov essentially called for intensive study of the literary heritage of the country's diverse regions.⁴ All too frequently, he claimed, "When people speak about Russian literature, they mean Great Russian; and by Great Russian they chiefly mean [the literature of] the capitals."⁵ This oddly circumscribed perception of literary geography, according to Piksanov, represented an unfortunate survival of Russia's despotic past. For centuries the country had suffered through "a process of centralization that subjugated smaller nationalities, independent regions (*oblasti*), and local economic life to the stern authority first of Moscow and then later of St. Petersburg, subjugating them, as much as possible, to one political and police uniform and mercilessly wiping away all local particulars." Now, however, that "the great Russian revolution . . . had broken up the previous despotism into its constituent parts," Piksanov called for a concerted campaign to redress centralist biases in the study of literature.⁶ For almost a hundred years, critics had spoken of a distinction between the literature of St. Petersburg and Moscow. It was time, Piksanov believed, to acknowledge that other cities and geographic regions had also produced unique literary traditions.

According to Piksanov, places like Kholmogory, Kazan, and Nizhni-Novgorod had contributed something palpable to Russian cultural life. They had nurtured young talent, providing a start to writers who, in many cases, later went on to establish successful careers in St. Petersburg or Moscow.⁷ When men like Mikhail Lomonosov, Sergei Aksakov, and Gorky arrived in the capitals, they brought with them at least some of the spirit and energy of their native regions. Regardless of how much they might later try "to free themselves from their provincialism," traces of this background remained. As Piksanov put it, "their origin inevitably affected their cultural output."⁸ With care, scholars could learn to read the clues and distinguish between the artistic efforts of true provincials, lifelong residents of the capitals, and assimilated arrivals; they could develop a method of studying the geographic extraction of texts. Considering current critical trends, this kind of investigation seemed particularly promising. Piksanov noted: "The sociological analysis of a work demands familiarity with its author and his socio-economic milieu. That inevitably leads the investigator away from the capital, to which the author has brought his creative work, and returns him [the investigator] to that region [*krai*] that raised him [the author]."[9] A writer's place of origin, in fact, generally served as a good indicator of class background. According to Piksanov, three distinct groups could be distinguished in nineteenth-century Russian literary society: writers raised on landed estates, authors from the capitals, and provincials. Those in the first category were generally nobles; the second represented the interests of the bourgeoisie; and the third, the provincials, expressed the cultural aspirations of Russia's *raznochintsy*.[10] In the contemporary literary scene, a slightly different pattern could be detected: in the provinces, the peasant's son had stepped forward to replace "the *raznochinets* -priest's son, the bureaucrat, and the petty-bourgeois in the conquest of culture"; in the capitals the burden of writing had started to shift to the factory worker; the old noble estate-writers had completely disappeared.[11] In other words, the great socialist revolution had transferred initiative in cultural affairs to new segments of the population. It had not, however, caused the fundamental differences between Russia's provinces and its central cities to disappear: geographic extraction still deserved to be considered as a factor in the analysis of texts.

Scholars, according to Piksanov, needed to regionalize Russian culture if they were ever really going to understand it. In each provincial area there were writers, institutions, and whole literary movements that had gone virtually unrecorded. Local *kraevedy*, Piksanov suggested, could play an important role in collecting information on such phenomena. While, in principle, almost any aspect of regional culture might prove of interest to these volunteers, certain patterns, when they appeared, deserved immediate attention. If a researcher noticed that a group of local cultural figures had been drawn together at a given point in history by an institution or a personal affinity, when he learned of a literary circle or theatrical club that had remained continuously in existence for several decades, he should suspect the presence of a "regional cultural nest." Piksanov went to great pains to explain that by this term he meant something other than "the mechanical aggregate of all cultural phenomena and agents" in a given area. The phrase signified a group that was in some sense united by common interests, where members worked in concert and shared certain goals. A researcher could identify "a regional cultural nest" by three principal traits:

it would have a distinct circle of participants, it would be continuously active, and it would train succeeding generations of artists.[12] Because they operated as collectives, these groups could accomplish far more than any single individual; they typically exerted enormous influence on local society as a whole, setting standards of taste and promoting the arts. Regional nests nurtured young artists, providing them with the support, encouragement, and basic skills they needed to move on to successful careers in Moscow and St. Petersburg. Any real study of the interaction between Russia's provinces and its capitals in the field of literature would have to take these groups into account.

Piksanov's ideas about "regional cultural nests" did not initially elicit much of a response from the leading spokesmen of the *kraevedenie* community. Coverage of the Second Conference in the Central Bureau's journals focused on other issues and speakers. The professor's paper was not among the dozen chosen for later publication, nor was it even extensively reviewed. It is impossible to say now what exactly motivated editorial decisions at the time, but several considerations may have figured in: Piksanov's relatively straightforward, sociological approach to the study of literature must have seemed primitive to anyone familiar with contemporary critical trends like formalism; his prose was cumbersome; and he apparently had not played a significant role in the organized *kraevedenie* movement of the early 1920s.[13] He was, in effect, another outsider with an agenda, a professor from a central university who required provincial manpower to complete a program of research. As such, he faced considerable competition from other scholars, many of whom had already spent several years working for the TSBK and cultivating a relationship with its network of local volunteers. In any case, in 1925 there were plenty of things to report on that might have seemed more important than Piksanov's "provincial nests": the Central Bureau was in the process of relocating to Leningrad and opening up a second periodical, local organizations faced increasing pressure to assist with industrialization drives, and the first signs of factionalism had begun to emerge within the bureau itself.[14] In the midst of all this turmoil, who had time to promote a new undertaking in the humanities? Passed over in the excitement, Piksanov quickly seems to have abandoned whatever interest he had in the local studies movement and moved on to find other outlets for his energy. His career was on the upswing, and he probably did not have time to contemplate another foray into the world of *kraevedenie*. In 1925 he was appointed Chairman of the Literature and Linguistics Department at the Second Moscow State University and began to work as an editor at the State Publishing House (*Gosizdat*).

Piksanov's speech at the Second Conference might well have been entirely forgotten, his concept of "provincial cultural nests" at best meriting a footnote in the history of local studies, if Grevs and Antsiferov had not intervened.[15] After the Excursion Institute collapsed at the end of 1924, both men began to play much larger roles in the *kraevedenie* movement, accepting posts with the Central Bureau. At this time, work in local studies by all accounts remained overwhelmingly concentrated in the natural sciences; projects in history and the arts were far less common, with certain fields, including literature, left completely unexplored. Committed to correcting this situation as quickly as possible, Grevs and Antsiferov embraced Piksanov as a potential ally. In articles and reviews published between 1926 and 1929, the two scholars repeatedly referred to their colleague's achievements. He had, they effusively proclaimed, succeeded in drawing attention to a "vital" and "as of yet little studied current in the development of spiritual life in the provinces"; he had opened up to the *kraevedy* "the alluring and promising task of working out a history of provincial literature."[16] Perhaps, they suggested, some of Piksanov's diatribes against centralist biases in literary criticism were a bit extreme, but, in general, his approach seemed almost perfectly suited to the needs of the *kraevedenie* movement. "One can be certain," Antsiferov remarked in a 1926 book, "that N. K. Piksanov's appeal will receive a warm response from historians of literature and the *kraevedy* of our provinces."[17] In order to ensure that volunteers from every area of Russia had the opportunity to participate in the drive, Antsiferov suggested taking an inclusive approach to the concept of literary nests. Any writer whose work contained descriptions of a given region (*krai*), who had lived in the area or even simply been born in it, represented a reasonable subject for study. Although, depending upon local circumstances, volunteers might choose to concentrate their efforts on a particular problem, ideally they ought to explore a broad range of issues relating to literature; they should investigate the lives of local writers and the ties that bound them to the community, learn about the intellectual and social milieu that existed in their area at various times, and study the image of their region as reflected in works of literature.

No doubt, Antsiferov and Grevs issued this enthusiastic endorsement of Piksanov's work to a large extent because they saw his "nests" as the key to developing a new, streamlined approach to literary geography. They had been conducting studies on related issues themselves for years, but had never really tried to gauge their explanations to a mass and overwhelmingly provincial audience like the *kraevedy*. While working for the Excursion

Institute, Antsiferov had urged his students to seek out the *Genius Loci* or spirit of their native city by gazing at architectural vistas and contemplating written descriptions of local sites. Their efforts, he had argued, would gradually lead them to some kind of revelation and personal enlightenment; they would develop a keener topographic sense and learn to be creative readers. All this mystical terminology, this talk of visions, inner growth, "souls," and "spirits," had no place in Piksanov's writing. He did not fill his articles with references to Pascal and Bergson, as Antsiferov often did, or use the minor deities of classical mythology to illustrate his argument.[18] Piksanov had reduced the study of literary topography to much more concrete terms, viewing it primarily as a means of achieving a single scholarly objective. In his articles and speeches, the professor urged the *kraevedy* to collect information on local cultural life, so that historians could at last construct a geographically unbiased account of the development of Russian literature.

Piksanov's positivist point of view and the fact that he wrote in the language of popular science represented assets in the context of the *kraevedenie* movement: his message was relatively easy to understand and could be quickly communicated to an army of unevenly trained local volunteers. Even the term Piksanov bragged of having coined himself, "provincial cultural nest," evoked clear associations and required little explanation.[19] So catchy that it sounded instantly familiar, it was just the sort of slogan that might inspire local volunteers to begin researching literary topics. In the second half of the 1920s, as the *kraevedy* came under increasing attack for "academicism" and "dilettantism," they in any case needed programs like Piksanov's that promised immediate, practical results. The professor's goal-oriented approach to the study of provincial literature and his willingness to tie his project to a concrete scholarly objective must have seemed quite felicitous. Moreover, the sincerity of Piksanov's commitment to the cause of regional culture in and of itself represented a significant selling point. Unlike Antsiferov and Grevs, who inevitably included pages of examples from St. Petersburg in any discussion of literary topography, Piksanov really wanted to talk about the provinces.

For all these reasons, promoting Piksanov made sense, even if it meant putting up with the less savory aspects of the professor's scholarship and career: his occasional forays into vulgar sociological analysis, his active participation in the anti-Formalist campaign of 1927, and the letter he sent to *Izvestiia* in February 1929 attacking the Academy of Sciences for failing to approve all the communist candidates at its recent elections.[20] Throughout it all, Grevs and Antsiferov continued to issue regular endorsements of Piksanov's work. In 1926, they urged him to take up his theory of nests again and fulfill his old promise to flesh it out into a book-length publication.[21] When Piksanov finally did find time to issue such a volume in 1928, *Regional Cultural Nests* (*Oblastnye kul'turnye gnezda*), Grevs and Antsiferov responded with a whole series of flattering comments and reviews, the last of which only appeared in June 1929.[22]

Grevs and Antsiferov clearly had high hopes for Piksanov's model in the late 1920s. They believed that it might help to attract the provincial masses to the study of literary topography. However, they did not in any way see the new drive to identify "cultural nests" as a replacement for their own earlier campaign to explore the landscape of the "monumental city." The two approaches in their minds were complementary; in every statement they made on literary *kraevedenie* in the second half of the 1920s, Grevs and Antsiferov referred not only to Piksanov's recent publications, but also to their own older articles and books. They probably reasoned that, although well-suited to the needs of the *kraevedy* of the provinces, Piksanov's work was unlikely to appeal to the members of the *kraevedenie* organizations that had opened in the nation's capitals in 1925. Volunteers in Moscow and Leningrad did not tend to see themselves or the topics they explored as "provincial" and would probably have little use for a theory that de-emphasized the role of Russia's traditional cultural centers.[23] It made sense, therefore, to offer the *kraevedy* of the capitals an alternative to Piksanov's system.

Out of everything they had written in the past, Antsiferov and Grevs put forward one piece particularly regularly as a model for literary *kraevedenie*: Antsiferov's book-length study *The Soul of Petersburg*. Composed largely in 1919, before excursion work at Narkompros had really taken off, it contained few references to pedagogical theory and therefore, no doubt, seemed particularly likely to appeal to the *kraevedy*. Although the volunteers active in local regional studies associations were often by profession educators, the *kraevedenie* movement as a whole had always been oriented more toward research than to teaching. Many members who were at least potentially interested in literary issues might well have been put off by even brief discussions of pedagogical issues. Therefore it made sense to draw their attention to Antsiferov's most famous essay rather than to his excursion primers. Although written long before Antsiferov joined the local studies movement—before, in fact, the Central Bureau and its network of affiliates had really even come into being—the *Soul of Petersburg* could still serve as an exemplar for contemporary *kraevedy*, guiding them in their first attempts to conduct serious literary research.

Two approaches developed outside the context of the organized regional studies movement, in other words, were promoted as models for the study of literary *kraevedenie* in the journals issued by the TSBK during the latter half of the 1920s: the interpretive techniques employed by Antsiferov in *The Soul of Petersburg* and Piksanov's work on cultural nests. In theory, volunteers could choose which system to follow based on their own personal inclinations and geographic biases. Relatively few local *kraevedy*, however, seem to have felt inspired to exercise this option: despite all the appeals made by Grevs and Antsiferov, TSBK affiliates apparently launched only a small number of projects relating to the study of literary topography during the 1920s. References to such work are few and far between in the journals and anthologies of the period. Provincial writers produced only a handful of articles on regional cultural nests; in Leningrad, aside from Antsiferov and Grevs, almost no one involved in the *kraevedenie* movement seemed inclined to conduct much literary research.[24]

Why didn't local *kraevedy* respond more enthusiastically to the proposals made by Grevs, Antsiferov, and Piksanov and take immediate steps to conduct practical literary research? No doubt, several factors combined to prevent the campaign from achieving greater success. The local studies movement had always tended to favor projects in the natural sciences and, no doubt, even in the best of circumstances, many volunteers would have shied away from the new initiatives in the humanities. In the late twenties, when *kraevedenie* organizations faced increasing pressure to contribute to the industrialization campaign, their reluctance probably increased. Everything from the natural inclinations and disciplinary biases of core volunteers to the latest missives from Moscow conspired to make new cultural initiatives unpopular. Moreover, between 1925 and 1929, the *kraevedenie* movement was in a constant state of turmoil. The great factional dispute between the Leningrad and Moscow branches of the TSBK and reorganization schemes absorbed a great deal of energy and resources, which might otherwise have gone to new programs. Regardless of how carefully Grevs, Antsiferov, and Piksanov tried to tailor their proposals to the needs and interests of local *kraevedy*, their efforts to encourage the TSBK's affiliates to conduct extensive literary research probably would have achieved only modest results in this hostile climate. Most significant attempts to study literary topography during the late 1920s—particularly in Leningrad—took place outside the context of the organized *kraevedenie* movement.

In Russia's old imperial capital, Antsiferov's work remained popular throughout the second half of the 1920s. His excursion primers, articles, and essays like *The Soul of Petersburg* had captured the imagination of the city's cultural workers. They were widely read and frequently discussed by the city's excursionists, museum employees, scholars, and critics. Given all the praise that Antsiferov's work received in this period, it is perhaps not surprising that other writers eventually appeared on the scene who seemed inclined to attempt something similar. In the late 1920s and early 1930s, several literary studies were published in Leningrad that, in terms of subject, style, or approach, at least to some extent recall Antsiferov's work. The most important of these were *City of Muses: Tsarskoe Selo in Poetry* (*Gorod muz: Tsarskoe Selo v poezii*) by Erikh Gollerbakh, a prominent art critic who worked primarily independently, and *Pushkin's Petersburg* (*Pushkinskii Peterburg*) by Andrei Iatsevich, a leading member and frequent officer of the Society of Old Petersburg. Neither of these writers had ever played a significant role in the *kraevedenie* movement or, for that matter, shown an interest in the excursion method. They apparently did not conceive of themselves as *kraevedy*. Gollerbakh at least seems to have viewed the regional studies movement with a certain amount of disdain and, on one occasion in his written work, mockingly derided its adherents as pedants.[25]

Gollerbakh's *City of Muses* and Iatsevich's *Pushkin's Petersburg* began to be perceived as classic works of "literary *kraevedenie*" only much later in the Soviet period. As I mentioned in the last chapter, local studies, which had, following the disastrous purge of 1930–1931, passed through a long period of dormancy, underwent an enthusiastic revival in the post-Stalin years. To some extent, this resurgence took place with the encouragement of the authorities; reprising a view that had been common in both the pre- and early post-Revolutionary era, some party ideologues, social theorists, and prominent educators asserted that local studies naturally fostered the emergence of stronger patriotic sentiments in the populace.[26] They dusted off Piksanov's ideas about provincial cultural nests and, in a somewhat modified form, introduced them, along with other principles and programs long associated with the term *kraevedenie*, into the curriculum at both grammar schools and higher educational institutions. In the 1960s Piksanov's ideas enjoyed far greater success than they had in the 1920s: a number of books appeared that attempted to describe the history and influence of various provincial cultural nests; clubs and study circles formed and attracted enthusiastic participants.[27]

In Leningrad, where studying local literary history became particularly popular, young enthusiasts digging through local libraries and archives swiftly discovered the books that had been written by their early-twentieth-century predecessors: Gollerbakh, Iatsevich, and Antsiferov. Because, as I have already noted, the meaning of the term *kraevedenie* had changed by the post-Stalin era, expanding to include almost anything that had ever been written about the city, the works these men had written could all now without hesitation be termed examples of literary *kraevedenie*. It no longer mattered when they had been written or whether or not the author had considered himself a *kraeved;* all the nice distinctions that had seemed so important to cultural workers in the 1920s had disappeared. The Excursion Institute and the Society for the Study and Preservation of Old Petersburg were now widely regarded as "centers of Russian *kraevedenie.*" All of Antsiferov's books, articles, and excursions, and everything Gollerbakh and Iatsevich wrote on the city's literature by default became classic works of literary *kraevedenie.*

This chapter considers three works that are often referred to as early masterpieces of "the Petersburg school of literary *kraevedenie*": Nikolai Antsiferov's *Soul of Petersburg,* Erikh Gollerbakh's *City of Muses,* and Andrei Iatsevich's *Pushkin's Petersburg.* Not really produced or even influenced by the organized local studies movement of the 1920s, aesthetically and philosophically distant from the form of provincial literary study inspired by Piksanov's theory of "cultural nests," these texts represent a unique indigenous tradition, the product of conditions and developments particular to early-twentieth-century St. Petersburg. Taken together, they constitute an excellent example of the kind of intellectually challenging, imaginative, and intensely personal cultural study with which the phrase "literary *kraevedenie*" ultimately became associated.

Nikolai Antsiferov spent the fall of 1919, the bleakest period of the Civil War, living in a small town near Pavlovsk with his wife Tatiana. They had recently lost two young children to dysentery and had accepted jobs at an orphanage in the hope of finding some purpose that would help them to overcome their grief. As Iudenich's troops advanced on Petrograd, the school was cut off without supplies, repeatedly shelled, and overrun first by one army and then by the other. Years later, Antsiferov would recall: "I looked in the direction of my beloved city, trying to understand what the glow [in the distance] meant, what it presaged for Petrograd! After all, its fate was being decided. I started to write about the city, about its tragic fate. And I called it the city of 'tragic imperialism,' like A. Akhmatova's 'City of glory and woe.' It was at this time, that I was working on the book that I later decided to call *The Soul of Petersburg.*"[28] In this brief passage, Antsiferov sketches out an entire scene for his reader, linking the composition of his most famous work to a particular time and place, to a specific visual and emotional perspective. The author describes how, from a vantage point outside Petrograd, he gazed back and contemplated his beloved city's fate, still undetermined in some sense perhaps, but clearly "tragic." It's hard to miss the apocalyptic undertones: the presumably reddish glow surrounding the old capital, the author looking back on a doomed metropolis.

What vista is it that Antsiferov recalls in this passage from his memoirs? Did he really stop at an overlook one afternoon in the fall of 1919 and gaze out toward the city? Perhaps, but it seems just as reasonable to read this scene more figuratively, to see it primarily as a statement on narrative perspective in *The Soul of Petersburg*. In his book-length essay, Antsiferov often speaks of Petrograd as though he were separated from it by a vast divide, as if the city had somehow crumbled or passed away, disappearing from view. "If Petersburg is not the capital, then there is no Petersburg," says Antsiferov, echoing a line from Andrei Bely's pre-Revolutionary novel on the city that had, with the transfer of the seat of government to Moscow in 1918, come to seem startlingly prescient. Closing the quotation, he then adds from his own point of view: "It [the city] only appears to exist."[29]

> The hubbub of hubbubs [*sueta suetstvii*] has disappeared.
> The trams crawl slowly. . . . The familiar din of arriving carts, cabs, and automobiles has disappeared. . . . Pedestrians walk right in the road, just as they do in the ancient cities of Italy. Vacant lots are everywhere. Wooden buildings, memories of "Old Petersburg" that had survived thanks to the fact that an inn or a tea-room had taken shelter in them . . . now have been torn down so that fuel for other buildings can be harvested from their remains: in the same way, the Samoyeds kill their dogs in periods of famine, so that they can feed the worst ones to the best. Greenery makes greater conquests all the time. In the spring grass covered the squares and streets, which were no longer being defended.[30]

Metaphorically, at least, the city has been overrun by a hostile invading army; it lies in ruins; it has started to cannibalize itself.

> The city's growth has ceased. Construction has died down. In all of Petersburg only one new structure is being erected. The granite material for it has been taken from the ruined fence of the Winter Palace. At one time, in this same way, the world of Christianity, as it was coming into being, took the columns and sarcophagi of the temples of the ancient world for its basilicas. A monument to the victims of the Revolution is slowly growing from the dust of the Field of Mars. Is it fated to become

a pedestal of new life, or will it remain a gravestone over the remains of Petersburg, the city of tragic imperialism?[31]

In published versions of *The Soul of Petersburg*, this anxious question falls about three pages from the end of the book and is immediately followed by the date: September 1919. It represents a tentative stopping place, a first conclusion, pegged to a specific moment in time. "Do you remember when we asked ourselves this question?" Antsiferov for an instant seems to prompt his reader, and then the text lurches forward again. Two brief sections stand as addenda at the end of *The Soul of Petersburg*—the first dated March 12, 1922; the second left undated.[32] In them Antsiferov speaks somewhat more confidently about his city's future, as though, perhaps, peace and the New Economic Policy had given him new hope: "More years will pass, and new structures will be created on the cleared sites, and the spring of young life will spout forth. The rebirth of Petersburg will begin. Petersburg will not be barren."[33] Even in the relatively bright 1922 conclusion, however, rebirth remains a matter for the future. Contemporary St. Petersburg still lies in ruins:

> Days and years pass by. The years are ages. The *destructio* of Petersburg continues. On Troitskaia Square the old circus buildings have been torn down. Behind them there is a row of buildings; a new square has taken shape. Behind it there is a three-story stone building that is all ruined inside, and through it a whole new vista of ruins opens up. And there, further off to one side, there is an enormous mass of uncompleted construction and a destroyed seven-story building, and then next to it there are the remains of the walls and the stairs of a small house, which look like the bared teeth of a skull.
>
> That is the place set aside for the new Petersburg! The old buildings that are still reminiscent of Northern Palmyra are disappearing. On the outskirts, by the Smolensk Cemetery, a new, tall building is being erected, the only one in the city: the Crematorium.
>
> Petropol is turning into a necropolis.[34]

Once again, Antsiferov has described the condition of the city in terms that are disturbingly corporeal: St. Petersburg is a mutilated corpse, a "skull" that now awaits disposal at the shiny new crematorium. Any examination of its physical remains, its severed staircases and collapsing walls, inevitably takes on the feel of an autopsy: there is, at least for now, no new life to investigate.

FIG. 6 Anna Ostroumova-Lebedeva, view of the river Fontanka.

The notion that war and revolution had brought destruction to St. Petersburg, transforming a once vibrant urban center into a desolate ruin, was by no means unique to Antsiferov. During the cold and hungry Civil War years, many Petrograd intellectuals came to view the old imperial capital as either dead or dying. In this period Evgeny Zamiatin wrote the famous short story "The Cave" (1922), in which he described Civil War Petrograd as a desolate wasteland caught in the crush of a second ice age; the graphic artists Mstislav Dobuzhinsky and Anna Ostroumova-Lebedeva produced volumes of sketches and lithographs of abandoned city streets; and Alexander Benois commented repeatedly in articles on the city's apparent demise.[35] Attempts to eulogize or memorialize the city and its disappearing culture were widespread. As noted in Chapter 3, new volunteers took up preservation work in a desperate attempt to save what remained of old Petersburg.

It seems important to emphasize that in this context *The Soul of Petersburg* does not represent a particularly nostalgic text. In it, Antsiferov spends little time extolling the glamorous past of the old capital and does not explicitly press his readers to take up traditional preservation work. Indeed, with all the images of skulls and half-eaten carcasses, Antsiferov's descriptions of Civil War–era Petrograd might fairly be accused of discouraging such efforts. They horrify and repulse with a morbidity so profound that they, if anything, seem calculated to remind readers of the impermanence of all purely material things.

The current state of the city as physical entity, the condition of concrete buildings, streets and squares, does not represent Antsiferov's primary concern in *The Soul of Petersburg*. Although anxiety about the fate of the architectural ensembles of the capital may well have played a role in motivating him to write, Antsiferov ultimately chose to devote relatively little space to accounts of the damage in the central districts of Petrograd. The citations I have included here represent the bulk of what Antsiferov had to say about physical conditions in the capital. In most of his essay Antsiferov focuses on something else: he talks about the city's "soul."

By this term, Antsiferov means that part of the city that affects us emotionally, its unique personality, its spirit or *genius*. Just as in Christian theology the human soul represents something purer and closer to the divine than the body it inhabits, Antsiferov depicts the soul of the city as both grander and less easily subject to destruction than any assemblage of buildings and monuments. In some sense, it constitutes the sum of all aspects of a municipality's life: "the forces of nature, the everyday life of its population, its growth and the character of its architectural landscape, its participation in the common life of the country, the spiritual existence of its citizens." "Concealed" deep within the "the material shell of the city," this soul can be discovered only through careful study and contemplation.[36] Although it grows and changes over time as a result of historical processes, it is also in some sense eternal. In his book Antsiferov uses the terms "spirit of place" (*dukh mestnosti*), "god of place" (*bozhestvo mestnosti*), and genius loci (Latin for "god of locality") in free variation with "soul of the city."[37] By introducing these synonyms, he encourages readers to view the soul as a kind of immortal force or being.

Antsiferov's ideas about the soul of the city owe much to the writing of Vernon Lee (born Violet Paget, 1856–1935), an English author best known for her travel sketches. In a collection of essays about Italy that was translated into Russian in 1914, Lee observed: "To certain among us, undeniably, places, localities (I can find no reverent and tender enough expression for them in our practical, personal language) become objects of intense and intimate feeling. Quite irrespective of their inhabitants, and virtually of their written history, they can touch us like living creatures; and one can have with them friendship of the deepest and most satisfying sort." Just like human companions, places could charm and comfort, "sing" in the memory "like melodies," and bring out, "even as melodies do when we hear or remember them, whatever small twitter of music there may be in our soul."³⁸ Noting that no adequate modern term existed for the ability of localities to affect us so favorably, Lee suggested borrowing the phrase genius loci from classical mythology. She employed the Roman term for the god of place cautiously, however, utterly rejecting the old custom of erecting statues personifying a given city or area. The images of the genius loci that graced monuments in many cities both ancient and modern struck Lee as almost blasphemous. She believed that a marble sculpture of a woman with a crown of walls and towers, like the famous statues on the Place de la Concorde in Paris, could never adequately embody or even illustrate the affective power of place.³⁹

> *Genius Loci.* A divinity, certainly, great or small as the case may be, and deserving of some silent worship. But, for mercy's sake, not a personification; not a man or a woman with mural crown and attributes, and detestable definite history, like the dreadful ladies who sit around the Place de la Concorde. To think of a place or a country in human shape is, for all the practice of rhetoricians, not to think of it at all. No, no. The *Genius Loci,* like all worthy divinities, is of the substance of our heart and mind, a spiritual reality. And as for visible embodiment, why that is the place itself, or the country; and the features and speech are the lie of the land, pitch of the streets, sound of the bells or of weirs; above all perhaps, that strangely impressive combination, noted by Virgil, of "rivers washing round old walls."⁴⁰

Lee urged her readers to go out and find the genius loci of their favorite city or place for themselves. Although in principle she believed that these spirits represented diffuse ethereal beings, coterminous with the territory they inhabited and hence equally present in every landmark and patch of earth, she readily admitted that they often seemed noticeably "nearer or more potent" at particular sites. A local deity might reveal itself most clearly "in some individual monument or feature of the landscape," "at a given turn of the road; or a path cut in terraces in a hillside, with a view of great distant mountains; or, again, in a church like Classe, near Ravenna." At such a site, Lee noted, "the genius of places often lurks . . . or, more strictly, *he is it.*"⁴¹

In his treatment of the soul of the city, Antsiferov relies heavily on Lee, borrowing both ideas and terminology, but he also introduces much that is new. He diverges from Lee's model most obviously in the sections of *The Soul of Petersburg* in which he offers advice on how to find the genius loci. There, two innovations seem particularly significant. First, although Antsiferov, like Lee, advises readers against attempting to establish contact with a local deity through the intermediacy of an idol erected in its honor, he apparently understands this injunction in a very limited sense: he shares Lee's disdain for personified images of localities like the statues on the Place de la Concorde, but he does not necessarily exclude other kinds of sculptural monuments from the list of places where the genius loci might make its presence felt.[42] Unlike Lee, who generally pictured herself communing with the spirit of a given locality at an isolated spring or by the bank of a river, perhaps in a picturesque, half-ruined church, in his book Antsiferov repeatedly identifies the soul of St. Petersburg with pieces of public statuary. The sphinxes on the Neva embankment, the rostral columns on the spit of St. Basil's island, the Shih Tza (Manchurian lions) by the cabin of Peter I, and, most important, Falconet's famous equestrian monument (the Bronze Horseman) serve in Antsiferov's text as emblems of St. Petersburg's nature and destiny.[43] Relics of or visual references to the great empires of the past, these statues remind us that St. Petersburg represents the physical manifestation of Russia's political aspirations, of its desire for "dominion over the sea," conquest and enrichment at the expense of its neighbors; that it is "a city of great struggle," brought into existence through a Herculean act of will. They also, however, suggest something darker: all of the references to past empires incorporated into the decoration of St. Petersburg, the Egyptian, Roman, and Chinese relics and motifs, can be read not only as testimony to the city's grandeur, but also as omens of potential ruin. As Antsiferov notes at the end of the brief section he devotes to Falconet's statue, there has always been a sense that "a great catastrophe hovers over it [St. Petersburg] like the spirit of implacable fate."[44]

Second, and more significantly, Antsiferov differs from Lee's model in his treatment of literary texts. Although Lee occasionally incorporated citations into her essays on Italy, using descriptions taken from works by Virgil and Dante to reinforce firsthand impressions of a given area, she did not spend much time analyzing the quotations themselves; physical exploration always remained her central concern. In *The Soul of Petersburg* Antsiferov, on the other hand, explicitly argues that the study of literature represents an essential part of the search for the genius loci. Noting that "for a real understanding of the soul of the city, personal impressions," in and of themselves, "are not enough," Antsiferov suggests that those interested in learning about the soul of the capital also "make use of the experience of others, of those who lived before us and knew Petersburg in the past." Russian "poetry and fiction," he notes, represents a particularly rich repository of "the traces Petersburg has left on people's souls."[45]

By far the greatest part of *The Soul of Petersburg* is devoted to the examination of literary texts. In the book, Antsiferov surveys descriptions of the capital in works by writers from Sumarokov to Mayakovsky, going to great pains to point out significant trends and common features. He argues that the representations of St. Petersburg recorded in books should not be viewed as the product of happenstance, "the creative caprice of colorfully manifested individualities"; behind them all, "one can sense a certain continuity, one could even say a regularity." "An unshakeable impression is created," notes Antsiferov, "that the soul of the city has its own fate and our writers, each in his own time, recorded a distinct moment in the history of [its] development."[46] In other words, the images of St. Petersburg found in classic works of Russian prose and poetry represent a coherent literary tradition, one that has gradually evolved and changed, but in every age remains concerned with the same basic issues. Moreover, these literary landscapes at least to some extent reflect underlying truths about the city. They can provide researchers with information about the old capital that could not be obtained through mere personal exploration of the city's external form. In them, not just the present moment, but also St. Petersburg's eternal nature is revealed. As Antsiferov notes in a brief explanation of his method: "The citations here should be considered not just as illustrations that elucidate one of the author's thoughts. Here they are displaying the image [*obraz*] itself and in this way replace pictures in the text."[47] In this passage, the repeated references to visual forms of representation, the juxtaposition of subjective "illustrations" and truly accurate "pictures," and the fact that the word *obraz* itself can mean "icon" as well as "image" in Russian, together seem calculated to call to mind traditional Orthodox beliefs regarding religious painting. Effectively, Antsiferov is suggesting that in *The Soul of Petersburg*, literary citations act almost as icons: functioning as a kind of open door, they offer readers a glimpse of a city that cannot possibly be swept away by the "cosmic wind" of war and revolution.[48]

In *The Soul of Petersburg,* Antsiferov traces the history of the city's image, as reflected in works of literature—much as one might, perhaps, survey centuries of icons of the Virgin or of a particularly revered saint.[49] Recognizing that the task he has set for himself is enormous, that he cannot possibly include "all of the rich material of the reflection of Petersburg into the consciousness of Russian society," he concentrates on establishing preliminary "landmarks" signifying stages in the image's development.[50] Hence, although Antsiferov was inclined to view all depictions of the city as potentially valuable, in *The Soul of Petersburg* he focused on works that, he felt, represented significant turning points; descriptions in which new features of the city's external appearance and new aspects of its soul were revealed. In the text, Antsiferov briefly characterizes descriptions of St. Petersburg by several dozen writers (Lomonosov, Derzhavin, Batiushkov, Odoevsky, Lermontov, Herzen, Garshin, Polonsky, for example); he analyzes the work of five in detail: the nineteenth-century masters Pushkin, Gogol, and Dostoevsky, and the early-twentieth-century symbolists Blok and Bely.[51]

What role did these individual writers play in shaping the image of St. Petersburg? Antsiferov addresses this issue in passing at several points in *The Soul of Petersburg* and, in general, appears to draw something of a distinction between Pushkin and all other St. Petersburg authors. Pushkin, Antsiferov tells us, is "the creator of the image of Petersburg to the same extent that Peter the Great is the builder of the city itself." Authors that came before him provided "only separate representations of what was most likely the idea of Northern Palmyra rather than its real existence." Pushkin, according to Antsiferov, endowed the image of St. Petersburg "with the force of independent existence." "His image of Petersburg sums up the work of the entire preceding century and is, at the same time, a prophesy about fate."[52] Pushkin, in other words, effectively engendered the image of St. Petersburg. After this primary act of creation, however, Antsiferov suggests that the image broke free and began to live "its own life, like the city itself, independent of the impressions of its individual inhabitants."[53] It evolved organically through various stages, becoming "business-like" and "hurried," "a foreigner to its own fatherland," or, on the other hand, "an elusive, beckoning, secret enigma."[54] "Of course," Antsiferov adds, "an individual contemplating the city places the stamp of his own individuality on the impression that has been reflected by him, but this stamp changes only the details."[55] In its essential features, the image of St. Petersburg exists in and of itself: it can be recorded well or badly, but in no sense should it be considered just the product of a particular author's vision. Hence, after describing the work of several minor nineteenth-century poets, Antsiferov can announce that their "persistent repetition" of the same motifs and attitudes "does not testify to a poverty of artistic imagination." The "homogeneity" instead points to "a certain objectivity of the image of Petersburg that has been sketched" by Russian writers.[56]

The methodological approach that Antsiferov adopts in *The Soul of Petersburg* depends entirely upon the notion that the descriptions of the northern capital found in individual works of literature are fundamentally reliable; that they accord with a larger tradition, the image of St. Petersburg, which in turn corresponds in some fashion to objective reality. Otherwise, how could the study of poetry or novels ever lead a person to a vision of the genius loci? Antsiferov clearly states in *The Soul of Petersburg* that he is using literature as a tool, a means of learning about the capital.[57] He is not studying the landscape of St. Petersburg in order to gain insight into the classic literary texts, as he later would in so many of his excursions. Nor is he analyzing the works of Dostoevsky and Pushkin for their own sake here. In *The Soul of Petersburg*, Antsiferov wants to find out what literature can tell him about St. Petersburg.

Why did Antsiferov focus so much attention on the role that works of art and, particularly, literature could play in the quest for the genius loci? Why did he not, like Lee, urge his readers to seek the soul of the city by visiting decaying churches or charming corners of local parks? Antsiferov's approach to the study of St. Petersburg, in part, I believe, reflects the influence of symbolist philosophy and aesthetic theory. As a young man Antsiferov attended meetings of both the St. Petersburg Religious-Philosophical Society and its most notable post-Revolutionary descendant, the *Voskresen'e* discussion circle organized by the philosopher Alexander Meier. He read and reread the work of Vladimir Soloviev, the nineteenth-century religious philosopher whose ideas exerted such a defining influence on Russia's symbolists, absorbing key concepts and vocabulary.[58] In his published and unpublished writing, Antsiferov alludes constantly to the notion of transcendence, to penetrating the veil that divides the material world from the eternal realm of spirit and finding the Logos of places or things.[59] He apparently accepted many basic elements of the symbolist principle of "life-creation" (*zhiznetvorchestvo*), believing that through specific creative acts and processes, including both romantic love and artistic work, man could transform the physical world, "spiritualizing" matter, and breaking the bonds of mortality.[60] Many of the manuscripts that Antsiferov wrote in the 1940s and 1950s contain reflections on the role that romantic love and memory can play in man's quest for immortality.[61] During the years in which he was working on *The Soul of Petersburg*, Antsiferov seems to have focused his attention more on the implications of life-creation for aesthetic theory.

In an influential 1890 treatise entitled "The General Meaning of Art" (*Obshchii smysl iskusstva*), Vladimir Soloviev defined the true task of art as the "transformation of physical life into its spiritual counterpart" through the incarnation of a "living idea" or "word" and argued that this process, if carried through completely, would automatically result in "immortalization."[62] "With the immediate and indivisible union in beauty of spiritual content and sensory expression, with their complete mutual penetration, the material phenomenon, which in reality has become beautiful, that is to say, actually has embodied in itself the idea, must become as permanent and immortal as the idea itself."[63] In other words, in an act of true creation, the artist breaks down the wall that divides spirit from flesh. The work he or she creates exists simultaneously in the material world and the heavenly realm of ideals. Although in one sense very much a physical object, the product of human effort, earthly observation and materials, it is also spiritually significant in that it bears within itself a unique idea or word.

In *The Soul of Petersburg* Antsiferov builds on Soloviev's ideas by considering the problem of art's meaning from the point of view of reception as opposed to creation. He looks not so much at how art is made, at the role of the poet/artist as a kind of shaman mediating between the here and now and some higher realm, but rather at the way in which the reader/viewer can participate in the process of revelation. How can and should works of art and literature affect us? In what way should we approach them so as to partake maximally of the mysteries they contain? Leading us past specific sculptural monuments and descriptions of St. Petersburg, Antsiferov shows us how we might, by contemplating specific artistic images, commune with the soul of the city, achieving a vision of an eternal, spiritualized St. Petersburg.

One form of art that might on the surface seem an ideal receptacle for the spirit of a city receives surprisingly little attention in Antsiferov's book. Although in "The General Meaning of Art," Soloviev specifically mentions architecture in the list of art forms he identifies as precursors to the "perfect beauty" that will ultimately transform the world by affecting a union between spiritual content and sensory expression, Antsiferov rarely links the facades of individual buildings or the city's great architectural ensembles with the genius loci in *The Soul of Petersburg*.[64] This choice cannot be explained on the basis of actual susceptibility to damage: realistically, a statue of a reforming tsar or a sphinx is just as easily destroyed as a line of buildings or a square. In all likelihood, Antsiferov avoided using architectural monuments as symbols because in his mind they seemed too physical in nature, part of the city's physiology, its muscular structure, its bones, and for this reason ill-suited to serve as expressions of its soul.[65]

When Antsiferov does connect an architectural detail, a building, or even, for that matter, a piece of public statuary to the genius loci, he often chooses to refer, directly or obliquely, to a famous literary description of the object within his text. He concludes his brief remarks on the Neva sphinxes with a citation from the Viacheslav Ivanov poem "The Sphinxes on the Neva" (*Sfinksy nad Nevoi*). After mentioning the Hermitage he cites Bunin.[66] It is almost as though, for Antsiferov, a reference to or the incantation of a literary citation in and of itself can help to spiritualize a given object or site, transforming it into a proper vessel or habitation for the soul of the city. This trend can be seen most clearly in the passages Antsiferov devotes to Falconet's monument to Peter I, the statue that Antsiferov most insistently and directly equates with the spirit of St. Petersburg. Antsiferov writes:

> If anyone happens to be alongside it [the statue] on a foul autumn evening when the sky has turned into chaos and moves on the earth, filling it with its confusion; the river, constricted by the granite, moans and thrashes about; sudden gusts of wind rock the street lamps and their swaying light makes the surrounding buildings stir,—let him look at that moment at the Bronze Horseman, at that fire turned into bronze with sharply etched and mighty forms. What strength he will sense, a passionate, stormy strength, calling him forward into the unknown; what great might, provoking the anxious question: what is next, what is up ahead? Victory or rupture and ruin?[67]

The references to "chaos," a stormy night, and a restless, thrashing river immediately call to mind Pushkin's *Bronze Horseman*. The questions Antsiferov raises resemble the famous back-to-back interrogatives from the poem: "Where are you galloping, proud steed, and where will you set down your hooves? Oh mighty master of fate! Was it not thus that you, on the brink of the very abyss on high, reared up Russia with your iron bridle?"[68] They also, perhaps even more clearly, evoke the famous allusion to and variation on the Pushkin passage in Andrei Bely's novel *Petersburg*:

> Russia, you are like a steed! Your two front hooves have leaped far off into the darkness, into the void, while your two rear hooves are firmly implanted in the granite soil.
>
> Do you too want to separate yourself from the rock that holds you, as some of your mad sons have separated themselves from the soil? Do you too want to separate yourself from the rock that holds you, and hang, bridle-less, suspended in air, and then plunge down into the chaos of

waters? Or, could it be that you want to hurtle through the air, cleaving the mists, to disappear in the clouds along with your sons?[69]

Obviously, when Antsiferov identified "the Bronze Horseman" with the genius loci of St. Petersburg, he understood the phrase as encompassing not just the statue, but also its literary reflection. He was paying homage to the creative accomplishments of Pushkin and Bely as much as to those of Falconet, realizing that in part through their efforts the monument had become richly invested with ideas: man's struggle with the elements, the eternal battle between order and chaos, Russia's uncertain destiny, the pain of the private individual who finds his dreams at odds with the forces of history.[70] They had helped to transform the statue from a mere physical entity, an edifice of metal and stone, into something of real spiritual significance.[71]

Literature, the word, is always center stage in Antsiferov's book. It represents the primary means of both spiritualizing and investigating space. In it he finds a St. Petersburg that is at once eternal and eminently mappable, a holy city ready to reveal itself to those who engage in purposeful contemplation. Like the excursion primers Antsiferov would write later in the 1920s, *The Soul of Petersburg* in a certain sense represents a how-to manual that provides readers with instruction in a specific investigative process. Here, however, Antsiferov addresses an audience of individual seekers rather than professional pedagogues; the approach he outlines is more personal and introspective, less clearly geared toward performance and display.

Of Antsiferov's immediate contemporaries, the writer whose work most clearly recalls *The Soul of Petersburg* is Erikh Gollerbakh. Best known in the West as a correspondent and friend of the philosopher Vasily Rozanov, Gollerbakh enjoyed a successful career in Russia as a literary critic, art historian, collector, and editor. In the early post-Revolutionary period, he served on the staff of a variety of cultural ventures, including the Artistic and Historical Commission in Tsarskoe Selo, the Department for the Preservation of Art and Antiquities in Petrograd, the Russian Museum, and the Petrograd branch of Gosizdat. Deeply attached to his birthplace and principal home for much of his early life, the imperial suburb of Tsarskoe Selo, Gollerbakh published a whole series of works in the 1920s and 1930s that focused on the area's cultural attractions and history: popular guides to the local palaces and parks, scholarly articles on specific architectural monuments, and a variety of books and pamphlets on the area's rich literary heritage, a topic for which he felt particular enthusiasm. The

FIG. 7 Erikh Gollerbakh, silhouette of the Pushkin monument in Tsarskoe Selo, frontispiece to the second edition of *City of Muses*, 1930.

most important of Gollerbakh's works on Tsarskoe Selo and Russian literature, *City of Muses*, was first published in 1927 and, garnered enough favorable attention in literary circles to merit releasing a second, significantly expanded edition three years later. Illustrated with a series of silhouettes made by the author himself, the second edition boasted a significantly revised and expanded text. Because it is more complete, it forms the basis for discussion here.[72]

In the preface to the second edition of *City of Muses*, Gollerbakh warns his readers to expect "more of a short story, than an 'investigation.'" "Let us agree," he notes, "with the Goncourts: *Il faut pour s'intéresser au passé qu'il nous revienne dans le coeur. Le passé qui ne revient que dans l'espirit est un passé mort.*"[73] Aiming to bring Tsarskoe Selo's past to life for his readers so that they might better understand and appreciate the many classic works of prose and poetry that paid homage to the area, Gollerbakh works in his book to capture the unique "physiognomies" of discrete literary epochs, revealing their principal characteristics. He offers his audience a series of loosely connected chapters, each of which focuses on a different period: the glorious reign of Catherine II, the great age of the Lyceum, the 1830s and 1840s, the 1890s, the years just before and immediately after the October Revolution. In every section, Gollerbakh weaves together diverse material, skillfully combining provocative general statements on artistic and literary trends; citations from poetry, memoirs, and the private letters of key historical figures; and vivid scenes of writers at work and at play in various corners of Tsarskoe Selo. Pushkin lies awake on his cot whispering to Pushchin through the walls of the Lyceum; Zhukovsky heads out into the imperial park for his evening constitutional; the light in Annensky's office burns through the night. Gollerbakh's approach to chronicling literary history encourages us to see our favorite writers as products of the sociocultural milieu and physical landscapes they inhabited: to recognize the role that both time and place can play in fueling literary creativity.

In the space of about a hundred and fifty years, from the late eighteenth to the early twentieth centuries, Gollerbakh assures us in his book, Tsarskoe Selo gave rise to something truly eternal, to a literary legacy that would never lose its luster. After the upheaval and destruction that took place in the wake of the Revolution, he suggests, this aspect of the area's past alone remained untarnished. Perhaps all the apocalyptic premonitions that had haunted men like Blok in the first years of the twentieth century had come true. Perhaps "someone's mighty callused hand had drawn a thick curtain made out of homespun cloth closed forever across the little stage called Tsarskoe Selo, upon which ... the tragicomedy of tsarist power had played itself out." Perhaps the area's great architectural ensembles, stripped of life, had come to resemble a silent, desolate "graveyard of memories."[74] Nonetheless, Gollerbakh insists, something still remains of the once vibrant cultural arena that Pushkin termed his "fatherland."[75] "What is dear to us in Tsarskoe Selo is not the 'imperial' but the eternal. More than anything else, in it [the city], the charm of literary achievement captivates."[76]

How does *City of Muses* compare to Antsiferov's *The Soul of Petersburg*? As the brief description provided above perhaps suggests, the books are similar in many key respects. Like *The Soul of Petersburg, City of Muses* is organized chronologically and represents, at least in part, an attempt to trace the evolution of the literary image of a geographical area, to set up "landmarks," identifying important stages and transition points.[77] Moreover, Antsiferov and Gollerbakh often rely upon the same imagery and terminology: like Antsiferov, Gollerbakh equates the October Revolution with the apocalypse; he associates the idea of imperial power with "tragedy"; and he talks about a genius loci discernible at least to sensitive residents.[78] Both writers speak of their cities as having physical "bodies," "souls," "images," "faces," and "fates"; both also suggest that by the end of the Civil War, in terms of their physical state, the areas they describe represented little more than "graveyards," inhospitable to new life. Statements concerning the general characteristics of population centers contained in the two books also often correspond. In *City of Muses,* for instance, we learn, just as we did in *The Soul of Petersburg,* that "every city has a secret predilection for a certain time of year"; it will look its best in spring perhaps, or in the winter when its buried under snow.[79]

Of course, there are real differences between the two books as well. In *The Soul of Petersburg,* Antsiferov focuses almost exclusively on an analysis of literary texts. Gollerbakh is more interested in the biographies of his authors, everyday life, and historical atmosphere. Perhaps the most striking difference between *The Soul of Petersburg* and *City of Muses* is that Gollerbakh inserts himself explicitly into his text, transforming it into a kind of literary memoir. He presents Tsarskoe Selo not just as the city of Pushkin and Annensky but also as his own. He tells us when he was born, reminisces about the teachers he had at school, and mentions his meetings with Rozanov. In the first person singular and often in parentheses, he talks to us about his love for the area: "The old park. . . . How many times, returning to you after an absence have I wanted to fall onto the gravel of your paths and kiss each piece of sand, each blade of grass. How many times have you cured my anxiety and melancholy, dispelled my nasty nightmares, with a whisper of your ancient trees, muffled the insinuating voices of trollops [*liarv*]." In *City of Muses,* Gollerbakh's relationship to the spirit of Tsarskoe Selo appears overwhelmingly passionate and sensual. The book reads as a kind of love letter, addressed to a long departed beloved: "Now in the lifeless nighttime quiet of my Leningrad apartment, in my office, which is growing cold as morning approaches, I see you, my city. I lean back into the embrace of my armchair, close my eyes, and return to the past." In effect, Tsarskoe Selo itself represents a vast alluring female body that the narrator can conjure up out of his adolescent memories. At one point he writes: "I sense you, my city, as I do my own body. I feel that broken bench as I would a scratch on my finger, that damaged statue as a hangnail. In the autumn, when the rains dig furrows in the walks and slobber all over the highway, I feel as though rainy dampness is depositing itself all over my body."[80] The city's vulnerability excites his empathy. She is the ultimate muse, and hence her role as the inspiration and point of origin of so much Russian poetry is only natural.

To what extent was Gollerbakh directly influenced by Antsiferov's work? Did he consciously use *The Soul of Petersburg* as a model when composing *City of Muses?* Despite the obvious similarities between the two texts, this question has, in recent years, excited a fair amount of critical debate. Gollerbakh's first work on the literary heritage of Tsarskoe Selo, a slim volume titled *Tsarskoe Selo in Poetry*, was published in 1922, the same year in which the first edition of *The Soul of the Petersburg* appeared. As a result, some scholars have been inclined to argue that Gollerbakh developed his interest in literary geography independently: they characterize the relation between *The Soul of Petersburg* and *City of Muses* as one of coincidental similarity rather than influence.[81] It seems worth noting, however, that Antsiferov's work was fairly well known in St. Petersburg even before 1922: he had given many public talks and excursions on literary topics between 1919 and 1921 and had published articles describing the St. Petersburg of Dostoevsky and Blok in 1921.[82] Moreover, Gollerbakh's 1922 book offers only a cursory discussion of Tsarskoe Selo's significance in Russian literary history.[83] More of an anthology of literary texts (with a brief introductory article) than a full study, it does not approximate *City of Muses* in terms of its complexity. Gollerbakh must have spent a great deal of time developing his ideas on the literary image of Tsarskoe Selo between 1922 and 1927, the year when the first edition of *City of Muses* appeared. It seems almost inconceivable that he did not stumble on the text of *The Soul of Petersburg* at some time in this process.

Andrei Iatsevich, the last writer I will discuss in this chapter, was, by nature, a popular historian. His most significant published work on the literature of the capital, *Pushkin's Petersburg* (1931), is primarily factual in orientation, devoid, for the most part of the abstract symbols and general statements on the nature of urban areas and literary images that fill the writing of Antsiferov and Gollerbakh.[84] In his book, Iatsevich traces the history of hundreds of individual buildings, providing for his readers out of this surfeit of detail a multifaceted view of daily life in Russia's northern capital during the time of Pushkin. Passing by the city's most famous monuments on the grounds that these "cathedrals and palaces" have already received ample attention, Iatsevich focuses primarily on structures that are less well-known to the public, "buildings . . . that are connected with the names of great people, their contemporaries, and the events of that [Pushkin's] epoch" but "have yet to find investigators."[85]

Working through a single more or less confined strip of territory at a time, Iatsevich, in the course of twelve chapters, traverses most of the central areas of early-nineteenth-century St. Petersburg. The first section of the book describes Kolomna, the region where Pushkin lived with his parents after leaving the Lyceum; the last reviews the history of the apartment house on the Moika where the poet died and talks about other nearby structures. The organizational scheme within each chapter is relatively loose: Iatsevich sometimes moves from house to house along one block; at other times, he skips from one street to another several blocks away to build on a particular association or follow a line of thought. Throughout the book, history remains the focus, not architecture or literature specifically. We learn who lived in every building, when and why houses were sold. We hear about young ladies who made disastrous marriages, corrupt officials, old women with superstitions, and the hostesses of prominent literary salons. Pushkin's friendships, romantic liaisons, and contacts with various political and artistic circles all receive attention. Iatsevich often mentions the demolition of buildings, but generally without particular sorrow. He seems to recognize that some change in a city's appearance is inevitable and, in any case, most of the houses he speaks about are not of great architectural or historical importance: their disappearance represents the end of a story, a little sad perhaps, but scarcely a great tragedy.

Of the writers of his own generation, Iatsevich seems to have the most in common with Stolpiansky, and perhaps that is only natural. The two men worked very closely together at the Society for the Study and Preservation of Old Petersburg during the late 1920s and the early 1930s. While Stolpiansky was chairman of the organization, Iatsevich served as his deputy. Although the relationship was not without its moments of tension, Iatsevich seems to have sincerely admired Stolpiansky as a scholar.[86] He turned to him for advice when he needed information on city history and was clearly very familiar with most of Stolpiansky's published work.[87]

Aside from their passion for historical anecdotes, Stolpiansky and Iatsevich favored similar organizational strategies in their writing. Many of the works that Stolpiansky wrote for his "Old Petersburg" series, like *Pushkin's Petersburg,* are organized, at least in part, geographically: the narrative moves from one house to the next until the history of an entire street or area has been covered.[88] This system makes it possible to incorporate a huge quantity of diverse material into a single volume. It can, however, result in the creation of texts that lack thematic coherence. In *Pushkin's Petersburg* Iatsevich's willingness to stray, on occasion, from the principle of geographic organization in order to follow particular themes or lines of thought, helps him to avoid this pitfall. Like Pyliaev, Iatsevich succeeds in weaving a vast array of historical anecdotes and details into a coherent portrait of an age.

Iatsevich's work represents an important turning point in the history of literary *kraevedenie.* Largely devoid of the lyricism and mysticism that characterized the essays of Gollerbakh and Antsiferov, it makes no mention of the genius loci and does not explicitly promote ritualized service to a cult of place: contemplation of the city's image at select shrines; the quest for personal revelation through carefully designed exercises. By the beginning of the 1930s, writers could no longer describe the experience of literary investigation in such spiritual terms. Works on literary Petersburg, almost by default, began to focus on providing detailed accounts of daily life in a given age. They documented how famous Russian writers lived, who they associated with, and what they would have seen outside their windows. They gave concrete addresses for the homes of both historical figures and literary characters, listed economic statistics, and assessed the level of technological and social development at the time. Most of all, they talked about opposition to tsarist tyranny and the history of the Russian revolutionary movement. All later Soviet works on St. Petersburg in the age of Pushkin would, like Iatsevich's *Pushkin's Petersburg*, devote huge amounts of space to discussions of the Decembrists, the evils of serfdom, censorship, and exile.[89]

This does not mean that later Soviet studies of literary St. Petersburg were necessarily bad or uninteresting to read. Many of the volumes, particularly those written during the post-Thaw years, contain fascinating pieces of information: they tell us about street lights and systems for paving roads, where unemployed servants went to find positions, and how books were bought and sold. Works like A. and M. Gordin's 1983 *A Journey to Pushkin's Petersburg* (*Puteshestvie v Pushkinskii Peterburg*) give readers a real sense of what it meant to live and work in the capital at the beginning of the nineteenth century: how typical citizens purchased clothes, what they ate, saw, and thought. The past fleshed out in this kind of glorious detail can be mesmerizing. Moreover, aside from merely providing entertainment, such historical sketches can enhance our understanding of classic works of literature. A well-constructed example of "literary *kraevedenie*" can teach us to detect the meanings hidden in seemingly inconsequential happenings, to understand the codes of etiquette and honor that governed society in a certain place and period of time; to distinguish between normal and extraordinary behavior. Without a gauge of this kind, how can we pretend to understand the motivation of characters in the work of Pushkin and Lermontov?

Because they recognized that the study of eighteenth- and nineteenth-century daily life offered these kinds of practical benefits, several decades ago a number of leading Russian scholars began writing historical sketches that in many ways resembled works of "literary *kraevedenie*." Members of the prestigious Tartu school of semiotics have been particularly active in this respect. In the last years of his life, Iurii Lotman, for example, wrote a series of essays on the culture of Russia's nobility in the eighteenth and early nineteenth centuries. In them, he generally used information gathered from literary texts and historical documents to reconstruct a particular cultural ritual and explore its significance for society as a whole: balls, duels, and dinner parties all attracted his attention at one time or another. In theory, Lotman usually examined these phenomena in the context of Russian society as a whole instead of confining his argument to a single city or geographic area as was customary for practitioners of literary *kraevedenie*. In practice, however, he almost always focused on one or the other of the nation's capitals, most frequently on St. Petersburg. Many of the essays he wrote for *Conversations about Russian Culture* (*Besedy o russkoi kul'ture*) can be read as studies of the northern capital; *High Society Dinners* (*Velikosvetskie obedy*), a book Lotman co-authored with Elena Pogosian, focuses explicitly on St. Petersburg.[90] In both these volumes, the city's past and the daily lives of its inhabitants 150 or even 250 years ago are chronicled, at least in part, in the hope of helping readers achieve a new understanding of classic literary texts. As Lotman explicitly states in the introduction to his *Conversations about Russian Culture:* "In order to understand the *meaning* of the behavior of living people and literary heroes of the past, it is essential to know their culture; their simple, customary lives, their habits, conceptions of the world, and so on, and so forth."[91]

Aside from writing studies that resemble, in terms of both their purpose and their basic design, the best examples of the historical approach to literary *kraevedenie*, Lotman and his colleagues at the Tartu school also showed a great deal of interest in Antsiferov's early work on literary topography. During the 1970s and 1980s, a number of leading semioticians were inspired by the example of *The Soul of Petersburg* to take a closer look at Silver Age descriptions of the northern capital. Expanding on and, in some key respects, modifying Antsiferov's basic thesis, these scholars developed a theory that they referred to as the "single Petersburg text" (*edinyi Peterburgskii tekst*).[92] Essentially, instead of arguing, as Antsiferov had, that the Petersburg theme had represented a fundamentally consistent literary tradition since the time of Pushkin, the semioticians suggested that the illusion of integrity had been, at least in part, created by Russia's symbolists. They had taken "the relatively motley heritage of the nineteenth century" and organized it, choosing from the vast array of works devoted to the "Petersburg theme" a short list that seemed significant and complementary: Pushkin's *Bronze Horseman* and "the Queen of Spades," Gogol's *Petersburg Tales,* and certain pieces by Dostoevsky.[93] "Semantically connected" in some key sense, these works, despite the fact that they had been written by many different authors, tended to address the same problems and use the same motifs. Effectively, they could be treated as a "single Petersburg text."[94] A writer like Andrei Bely could, in his novel *Petersburg*, alternate references to a variety of works and authors, shifting almost seamlessly from one to the next; he could create symbols that simultaneously suggested allusions to several classic texts. The nineteenth-century tradition, according to the semioticians, when understood in this restrictive sense, effectively functioned as a kind of "code": a shorthand that the symbolists employed for sketching out ideas and images.[95]

Soviet semioticians admired *The Soul of Petersburg* enormously, in part because they saw it as a "key" that could help both readers and critics understand works like Bely's *Petersburg*. Antsiferov's methodical account of the evolution of the capital's image in Russian literature had helped to draw attention to the motifs that dominated the "single text": petty officials, the fantastic, the city as a spectral vision liable to evaporate, Peter I as demiurge, the coming apocalypse, flood and ruin. Perhaps Antsiferov, members of the Moscow-Tartu School thought, had not fully recognized the extent to which the symbolists had actively reshaped the legacy of the nineteenth century; he had, nonetheless, created the basic scholarly foundation on which all later efforts to study the image of St. Petersburg depended. As the semioticians repeatedly and openly acknowledged in their articles, they were, in many ways, enormously indebted to *The Soul of Petersburg*: it was the first work in which "the question of the 'poetics of St. Petersburg' had been raised in the framework of an academic investigation"; the source for many basic concepts and ideas.[96]

It is interesting to note that, for all their open admiration of Antsiferov, the Tartu semioticians embraced his legacy rather selectively. They tended to ignore almost entirely his mystical beliefs about the genius loci, his conviction that cities represented living entities with faces, bodies, souls, and even, potentially, tragic destinies. Unlike Antsiferov, the semioticians did not send their readers off to commune with the spirit of the northern capital; they did not understand the world in pantheistic terms. For them, the cult of Petersburg represented a fascinating subject for scientific inquiry: it did not occur to them to profess faith in it themselves. They wanted instead to analyze it, to discover its essential parts, and identify their significance. What forces and pressures in Russian society lay behind the widespread belief that St. Petersburg would one day be swept away in an apocalyptic flood? Why did most accounts of the city's construction emphasize the fact that it had arisen "almost magically" overnight? Antsiferov might raise these same questions in his essays, but at some point he always stopped analyzing the processes that produced a particular set of cultural beliefs and began professing them himself. He was an insider, a cleric in the service of the cult of Petersburg aside from being its student.

The Tartu semioticians saw the world in less obviously supernatural terms. For them, the body of St. Petersburg, the city's myth, and its "image" or literary reflection all represented acts of human communication, vast symbolic texts that needed to be deciphered, rather than independent, organically developing entities. What had changed by the middle of the twentieth century? Why had cultural commentators stopped trying to experience and describe transcendental visions? Why did they no longer approach the cult of St. Petersburg from a subjective, empathetic perspective? Several decades of Soviet rule had no doubt played a role: even scholars who did not accept the official ideology might find it difficult to escape its influence completely, to think in terms other than those of positivism and materialism. The mystical, symbolic language favored by essayists like Antsiferov and Gollerbakh had disappeared long ago; read in the pages of a book it seemed strange and unfamiliar, as ancient and at least initially inscrutable as the expressions of the Old Russian chronicles. It could be analyzed and deciphered, but it did not represent a viable form of modern communication. By the second half of the twentieth century, cultural commentary had become a business for professionals with academic degrees and recognizable credentials. Trained to think of themselves as scholars and to aspire to scientific standards of accuracy and objectivity in their work, to denigrate anything that was not proved beyond a shadow of a doubt, that was not adequately supported by evidence or reasoned out, they could hardly be expected to adopt intuition and sympathetic feeling as methods of discovery.

Conclusion

What does the story of *kraevedenie* suggest about the nature of disciplines in general and about identity disciplines specifically? To what extent does Russian local studies represent an exceptional phenomenon, and in what ways is it comparable to other fields of study? In this conclusion I will turn from the specific to the general and offer some preliminary inferences.

First, the account of the development of modern *kraevedenie* that I have provided here accords well with contemporary Western theories of disciplinary formation. Researchers today rarely advance single-cause explanations of the genesis of disciplines, treating the emergence of a new field as the direct result of a particular scientific discovery, theoretical development, or the achievements of a certain school of founding luminaries. In the wake of Foucault's work, most instead tend to perceive disciplines as complex cultural constructs that arise out of a web of social relations specific to a given time and place and which, hence, cannot be said to stem from any single source. "No one," modern scholars of disciplinary studies like to remind us, "creates disciplines." As Timothy Lenoir explains in one article:

the heterogeneity and dispersion of interlocking elements in discursive formations . . . implies that the teleological unfolding of a core idea or the persistent efforts of single researchers, indeed even groups of single researchers in the same field, are insufficient to found disciplines. The multidimensional linkages and exclusions of and between different discursive practices required for the creation of a discipline exceed the power of individuals to engineer and orchestrate. The difficulty with founder narratives, then, is not simply the complexity of the task of building disciplines; the problem is that disciplines do not have single, originary sources but are more appropriately grasped as interactive system effects.[1]

Disciplines, in other words, are best understood as by-products of social exchange, of interaction between communities of scholars, public and private agencies, institutions, and interest groups. The boundaries which contain them arise gradually as the result of a myriad of small acts: individual and institutional choices and statements, attempts at self-definition or self-assertion; alliances forged or broken; efforts to secure support, set standards, husband resources, take advantage of new discoveries and theoretical developments, and address pressing cultural, economic, or political concerns.

Because so many factors play a role in their formation, because they grow out of spontaneous social interaction rather than in accordance with any fixed plan, disciplinary constructs will often, particularly in the early stages of their development, resemble ungainly conglomerates. Most, like *kraevedenie,* will combine within themselves elements that might reasonably be judged heterogeneous, groups of researchers, theories, and works of scholarship that proceed from different intellectual traditions and are in significant respects dissimilar. It takes time for the differences between these components to blur, for the new field of specialization to coalesce and start to be perceived as natural. First the emerging discipline must acquire independent institutions, traditions, and standards; scholars associated with it have to forget old allegiances and accept their new collective identity; they must come to perceive the commonalities they share as more important than any dissimilarities and begin to promote the development of the new category actively by writing about its history and goals, recruiting students, and lobbying for funding. For this reason, as Joseph Kiger has pointed out, age and disciplinary status are necessarily correlated: relatively new formations are often not recognized as true disciplines—even by insiders.² In many cases, more than one generation must pass before a discipline comes into its own.

Identity fields, as I noted in the introduction to this book, may take a particularly long time to win recognition as disciplines because of the peculiarities of their structure. To both internal and external observers they often seem profoundly amorphous, communities of scholars united by little more than a desire to explore a particular form of selfhood. Their obvious connection to historically and culturally contingent notions of identity, their inevitable association with some crusade for minority rights, social and political equality, or the protection of a particular cultural tradition, can so dominate discussion that other defining characteristics pass unobserved.

Like other kinds of disciplinary formations, identity fields, however, can and do give rise to departments, centers, institutes, degree programs, professional organizations, publishing venues, and funding lines. They are generally associated with specific theories, methods, techniques, and discursive strategies. Scholars working in them devise mechanisms for training, examining, and accrediting successors; they employ distinctive terminology; by referring to certain books and writers more than others, they create disciplinary canons and pantheons. As they struggle to make sense of their past, they gradually construct collective mythic narratives that explain the origin, history and purpose of their respective disciplines. Identity fields, in other words, can come to exhibit many of the structural attributes associated with true disciplinarity. Scholars working in a single field will in many cases share institutional allegiances and traditions as well as interests, perceptions, values, and attitudes: they will be bound together by a complex web of overlapping ties.

In this monograph I have argued that one of the unifying factors which helped draw Russian *kraevedenie* together, allowing its constituent parts to cohere enough to begin to give rise to this kind of developed superstructure, was literary. Most of the researchers commonly identified as forefathers of modern *kraevedenie* shared an interest in a class of texts known in Russian as *putevoditeli*. Preservationists, excursionists, and activists associated with the Central Bureau of *Kraevedenie* all composed and used such works as sources. Appreciation of this kind of descriptive literature represented one of the most obvious similarities between these groups, part of what allowed them, despite very real differences, ultimately to be subsumed into a single category. Because an interest in guidebooks represented one of the commonalities that united many of the key components from which modern *kraevedenie* grew, it inevitably came to serve as one of the discipline's defining characteristics. Each generation of *kraevedy* emulated its predecessors, following patterns and building upon traditions established during the period of *kraevedenie's* formation. Like Benois, Kurbatov, Stolpiansky, and Antsiferov, modern *kraevedy* both wrote and studied guides. As a result, over time, *kraevedenie* and the guidebook became so closely associated that today Russian publishers, librarians, and booksellers regularly classify guidebooks as works of *kraevedenie*.

Few obvious parallels exist for this situation in other disciplines. Most contemporary fields of specialization are distinguished by their research focus, methods, jargon, and evaluative norms but not by an association with a specific textual form. What do sociologists, chemists, and political scientists produce that is characteristic of their respective disciplines? Although one can certainly argue that in each of these fields researchers organize the books and articles they write a little differently, such distinctions exist on a subgeneric level. The same terminology is typically used to describe studies written by both political scientists and sociologists; a phrase like "refereed article" or "scholarly monograph" calls to mind no particular discipline. It would be fair to say that literary form plays a more obvious organizational role in the case of *kraevedenie* than it does in most other knowledge systems.

If we understand disciplines as cultural constructs that evolve out of social relations specific to a particular time and place, then it becomes reasonable to ask: To what extent will these formations reflect the values and concerns of the societies from which they emerged? The work of Michel Foucault suggests that linkages will often exist on numerous levels: a discipline may arise out of the quest for a solution to concrete social problems; it may reflect or reinforce prevalent biases, oppositions, and distinctions; it may depend on a particular epistemological framework or world view.[3] In the case of *kraevedenie* at least one connection to Russian social reality is fairly obvious: concerns central to the discipline mirror obsessions prevalent among Russia's educated elite throughout both the nineteenth and twentieth centuries. *Kraevedy* study local regions, cities, and villages from a holistic perspective. They consider how human society and the environment affect each other, what features distinguish particular population groups and areas, and the way in which local myths and descriptive conventions emerge and evolve. They trace and, in some cases, obviously attempt to manipulate the development of regional and national patriotic sentiment. As such, their work inevitably touches upon the problem of local particularity. Do all human societies follow similar paths of development or can individual cities, regions, and countries be said to have a special destiny, character, and historic role? Should developing areas strive to emulate their most powerful neighbors or should they rather confine themselves to building upon indigenous traditions? How can regional variation and national type be reconciled? To what extent will the cities and areas that make up a country share similar characteristics and in what ways might they differ?

Such questions call to mind the persistent debates on Russia's national character and destiny that erupted as a result of the dramatic reforms introduced by Peter I in the early eighteenth century and, in the 1830s, culminated in the rise of Slavophilism and Westernism as intellectual movements. Although often portrayed as polar opposites, both the Slavophiles and the Westernizers shared an interest in the exploration and description of Russia's diverse regions. They reviewed and actively promoted the composition of various forms of geographic literature, including texts that later came to be categorized as guidebooks.[4] In the sketches and polemical essays that they wrote themselves, they often characterized and compared various cities and areas, focusing particular attention on the capitals, Moscow and St. Petersburg.[5] Each camp tended to see geographic description as a means of addressing larger issues, of articulating its views on the nature of Russianness, progress, and development. Did Peter I's efforts to reform and modernize Russian society represent a great leap forward or a tragic miscalculation? What role could Russia expect to play in world history in the future? What areas of Russian territory and what aspects of Russian culture deserved the greatest praise? Should the Western-looking capital of St. Petersburg serve as the model for all development or did older regions hold the key to the nation's future? In their descriptions of Russia and its people, the Slavophiles and Westernizers posed answers to these questions, speaking always in terms of oppositions between center and periphery, tradition and reform, Russia and the West.

Long after the original circles of Slavophiles and Westernizers disappeared, the ideas articulated by each camp, the terms and discursive forms employed in their debate, retained their cultural currency. Throughout the nineteenth century they resurfaced regularly in newspaper articles, works of social theory, literary criticism, history, fiction, sketches, and even guidebooks. New groups of writers and intellectuals who defended views reminiscent of Slavophilism or Westernism regularly appeared; old questions and issues generated new controversy. *Kraevedenie* itself might reasonably be termed an outgrowth of this persistent dialogue. In it the discursive forms associated with Slavophilism and Westernism were, in a sense, institutionalized and disciplined; the efforts of generations of Russian intellectuals to promote the study, description, and appreciation of the motherland at last found structural expression.

Kraevedenie's rootedness, the fact that it seemed so organically connected to long-standing domestic cultural traditions and societal debates, made it easy for early practitioners to envisage the discipline as having an elaborate prehistory. In the 1920s, as I have already noted, researchers associated with the Central Bureau of *Kraevedenie* began to look back to preceding centuries in search of possible ancestors. Generally the identifications they made have been accepted by later generations of *kraevedy* and to some extent even by the population of the Russian Federation at large. Russians today often classify eighteenth- and nineteenth-century investigators of discrete geographic localities as *kraevedy,* particularly if they perceive their work as having in some way advanced the development of the *putevoditel'* as a literary tradition.

By claiming that *kraevedenie* in many respects represents a profoundly Russian discipline, by emphasizing the fact that it emerged out of long-standing domestic cultural dialogue, that it was in part defined by its association with a literary form that had, since the end of the eighteenth century, enjoyed substantial popularity with Russian readers, I do not mean to suggest that the discipline entirely lacked foreign antecedents and influences. Of course, the example of *Heimatkunde* in Germany played a role in prompting the emergence of *kraevedenie* in Russia. In the first two decades of the twentieth century, Russian pedagogical magazines regularly published reports on the homeland studies movement in Germany and encouraged domestic educators to implement related reforms. When officials at the Commissariat of Enlightenment took steps to organize the First Conference of Scientific Societies for the Study of Local Regions in December 1921, they may well have been thinking in part of the positive role that *Heimatkunde* had come to play in provincial cultural life in Germany, of how German regional societies had built and maintained museums, spearheaded preservation campaigns, and implemented significant educational initiatives. They clearly hoped that by linking together voluntary cultural and scholarly organizations that existed throughout the Soviet territory, they would encourage a similar pattern of development.

It is important to note, however, that the influence of *Heimatkunde* on *kraevedenie* did not extend much beyond such initial contacts. During the early 1920s, as Russian local studies grew in importance and prestige, as the term *kraevedenie* began assume its modern connotations, expanding to include movements and groups not initially associated with the Central Bureau and its affiliates or, for that matter, with pre-Revolutionary pedagogical *rodinovedenie,* practitioners largely ceased to make reference to German *Heimatkunde.* Political circumstances undoubtedly played a part in this shift. After the Revolution,

Russian educators and cultural workers gradually lost contact with friends and colleagues in Western Europe; they no longer had such easy access to current publications from abroad; the dictates of Bolshevik ideology often discouraged them from acknowledging connections between their work and cultural or scientific trends in the capitalist countries of the West. It also seems likely, however, that Soviet *kraevedy* stopped talking about *Heimatkunde,* because, as the concept of what constituted *kraevedenie* expanded, the association between this form of regional scholarship and its German precursor began to appear more tenuous. Only some of the elements and trends that came to be identified as forms of *kraevedenie* in the 1920s had arisen under the influence of *Heimatkunde.* A number of approaches to regional investigation that evolved in Russia, including most particularly forms of excursion work and preservationism practiced in St. Petersburg and Moscow, may have seemed to many experts incompatible in spirit with the German provincial science.

From the early 1920s on, *kraevedenie* took a largely independent course of development. It evolved in isolation from *Heimatkunde* and all other Western forms of regional research. Shaped by unique historical pressures and a distinctive social environment, it assumed different functions and acquired its own traditions. It absorbed both high and low cultural trends; movements, programs, and approaches developed in Russia's historical capitals and those more typically associated with provincial areas; forms of research undertaken, as a rule, by professionals and various amateur endeavors. Subjected to a truly vicious purge in the early 1930s, it lost much of its impetus toward growth and devolved into an intellectual backwater. It did not undergo a significant revival until the post-Stalin years and even then was often viewed by outsiders with a certain amount of condescension because of its checkered history and its association with amateurism. In part for this reason, *kraevedenie* generally received less attention than better established disciplines and was less strictly regulated. It came to serve a convenient outlet for various sorts of frustrated intellectuals in the late Soviet period: scholars interested in studying the cultural heritage, ecology, or geography of some segment of Soviet territory (a given city, region, or even autonomous republic) often found that they could say more as *kraevedy* than as historians, ethnographers, and geographers. In at least small ways, the field represented a forum for the expression of anticentrist sentiments, a nexus of resistance to the dictates of the Kremlin and to the hegemony of official Soviet (as opposed to regional) cultural models.

Freed from essentially all outside restraint with the advent of *glasnost* and perestroika, *kraevedenie* underwent yet another renaissance, capturing the imagination of large sectors of the population. In many areas of the Soviet Union in the late 1980s and the early 1990s, the study of local history, cultural traditions, and ecological problems became enormously fashionable. Publishing houses raced to get both old and new guidebooks into print, in some cases releasing books in editions of more than 100,000 copies. New preservation societies and study circles focusing on regional history arose; veteran *kraevedy* emerged as recognized authorities and, to some extent, local celebrities. They appeared on television and the radio constantly; they had regular bylines in regional newspapers; they served on committees charged with determining the fate of Soviet-era monuments, played an important role in the drive to restore pre-Revolutionary toponyms in many areas, and drafted educational programs for the schools.

During the very early post-Soviet period, interest in *kraevedenie* was often taken as a strong indicator of liberal political views. In their scholarly work and in the presentations they made to the media, Russian *kraevedy* constantly pointed to the havoc wrecked by the old Soviet system of economic and political centralization. They documented ecological disasters and the destruction of architectural landmarks; they fought for the return of discarded street names and long hidden Tsarist monuments; they spoke of the disregard party leaders and government officials had often shown for local needs, traditions, and aspirations. As a result they were often seen as (and in many cases perceived themselves to be) strong supporters of the liberal reforms introduced by the Yeltsin government. This situation began to change in 1993, the year in which Yeltsin ordered tanks to shell the White House, headquarters to the Russian parliament, killing, by official counts, 144 individuals. In many provincial areas political activists understood the great conflict that raged in Moscow between the executive and legislative branches as a struggle between the central government and local interests and spoke ominously of the return of Soviet-style centralization. The new constitution that the Yeltsin administration pushed through in the aftermath of the White House tragedy did little to calm such fears: it transferred vast powers to the hands of the president, restricting in important respects the prerogatives of regional representatives and officials.

Throughout the mid- and late-1990s tensions between the central government in Moscow and various regional interests grew. Spates of hostile editorials filled the papers following particularly controversial presidential acts and campaigns; Yeltsin and his associates, critics argued, showed as little tolerance for local initiative as Soviet leaders and displayed the same propensity to micromanage regional affairs. As the controversy surrounding renewed centralization escalated, *kraevedenie,* as might perhaps be expected, gradually resumed its traditional function as a forum for the expression of opposition to the central government. Although some self-identified *kraevedy* maintained a "liberal" stance and defended the president's policies as essential to the implementation of fundamental economic and political reforms, contrary views also began to be voiced. At conferences devoted to regional studies, in guidebooks written for Russian readers, published collections of articles, and textbooks, *kraevedy* more and more frequently expressed anxiety about the role of Moscow (that is, the center) in Russian culture. They described the problems and suffering caused by Muscovite interference in the affairs of other cities and regions in the past; they made veiled references to present power struggles. Anticentrist rhetoric surfaced with particular regularity in studies and discussions of the cultural history of cities like St. Petersburg and Novgorod that once rivaled Moscow in influence and had, at least by some accounts, been terrorized in various periods by the agents of the capital. Ivan IV's great purge of Novgorod in the sixteenth century, the imprisonment and execution of vast numbers of local inhabitants in both cities during the Stalin years, the failure of the center to protect western areas of the Soviet Union during World War II testified, some researchers implied, to Moscow's constant jealousy and intolerance toward all former and potential rivals.[6]

By some measures, interest in *kraevedenie* tapered off during the mid- and late 1990s: Russian-language guidebooks and other publications on regional history and culture sold less well; attendance at and interest in meetings concerning preservation work and ecological issues declined. These changes almost certainly took place as a result of larger processes in Russian society: many families had little disposable income and purchased fewer books; struggling to make ends meet, Russians worked longer hours and had less time for both reading and social activism; economic turmoil and political corruption led to widespread despair; when they did rest from their labors, Russians sought escape as often as enlightenment. Access to both Western and domestically produced popular culture dramatically improved; the social mechanisms that had encouraged virtually universal interest in high culture and academic affairs during the Soviet period broke down. As a result, mass participation in many self-educational endeavors and voluntary cultural projects declined: enrollment for adult enrichment courses at most major museums fell; study circles at cultural centers collapsed; sales of books in many academic fields dwindled.

In as much as similar trends affected a wide variety of other fields and cultural endeavors, the decline in the involvement of adult non-specialists in regional studies that took place in the mid- and late 1990s probably should not be taken as a sign that the discipline itself has entered a significant crisis. By many other indicators, *kraevedenie* has continued to flourish throughout the last decade. Conferences are proliferating; new publications appear regularly (albeit in small editions); academic sections and centers devoted to *kraevedenie* are gradually growing. In many cities, including St. Petersburg, *kraevedenie* has come to represent a substantial, mandatory component of the elementary- and high-school curriculum. Students receive at least an hour a week of instruction in local history, geography, and culture. In some areas specialized academies have opened in which *kraevedenie* represents the primary focus of the curriculum. Math teachers have their students complete word problems based city geography and history, calculating the ages of various buildings and architects. In Russian grammar classes, students compose participle-laden essays about favorite monuments or punctuate preprinted texts about particularly noteworthy sites or events. Music teachers tell their pupils about local ensembles; art teachers take students out to sketch the facades of famous buildings or panoramic views.[7] In St. Petersburg middle- and high-school students in both regular and specialized schools typically read excerpts from key works by Benois, Kurbatov, Antsiferov, and Stolpiansky. Anthologies and textbooks containing fragments of famous guidebooks, essays, and classic literary descriptions of the city are regularly published for their benefit.[8]

Advocates of both the creation of discrete courses in regional studies and the introduction of local materials throughout the school curriculum often contend that *kraevedenie* by its very nature advances the growth of national patriotic sentiment, that the study of local history and culture invariably helps to instill in the young sincere regard for motherland as a whole. This argument is by no means new: as I noted in the body of this manuscript, during the first decades of the twentieth century and the post-Stalin years Russian educators interested in local studies frequently advanced similar claims.[9] Only by learning to love their native city or region, they asserted, could students gain a true attachment to the nation as a whole.

Doubtless a local studies curriculum can act this way. If taught to see what is close at hand as valuable and interesting not just for its intrinsic properties but also because it represents part of a larger (and even more fascinating) whole, many students of *kraevedenie* probably will make the leap from love of neighborhood, city and region to grander forms of geographic attachment. But is this really the primary thrust of *kraevedenie* today? Has local studies in Russia ever consistently functioned in this way? *Kraevedenie* is a complex and ambiguous phenomenon. Although often promoted as an aid to the unification of a vast and diverse state, it has so frequently served as a outlet for regionalist and separatist aspirations that it on balance appears at least as conducive to division as to consolidation. It fosters local pride and rivalries far more obviously than national patriotic sentiment. In this respect, *kraevedenie* may well differ from its closest foreign cousin, *Heimatkunde*, which, many scholars today believe, played an important role in the unification of the modern German state in the late nineteenth century.[10]

In recent years, Russian *kraevedy* have taken some tentative steps to forge ties with their most obvious counterparts in countries like Germany, France, and the United States. They have both participated in and organized international conferences on the problem of regional research; they occasionally invite foreign academics who work on topics unrelated to Russian territory to participate in publications.[11] For the most part, however, contacts with practitioners of other forms of local scholarship have remained fairly tentative and have tended to call attention to *kraevedenie*'s particularity as much as to any larger commonality of interests. *Kraevedenie*'s unusually dramatic history and its connection to various forms of political activism set it apart from many of its most obvious Western counterparts. Viewed from the perspective of social functionality as opposed to thematic focus, in many Western countries, including, most notably, the United States, identity disciplines which explore gender, sexual preference, ethnicity, and race represent closer counterparts to *kraevedenie* than those focusing on regionalism. They seem more obviously relevant to contemporary political and cultural debate; they are more frequently implicated in the struggle between forces for and against fundamental social change.

Perhaps this should come as no surprise. In the United States, perhaps the most significant and lasting cultural debate in our brief history revolves around the question of individual and group rights. Since our nation's conception we have struggled to define equality and asked ourselves to which segments of our population it should extend. Some of the most obvious fissures in our body politic today mark differences in racial and ethnic identity, gender and, now to some extent, sexual preference. In Russia, although the issue of individual and group rights has and does receive substantial attention, the problem of backwardness might arguably be said to have figured more prominently in the national narrative. Time and time again over the course of the last three centuries Russian intellectuals have raised the issue of development. They have tried to isolate Russia's position in relationship to various western countries—

is it ahead, behind, or on some separate continuum entirely? They have asked themselves whether the state should follow in the footsteps of Germany, England, France, and the United States or remain true to native cultural traditions. This great dialogue about models of development, as I suggested earlier in this conclusion, has frequently been conducted through the medium of geographic description. In the works they composed about Moscow, St. Petersburg, and the provinces, Russian writers and social thinkers, beginning in the eighteenth century, commented upon their homeland's state and destiny. When they pointed to positive or negative developments, when they praised or excoriated specific aspects of local life, they also, by implication, took positions on larger problems and issues: the success or failure of national political, economic, and social reforms; the desirability of continued Westernization or modernization. As a result, both regional landscapes and identities became imbued with a different significance in Russian culture than in many other societies. Identification as a Muscovite, a Petersburger, or a resident of the provinces came, in many instances, to imply something about ideological orientation (support of/association with a particular model of development) as well as place of origin or domicile and habits (speech patterns, manners, prevailing forms of dress).

In Russia, the associations evoked by specific landscapes and local identity markers have periodically shifted in response to changes in social and political circumstances. For example, after Petersburg lost its status as capital in 1918, the city and its citizens gradually ceased to be perceived as representative of bureaucracy and imperial might. Similarly, since the collapse of the Soviet Union, Moscow has largely replaced Petersburg as the most "Western" Russian city, and its denizens, like their northern counterpars in the nineteenth century, have increasingly acquired a reputation as "foreigners to their own fatherland."[12] In such instances, the concrete meaning assigned to specific geographic markers has changed, but the terms themselves have not lost any of their overall cultural significance. In every period in modern Russian history, including the present post-Soviet age, regional landscapes and identity categories have remained semantically charged. Small wonder that *kraevedenie*, a discipline that simultaneously explores and promotes local attachments, has thrived in this cultural environment.

Over the course of the last century identity disciplines have come to enjoy enormous popularity in many parts of the globe. It is as if, having achieved passable knowledge of physical existence and tested the most obvious avenues of philosophical and theological speculation, we have turned at last to contemplate the basic vocabulary of selfhood, the terms and categories that human beings employ in their quest to distinguish between self and other. In the West we have begun to ask ourselves whether race represents a cultural construct or has some basis in nature. We interrogate, explore, and manipulate gender and sexual stereotypes. In Russia scholars look at the way in which local landscapes can give rise to myths and patterns of identity, what it means to be a Muscovite, a Petersburger, or an Odessan; they investigate the connections that bind human beings to the regions they inhabit.

Because identity constructs are by no means universal, because cultures around the globe understand and weight even basic concepts like race and sex very differently, one must expect at least some variation in the way in which selfhood is studied in various lands. Disciplines that first emerged in the West, like gender studies, may take on new features and evolve in unexpected ways when transplanted to other environments. Native-born identity disciplines will sometimes persist and even flourish in countries like Russia despite the pressures of Westernization. Although the economic and political dominance of the great democracies of the West and the present system for distributing academic and cultural aid internationally both tend to promote the homogenization of systems of scholarly inquiry, it seems unlikely that cultural differences in the pursuit of knowledge will ever entirely disappear. Disciplines are, like most complex social structures, tremendously resilient: they can adapt and change to accommodate new scientific discoveries, fiscal, political or cultural realities, but, unless they completely cease to express the needs, aspirations, and obsessions of the societies they inhabit, they are unlikely to die away entirely.

NOTES

INTRODUCTION

1. In Bulgaria, for instance, an equivalent discipline known as *kraeznanie* emerged as an organized entity in the years following World War II, presumably, at least in part, under Soviet influence. As Aleksandur Kovachev points out, the word *kraeznanie* rarely appears in Bulgarian publications before this period. Although certainly a phenomenon can exist before it is named, the appearance of terminology often signals a new stage of self-awareness and hence formal organization. *Bulgarskoto kraeznanie v perioda 1878–1912 g.* (Veliko Turnovo: n.p., 1999), 4.

2. *Sovetskii entsiklopedicheskii slovar'*, 4th ed., A. M. Prokhorov (Moscow: Sovetskaia entsiklopediia, 1987), 643. See also the definitions provided in S. I. Ozhigov's *Slovar' russkogo iazyka* and N. A. Milonov, *Literaturnoe kraevedenie* (Moscow: Prosveshchenie, 1985), 3.

3. *Sovetskii entsiklopedicheskii slovar'*, 643.

4. For an account of the history and significance of *Heimatkunde*, see Alon Confino, *The Nation as Local Metaphor: Württemberg, Imperial Germany, and National Memory, 1871–1918* (Chapel Hill: University of North Carolina Press, 1997).

5. For a discussion of the role of identity in lesbian and gay studies, see Ed Cohen, "Are We (Not) What We Are Becoming? Gay 'Identity,' 'Gay Studies,' and the Disciplining of Knowledge," in *Knowledges: Historical and Critical Studies in Disciplinarity*, ed. Ellen Messer-Davidow, David R. Shumway, and David J. Sylvan, 397–421, Knowledge: Disciplinarity and Beyond (Charlottesville: University of Virginia Press, 1993).

6. Jack Amarglio, Stephen Resnick, and Richard D. Wolff, "Division and Difference in the 'Discipline' of Economics," in Messer-Davidow, Shumway, and Sylvan, eds., *Knowledges*, 150–84; Julie Thompson Klein, "Blurring, Cracking, and Crossing: Permeation and the Fracturing of Discipline," in Messer-Davidow, Shumway, and Sylvan, eds., *Knowledges*, 197–98; and James C. Raymond, ed., *English as a Discipline; or, Is there a Plot in the Play?* (Tuscaloosa: University of Alabama Press,

1996). Attempts to argue for internal intellectual consistency as an inherent attribute of "true" disciplinarity seem, at least in some cases, founded on a misreading of Michel Foucault. Foucault argued that a specific kind of unity represented an intrinsic property of individualized discourses, but it was not a simplistic unity of concepts, themes, or style. He allowed for a great deal of heterogeneity within discourses. The unity that he perceived as holding individualized discursive formations together lay outside the boundaries of the discourse, in the rules and relations that governed its formation. *The Archeology of Knowledge and the Discourse on Language,* trans. A. M. Sheridan Smith (New York: Pantheon Books, 1972), 72.

7. Timothy Lenoir, "The Discipline of Nature and the Nature of Disciplines," in Messer-Davidow, Shumway, and Sylvan, eds., *Knowledges,* 72, 76, 80.

8. Cohen, "Are We (Not) What We Are Becoming?" in Messer-Davidow, Shumway, and Sylvan, eds., *Knowledges,* 406–7; Keith W. Hoskin, "Education and the Genesis of Disciplinarity: The Unexpected Reversal," in Messer-Davidow, Shumway, and Sylvan, eds., *Knowledges,* 272–74; David R. Shumway and Ellen Messer-Davidow, "Disciplinarity: An Introduction," *Poetics Today* 12, no. 2 (1991): 212.

9. See, for instance, the description of the organization of the Fifth Annual Lesbian and Gay Studies Conference in Cohen, "Are We (Not) What We Are Becoming?" in Messer-Davidow, Shumway, and Sylvan, *Knowledges,* 418–19.

10. Confino, *The Nation as Local Metaphor,* 9–13.

11. Lev Lur'e and Alexander Kobak, "Rozhdenie i gibel' peterburgskoi idei," *Muzei i gorod,* special issue of *Ars,* no. 2 (1993): 26–27.

12. In June 2000, Lev Lur'e delivered a paper touching upon this issue at an international seminar on *kraevedenie* and Western forms of regional scholarship that was held at the Marble Palace in St. Petersburg. His paper was entitled, "Ispol'zovanie regional'nogo istoricheskogo mifa v sovremennoi politicheskoi bor'be."

13. Foucault, *The Archeology of Knowledge,* 40–44.

14. The city has borne several different names over the course of its three-hundred-year history: from 1914 to 1924 it was known as Petrograd; from 1924 until the end of the Soviet period it bore the name Leningrad; in 1991 the pre-Revolutionary toponym St. Petersburg was restored. In this book, I will shift between the names St. Petersburg, Petrograd, and Leningrad depending upon the period under discussion. In contexts where more than one name might reasonably be used, I will generally favor "St. Petersburg."

15. Celia Applegate, *A Nation of Provincials: The German Idea of Heimat* (Berkeley and Los Angeles: University of California Press, 1990); Confino, *The Nation as Local Metaphor.*

16. When we deem something "influential," we suggest that it is atypical: we imply that it establishes norms instead of adhering to them. For all of its much ballyhooed "uniqueness," St. Petersburg has exerted a pronounced architectural and cultural influence on other Russian population centers throughout its history.

17. As I explain in Chapter 1, I believe that in at least some periods of time and in the case of certain writers the *putevoditel'* has transcended the norms of the nonaesthetic and nonliterary and acquired some of the functionality and characteristics of a true artistic medium. That being said, when I employ the word "literary" here, I am thinking primarily of the less-elevated meanings assigned to the word "literature," form or body of writing as opposed to imaginative work of recognized artistic value.

18. Most *putevoditeli* describe geographic areas, cities, museums, monuments, or other sites. The term, however, can also be used to refer to certain forms of bibliographic literature, including guides to library and archival collections and surveys of current research in a single scientific field.

CHAPTER 1

1. The text appeared under the initials "H. G." *Exacte Relation von der von Sr. Czaarschen Majestät Petro Alexiowitz, an dem grossen Newa Strohm und der Ost-See neu erbaueten Vestung und Stadt St. Petersburg, wie auch vom dem Castel Cron Schloss und derselben umliegenden Gegend, Ferner Relation von den uhralten russischen Gebrauch der Wasser Weyh und Heiligung, Nebst einigen besondern Anmerkungen auffgezeichnet* (Leipzig: n.p., 1713).

2. Introduction to *Peterburg Petra I v inostrannykh opisaniiakh: Vvedenie, teksty, kommentarii*, ed. Iu. N. Bespiatykh, Panorama istorii (Leningrad: Nauka, 1991), 10.

3. P. N. Stolpiansky, *Peterburg: Kak voznik, osnovalsia i ros Sankt-Piterburkh*, Liki goroda (St. Petersburg: Nega, 1995), 116–17.

4. As James Cracraft notes, some European visitors did write negative accounts of St. Petersburg: "St. Petersburg: The Russian Cosmopolis," in *Russia Engages the World, 1453–1825*, ed. Cynthia Hyla Whittaker (Cambridge: Harvard University Press, 2003), 42–43.

5. See Iurii Bespiatykh's comments on Elizabeth Justice's *A Voyage to Russia* (York: n.p., 1739) in the introduction to *Peterburg Anny Ioannovny v inostrannykh opisaniiakh: Vvedenie, teksty, kommentarii*, ed. Iu. N. Bespiatykh (St. Petersburg: BLITS, 1997), 12.

6. "O zachatii i zdanii tsarstvuiushchego grada Sanktpeterburga v leto ot pervogo dni Adama 7211. Po rozhdestve Iisus Khristove 1703," in Bespiatykh, ed., *Peterburg Petra I*, 258–62.

7. Excerpt from Feofan Prokopovich, *Istoriia imperatora Petra Velikogo ot rozhdeniia ego do Poltavskoi batalii i vziatiia v plen ostal'nykh shvedskikh voisk pri Perevolochne, vkliuchitel'no*, 2nd ed. (Moscow: n.p., 1788), 82–89, reprinted in Bespiatykh, ed., *Peterburg Petra I*, 255–57.

8. *Die so genannte Moscowitische Brieffe, oder die, wider die löbliche Russische Nation von einem aus der andern Welt zurück gekommenen Italiäner ausgesprengte abendtheurliche Verläumdungen und Tausend-Lügen aus dem Französischen übersetzt, mit einem zulänglichen Register versehen, und dem Brieffsteller so wohl, als seinen gleichgesinnten Freunden, mit dienlichen Erinnerungen wieder heimgeschickt von einem*

Teutschen (Frankfurt and Leipzig: n.p., 1738). For facts regarding the book's publication I rely on Iu. Bespiatykh's introduction to *Peterburg Anny Ioannovny*, 34–36.

9. Most later Romanovs worked very hard to create the impression among their subjects that they were carrying on the policies of Peter I. As Richard Wortman has shown, they constantly linked their own names and faces to Peter's in sculptural monuments, paintings, and firework displays, creating a powerful symbolic web that insured that any reference to the great deeds of Peter also tended to reflect positively on the dynasty in general. *Scenarios of Power: Myth and Ceremony in Russian Monarchy*, vol. 1 (Princeton: Princeton University Press, 1995), 85.

10. See, for instance, "O zachatii i zdanii tsarstvuiushchego grada Sanktpeterburga v leto ot pervogo dni Adama 7211. Po rozhdestve Iisus Khristove 1703," in Bespiatykh, ed., *Peterburg Petra I*, 261.

11. Christopher Ely, *This Meager Nature: Landscape and National Identity in Imperial Russia* (Dekalb: Northern Illinois University Press, 2002), 36–37. As I note later in this chapter, more negative assessments of the reforms do figure in the folk tradition. See Iurii M. Lotman and Boris Uspensky, "Otzvuki kontseptsii 'Moskva—tretii Rim' v ideologii Petra Pervogo," in *Iu. M. Lotman: Izbrannye stat'i*, 3 vols. (Tallinn: Aleksandra, 1993), 3:203.

12. P. N. Petrov, *Istoriia Sankt-Peterburga s osnovaniia goroda do vvedeniia v deistvie vybornogo gorodskogo upravleniia, po uchrezhdeniiam o guberniiakh, 1703–1782* (St. Petersburg: Tipografiia Glazunova, 1884), 6.

13. M. I. Slukhovsky, "K biografii pervogo russkogo knigoveda A. I. Bogdanova," in *Kniga: Issledovaniia i materialy*, vol. 26 (Moscow: Kniga, 1973), 208.

14. Andrei I. Bogdanov, *Opisanie Sanktpeterburga. Polnoe izdanie unikal'nogo rossiiskogo istoriko-geograficheskogo truda serediny XVIII veka*, ed. K. I. Logachev and V. S. Sobolev (St. Petersburg: Severo-Zapadnaia Bibleiskaia Komissiia, Sankt-Peterburgskii filial Arkhiva RAN, 1997), 99. The phrase *Tsarstvuiushchii Grad* is a reference to Constantinople, also known in Russia as Tsargrad (present-day Istanbul, Turkey).

15. Ibid., 106, 123, 138, 340, 370–71.

16. Slukhovsky, "K biografii pervogo russkogo knigoveda A. I. Bogdanova," 208.

17. A. I. Bogdanov, *Istoricheskoe, geograficheskoe i topograficheskoe opisanie Sanktpeterburga ot nachala zavedeniia ego s 1703 po 1751 god*, ed. and suppl. Vasily Ruban (St. Petersburg: n.p., 1779). In 1778 a brief excerpt from Bogdanov's work was published in *Mesiatseslov na leto ot rozhdestva Khristova 1778*. For more information on this, see I. N. Koblents, *Andrei Ivanovich Bogdanov, 1692–1766* (Moscow: Izdatel'stvo AN SSSR, 1958), 58.

18. I. N. Koblents, *Andrei Ivanovich Bogdanov*, 58–60.

19. *Syn otechestva*, no. 8 (1839): 8–10, as noted in I. N. Koblents, *Andrei Ivanovich Bogdanov*, 60.

20. A. A. Titov, ed., *Dopolnenie k istoricheskomu, geograficheskomu i topograficheskomu opisaniiu Sanktpeterburga s 1751 po 1762 goda sochinennoe A. Bogdanovym, Izdanie*

glasnogo Sankt- Peterburgskoi gorodskoi dumy P. A. Fokina v pamiat' dvukhsotletnego iubileia (Moscow: Tipo-litografiia I. M. Mashistova, 1903).

21. I. G. Georgi, *Opisanie rossiisko-imperatorskogo stolichnogo goroda Sankt-Peterburga i dostopamiatnostei v okrestnostiakh onogo, s planom*, Mramornaia seriia (St. Petersburg: Liga, 1996), 24.

22. Ibid., 20–21, 22.

23. Ibid., 19.

24. Ibid, 53. St. Petersburg briefly fell into decline after the death of Peter I in 1725. Under Peter II, the Russian court relocated to Moscow. Although the city regained its status and prestige soon after Anna Ioannovna ascended to the throne in 1730, for political reasons Georgi chooses to imply that it remained in decline for far longer. He suggests that only two tsars—Peter I and the present monarch Catherine II—have committed adequate resources to the city.

25. Ibid., 80–81, 91, 109, 119, 121, 125.

26. Ibid., 53.

27. "S chego nachinalas' peterburgiana: Opisanie putevoditelei po gorodu s momenta ikh vozniknoveniia do serediny XIX stoletiia," in *Nevskii Arkhiv: Istoriko-kraevedcheskii sbornik*, issue 3, ed. A. I. Dobkin and A. V. Kobak (St. Petersburg: Atheneum-Feniks, 1997), 485.

28. *Putevoditel' k drevnostiam i dostopamiatnostiam moskovskim, rukovodstvuiushchii liubopytstvuiushchego po chetyrem chastiam seia stolitsy k dee—mesto—opisatel'nomu poznaniiu vsekh zasluzhivaiushikh primechanie mest i zdanii* (Moscow: Universitetskaia tipografiia u V. Okorokova, 1792). See Iurii Aleksandrov, *Moskva: Dialog putevoditelei* (Moscow: Moskovskii rabochii, 1986), 20.

29. *Moskva ili istoricheskii putevoditel' po znamenitoi stolitse Gosudarstva, zakliuchaiushchii v sebe: 1e Istoriiu sego prestol'nogo goroda ot nachala onogo do nashikh vremen; 2e podrobnoe opisanie vsekh vazhnikh sobytii, sluchivshikhsia v onom; 3e opisanie nakhodivshchikhsia v nem redkostei, monastyrei, tserkvei i raznykh zdanii i pamiatnikov, s pokazaniem vremeni i prichin ikh osnovaniia; 4e svedenie o vsekh mestakh, zamechatel'nykh po kakomu nibud' Istoricheskomu proizshestviiu; 5e obychai drevnikh vremen; 6e razlichnye tserkovnye i grazhdanskie tserimonialy; 7e bogatstvo i shtat Dvora Tsarskogo; 8e opisanie odezhdy, monetnogo kursa i tsen proizvedenii, k raznym vremenam otnosiashchikhsia; 9e biografii Metropolitov i Patriarkhov; 10e statisticheskoe i topograficheskoe obozrenie sei stolitsy v nyneshnem ee sostoianii* (Moscow: Tipografiia S. Selivanovskogo, 1827).

30. In the introduction to this book, Shreder mentions that he would like to publish a second volume devoted to the imperial suburbs surrounding the capital eventually. This plan was never realized. The one-volume guide that does exist focuses entirely on St. Petersburg proper. *Noveishii putevoditel' po Sankt-Peterburgu s istoricheskimi ukazaniiami* (St. Petersburg: Pervyi kadetskii korpus, 1820), vii.

31. Pavel Svin'in, *Dostopamiatnosti Sanktpeterburga i ego okrestnostei* (St. Petersburg: Tipografiia V. Plavil'shchikova, 1816), 1:4; Shreder, *Noveishii putevoditel'*, iii-iv. Svinin's

work initially appeared as a bilingual edition with French and Russian texts on facing pages.

32. Svin'in *Dostopamiatnosti Sanktpeterburga*, 1:72; 3: 44; Shreder, *Noveishii putevoditel'*, 5, 49, 54, 146.

33. *Dostopamiatnosti Sanktpeterburga*, 4:22.

34. See, for instance, Svin'in, *Dostopamiatnosti Sanktpeterburga*, 3:122–38; Shreder *Noveishii putevoditel'*, 10–11, 99, 115–16.

35. Hubertus F. Jahn, "'Us': Russians on Russianness," in *National Identity in Russian Culture: An Introduction*, ed. Simon Franklin and Emma Widdis (Cambridge: Cambridge University Press, 2004), 58–62; Christopher Ely, *This Meager Nature*, 37.

36. *Dostopamiatnosti Sanktpeterburga*, 2: 96, 130. Exaggeration represented Svinin's hallmark as a writer. A minor figure in nineteenth-century literary history, he was the subject of many vicious epigrams and, rumor has it, served as the model for the character Khlestakov in Gogol's *The Inspector General*. Svinin did perform one great service to the literary world: in 1820 he founded the journal *Notes of the Fatherland* (*Otechestvennye zapiski*). V. Danilov, "Dedushka russkikh istoricheskikh zhurnalov: 'Otechestvennye zapiski' P. P. Svin'ina," *Istoricheskii vestnik* (July 1915): 109–29.

37. *Noveishii putevoditel'*, 10–12, 87–88, 215.

38. Svin'in, *Dostopamiatnosti Sanktpeterburga*, 1: 2–4.

39. Gavrila Derzhavin, "Shestvie po Volkhovu Rossiiskoi Amfitrity," in *Peterburg v russkoi poezii XVIII-nachalo XX veka*, ed. M. V. Otradin (Leningrad: Izdatel'stvo Leningradskogo universiteta, 1988), 45.

40. Mikhail Lomonosov, "Oda na den' vosshestviia na prestol ee velichestva gosudaryni imperatritsy Elizavety Petrovny 1748 goda," in Mikhail Lomonosov, *Izbrannye proizvedeniia*, ed. A. A. Morozova, Biblioteka poeta, Bol'shaia seriia, 2nd ed. (Moscow: Sovetskii pisatel', 1965), 133.

41. Julie Buckler argues that eighteenth-century literary works describe St. Petersburg in a more eclectic manner than scholars have generally recognized. Poets often wrote about the city in middle as well as high generic registers; within the context of a single poem they might shift from the odic to a softer elegiac or idyllic tone. Buckler's point is well taken, but I would note that the authors she cites all remain overwhelmingly positive in their appraisal of the city. Although perhaps to some extent eclectic in form, descriptions of St. Petersburg in eighteenth-century literary works are remarkably consistent in their ideological orientation. *Mapping St. Petersburg: Imperial Text and Cityshape* (Princeton: Princeton University Press, 2005), 67–73.

42. See, for instance K. N. Batiushkov, "Progulka v Akademiiu Khudozhestv," in *Peterburg v russkom ocherke XIX veka*, ed. M. V. Otradin (Leningrad: Izdatel'stvo Leningradskogo universiteta, 1984), 25–31; Petr Viazemsky, "Peterburg," in Otradin, ed., *Peterburg v russkoi poezii*, 67–70.

43. Kondratii Ryleev, "Davno mne serdtse govorilo," in Otradin, ed., *Peterburg v russkoi poezii*, 59–60; Alexander Bestuzhev-Marlinsky, "Podrazhanie pervoi satire

Bualo," in Otradin, ed., *Peterburg v russkoi poezii,* 57; Alexander Pushkin, "Volnost'," in Otradin, ed., *Peterburg v russkoi poezii,* 80.

44. Alexander Pushkin, *The Bronze Horseman,* trans. Charles Johnston, in *An Anthology of Russian Literature from Earliest Writings to Modern Fiction: Introduction to a Culture,* ed. Nicholas Rzhevsky (Armonk, N.Y.: M. E. Sharpe, 1996), 122, 128–29.

45. With the exception of "The Overcoat," Gogol's Petersburg Tales were composed between 1833 and 1835 and published in 1835 and 1836. Gogol worked on various drafts of the "Overcoat" from 1839 to 1842. It first appeared in the 1842 edition of his collected works. Dostoevsky completed his first novel *Poor Folk* in 1845 and published it in 1846.

46. Iurii M. Lotman, "Simvolika Peterburga i problemy semiotiki goroda," in *Iu. M. Lotman: Izbrannye stat'i,* 2: 13; Iurii M. Lotman and Boris A. Uspensky, "Otzvuki kontseptsii 'Moskva—tretii Rim' v ideologii Petra Pervogo," in *Iu. M. Lotman: Izbrannye stat'i,* 3: 203.

47. *Panorama Sanktpeterburga,* 3 vols. (St. Petersburg: Tipografiia vdovy Pliushara s synom, 1834), 3:12–210. Enormously generically complex as a work, *Panorama* attempts to meet multiple needs simultaneously. In the introduction Bashutsky himself implies that it represents a cross between a traditional history, a statistical compendium, and a guidebook. He specifically notes that he chose a small typeface so that readers could carry individual volumes on tours. A planned fourth volume would have contained more material for sightseers, including detailed descriptions of local architecture and a series of historical excursions. Financial problems prevented its publication. N. G. Okhotin, "A. P. Bashutskii i ego kniga," in *Nashi spisannye s natury russkimi,* facsimile edition with extensive commentary, 2 vols. (1841–42; reprint, Moscow: Kniga, 1986), 2:8–9. See page viii and xiii of the introduction to volume one of *Panorama* for Bashutsky's comments.

48. *Opisanie Sanktpeterburga i uezdnykh gorodov S. Peterburgskoi gubernii,* 4 vols. (St. Petersburg: Tipografiia S. Peterburgskogo gubernskogo pravleniia, 1841), 3:1–55.

49. In the last chapter of this book I discuss a number of books conventionally classified as guidebooks in which the image of the city of St. Petersburg is suffused with horror and pathos. Written during the difficult Civil War years, a time in which many Russian intellectuals came to perceive the northern capital as dead or dying, these texts treat St. Petersburg as a lifeless ruin. It is worth noting, however, that even in these grim works, St. Petersburg's past, its cultural legacy, is, as in a eulogy, extolled.

50. One can, of course, imagine a guide in which the author provides advice on how to minimize the discomforts of life in a city viewed as profoundly disagreeable without making any effort to extol its virtues or detail noteworthy sites. Such a work would, however, effectively overturn the discursive conventions standard to both the Russian *putevoditel'* and the American/Western European guidebook. Isn't this why we find the description of the armchair travel guides in Anne Tyler's novel *The Accidental Tourist* so witty? In having her character write joyless guides for the business traveler, Tyler simultaneously pokes fun at American xenophobia and, by negating it, at the

relentlessly enthusiastic tone we associate with the guidebook as a genre. *The Accidental Tourist* (Ontario: Penguin, 1986), 12–13.

51. See, for instance, the introduction to Ivan Pushkarev, *Opisanie Sanktpeterburga i uezdnykh gorodov S. Peterburgskoi gubernii*, vol. 1 (St. Petersburg: privately published, 1839).

52. Gary Saul Morson, *The Boundaries of Genre: Dostoevsky's Diary of a Writer and the Traditions of Literary Utopia* (Evanston: Northwestern University Press, 1981), 15.

53. Viktor Bur'ianov, *Progulka s det'mi po S.-Peterburgu i ego okrestnostiam*, 3 vols. (St. Petersburg: Tipografiia glavnogo upravleniia putei soobshcheniia i publichnikh zdanii, 1838), 1:2, 228–29; 3:19, 143.

54. *Panorama Sankt Peterburga*, 3:111–48; 2:194–271. The Prince-Pope was the head of the Most Drunken Synod of Fools and Jesters, a forum for drunken revelry created by Peter I as a parody of the rites and ceremonies of the official Orthodox Church.

55. Bashutsky, for instance, contributed to the development of the sketch as well as the guidebook. In the early 1840s he published the anthology *Our Folk Sketched from Nature by Russians* (Nashi spisannye s natury russkimi), which was modeled after the well-known French edition, *Les Français et les Anglais peints par eux-mêmes*. The section of Ivan Pushkarev's *Opisanie Sanktpeterburga i uezdnykh gorodov S. Peterburgskoi gubernii* entitled "Melkaia promyshlennost' i sharlatanstvo v S. Peterburge" (3:1–55) might reasonably be termed a sketch.

56. Morson, *The Boundaries of Genre*, 15–16.

57. V. G. Belinsky, introduction to *Fiziologiia Peterburga*, Literaturnye pamiatniki (Moscow: Nauka, 1991), 7.

58. Ibid., 12.

59. Review of *Fiziologiia Peterburga, sostavlennaia iz trudov russkikh literatorov*, ch. 1, in Konstantin Aksakov and Ivan Aksakov, *Literaturnaia kritika* (Moscow: Sovremennik, 1981), 161–66.

60. In fact, the last paragraph of Aksakov's review, although negative in its assessment of the role of St. Petersburg in Russian culture, acknowledges and might be interpreted as encouraging the depiction of Russia's diverse regions: "Since the notion of national character appeared in Russian literature, individual regions of enormous Russia have also begun to express their particularity in literature. In accordance with this general trend, Petersburg has expressed itself in literary activity, imparting to it its particular character. Concentrating in itself all the wealth of Russia, it has increased commerce in books and imparted this commercial character to literature." Ibid., 166.

61. See, for instance, V. G. Belinsky, "Moskva i Peterburg," in *Fiziologiia Peterburga*, 14; A. I. Gertsen, "Moskva i Peterburg," in Otradin, ed., *Peterburg v russkom ocherke XIX veka*, 51–58.

62. See, for instance, E. Karnovich, *Sanktpeterburg v statisticheskom otnoshenii* (St. Petersburg: Voennaia tipografiia, 1860); *Sanktpeterburg. Issledovanie po istorii, topografii*

i statistike stolitsy. Izdanie Tsentral'nogo komiteta Ministerstva vnutrennikh del (St. Petersburg: Tipografiia V. Bezobrazova, 1870).

63. It seems worth noting that in Moscow the guidebook tradition flourished in the latter half of the nineteenth century. Two factors probably explain its continued growth: the image of Moscow was not as problematized as that of St. Petersburg in this period; the southern capital figured less prominently in works of Russian literature than its northern counterpart, so guidebook writers faced somewhat less competition. For a survey of guides to Moscow from the second half of the nineteenth century, see Aleksandrov, *Moskva: Dialog putevoditelei,* 27–32.

64. "Mikhail Ivanovich Semevskii: Biograficheskii ocherk," in *Pavlovsk: Ocherk istorii i opisanii, 1777–1787,* ed. A. A. Alekseev (1887; reprint, St. Petersburg: Liuks Plius, 1997), 586–87.

65. Ibid., 591–92.

66. Some new guides to present-day St. Petersburg also emerged in this period. See, for instance, V. O. Mikhnevich, *Peterburg ves' na ladoni, s planom Peterburga, ego panoramoi s ptich'ego poleta, 22 kartinkami i s pribavleniem kalendaria* (St. Petersburg: Izdanie knigoprodavtsa N.N. Plotnikova, 1874). Sketches focusing on contemporary life, including many works depicting the capital's "underbelly" and lower classes, also continued to appear. Two of the best late-nineteenth-century collections of physiological sketches are A. A. Bakhtiarov, *Briukho Peterburga: Ocherki stolichnoi zhizni* (St. Petersburg: Izdanie F. Pavlenkova, 1888); N. N. Zhivotov, *Peterburgskie profili,* 4 vols. (St. Petersburg: n.p., 1894–95).

67. *Opisanie Petergofa, 1501–1868* (1868; reprint, St. Petersburg: Aurora, 1991).

68. "Mikhail Ivanovich Semevskii: Biograficheskii ocherk," in *Pavlovsk: Ocherk istorii i opisanii,* 595–96.

69. Geirot, *Opisanie Petergofa,* 106; Semevsky, *Pavlovsk,* 47, 56–57.

70. Geirot, *Opisanie Petergofa,* 106–8; Semevsky, *Pavlovsk,* 115–17.

71. "Mikhail Ivanovich Semevskii: Biograficheskii ocherk," in Semevsky, *Pavlovsk,* 596.

72. *Staryi Peterburg,* Mramornaia seriia (1889; reprint, Leningrad: Titul, 1990), 78.

73. Ibid., 312.

74. Ibid., 73, 154, 442.

75. See, for instance, Viktor Bur'ianov, *Progulka s det'mi po S.-Peterburgu i ego okrestnostiam,* 3 vols. (St. Petersburg: Tipografiia glavnogo upravleniia putei soobshcheniia i publichnikh zdanii, 1838), 1:33, 43.

76. A. I. Gertsen, "Moskva i Peterburg," in Otradin, ed., *Peterburg v russkom ocherke XIX veka,* 52.

CHAPTER 2

1. See, for instance, Vsevolod Petrov, "The World of Art Movement," in Vsevolod Petrov and Alexander Kamensky, *The World of Art Movement in Early-Twentieth-Century Russia* (Leningrad: Aurora, 1991), 134.

2. Benois's first article on "old Petersburg" appeared in *World of Art*, no. 15 (1899) under the pseudonym B. Veniaminov. Igor Grabar and Ivan Fomin also contributed articles praising the artistic legacy of the early nineteenth century. Fomin's work focused on Moscow.

3. "Monplezir," *Mir iskusstva*, nos. 2–3 (1901): 121–22.

4. A. Benois, "Arkhitektura Peterburga," *Mir iskusstva*, [no. 4] (1902): 84.

5. B. Veniaminov [A. Benois], "Agoniia Peterburga," *Mir iskusstva*, no. 15 (1899): 17.

6. "Zhivopisnyi Peterburg," in *Skaz o Sankt-Peterburkhe: Iz istorii goroda Sankt-Peterburga v bytnost' ego stolitseiu gosudarstva rossiiskogo. Sbornik podlinnykh povestvovanii sostavlennykh dlia pol'zy i udovol'stviia pochtennykh gorozhan i uvazhaemykh gospod puteshestvennikov* (Leningrad: Askat, 1991), 132. The article initially appeared in *Mir iskusstva*, no. 1 (1902): 1–5.

7. I refer to the monuments by Carlo Rastrelli and Étienne-Maurice Falconet. See George Hamilton Heard, *The Art and Architecture of Russia*, The Pelican History of Art (New York: Penguin, 1983), 352–54. In the case of the Falconet monument, scholars have interpreted Peter I's dress in various ways. The laurel wreath on the tsar's head suggests a connection to Rome. The smock, cloak, and boots the tsar wears and the bearskin that serves as his saddle, as Julie Buckler notes, seem more "folkloric" and perhaps link Peter I to Alexander Nevsky. Taken as a whole, the statue clearly recalls the monument to Marcus Aurelius on the Capitoline in Rome. Buckler, *Mapping St. Petersburg*, 73.

8. Igor Grabar described Rossi's work in the following terms: "What scope, what an expanse of architectural designs! This man was bursting to build whole squares and streets. The Romans—those were his teachers, and he wanted his architecture to be comparable to theirs. The grandeur and splendor of Roman constructions of the time of Agrippa, Hadrian, and Caracalla attracted his imagination, and he dreamed of making Petersburg into a second Rome." *Peterburgskaia arkhitektura v XVIII i XIX vekakh*, reprint of *Istoriia russkogo iskusstva*, vol. 3 (St. Petersburg: Lenizdat, 1994), 354.

9. In their ornately decorated compositions, late-nineteenth-century architects were specifically reacting against the clean, forbidding lines and uniform facades of St. Petersburg's vast Empire ensembles. In a larger sense, however, their work also signals a revolt against classical standards in general. The great palaces built in the "early classical" style during the reigns of Catherine II and Paul were, to a certain extent, also under attack. Advocates of the neo-Russian look often went even further, rejecting everything built in an "alien," imported style.

10. Richard Wortman speaks extensively about the political implications of the neo-Russian style in his article, "Moscow and Petersburg: The Problem of Political Center in Tsarist Russia, 1881–1914," in *Rites of Power: Symbolism, Ritual and Politics since the Middle Ages*, ed. Sean Wilentz (Philadelphia: University of Pennsylvania Press, 1985), 244–71.

11. "Zhivopisnyi Peterburg," *Skaz o Sankt-Peterburkhe*, 134.

12. Ibid., 138.

13. Ibid., 138, 136.

14. In a 1984 article, Leonid Dolgopolov suggests that, in his critical prose, Alexander Benois focused solely on St. Petersburg's magnificent "external appearance" and failed to detect the "hidden essence" that had preoccupied Russian writers from Pushkin to Bely. Dolgopolov claims, however, that in his work as a visual artist, particularly his illustrations for Pushkin's "Bronze Horseman," Benois transcended the limits of his own perspective, abandoning "the idealistic attitude to the city that was characteristic of the eighteenth century and had been resurrected in the 'retrospective' works of the 'World of Art' group," and rejoining the main line of Russian cultural development. As will be seen, I feel Dolgopolov goes too far in his analysis. "Peterburg Aleksandra Benua," *Leningradskaia panorama*, ed. Ia. A. Gordin (Leningrad: Sovetskii pisatel', 1984) 391, 401, 403.

15. "Zhivopisnyi Peterburg," in *Skaz o Sankt-Peterburkhe*, 132–33.

16. Ibid., 133.

17. Even before the first issue of *World of Art* appeared, Benois worried that the periodical might prove too contemporary in its orientation to suit his inclinations. See the citations from Benois's correspondence provided in N. Lapshina, *Mir iskusstva: Ocherki istorii i tvorcheskoi praktiki* (Moscow: Iskusstvo, 1977), 42–43.

18. *Moi vospominaniia*, 2:314.

19. See, for instance, ibid., 2:313.

20. Ibid., 2:361.

21. The magazine attracted favorable attention and subscriptions grew. It did not, however, make money. Adrian Prakhov, the art historian who succeeded Benois as editor at *Art Treasures of Russia* in 1903, complained that his predecessor had run up an enormous deficit. The great art journals of the turn of the century rarely proved profitable due to the enormous cost of creating quality reproductions. *World of Art*, *Art Treasures of Russia*, and *Bygone Years* all struggled financially. "Deiatel'nost' imperatorskogo obshchestva pooshchreniia khudozhestv," *Khudozhestvennye sokrovishcha Rossii*, nos. 11–12 (1907): 232–33.

22. In 1901, the bulk of the reproductions and photographs included in *World of Art* began to appear in a single block at the beginning of each issue. The major articles and the chronicle of current events would then follow.

23. Issues 1 and 2–3 for the year 1903 explore the topic "Peter I: Material for an Illustration of His Time." These issues were almost entirely assembled by Benois, but were printed after he had resigned from his post as editor at the magazine. On the mask, see "Gipsovaia golova Petra I v Imperatorskom Ermitazhe," *Khudozhestvennye sokrovishcha Rossii*, nos. 2–3 (1903): 83–84.

24. See, for instance, *Mir iskusstva*, no. 1 (1902) on St. Petersburg and nos. 8–9 (1902), which focused on a Western European art exhibit. As I have already mentioned,

World of Art had experimented with thematic issues even before the emergence of *Art Treasures of Russia*.

25. See, respectively, the issues for July–September for 1907, 1908, 1914, and 1916.

26. Igor' Grabar', rev. of *Pavlovsk* by V. Kurbatov, *Starye gody* (April 1912): 52. The review includes some general remarks on the shortcomings of available sources on St. Petersburg. Grabar cites Petrov's *Istoriia S.-Peterburga* as an example of a work with a particularly inadequate scholarly apparatus.

27. Review of *Ob'iasnitel'nyi putevoditel' po khudozhestvennym sobraniiam Peterburga*, by D. D. Ivanov, *Mir iskusstva*, no. 6 (1904): 126–27.

28. See, for instance, V. Kurbatov, *Peterburg: Khudozhestvenno-istoricheskii ocherk i obzor khudozhestvennogo bogatstva stolitsy* (St. Petersburg: Lenizdat, 1993), 3, 8, 30, 40, 109.

29. For Benois's account of the conflict, see *Moi vospominaniia*, 2:382. For the original review, see "Frantsuzskaia vystavka," *Mir iskusstva*, no. 1 (1903): 13–15. Prakhov had run the art department of the journal *Pchela*, or *Russkaia illiustratsiia*, as it was also known, in the 1870s. He was a professor at St. Petersburg University and a popular lecturer. Like Benois, he had occasionally helped Princess Maria Tenisheva purchase art for her collection during the late 1890s.

30. See, for instance, *Moi vospominaniia*, 2:391–92.

31. *Khudozhestvennye sokrovishcha Rossii*, nos. 9–12 (1903). The issue was republished in the late 1990s as part of a larger collection of material on Pavlovsk: Iu. V. Mudrov, ed., *Pavlovsk: Imperatorskii dvorets, stranitsy istorii* (St. Petersburg: Art-palas, 1997). In 1905, Prakhov put together another thematic issue on Pavlovsk, this time focusing on the imperial park and the monuments it contained. *Khudozhestvennye sokrovisha*, nos. 6–8 (1905).

32. *Khudozhestvennye sokrovishcha Rossii*, nos. 9, 10, 11, and 12 (1904). Although these issues primarily focus on the palace complex, they also contain some articles on other subjects.

33. Both Iaremich and Kurbatov were minor figures in the World of Art movement and regularly attended the editorial meetings of Diaghilev's magazine. I will speak briefly about Kurbatov in Chapter 3. Iaremich is principally known as an illustrator, art historian, and collector. He served as the curator of the drawing department at the Hermitage after the Revolution. Benois, *Moi vospominaniia*, 2: 283, 378, 430–31, 680; M. V. Dobuzhinsky, *Vospominaniia*, ed. G. I. Chugunov (Moscow: Nauka, 1987), 210, 416.

34. Dobuzhinsky, *Vospominaniia*, 198.

35. *World of Art*, no. 2 (1904): unnumbered page.

36. Benois did, however, continue to collect material on Tsarskoe Selo on his own. In 1910 he published a spectacular volume on the palace complex: *Tsarskoe Selo v tsarstvovanii imperatritsy Elisavety Petrovny* (St. Petersburg: Golike i Vil'borg, 1910). For a description of Benois's research process, see his *Moi vospominaniia*, 2:405.

37. For a more detailed account of the journal's financial difficulties, see John E. Bowlt, *The Silver Age: Russian Art of the Early Twentieth Century and the "World of Art" Group,* ORP Studies in Russian Art History (Newtonville, Mass.: Oriental Research Partners, 1982), 62–65.

38. *Moi vospominaniia,* 2:410.

39. "Deiatel'nost' imperatorskogo obshchestva pooshchreniia khudozhestv," *Khudozhestvennye sokrovishcha Rossii,* nos. 11–12 (1907): 233.

40. Ibid.

41. *Moi vospominaniia,* 2:336.

42. *Starye gody* (February 1907): 75. See also the programmatic statement written by the journal's first editor V. A. Vereshchagin for the first issue: "Starye gody," *Starye gody* (January 1907): 1.

43. "Khronika," *Starye gody* (May 1907): 175; V. Kurbatov, "Proekt porchi inzhenernogo zamka," *Starye gody* (July–September 1907): 446.

44. "Dvortsovye stroitel'stva imperatora Nikolaia I," *Starye gody* (July–September 1913): 173.

45. Ibid., 174. Baron Nikolai Vrangel also contributed a substantial article to the same thematic issue. Like Benois and Lanceray, he opens his piece by acknowledging that tastes change with each passing generation. He suggests, however, that at times the "children" may be too enthusiastic in their pursuit of novelty and by accident may destroy the old temples of art. Vrangel seems to have seen his colleagues' attempts to reconsider the role of Nicholas I in Russian culture as fraught with this kind of danger. "Iskusstvo i gosudar' Nikolai Pavlovich," *Starye gody* (July–September 1913): 54.

46. In her book on St. Petersburg, Katerina Clark suggests that Benois and his fellow preservationists had "a distinctly utopian streak," that they had a clear vision of how they wanted St. Petersburg to look and sought to establish in the city a "static, monumental landscape" through a process of "spatial purification." Preservationism, Clark suggests, was "about power and control," a form of "national aggrandizement and centralization," and hence might, in some respects, be equated with the later socialist realist tradition and the values of Stalinism. I believe this argument fails to take into account the evolution of preservationist thinking in the second decade of the twentieth century. *Petersburg: Crucible of Cultural Revolution* (Cambridge: Harvard University Press, 1995), 63, 60, 64, 73.

47. The summer 1914 thematic issue of *Bygone Years* was republished as a book in 1995. The publication statistics I cite here are taken from the introduction to the volume. I. A., "Zhurnal 'Starye gody' i ego avtory," *Gatchina pri Pavle Petroviche Tsesareviche i Imperatore,* Mramornaia seriia (St. Petersburg: Liga, 1995), 4. In comparison, *World of Art* rarely had more than a thousand subscribers. Bowlt, *The Silver Age,* 62.

48. While working on *Bygone Years,* Sergei Troinitsky and Baron Nikolai Vrangel filled posts at the Hermitage. Benois published a guide to the museum's painting galleries in 1911, allowing visitors unprecedented access to basic information on the

collection. Vrangel cataloged the holdings of the Academy of Arts. S. Makovsky went on to edit the art journals *Apollo* (*Apollon*) in 1909 and *The Russian Icon* (*Russkaia ikona*) in 1913.

49. For a discussion of the meanings assigned to the terms *obshchestvo* and *obshchestvennost'*, see Abbott Gleason, "The Terms of Russian Social History," in *Between Tsar and People: Educated Society and the Quest for Public Identity in Late Imperial Russia*, ed. Edith W. Clowes, Samuel D. Kassow, and James L. West (Princeton: Princeton University Press, 1991), 15–27.

50. "Voluntary Associations, Civic Culture, and *Obshchestvennost'* in Moscow," in Clowes, Kassow, and West, eds., *Between Tsar and People*, 139.

51. V. Kurbatov, "Zapozdalye zaboty," *Starye gody* (July–September 1909): 482; *Starye gody* (May–June 1910): 80.

52. V., "Okhrana pamiatnikov stariny," *Starye gody* (May 1909): 146–47; *Starye gody* (December 1909): 694; "Zashchita stariny," *Starye gody* (April 1910): 45; "Butaforskii proekt," *Starye gody* (April 1911): 55–57; *Starye gody* (June 1911): 45; V. Vereshchagin, "Zakonoproekt ob okhrane stariny," *Starye gody* (March 1912): 49–54; "Zakon ob okhrane stariny," *Starye gody* (February 1914): 47–50.

53. N. N. Vrangel', "Zashchita stariny," *Starye gody* (April 1910): 45.

54. *Starye gody* (April 1907): 142–43.

55. *Starye gody* (November 1907): 578–79; I. F., "V Komissii po izucheniiu i opisaniiu starogo Peterburga," *Starye gody* (July–September 1908): 573.

56. My account of the organization of the museum is drawn primarily from A. M. Blinov, "Eti liudi byli podvizhnikami . . . ," *Leningradskaia panorama*, no. 9 (1988): 38–39; Al'bina Pavelkina, "Muzei Starogo Peterburga," *Muzei i gorod*, special issue of *Ars*, no. 2 (1993): 10–15.

57. This overlap in personnel makes it virtually impossible at times to determine which organization was in charge of work at a given site or had suggested a certain project. When a group of well-known preservationists arrived to measure a building and remove valuable decorative details, were they there as representatives of the Commission for the Study and Description of Old Petersburg or as members of the Council of the Museum of Old Petersburg? It seems likely, in many cases, that the preservationists themselves did not know.

58. *Starye gody* (November 1907): 578; *Starye gody* (March 1912): 56.

59. *Starye gody* (May 1911): 48.

60. A. M. Blinov, "Eti liudi byli podvizhnikami . . . ," *Leningradskaia panorama*, no. 9 (1988): 39.

61. "Russia's Unrealized Civil Society," in Clowes, Kassow, and West, eds., *Between Tsar and People*, 367–68; James L. West, "The Riabushinsky Circle: *Burzhuaziia* and *Obshchestvennost'* in Late Imperial Russia," in Clowes, Kasow, and West, eds., *Between Tsar and People*, 55.

CHAPTER 3

1. The commission was later expanded. Benois, "Revoliutsiia v khudozhestvennom mire," in *Aleksandr Benua razmyshliaet,* ed. I. S. Zil'bershtein and A. N. Savinov (Moscow: Sovetskii khudozhnik, 1968), 144–45.

2. V. P. Lapshin, *Khudozhestvennaia zhizn' Moskvy i Petrograda v 1917 godu* (Moscow: Sovetskii khudozhnik, 1983), 88.

3. I have taken this phrase from a negative reference to the Gorky Commission printed in the newspaper *Den'* on March 12, 1917, and cited in Lapshin, *Khudozhestvennaia zhizn',* 90.

4. "K deiateliam iskusstva," TsGIA f. 794, op. 1, ed. khr. 13, l. 13, quoted in Lapshin, *Khudozhestvennaia zhizn',* 94.

5. The Gorky Commission also made some effort to extend its reach to the provinces, sending Georgy Lukomsky and Georgy Narbut, for instance, to inspect palaces in Tver and Kiev. Within Petrograd, the commission participated in contemporary cultural initiatives as well as preservation efforts; it helped to select a burial site for those who had fallen in the Revolution, designed decorations for a First of May celebration in Tsarskoe Selo, and proposed a major reform of the Academy of the Arts.

6. *Rech',* March 11, 1917, and April 21, 1917, quoted in Lapshin, *Khudozhestvennaia zhizn',* 83.

7. *Revolutionary Dreams: Utopian Vision and Experimental Life in the Russian Revolution* (New York: Oxford University Press, 1989), 64.

8. Unfortunately, the space the Gorky Commission found for the Museum of Old Petersburg was both small and expensive. By the fall of 1918 the repository desperately needed to move again. See the questionnaire filled out by the museum's administration on March 1, 1921, for KUINS: AAN, SPb f. 155, op. 3, ed. khr. 47, l. 232.

9. Benois, "Revoliutsiia v khudozhestvennom mire," in *Aleksandr Benua razmyshliaet,* 142.

10. *Arkhitekturno-khudozhestvennyi ezhenedel'nik,* nos. 15–17 (1917), as cited in Lapshin, *Khudozhestvennaia zhizn',* 149.

11. Lapshin, *Khudozhestvennaia zhizn',* 378.

12. Lukomsky headed the commission in Tsarskoe Selo. Veiner worked under the direction of V. P. Zubov in Gatchina. Iu. N. Zhukov, *Stanovlenie i deiatel'nost' sovetskikh organov okhrany pamiatnikov istorii i kul'tury, 1917–1920 gg.,* ed. I. M. Katuntseva (Moscow: Nauka, 1989), 53, 144.

13. Benois, "Dvortsy-muzei," in *Aleksandr Benua razmyshliaet,* 73.

14. Vereshchagin had held the rank of *hofmeister* at court and had served in both the Ministry of Justice and the State Soviet before the Revolution. By all accounts he had little sympathy for the Bolsheviks.

15. TsGALI, SPb f. 2816, op. 2, d. 15, l. 68, quoted in Lapshin, *Khudozhestvennaia zhizn'*, 143.

16. See, for instance, Benois's correspondence from this period: *Aleksandr Benua razmyshliaet*, 525–28.

17. The behavior of the preservationists is in many ways comparable to that of the Academy of Sciences. Despite the fact that they, in many cases, viewed the Bolshevik regime negatively, academicians voted to cooperate rather than strike in 1918. They viewed the mission of their institution as too important to set aside for any reason. Vera Tolz, "The Formation of the Soviet Academy of Sciences," in *Academia in Upheaval: Origins, Transfers, and Transformations of the Communist Academic Regime in Russia and East Central Europe*, ed. Michael David-Fox and György Péteri (Westport, Conn.: Bergin and Garvey, 2000), 43–44.

18. Benois served as the head of the painting department at the Hermitage from 1918 until he emigrated to Europe in the mid-1920s. After the last artistic-historical commission was liquidated in the fall of 1918, Vereshchagin joined the staff of the structure that replaced them: the Petrograd Department of Museum Affairs and the Preservation of Monuments of Art and Antiquity (*Petrogradskii otdel po delam muzeev i okhrane pamiatnikov iskusstva i stariny*). Troinitsky held the post of director of the Hermitage from 1918 to 1927. In the post-Revolutionary era, Veiner served as the director of the Museum of Old Petersburg and was a member of the board of the Museum of the City. Zhukov, *Stanovlenie i deiatel'nost'*, 173–74.

19. *Muzei Goroda k oktiabriu 1927* (Leningrad: Izdanie Muzeia Goroda, 1928), 9.

20. V. Kurbatov, *Pavlovsk: Khudozhestvenno-istoricheskii ocherk i putevoditel'* (St. Petersburg: Izdanie obshchiny sv. Evgenii Krasnogo Kresta, 1912); V. Kurbatov, *Peterburg: Khudozhestvenno-istoricheskii ocherk* (St. Petersburg: Izdanie obshchiny sv. Evgenii Krasnogo Kresta, 1913); V. Kurbatov, *Sady i parki* ([Petrograd]: M. O. Vol'f, 1916).

21. For information on Kurbatov's contacts with Narkompros, see AAN, SPb f. 858, op. 2, ed. khr. 1, l. 68. Kurbatov's contributions to art history are particularly impressive given the fact that it did not represent his primary profession. A student of Dmitri Mendeleev, he worked throughout his adult life as a chemist. In 1918, when Menzhinskaia first approached him for help, he was head of the physical and colloidal chemistry lab at Petrograd's Technological Institute. N. A. Kostrigina, "V. Ia. Kurbatov—khimik," in *Antsiferovskie chteniia: Materialy i tezisy konferentsii (20–22 dekabria 1989 g.)*, ed. A. I. Dobkin and A. V. Kobak (Leningrad: Leningradskoe otdelenie Sovetskogo fonda kul'tury, 1989), 56–58.

22. In November 1918, an official decree granted the museum possession of the adjacent mansion of Countess N. F. Karlova as well. Galina Popova, "Muzei Goroda," *Muzei i gorod*, spec. issue of *Ars*, no. 2 (1993): 16. See also an untitled internal report in the fund of the Museum of the City: TsGALI, SPb f. 72, op. 1, d. 3, ll. 38–41.

23. It took several years for the museum to clear old tenants from the buildings placed under its control. Other less fortunate Soviet organizations regularly tried to wrest

away some section of the territory. The museum rented or loaned out space to the Central Station for School Excursions in the Humanities, the Society of Old Petersburg-New Leningrad, and various regional studies (*kraevedenie*) organizations in certain periods. L. A. Il'in, "Doklad zaveduiushchemu otdelom obrazovaniia Petrosoveta," August 2, 1920, TsGALI, SPb f. 72, op. 1, d. 3, l. 3; "Protokoly obshchikh sobranii sluzhashchikh Muzeia i zasedanii komiteta sluzhashchikh," TsGALI, SPb f. 72, op. 1, d. 9.

24. Initially, the primary administrative body at the museum was known as the working board or commission (*rabochaia kollegiia* or *rabochaia komissiia*). Later it was renamed the Museum Council (*sovet*). For the sake of simplicity, I will always refer to this entity as the "board." "Ot rabochei komissii Muzeia Goroda Komissaru narodnogo prosveshcheniia," September 30, 1918, TsGALI, SPb f. 72, op. 1, d. 3, l. 30.

25. "Muzei Goroda," *Muzei*, no. 1 (1923): 71–72.

26. Report by Lev Il'in, "Istoriia vozniknoveniia Muzeia Goroda," November 29, [1918], TsGALI, SPb f. 72, op. 1, d. 3, l. 52. See also *Muzei Goroda k oktiabriu 1927*, 11.

27. The Museum of the City was repeatedly restructured between 1918 and 1931. The department names I have listed here are taken from the description of the museum published in 1927 in honor of the tenth anniversary of the October Revolution. *Muzei Goroda k oktiabriu 1927*, 36, 54–55, 63.

28. "V Komissariat po narodnomu prosveshcheniiu—Dokladnaia zapiska ob organizatsii gorodskogo muzeia," TsGALI, SPb f. 72, op. 1, d. 1, ll. 27–28.

29. *Muzei Goroda k oktiabriu 1927*, 97–101, 65–87.

30. TsGALI, SPb f. 72, op. 1, d. 6, l. 36; l. 50.

31. On Veiner's arrest and probable execution, see "Protokol zasedaniia soveta muzeia," August 19, 1925, TsGALI, SPb f. 72, op. 1, d. 166, l. 31. Benois, *Moi vospominaniia*, 2:336; Benois, "Pamiati P. P. Veinera," *Poslednie novosti* [Paris], February 11, 1931.

32. G. G. Meklenberg-Strelitsky was the grandson of Grand Prince Mikhail Pavlovich (the brother of Nicholas I). For information on his life and that of his wife, see Popova, "Muzei Goroda," 17–18.

33. "Protokol zasedaniia soveta muzeia," August 22, 1923, TsGALI, SPb f. 72, op. 1, d. 119, l. 35 obr.

34. According to one of the museum's annual reports, during a twelve-month period between 1925 and 1926 more than eighteen thousand visitors went through the historical rooms in the Anichkov Palace. In contrast, 2,402 visitors were reported at the architecture department; 2,764 at the Museum of Old Petersburg; 3,013 at the Department of Interior Furnishings; 5,078 at the Library and Reference Department; and 11,791 at the Department of Communal Hygiene (a popular destination for school excursions). No figures whatsoever were reported for the Technical Department. Entrance fees for each department were paid separately and varied widely, with admission to historical exhibits costing more. TsGALI, SPb f. 72, op. 1, d. 148, l. 60.

35. "Doklad khudozhestvennoi podkomissii," TsGALI, SPb f. 72, op. 1, d. 10, l. 14.

36. Ibid.

37. Occasionally arguments between the two groups did break out at board meetings. For instance, in August and November 1923, E. K. Zamyslovskaia, the head of the museum's Cultural-Enlightenment Department, sharply criticized the Department of Interior Furnishings for failing to illustrate the living conditions of the poor. "Protokol zasedaniia soveta muzeia," August 22, 1923, TsGALI, SPb f. 72, op. 1, d. 119, ll. 35–36; "Protokol zasedaniia soveta muzeia," November 14, 1923, TsGALI, SPb f. 72, op. 1, d. 119, ll. 90–91.

38. The museum became heavily involved in issues of communal management after it left the jurisdiction of Narkompros in 1920 and became an affiliate of the Petrograd Gubernia Soviet of Communal Management (Petrogubkomkhoz: *Petrogradskii gubernskii sovet kommunal'nogo khoziaistva*). The name of the museum's parent organization changed repeatedly in the 1920s. Petrogubkomkhoz, Petrogubotkomkhoz, Lengubotkomkhoz, Lengorotkomkhoz, and Lenoblotkomkhoz all essentially represent the same administrative entity. For information on the name changes, see the inventory (*opis'*) of the aforementioned fund.

39. *Muzei Goroda k oktiabriu 1927*, 19; "Protokol zasedaniia soveta muzeia," May 7, 1924, TsGALI, SPb f. 72, op. 1, d. 150, l. 57.

40. "Protokol zasedaniia soveta muzeia," November 15, 1924, TsGALI, SPb f. 72, op. 1, d. 150, ll. 120–21.

41. Introduction to *Russia in the Era of NEP: Explorations in Soviet Society and Culture*, ed. Sheila Fitzpatrick, Alexander Rabinowitz, and Richard Stites (Bloomington: Indiana University Press, 1991), 10.

42. "Akt obsledovaniia 'Muzeia Goroda' pri otkomkhoze chlenami sektsii kommunal'nogo khoziaistva Leniigradskogo Soveta XI sozyva," TsGALI, SPb f. 72, op. 1, d. 3, ll. 72–75.

43. "Doklad Leningradskogo oblastnogo otdela raboche-krest'ianskoi inspektsii," undated, TsGALI, SPb f. 72, op. 1, d. 3, l. 66.

44. TsGALI, SPb f. 72, op. 1, d. 3, l. 65 obr; Popova, "Muzei Goroda," 21.

45. In 1931, the Museum of the City was renamed "the Museum of the Socialist Reconstruction of the City" (*Muzei sotsialisticheskoi rekonstruktsii goroda*) and placed under the jurisdiction of the Leningrad Soviet of Workers, Peasants, and Red Army Deputies. In 1933 it was again given a new name: "the Museum of Construction and City Management" (*Muzei stroitel'stva i gorodskogo khoziaistva*). TsGALI, SPb *Opis'*, f. 72.

46. For a full list of council members, see *Obshchestvo "Staryi Peterburg", 1921–1923 gg.* (Petrograd: Gos. uchebno-prakticheskaia shkola, 1923), 11.

47. In 1922, a second election was held and the composition of the council changed significantly with individuals involved in day-to-day operations largely replacing cultural luminaries. Ibid., 15.

48. The society restored, among other things, the Bezobrazov estate, Falconet's monument to Peter I (the Bronze Horseman), and a secret chapel used by Old Believers

for over one hundred years. It opened a museum of nineteenth-century daily life on Vasilievsky Island (*Dom Kovriginykh*) and created the first cemetery museum in all of Russia (Lazarevskoe cemetery in the Alexander Nevsky Monastery). Ibid., 22–25.

49. In the summer of 1922, the society ran a follow-up to the 1921 Pavlovsk seminar, this time focusing specifically on excursions and other forms of practical work. In 1923, it sponsored a summer seminar in Peterhof as well as in Pavlovsk and opened an experimental excursion base at Oranienbaum. I will discuss the society's contributions to excursion work in somewhat more detail in Chapter 5.

50. "Protokoly zasedanii komissii po ispuskaniiu sredstv i komiteta pomoshchi," September 1922–August 1924, TsGALI, SPb f. 32, op. 1, d. 74; "Otchety o deiatel'nosti komiteta," March 1922–June 1924, TsGALI, SPb f. 32, op. 1, d. 75.

51. *Obshchestvo "Staryi Peterburg", 1921–1923 gg.*, 14–15.

52. Ibid., 10.

53. The society initially was not directly affiliated with any government agency. As a voluntary scholarly association, it had to file a copy of its statutes with the Administrative Department of the Petrograd Soviet and undergo a formal registration process when it was created in the fall of 1921. Once these steps were completed, it was able to operate essentially autonomously. Ibid., 11, 16.

54. *Science for the Masses: The Bolshevik State, Public Science, and the Popular Imagination, 1917–1934* (College Station: Texas A & M University Press, 2003), 39.

55. "Protokol zasedaniia soveta obshchestva," April 1, 1924, TsGALI, SPb f. 32, op. 1, d. 1, l. 34; "Protokol zasedaniia soveta muzeia," May 7, 1924, TsGALI, SPb f. 72. op. 1, d. 150, l. 57.

56. Both the summer seminars and the popular festival (*narodnye gulian'ia*) were expected to generate income. "Protokol zasedaniia soveta obshchestva," June 17, 1924, TsGALI, SPb f. 32, op. 1, d. 1, l. 64 obr.

57. "Protokol zasedaniia soveta obshchestva," June 17, 1924, TsGALI, SPb f. 32, op. 1, d. 1, l. 64 obr.

58. "Tezisy doklada S. N. Zharnovskogo," September 18, 1924, TsGALI, SPb f. 32, op. 1, d. 1, l. 84.

59. The experience of imprisonment played at least as much of a role in Stolpiansky's defection as the collapse of the Revolution of 1905. Locked up with a group of young radicals whom he considered hopelessly naive, Stolpiansky quickly became disillusioned with the cause for which he had sacrificed so much. See Stolpiansky's correspondence with family members: P. N. Stolpiansky, "Pis'mo M. G. Stolpianskoi," May 20, 1907, OR RNB f. 741, op. 2, ed. khr. 447; "Pis'ma k ottsu N. P. Stolpianskomu," OR RNB f. 741, op. 2, ed. khr. 448.

60. Stolpiansky's diary for 1921 and 1922 provides insight into his state of mind. It contains a good deal of direct criticism of the Bolshevik regime and details his increasingly desperate efforts to support his family. OR RNB f. 741, op. 2, ed. khr. 31, ll. 8, 17–19. Stolpiansky's revolutionary guides include *Revoliutsionnyi Peterburg: U*

kolibeli russkoi svobody (Petrograd: Kolos, 1922) and *Staryi Peterburg: Kolybel' russkoi svobody (Delo 1 marta 1881)* (Petrograd: Gosizdat, 1922).

61. See the minutes for meetings held on February 3 and 10 in TsGALI, SPb f. 32, op. 1, d. 18, ll. 3–4.

62. In the official inventory of the fund of the society in TsGALI, SPb, the date of the adoption of the new name is listed as April 1, 1924. I have taken the date I provide here from the society's report for 1923–25. TsGALI, SPb f. 32, op. 1, d. 3, l. 114.

63. The society's financial prospects grew even bleaker when Gubispolkom barred its committee from engaging in commercial operations in October 1925. The committee had to liquidate all of its remaining stock out of season in order to put together investment capital so that it could start up ventures in manufacturing—the only sphere, according to the decree, in which it was allowed to operate. None of its investments paid off, and, in May 1926, the committee was liquidated. "V Leningradskii Gubispolkom—Dokladnaia zapiska ob okazanii sodeistviia obshchestvu," n.d., TsGALI, SPb f. 32 op. 1, d. 11, ll. 15–16; "Protokol zasedaniia obshchego sobraniia chlenov obshchestva," May 11, 1926, TsGALI, SPb f. 32 op. 1, d. 17, l. 32.

64. By March 1926 the society's financial situation was so dire that it was renting out its typewriter. In May, the society's assets were seized and sold at auction to liquidate the debts of its bankrupt committee. Although the society protested, arguing that it could not be held legally responsible for the committee's obligations, it was not able to secure the return of its property. TsGALI, SPb f. 32, op. 1, d. 1, ll. 157–83.

65. See the society's reports for 1928–35: OR RNB f. 443, ed. khr. 109–13.

66. A. G. Iatsevich, "Pis'ma k P. N. Stolpianskomu, 1926–1936 gg.," OR RNB f. 741, op. 1, ed. khr. 361.

67. Andrews, *Science for the Masses*, 47, 9.

68. See, for instance, Michael David-Fox, "The Assault on the Universities and the Dynamics of Stalin's 'Great Break,' 1928–1932," in David-Fox and Péteri, eds., *Academia in Upheaval*, 77; Lewis H. Siegelbaum, *Soviet State and Society Between Revolutions, 1918–1929* (Cambridge: Cambridge University Press, 1992), 221; Sheila Fitzpatrick, *The Cultural Front: Power and Culture in Revolutionary Russia* (Ithaca: Cornell University Press, 1992), 41.

69. *Storming the Heavens: The League of the Militant Godless* (Ithaca: Cornell University Press, 1998), 67.

70. Ibid., 44–45.

71. "The 'Quiet Revolution' in Soviet Intellectual Life," in Fitzpatrick, Rabinowitz, and Stites, eds., *Russia in the Era of NEP*, 213.

CHAPTER 4

1. Antsiferov's most famous work, *The Soul of Petersburg* (*Dusha Peterburga*), is not really a product of his experiences as an excursionist and therefore is not mentioned here. It is discussed in Chapter 7.

2. See, for instance, N. P. Antsiferov, *Nepostizhimyi gorod . . . Dusha Peterburga; Peterburg Dostoevskogo; Peterburg Pushkina*, ed. M. B. Verblovskaia (St. Petersburg: Lenizdat, 1991)—100,000 copies printed. N. P. Antsiferov, *Dusha Peterburga. Peterburg Dostoevskogo. Byl' i mif Peterburga*, reprint of 1922, 1923, 1924 editions, ed. E. B. Pokrovskaia (Moscow: Kniga, 1991)—10,000 copies. When Brokhaus-Efron first published Antsiferov's books in the 1920s, each had a run of 2,000 copies.

3. See, for instance, A. I. Dobkin, introduction to N. P. Antsiferov, *Iz dum o bylom: Vospominaniia*, ed. A. I. Dobkin (Moscow: Feniks; Kul'turnaia initsiativa, 1992), 3–4.

4. Only one of Grevs's published scholarly works focuses on the capital. A brief essay entitled "Turgenev i Peterburg," it is included as an appendix in Grevs's monograph *Turgenev i Italiia* (Leningrad: Brokgauz i Efron, 1925), 105–25. The history and philology departments of St. Petersburg University were combined in the late nineteenth and early twentieth centuries, which probably encouraged faculty to work in both disciplines. Although his primary specialty was medieval history, Grevs wrote about and led seminars on literary topics throughout his career. See Antsiferov, *Iz dum o bylom*, 171–73, 277–80.

5. For the details of Grevs's biography, see E. Ch. Skrzhinskaia, "Ivan Mikhailovich Grevs: Biograficheskii ocherk," in I. M. Grevs, *Tatsit* (Moscow: AN SSSR, 1946), 223–48.

6. The German historian Otto Girschfeld published the article in question in the journal *Klio* in 1901. See Skrzhinskaia for a more detailed treatment of this crisis. Ibid., 237.

7. Skrzhinskaia suggests that Grevs flirted with radical groups, including the terrorist organization People's Will (*Narodnaia volia*), throughout his student years. In his memoirs Grevs himself claimed to have participated only slightly in the revolutionary cause and to have become disillusioned as early as the 1880s. At about this time, he grew close to Fyodor and Sergei Oldenburg, helping them to found the Student Scientific-Literary Society, an organization that tried to draw students away from terrorist circles. Regardless, Grevs's name apparently remained on some sort of official watch list and, after the 1899 demonstration, he was dismissed from the university. Ibid., 229; AAN, SPb f. 726, op. 1, ed. khr. 15/1.

8. Grevs had some interest in educational travel even before his dismissal from the university. As he notes in his unfinished memoirs, however, he initially viewed excursions as a valuable broadening experience for young teachers and emphasized the virtues of relaxed recreation as opposed to scholarly preparation. AAN, SPb f. 726, op. 1, ed. khr. 187, l. 213. See also "Proekt obrazovatel'no-uveselitel'noi poezdki iz S.-Peterburga v Parizh. Letom 1896," AAN, SPb f. 726, op. 1, ed. khr. 205, ll. 1–2.

9. Some sources list 1896 as the year the school opened. I base my account on *Pamiatnaia knizhka Tenishevskogo uchilishcha v S.-Peterburge za 1900/1 uchebnyi god. God 1-yi* (St. Petersburg: Obshchestvennaia pol'za, 1902), 5–7. Prince Viacheslav Tenishev

was the husband of Maria Tenisheva, the mistress of the Talashkino arts community and the financial backer of the journal *World of Art.*

10. The Tenishev School agitated against bookishness in education and standardized textbooks, not books per se. Reading played an important role in the educational process. In terms of the quality of both its teachers and the students it graduated, the Tenishev School might fairly be compared to the Lyceum in Tsarskoe Selo. Its students included Vladimir Nabokov, Osip Mandelstam, Lydia and Nikolai Chukovsky, Daniil. A. Granin, and a number of prominent Soviet scientists. Iurii Tynianov and Nikolai Antsiferov both taught there at various times. Kornei Chukovsky staged stories in the school theater with children in the lower grades.

11. "Neskol'ko teoreticheskikh zamechanii ob obshcheobrazovatel'nom znachenii ekskursii," in *Pamiatnaia knizhka Tenishevskogo uchilishcha za 1900/1,* 108.

12. "Rospisanie ekskursii, proizvedennykh vesnoi 1901 goda," in *Pamiatnaia knizhka Tenishevskogo uchilishcha za 1900/1,* 112.

13. An unpublished report Grevs read at the Tenishev School indicates that he was beginning to address key methodological issues in this period. He notes that excursions need to be planned and integrated into the curriculum. He also suggests creating a unified program of field trips for the school that begins with tours of local sites for the younger grades and then gradually expands to more distant objects. The term "excursion" remains undefined, however, and again there is no attempt to outline specific procedures for conducting them. "K voprosu ob organizatsii istoricheskikh ekskursii. Dolozheno v zasedanii popechitel'nogo soveta 13 fevralia, 1901," AAN SPb f. 726, op. 1, ed. khr. 171.

14. N. N., "Ekskursionnoe delo v Rossii i zagranitsei," in *Shkol'nye ekskursii, ikh znacherie i organizatsiia,* ed. B. E. Raikov, Pedagogicheskii ezhegodnik izdavaemyi pri S.-Peterburgskom Lesnom kommercheskom uchilishche, vol. 2 (St. Petersburg: Tipografiia B. M. Vol'fa, 1910), 249–50; B. F. Omel'chenko, *Ekskursionnoe obshchenie: Poznanie, vospitanie, otdykh* (Moscow: Nauka, 1991), 9.

15. *K teorii i praktike "ekskursii"* (St. Petersburg: Senatskaia tipografiia, 1910), 12–13.

16. Rome, the only exception, was added to the list as a concession to the natural inclinations of the group. Ibid., 44.

17. Ibid., 16.

18. Antsiferov, *Iz dum o bylom,* 280.

19. For Grevs's notes for the trip, see AAN, SPb f. 726, op. 1, ed. khr. 187. Grevs began to write a memoir of the trip several times. The fragmentary drafts that survive provide good coverage of Grevs's own preparatory work. AAN, SPb f. 726, op. 1, ed. khr. 188.

20. *Russian Teachers and Peasant Revolution: The Politics of Education in 1905* (Bloomington: Indiana University Press, 1989), 31–54, 197–213.

21. In articles throughout his career, Grevs emphasized the importance of long-term excursions, particularly to foreign lands. Even in 1922, despite the obvious

problems associated with sending student groups abroad, Grevs continued to insist that such trips were essential and teachers should not abandon attempts to organize them. I. M. Grevs, "Dal'nie gumanitarnye ekskursii i ikh vospitatel'no-obrazovatel'nyi smysl," *Ekskursionnoe delo,* nos. 4–6 (1922): 12.

22. "Ekskursionnoe delo v Rossii i zagranitsei," in Raikov, ed., *Shkol'nye ekskursii,* 1st ed., 250.

23. For a defense of the value of museum excursions, see V. Ul'iansky, "Politekhnicheskii muzei, kak material dlia uchenicheskikh ekskursii," *Ekskursionnyi vestnik,* no. 1 (1914): 16–32.

24. In 1915 and 1916 the *Excursion Herald* appeared under the title *Walking through Rus and Abroad* (*Khozhdenie po Rusi i za rubezh*) with the original name now listed second. Many of the same people continued to contribute, but, perhaps because of wartime conditions, printing quality declined and issues emerged with significant delays.

25. "Ot redaktsii," *Ekskursionnyi vestnik,* no. 1 (1914): 5.

26. I. M. Grevs, *Kraevedenie v sovremennoi germanskoi shkole* (Leningrad: Brokgauz-Efron, 1926), 17.

27. D. Zolotarev, "K voprosu ob organizatsii uchebno-obrazovatel'nykh ekskursii," *Russkii ekskursant,* no. 2 (1914): 8. In this passage Zolotarev is specifically responding to and cites from G. G. Sherenburg's article "Tsel' i kharakter geograficheskikh ekskursii," published in the third volume of *Trudy Obshchestva zemlevedeniia pri S.-Peterburgskom universitete.*

28. The *Excursion Herald* often suggested exactly the opposite, sometimes even hinting that poorly planned trips might damage the minds of students by indulging their penchant for superficial observation. G. Gordon, "Ekskursiia v Aziatskii zal Muzeia iziashchnykh iskusstv imeni Aleksandra III v Moskve," *Ekskursionnyi vestnik,* no. 2 (1914): 112.

29. "1500 verst peshkom po beregu Volgi (Opyt organizatsii peshekhodnykh ekskursii s det'mi)," *Russkii ekskursant,* no. 1 (1914): 54–66; no. 2 (1914): 43–54.

30. "Zemskie ekskursii Voronezhskoi gubernii," *Russkii ekskursant,* no. 5 (1915): 307–14; "Bytovye ekskursii," *Russkii ekskursant,* no. 9 (1915): 491–94.

31. When the first issue of *The Russian Excursionist* came out, the *Herald* published an extremely critical review that jokingly dismissed Studitsky's walking tours as a threat to the railroads, questioned the value of printing travel notes by grade school students, and mocked a brief poem included in the issue. With particular glee the author S. Gintovt recounted the highlights of an article by the headmistress at a coeducational gymnasium who seems to have viewed excursions primarily as a way of distracting students from their dangerous preoccupation with card games. *Ekskursionnyi vestnik,* no. 3 (1914): 130–32.

32. For coverage of the debate over professional schools in Narkompros, see Sheila Fitzpatrick, *The Commissariat of Enlightenment* (Cambridge: Cambridge University Press, 1970), 29–33.

33. *Metodika i tekhnika vedeniia ekskursii,* 2nd ed. (Petrograd: Vremia, 1922), 8, quoted in I. M. Grevs, "Priroda 'ekskursionnosti' i glavnye tipy 'ekskursii v kul'turu'," in Grevs, ed., *Ekskursii v kul'turu* (Moscow: Mir, 1925), 10.

34. "Dva pedagogicheskikh ideala," *Pedagogicheskaia mysl',* nos. 1–4 (1921): 17.

35. "Chto est' trudovaia shkola?" *Pedagogicheskaia mysl',* nos. 3–4 (1922): 8.

36. *Pedagogical Thought* (1918–24) served as an important forum for the complaints of veteran reformers. When it opened in 1918, it effectively replaced a whole series of older liberal educational journals, absorbing the editorial staffs of *Russkaia shkola, Pedagogicheskii sbornik, Shkola i zhizn', Vospitanie i obuchenie,* and *Narodnoe obrazovanie* virtually wholesale. Grevs was a regular contributor, and by 1922 is listed as one of three editors. For information on the journal's history, see "Na vernom-li my puti?" *Pedagogicheskaia mysl',* nos. 5–8 (1918): 154–56.

37. The Lesnoe Commercial School opened in 1904 with a curriculum and philosophy drawn from the experience of the Tenishev School. Consultants, supporters, and even faculty members at the two schools often overlapped. The faculty at Lesnoe put together the single most important pre-Revolutionary collection of articles on excursion work: B. E. Raikov, ed., *Shkol'nye ekskursii, ikh znachenie i organizatsiia* (St. Petersburg: Tipografiia B. M. Vol'fa, 1910). It was reissued by the State Publishing House (Gosizdat) in a substantially expanded and revised form in 1921.

38. As Sheila Fitzpatrick notes, Narkompros withdrew from Petrograd rather slowly. Until early 1919, the Commissar of Enlightenment Lunacharsky retained his primary residence in the city and personally controlled the local schools. Fitzpatrick, *The Commissariat of Enlightenment,* 18.

39. While certainly worthy of independent study, the Moscow excursion movement comes off as less pedagogically grounded than that of Petrograd. When local schools of thought emerged, they often expressed extremist ideas. One group demanded that all instruction in the schools take the form of excursions; another wanted to reduce all tours involving art to exercises in appreciation. Revolutionary routes appeared quite early. See A. Ia. Zaks, "Opyt izucheniia i propagandy istorii revoliutsionnoi Moskvy v 20-e gody XX v.," in *Iz istorii ekonomicheskoi i obshchestvennoi zhizni Rossii. Sbornik statei k 90-letiiu Akademika Druzhinina* (Moscow: Nauka, 1976), 273–86.

40. Some kind of excursion structure also existed within Petroprofobr to serve the Schools of Working Youth (*shkoly rabochei molodezhi*). See E. Krasnukha, "Ekskursionnoe delo v Petrograde," *Ekskursionnyi vestnik,* no. 1 (1922): 6.

41. Fitzpatrick, *The Commissariat of Enlightenment,* 188–209.

42. The Excursion Section of the Collegium of the United Labor School published its own magazine in 1921 and 1922, *Excursion Matters* (*Ekskursionnoe delo*). "The excursion chronicle" at the back of each issue contains reports on work at various stations. Unless otherwise noted, information on the stations is drawn from these chronicles.

43. The Pavlovsk courses accepted one hundred and fifty teachers in the summer of 1919 and two hundred in 1920. For more information on these courses and their pre-

Revolutionary antecedents, see I. I. Poliansky, "Opyt novoi organizatsii ekskursionnogo dela v shkolakh," *Ekskursionnoe delo,* no. 1 (1921): 18, and also the review of this article by B. Raikov in *Ekskursionnyi vestnik,* no. 1 (1922): 8.

44. For an account of the problems faced by the stations, see K. M. Deriugin, "Petergofskaia ekskursionnaia stantsiia," *Ekskursionnoe delo,* no. 1 (1921): 94–106.

45. In 1921 the word "instruktorskaia" was added to the name of the station, drawing attention to its teacher-training work. P. Koval'skaia-Il'ina, "Tsentral'naia instruktorskaia stantsiia gumanitarnykh ekskursii," *Ekskursionnoe delo,* nos. 2–3 (1921): 192–96.

46. I. I. Poliansky, "Opyt novoi organizatsii ekskursionnogo dela v shkolakh," *Ekskursionnoe delo,* no. 1 (1921): 18.

47. Financed and run in part from Petrograd, the Pskov station boasted programs in both the humanities and natural sciences, but focused primarily on history. V. A. Fedorov, "Pskovskaia ekskursionnaia stantsiia i ekskursii po gorodu Pskovu," *Ekskursionnoe delo,* nos. 2–3 (1921): 196–203; V. A. Fedorov, "Rabota Pskovskoi ekskursionnoi stantsii v 1921 i 1922 gg.," *Ekskursionnoe delo,* nos. 4–6 (1922): 282–84.

48. "Deiatel'nost' Muzeinogo otdela po organizatsii shkol'nykh ekskursii," *Ekskursionnoe delo,* nos. 2–3 (1921): 207.

49. In 1910 a group of university students, including a number of participants in Grevs's seminars, formed a study circle with the aim of crafting educational tours of the Hermitage for workers. Their scheme was never fully realized, but they did conduct a couple of excursions. In at least one case, they were invited by the administration of the Hermitage, which had no staff of guides itself and was unsure how to handle requests for tours. A similar privately organized study circle took shape at the Russian Museum in the same period. If anything, the existence of these groups highlights the failure of the museums themselves to assume a more active educational role. Antsiferov, *Iz dum o bylom,* 202–14.

50. "Deiatel'nost' Muzeinogo otdela po organizatsii shkol'nykh ekskursii," *Ekskursionnoe delo,* nos. 2–3 (1921): 209.

51. Ia. A. Veinert, "Obshchaia soglasovannaia programma khudozhestvenno-istoricheskikh ekskursii," in *Shkol'nye ekskursii, ikh znachenie i organizatsiia: Sbornik nauchno-pedagogicheskikh statei,* ed. B. E. Raikov, 2nd enl. ed. (Petrograd: Gosizdat, 1921), 397–406.

52. "Deiatel'nost' Muzeinogo otdela po organizatsii shkol'nykh ekskursii," *Ekskursionnoe delo,* nos. 2–3 (1921): 209–10.

53. These remarks appear in the final report of a seminar for the preparation of tour guides for the historic rooms of the Winter Palace run by the Society for the Study, Popularization, and Artistic Preservation of Old Petersburg. OR RNB f. 741, op. 2, ed. khr. 663, l. 1.

54. See the detailed records Petr Stolpiansky kept of his activities throughout the 1920s: OR RNB f. 741, op. 2, ed. khr. 416–17, 419–20. The problem is also mentioned

in the minutes of meetings at the Petrograd Excursion Institute: TsGALI, SPb f. 53, op. 1, d. 33, l. 90; f. 53, op. 1, d. 27, l. 22 obr; f. 53, op. 1, d. 76, l. 66.

55. Emma Krasnukha, "Ekskursionnoe delo v Petrograde," *Ekskursionnyi vestnik*, no. 1 (1922): 5–6. Politprosvet's Central Excursion Base in the House of the Excursionist put out its own publication in 1925 and 1926, *Sputnik ekskursanta*.

56. Ibid., 6. For information on a conflict with another excursion provider, see TsGALI, SPb f. 32, op. 1, d. 1, l. 18 obr.; l. 20.

57. TsGALI, SPb f. 53, op. 1, d. 1–2.

58. "Protokol zasedaniia vremennogo pravleniia Vysshego ekskursionnogo instituta, " July 25, 1921, TsGALI, SPb f. 53, op. 1, d. 5, l. 42; "Protokol zasedaniia pravleniia Instituta," August 21, 1922, TsGALI, SPb f. 53, op. 1, d. 7, l. 69.

59. "Tsel' i zadachi 'Russkogo ekskursanta,'" *Russkii Ekskursant*, no. 1 (1914): 3.

60. Ibid., 3–4.

61. From an explanatory note prefacing a draft of the institute statutes. TsGALI, SPb f. 53, op. 1, d. 2, l. 1.

62. "Protokoly zasedanii nauchno-pedagogicheskoi sektsii gosudarstvennogo uchenogo soveta (Moskva) ob organizatsii ekskursionnogo instituta v Petrograde," TsGALI, SPb f. 53, op. 1, d. 3.

63. Lack of funding led to the demise of *The Excursion Herald*. Collections put together by institute faculty included *Ekonomiko-tekhnicheskie ekskursii* (Petrograd: Petrogradskii ekskursionnyi institut, 1923); B. E. Raikov, ed., *Estestvenno-istoricheskie ekskursii po Petrogradu* (Petrograd: n. p., 1923); I. M. Grevs, ed., *Ekskursii v kul'turu* (Moscow: Mir, 1925).

64. The Northern expedition was organized in conjunction with the Moscow Museum and Excursion Institute run by A. Ia. Zaks. "Protokol zasedaniia soveta instituta," September 11, 1922, TsGALI, SPb f. 53, op. 1, d. 27, l. 5.

65. "Protokol zasedaniia gumanitarnogo otdela," n.d., TsGALI, SPb f. 53, op. 1, d. 33, l. 88.

66. I. M. Grevs, "Priroda 'ekskursionnosti' i glavnye tipy 'ekskursii v kul'turu," in I. M. Grevs, ed., *Ekskursii v kul'turu* (Moscow: Mir, 1925), 11–12, 13.

67. "Monumental'nyi gorod i istoricheskie ekskursii," *Ekskursionnoe delo*, no. 1 (1921): 25–26.

68. Ibd., 30–31.

69. Ibid., 21.

70. Ibid., 22.

71. Ibid., 27.

CHAPTER 5

1. *Byl' i mif Peterburga*, in *Dusha Peterburga. Peterburg Dostoevskogo. Byl' i mif Peterburga*, reprint of 1922, 1923, 1924 editions, ed. E. B. Pokrovskaia (Moscow: Kniga, 1991), 9.

2. Ibid., 23–24.

3. "Monumental'nyi gorod i istoricheskie ekskursii," *Ekskursionnoe delo*, no. 1 (1921): 26.

4. See, for instance, *Byl' i mif Peterburga*, 28.

5. Ibid., 44.

6. See, for instance, N. Z. Kerov, "Ekskursiia v podmoskovnye 'dvorianskie gnezda'," *Ekskursionnyi vestnik*, no. 3 (1914): 43–71; S. Zolotarev, "Odin iz obrazovatel'nykh elementov ekskursii," *Russkii ekskursant*, no. 5 (1916): 7.

7. "Literaturnye ekskursii," in B.E. Raikov, ed., *Shkol'nye ekskursii*, 1st ed., 221.

8. *Teoriia i praktika literaturnykh ekskursii* (Leningrad: Seiatel', 1926), 5. Throughout the discussion of this work that follows, page numbers will be given parenthetically.

9. See, for instance, the articles in *Semiotika goroda i gorodskoi kul'tury: Peterburg, Trudy po znakovym sistemam XVIII v., Uchenye zapiski Tartuskogo gosudarstvennogo universiteta* (Tartu: Tartuskii gosudarstvennyi universitet, 1984).

10. *Byl' i mif Peterburga*, 58. Page numbers will be given parenthetically throughout the rest of this examination of *Byl' i mif*.

11. *Peterburg Dostoevskogo* in *Nepostizhimyi gorod . . . Dusha Peterburga; Peterburg Doestoevskogo; Peterburg Pushkina*, ed. A. M. Konechny and K. A. Kumpan (Leningrad: Lenizdat, 1991), 209.

12. F. M. Dostoevsky, *Prestuplenie i nakazanie*, in *Polnoe sobranie sochinenii*, (Leningrad: Nauka, 1972–88), 6:391, 389, cited in Antsiferov, *Peterburg Dostoevskogo*, in *Nepostizhimyi gorod*, 236.

13. Ibid., 392, cited in N. P. Antsiferov, *Peterburg Dostoevskogo*, in *Nepostizhimyi gorod*, 239.

14. N. P. Antsiferov, *Peterburg Dostoevskogo*, in *Nepostizhimyi gorod*, 235–36. Page numbers will be given parenthetically throughout the rest of this discussion of Antsiferov's *Peterburg Dostoevskogo*.

15. B. E. Raikov, ed., *Voprosy ekskursionnogo dela* (Petrograd: Nachatki znaniia, 1923), 131.

16. N. P. Antsiferov, "Ulitsa rynkov (Sadovaia, nyne ul. 3-go iiulia v Leningrade): Kraevedcheskii material dlia ekskursii po sotsial'nomu i ekonomicheskomu bytu," in I. M. Grevs, ed., *Po ochagam kul'tury: Novye temy dlia ekskursii po gorodu. Metodicheskii sbornik*, ed. I. M. Grevs (Leningrad: Seiatel', 1926), 57–108.

17. N. P. Antsiferov, "Nasha ulitsa: Opyt podkhoda k izucheniiu goroda," in *Ekskursii v sovremennost'*, ed. N. A. Kuznetsov and K. V. Polzikova-Rubets, Ekskursionnaia praktika Leningradskogo Gubsotsvosa (Leningrad: Knizhnyi sektor Gubono, 1925), 26.

18. "Ekskursii v oblast' finansovogo kapitalizma," in Grevs, ed., *Po ochagam kul'tury*, 119.

19. "Aristokraticheskaia Ispaniia i gorodskaia Gollandiia," in Petri and Antsiferov, *Istoricheskie ekskursii po Ermitazhu* (Leningrad: Priboi, 1924), 10.

20. Ibid., 12.

21. "Frantsuzskoe obshchestvo v epokhu absolutizma," in Petri and Antsiferov, *Istoricheskie ekskursii po Ermitazhu*, 30–31.

22. Ibid., 35.

23. *Ekskursiia na gosudarstvennyi farforovyi zavod* (Leningrad: Priboi, 1924).

24. In 1926 the Central School Excursion Station published a whole series of anthologies that focused on the everyday. See, for instance, K. V. Polzikova-Rubets, ed., *Ekskursionnaia praktika. Sbornik 1: Temy "rynok", "kooperativ" i "khlebozavod"*, Sborniki Leningradskoi shkol'noi ekskursionnoi stantsii (Leningrad: Seiatel', 1926).

25. A. A. Iakhontov, "Kraevedenie i shkola," in *Dnevnik Vserossiiskoi konferentsii nauchnykh obshchestv po izucheniiu mestnogo kraia sozyvaemoi Akademicheskim tsentrom Narkomprosa v Moskve, 10–20 dekabria, 1921*, 5 issues (Moscow: Pechatnyi tekhnik, 1921), 3:39–41.

26. K. V. Polzikova-Rubets, "Ekskursiia po tsentral'noi chasti goroda," in K.V. Polzikova-Rubets, ed., *Ekskursionnaia praktika. Sbornik 3*, 6–7.

27. *The Birth of the Propaganda State: Soviet Methods of Mass Mobilization, 1917–1929* (Cambridge: Cambridge University Press, 1985), 15, 127–28.

28. *Byl' i mif Peterburga*, 6.

29. Ibid.

30. "Otchet o deiatel'nosti obshchestva za 1921–1923," TsGALI, SPb f. 32, op. 1, d. 3, l. 17.

31. "Protokoly zasedanii soveta obshchestva," spring 1924, TsGALI, SPb f. 32, op. 1, d. 1, ll. 18–27, 49–51; "Protokoly zasedanii ekskursionnogo biuro obshchestva i mezhduvedomstvennoi komissii ekskursionnogo seminariia," January 1923–March 1924, TsGALI, SPb f. 32, op. 1, d. 18.

32. "Protokol zasedaniia soveta obshchestva," June 25, 1925, TsGALI, SPb f. 32, op. 1, d. 1, l. 93.

33. "Protokoly zasedanii pravleniia instituta," March–July 1922, TsGALI, SPb f. 53, op. 1, d. 7, ll. 45–64; "Protokol zasedaniia pravleniia instituta o sokrashchenii shtata i prilozheniia k nemu," June–July 1922, TsGALI, SPb f. 53, op. 1, d. 29.

34. "Protokoly zasedanii soveta instituta," June–September 1924, TsGALI, SPb f. 53, op. 1, d. 27, ll. 31–38.

35. OR RNB f. 741, op. 2, ed. khr. 410, l. 4. Unfortunately no year is listed on the document. It probably dates to the late 1920s when Stolpiansky regularly appeared before union and factory groups. Stolpiansky is listed as working with the Union of Metalworkers during this period.

36. L. Gurvich, *Ocherednye zadachi turisticheskogo dvizheniia*, 2nd ed., Biblioteka proletarskogo turista (Moscow: Ogiz fizkul'tura i turizm, 1931). Traditionally, the

creation of OPTE is considered the true beginning of the Soviet mass tourism movement. See Omel'chenko, *Ekskursionnoe obshchenie*, 14–15.

37. N. Sobolev-Tomilin, *Sputnik turista po Leningradu i okrestnostiam* (Leningrad: Ogiz fizkul'tura i turizm, 1932), 58–150.

38. I. Ia. Eliashevich, ed., *Sputnik bezbozhnika po Leningradu* (Leningrad: Priboi, 1930), 11–12, 19.

39. P. Surozhsky, *V gorode Lenina: Putevka pervaia,* Po zemle sovetskoi (Moscow: Molodaia gvardiia, 1925), 7.

40. Ibid., 19.

41. Ibid.

42. Ibid., 26.

43. See, for instance, *Okrestnosti Leningrada: Samoobrazovatel'naia ekskursiia,* V pomoshch' ekskursantu (Leningrad: Priboi, 1927); A. P. Pressman, *Peterburg-Leningrad v proshlom i nastoiashchem: Posobie dlia ekskursantov i turistov* (Leningrad: Leningradskii oblastnoi otdel narodnogo obrazovaniia Politprosvet, 1928).

44. S. P. Lebedinsky, "Muzei Leningrada," in M. G. Vigand, ed., *Putevoditel' po Leningradu s prilozheniem novogo plana g. Leningrada* (Leningrad: Lenoblispolkom i Lensovet, 1933), 85. See also, *Sbornik postanovlenii po muzeinomu stroitel'stvu RSFSR, 1931–1934* (Moscow: Narkompros muzeinyi otdel, 1934), 6.

45. A. B. Gilenson, ed., *V pomoshch' rabotniku muzeia: Zakony, rasporiazheniia, raz"iasneniia po muzeinomu stroitel'stvu* (Moscow: Narkompros RSFSR, 1936), 45–49.

46. The archive of V. M. Losev contains a number of examples. See, for instance, "Plan ekskursii po gorodu, organizuemykh dlia slushatelei tsikla 'Peterburg-Leningrad' Leningradskim lektoriem," mid-1930s, OR RNB f. 443, op. 1, ed. khr. 153. Excursion plans, while elevated to unexpected prominence in the early 1930s, were not entirely new; they had been used on a limited basis at the Excursion Institute, particularly in connection with a certification program that staff ran for guides in 1923 and 1924. Applicants submitted folders of materials that included a description of at least one route, often given in a column format similar to the one described here. Times, however, rarely appear in these early outlines and, when they do, clearly represent rough estimates, calculated to the nearest five-minute mark. Unlike later plans, these documents did not function as rigid schedules. TsGALI, SPb f. 53, op. 1, d. 60.

47. I rely partly on interviews with practicing guides. A good written description of the process of developing a topic is included in K. G. Levykina and V. Kherbsta, eds., *Muzeevedenie: Muzei istoricheskogo profilia* (Moscw: Vysshaia shkola, 1988), 281–82.

CHAPTER 6

1. "Protokol zasedaniia pravleniia instituta," April 24, 1922, TsGALI SPb f. 53, d. 7, ll. 45–50.

2. See, for instance, debates on institute involvement in the Fourth Session of the Central Bureau of *Kraevedenie* (March 1923). "Protokol zasedaniia organizatsionnogo biuro po sozyvu v Petrograde ekskursionnoi konferentsii," February 15, 1923, TsGALI, SPb f. 53, d. 64, ll. 1–3.

3. *Voprosy ekskursionnogo dela. Po dannym petrogradskoi ekskursionnoi konferentsii 10–12 marta 1923 g.*, ed. B. E. Raikov (Petrograd: Nachatki znanii, 1923), 3–4.

4. In a 1932 article, I. Klabunovsky claimed that one experienced *kraeved* had collected 150 separate definitions for *kraevedenie*. "V bor'be za printsipy sovetskogo kraevedeniia," *Sovetskoe kraevedenie*, nos. 11–12 (1932): 6.

5. I. M. Grevs, "Kraevedenie i ekskursionnoe delo," in Raikov, ed., *Voprosy ekskursionnogo dela*, 3.

6. See I. M. Grevs, *Kraevedenie v sovremennoi germanskoi shkole* (Leningrad: Brokgauz-Efron, 1926); N. Dukhovnitsky, "Rodinovedenie v vysshikh nachal'nykh uchilishchakh," *Russkii ekskursant*, no. 9 (1916): 7–11.

7. Ivan Grevs argues that attempts to differentiate between *rodinovedenie* and *kraevedenie* are futile; both terms promote the same principle of localization. Grevs is certainly right if we look at the implications of *kraevedenie/rodinovedenie* for the schools. In terms of broader organizational issues, however, there are enormous differences between pre-Revolutionary *rodinovedenie* and the *kraevedenie* movement of the 1920s. *Kraevedenie v sovremennoi germanskoi shkole*, 12.

8. "Tsentral'noe biuro kraevedeniia," *Kraevedenie*, no. 1 (1923): 47.

9. "K izucheniiu naseleniia Rossii," *Kraevedenie*, no. 1 (1923): 19, 25.

10. "Ot redaktsii," *Izvestiia TSBK*, no. 1 (1925): 2.

11. B. E. Raikov, "Eshche po povodu peredachi kraevednykh organizatsii Narkomprosu," *Izvestiia TSBK*, no. 9 (1928): 300.

12. N. Vladimirsky, "K ponimaniiu kraevedcheskogo dvizheniia," *Kraevedenie*, no. 3 (1924): 217–18.

13. S. Bezbakh, *K istorii kraevedcheskoi raboty v Leningrade: Obshchestvo "Staryi Peterburg—Novyi Leningrad". Otdelenie Obshchestva v severnykh okrestnostiakh* (Leningrad: [Obshchestvo "Staryi Peterburg–Novyi Leningrad"], 1926).

14. "Tsentral'noe biuro kraevedeniia," *Kraevedenie*, no. 1 (1923): 50. See also K. I. Vorob'ev, "Kraevedcheskaia rabota studencheskikh organizatsii Leningrada, Saratova i Nizhnego Novgoroda," *Izvestiia TSBK* no. 9 (1928): 18.

15. *Izvestiia TSBK*, no. 1 (1925): 6–7. "Otchet o deiatel'nosti Tsentral'nogo biuro kraevedeniia za pervoe polugodie 1925 goda," *Izvestiia TSBK*, no. 2 (1925): 38.

16. On the situation in Moscow, see M. Ia. Fenomenov, "Zadachi gubernskogo obshchestva izucheniia mestnogo kraia v dele planovoi organizatsii kraevednoi raboty," *Kraevedenie*, no. 2 (1926): 153–65. Fenomenov notes the existence of three separate centers of *kraevedenie* in Moscow, one apparently created in 1924, the others in 1925.

17. "Leningrad," *Izvestiia TSBK*, no. 2 (1927): 51–52.

18. See, for instance, I. M. Grevs, "Istoriia v kraevedenii," *Kraevedenie*, no. 4 (1926): 487–508.

19. I. A. Butin, ed., *Leningrad: Kraevednyi sbornik (Posobie dlia shkol I-oi i II-oi stupeni)* (Leningrad: Izd. Leningradskogo oblono, 1928).

20. M. I. Uspensky, "Literaturno-etnograficheskaia ekspeditsiia 1856," *Kraevedenie*, no. 3 (1928): 149–56; D. O. Sviatsky, "M. V. Lomonosov i kraevedenie (Stranichka iz istorii kraevedeniia v Rossii)," *Kraevedenie*, no. 4 (1924): 369–74.

21. "Tsentral'noe biuro kraevedeniia," *Kraevedenie*, no. 1 (1923): 48; D. O. Sviatsky, "Sovremennoe polozhenie raboty kraevykh organizatsii," *Kraevedenie*, no. 2 (1926): 237.

22. D. O. Sviatsky, "Sovremennoe polozhenie raboty kraevykh organizatsii," *Kraevedenie*, no. 2 (1926): 238.

23. See A. I. Dobkin's commentary on Antsiferov, *Iz dum o bylom*, 448. In *Models of Nature*, Douglas Weiner gives a significantly higher estimate of peak membership. Citing a decree of the presidium of the Central Bureau of *Kraevedenie*, he notes that in 1931 the organization claimed 115,000 members organized into 2,700 cells and affiliates. See "Postanovlenie Prezidiuma TSBK 25-ogo marta 1931 g.," *Sovetskoe kraevedenie* (1931): 64, cited in *Models of Nature* (Bloomington: Indiana University Press, 1988), 274.

24. I write "Russian" consciously; the movement remained concentrated in the RSFSR throughout the early 1920s. Of the 1,405 societies, circles, and museums devoted to *kraevedenie* on March 1, 1926, according to the Central Bureau only 25 percent were located outside Russian territory. "Sovremennoe polozhenie raboty kraevedcheskikh organizatsii v RSFSR," *Kraevedenie*, no. 2 (1926): 237.

25. Proletkult was a broad-based organization dedicated to fostering the development of "proletarian culture." It sprang up early in 1917 and initially had the support of some prominent Bolsheviks. After the October Revolution, it became part of the newly created Commissariat of Enlightenment. It regularly, however, refused to submit to Narkompros directives and in 1920 was effectively shut down by Bolshevik leaders.

26. N. P. Antsiferov, "Kraevedenie kak istoriko-kul'turnoe iavlenie," *Izvestiia TSBK*, no. 3 (1927): 84.

27. Tatiana Khorkhordina, *Istoriia otechestva i arkhivy: 1917–1980-e gody* (Moscow: RGGU, 1994), 124–32. For coverage of the controversy in the *kraevedenie* press, see I. Maiakovsky, "Arkhivy, kak odna iz oblastei kraevedcheskoi raboty," *Kraevedenie*, no. 1 (1927): 47–62; "K voprosu o khranenii arkhivnykh materialov," *Izvestiia TSBK*, no. 5 (1927): 154–55; "O sdache uchrezhdeniiami Glavnauki arkhivnykh materialov organam Tsentrarkhiva RSFSR," *Izvestiia TSBK*, no. 9 (1927): 305–6.

28. "Polozhenie o Tsentral'nom biuro kraevedeniia pri Rossiiskoi akademii nauk," *Kraevedenie*, no. 2 (1923): 209–10.

29. The break with the Academy of Sciences was amicable. Academicians like Nikolai Marr, Sergei Oldenburg, and Alexander Fersman remained members of the bureau even after the split. Others volunteered their time or contributed to the

movement's periodicals. "Rezoliutsii," *Dnevnik Vtoroi vsesoiuznoi konferentsii po kraevedeniiu*, 4 issues (Moscow: Mospoligraf, 1924), 4:17. For later debate on the merits of the move, see "VI-ia sessiia (plenum) Tsentral'nogo biuro kraevedeniia," *Izvestiia* TSBK, no. 1 (1926): 20.

30. My figures are drawn from the lists given in "Vtoraia vsesoiuznaia konferentsiia po kraevedeniiu," *Kraevedenie*, nos. 1–2 (1925): 103–4. A slightly different figure is given in "Otchet o deiatel'nosti Moskovskogo otdeleniia Tsentral'nogo biuro kraevedeniia (MOTSBK)," *Biulleten' Tret'ei vserossiiskoi konferentsii po kraevedeniiu*, 6 issues (Moscow: TSBK, 1927), 5:121.

31. Getting provincial members elected proved difficult and slow. The majority of *kraevedenie* organizations still had not chosen delegates a year after the Second Conference, so, in January 1926, the Central Bureau of *Kraevedenie* abandoned formal election procedures and mailed out invitations to the Sixth Session to oblast and gubernia *kraevedenie* organizations, suggesting that they, in consultation with other groups in their area, appoint a member to attend. "VI-ia sessia (plenum) TSBK," *Izvestiia* TSBK, no. 1 (1926): 2.

32. "Rezoliutsii plenuma," *Dnevnik Vtoroi vsesoiuznoi konferentsii po kraevedeniiu*, 4:17.

33. See the remarks of the Moscow delegate V. D. Vilensky-Sibiriakov in "VI sessiia (plenum) Tsentral'nogo biuro kraevedeniia," *Izvestiia* TSBK, no. 1 (1926): 6–7.

34. "VI sessiia (plenum) Tsentral'nogo biuro kraevedeniia," *Izvestiia* TSBK, no. 1 (1926): 4.

35. Ibid., 4.

36. Ibid., 6.

37. Boris Sokolov was a full member of the Central Bureau. Mikhail Fenomenov's name is not included in the lists of bureau members published between 1924 and 1927. He probably attended the Sixth Session in some other capacity. See "Sostav Tsentral'nogo biuro kraevedeniia," *Dnevnik Vtoroi vsesoiuznoi konferentsii po kraevedeniiu*, 4:2–3; *Biulleten' Tret'ei vserossiiskoi konferentsii po kraevedeniiu*, 1:4–6. For the last day of debates at the Sixth Session, see "VI sessiia (plenum) Tsentral'nogo biuro kraevedeniia," *Izvestiia* TSBK, no.1 (1926): 17–21.

38. "Rezoliutsii Sessii," *Izvestiia* TSBK, no.1 (1926): 23–24.

39. A. Pinkevich, "Otchet o deiatel'nosti Moskovskogo otdeleniia Tsentral'nogo biuro kraevedeniia (MOTSBK)," *Biulleten' Tret'ei vserossiiskoi konferentsii po kraevedeniiu*, 5:121.

40. Ibid., 5:121–24.

41. "Rezoliutsii III-i vserossiiskoi konferentsii po kraevedeniiu po osnovnym dokladam Glavnauki, TSBK i po organizatsionnym voprosam," *Izvestiia* TSBK, no. 10 (1927): 346.

42. "III vserossiiskaia konferentsiia po kraevedeniiu," *Kraevedenie*, no. 1 (1928): 43–46.

43. "Obrashchenie akad. S. F. Ol'denburga k III vserossiiskoi konferentsii po kraevedeniiu," *Izvestiia* TSBK, no. 10 (1927): 351.

44. "Telegramma akad. S. F. Ol'denburgu ot TSBK," *Izvestiia TSBK*, no. 10 (1927): 352.

45. "III-ia vserossiiskaia konferentsiia po kraevedeniiu," *Izvestiia TSBK*, no. 10 (1927): 345.

46. *Kraevedenie*, the bureau's first periodical, appeared irregularly from 1923 to 1929. It printed full scholarly articles and large numbers of book reviews. Thick and expensive to publish, it had a subscription price that was too high for many local organizations. At the Second Conference in 1924, delegates voted to create a second, less ambitious journal that might appear more regularly and could be sold for less. Known as *Izvestiia Tsentral'nogo biuro kraevedeniia*, it ran from 1925 to 1929. On the creation of *Izvestiia TSBK*, see "Ot redaktsii," *Izvestiia TSBK*, no. 1 (1925): 1–3. On the division of responsibilities following the Third Conference, see "Deiatel'nost' TSBK," *Izvestiia TSBK*, no. 2 (1928): 14–18.

47. "Postanovlenie Soveta narodnykh komissarov RSFSR o poriadke proizvodstva kraevedcheskikh rabot na territorii RSFSR," *Izvestiia TSBK*, no. 8 (1927): 272–73.

48. "Po povodu postanovleniia Sovnarkoma RSFSR 'O poriadke proizvodstva kraevedcheskikh rabot na territorii RSFSR," *Izvestiia TSBK*, no. 8 (1927): 273–74. At the Sixth Session of the Central Bureau in January 1926, Pavlov-Silvansky, as I noted, sided with the Leningrad delegates. Perhaps by 1927 he had collapsed under pressure. It is possible, however, that he sincerely believed that subordination to Narkompros would help the *kraevedenie* movement. In the late 1920s Russian cultural organizations faced difficult choices: each time they found themselves under attack, members had to decide whether to compromise, seek the protection of a more powerful official structure, or try to wait out the situation. Well-intentioned people often disagreed about what constituted the correct course of action.

49. "Eshche po povodu peredachi kraevednykh organizatsii Narkomprosu," *Izvestiia TSBK*, no. 9 (1927): 301–2. Raikov's letter is followed by a rebuttal from Pavlov-Silvansky.

50. During the early stages of the cultural revolution, Moscow often manipulated provincial votes to gain leverage against Leningrad-based institutions. For a discussion of this and examples, see the preface to *Akademicheskoe delo: 1929–1931*, issue 1 (St. Petersburg: Biblioteka Rossiiskoi akademii nauk, 1993), xvii.

51. "Leningradskaia gruppa TSBK (Za period ianvaria—mart 1928)," *Izvestiia TSBK*, no. 5 (1928): 14. Indeed, bibliographical work ground to a virtual standstill once Moscow took over.

52. Ibid., 11.

53. "Leningradskaia gruppa (Obzor raboty za 1927–1928 g.)," *Izvestiia TSBK*, no. 2 (1929): 10. Italics added.

54. Actually individual *kraevedy* were already being arrested in large numbers between 1927 and 1929, both because of their resistance to archival policies and on other unrelated charges. The authorities, however, generally maintained a tolerant attitude

to the movement as a whole during this early period, even allowing some enthusiasts to continue to pursue their hobby while serving out their sentences in labor camps. D. Drialitsyn, "Iz istorii Solovetskogo obshchestva kraevedeniia (SOK)," in *Antsiferovskie chteniia*, 68–71; *Izvestiia TsBK*, no. 5 (1926): 139–40.

55. The Black Hundreds were reactionary bands that conducted a campaign of terror against Jews, liberals, and intellectuals after the 1905 Revolution. Sergei Tolstov, *Vvedenie v sovetskoe kraevedenie*, cited in M. Briansky, "Pervyi kurs sovetskogo kraevedeniia (Sergei Tolstov—vvedenie v sovetskoe kraevedenie)," *Sovetskoe kraevedenie*, no. 10 (1932): 16.

56. D. O. Sviatsky was kept in prisons and camps from 1930 to 1932. I. M. Grevs was held briefly and then released. See the notes provided by A. I. Dobkin inAntsiferov, *Iz dum o bylom*, 473, 499.

57. Antsiferov attended Alexander Meier's *Voskresen'e* (Sunday) discussion circle between 1918 and 1925. In the last few years, he came infrequently, gradually losing interest in the group. Other participants included Mikhail Bakhtin and Sergei Askoldov. See Antsiferov, *Iz dum o bylom*, 323–37.

58. Antsiferov, *Iz dum o bylom*, 354. The pun hinges on the similarity between the words "to know" (*védenie/vedat'*) and "to lead or guide" (*vedénie/vesti*). One approximate translation might be: "only then will our knowledge of local regions lead somewhere."

59. Ibid., 362.

60. The Academy of Sciences finally moved its primary base of operations to Moscow in 1934 after the purges of the early 1930s had completely destroyed its illusions of independence.

61. "The Formation of the Soviet Academy of Sciences: Bolsheviks and Academicians in the 1920s and 1930s," in David-Fox and Péteri, eds., *Academia in Upheaval*, 40–41.

62. Four additional employees were listed as candidates for party membership. Preface to *Akademicheskoe delo 1929–1931 gg.*, xiii.

63. Hostility to both the process of compromise and to its negotiators was common at the time. One epigram popular in academic circles, for instance, reads: "The academician Oldengrad [Oldenburg]/licks the communists on the ass/Their fronts are licked/by his secretary Molas." Traditionally, the verses are attributed to Sergei Platonov. Although a moderate himself and directly involved in negotiations on more than one occasion, Platonov may well have felt a great deal of bitterness about the compromises that were being made. F. F. Perchenok, "Akademiia nauk na 'velikom perelome,'" in *Zven'ia: Istoricheskii al'manakh*, issue 1 (Moscow: Progress-Feniks-Atheneum, 1991), 209.

64. F. F. Perchenok, "Akademiia nauk na 'velikom perelome," in *Zven'ia*, 1:221.

65. I. Klabunovsky, "V bor'be za printsipy sovetskogo kraevedeniia," *Sovetskoe kraevedenie*, nos. 11–12 (1932): 6. The old publications, *Kraevedenie* and *News of the TsBK*, were replaced by *Soviet Kraevedenie* (*Sovetskoe kraevedenie*) in 1930. It initially served as

an organ of both the Central Bureau and of the *kraevedenie* section of the Communist Academy, which had been organized in the fall of 1929. In 1931 the *kraevedenie* section was reorganized into the Society of Marxist *Kraevedy* at the Communist Academy (*Obshchestvo kraevedov-marksistov pri Komakademii* [OKRAM]). A year later this second organization was transformed into the Central Scientific Research Institute on the Methods of *Kraevedenie* Work (*Tsentral'nyi nauchno-issledovatel'skii institut metodov kraevedcheskoi raboty* [TSNIMKR]). In all cases the Marxist organization was supposed to provide the TSBK with methodological supervision. See R. Gel'gardt, "TSBK i Vsesoiuznaia akademiia nauk," *Sovetskoe kraevedenie*, no. 8 (1934): 3–12.

66. "Na putiakh sotsialisticheskogo stroitel'stva," *Sovetskoe kraevedenie*, nos. 1–2 (1930): 5.

67. M. Fenomenov, "Chto pishut v sovetskikh gazetakh o kraevednoi rabote?" *Sovetskoe kraevedenie*, no. 4 (1934): 34.

68. M. P. Potemkin, "X plenum TSBK," *Sovetskoe kraevedenie*, no. 2 (1931): 2–4; "Organizovanno provesti kraevednye konferentsii," *Sovetskoe kraevedenie*, no. 8 (1934): 1. See also O. V. Ionova's treatment of this crisis in her historical survey, "Iz istorii stroitel'stva kraevedcheskikh muzeev RSFSR," in *Ocherki istorii muzeinogo dela v SSSR*, issue 5, Trudy NII muzeevedeniia (Moscow: Sovetskaia Rossiia, 1961), 152.

69. On wartime *kraevedenie*, see N. V. Fatigarova, "Muzeinoe delo v RSFSR v gody Velikoi Otechestvennoi voiny (Aspekty gosudarstvennoi politiki)," in *Muzei i vlast'*, part 1, ed. S. A. Kasparinskaia (Moscow: NII kul'tury, 1991), 199–203.

70. In *Models of Nature*, Douglas Weiner concludes a brief description of the purge of 1930–31 by noting that "this political hullabaloo, while disruptive in a general sense, affected the actual policies of the TSBK surprisingly little." Weiner's point seems to be that the hard-liners at the Communist Academy who led the attack later fell victim to charges of extremism; as was generally the case in the cultural revolution, the opinions of moderate party members ultimately won out. I agree but think it is important not to lose sight of the lasting damage caused by the purge; *kraevedenie* as an independent movement was thoroughly crushed. Work in the humanities and social sciences was particularly affected. Even "moderate" Marxists wanted *kraevedy* to work on projects that promised practical benefits. *Models of Nature* (Bloomington: Indiana University Press, 1988), 140.

71. See, for instance: O. V. Ionova, "Sozdanie seti kraevedcheskikh muzeev v pervykh desiat' let sovetskoi vlasti," in *Ocherki istorii muzeinogo dela v SSSR*, issue 1, Trudy NII muzeevedeniia (Moscow: Gosizdat kul'turno-prosvetitel'noi literatury, 1957), 37–72.

72. Lev Lur'e and Alexander Kobak, "Rozhdenie i gibel' peterburgskoi idei," *Muzei i gorod*, spec. issue of *Ars*, no. 2 (1993): 26.

73. M. A. Tikhomirova, *Pamiatniki. Liudi. Sobytiia: Iz zapisok muzeinogo rabotnika*, 2nd enl. ed. (Leningrad: Khudozhnik RSFSR, 1984), 60, cited in "Muzeinoe delo v RSFSR v gody Velikoi Otechestvennoi voiny (Aspekty gosudarstvennoi politiki)," by N. V. Fatigarova, *Muzei i vlast'*, ed. S. A. Kasparinskaia, 198.

74. The palace in Pavlovsk finally reopened in 1957, the same year in which Ionova's first article on the history of the *kraevedenie* movement appeared. The Catherine Palace in Pushkin opened two years later. O. V. Ionova, "Sozdanie seti kraevedcheskikh muzeev v pervykh desiat' let sovetskoi vlasti," in *Ocherki istorii muzeinogo dela v SSSR*, 1:37–72.

75. Lev Lur'e and Alexander Kobak, "Rozhdenie i gibel' peterburgskoi idei," 26–27.

76. Lur'e and Kobak directly equate the *kraevedy* in Leningrad with Moscow's dissidents. They note that in each city the opposition focused on different problems: in Moscow discussion revolved around religion and politics; in Leningrad cultural issues were primary. Although interesting, this remark tends to obscure the fact that an active *kraevedenie* movement existed in Moscow in the post-Thaw years. Ibid., 27.

77. Antsiferov was arrested for the first time in 1925 and briefly exiled to Novosibirsk and Omsk. In 1929 he was picked up in connection with Alexander Meier's philosophical discussion circle and sentenced to three years in a labor camp. After serving ten months in Kem, he was arrested during a camp-wide investigation, a year was added to his sentence and he was transferred to Solovki. Several months later he was sent back to Leningrad for interrogation in connection with the purge of the Academy of Sciences. In 1931, his sentence was increased to five years, and he was sent to Medvezhii Gor to work on the White Sea Canal construction site. Freed in 1933, Antsiferov moved to Moscow in the hopes of avoiding rearrest. In 1937 he was picked up again. See the timeline provided by A. I. Dobkin in Antsiferov, *Iz dum o bylom*, 411–17.

78. Antsiferov's first wife died of tuberculosis while he was in the camps in 1929.

79. A. I. Dobkin, introduction to Antsiferov, *Iz dum o bylom*, 6–9.

80. N. P. Antsiferov, *Puti izucheniia goroda, kak sotsial'nogo organizma: Opyt kompleksnogo podkhoda*, 2nd rev. and enl. ed. (Leningrad: Seiatel', 1926).

81. N. and T. Antsiferov, *Kniga o gorode 1: Gorod kak vyrazitel' smeniaiushchikhsia kul'tur* (Leningrad: Brokgauz-Efron, 1926), 25–26; N. and T. Antsiferov, *Kniga o gorode 2: Sovremennye goroda* (Leningrad: Brokgauz-Efron, 1926); N. and T. Antsiferov, *Kniga o gorode 3: Zhizn' goroda* (Leningrad: Brokgauz-Efron, 1927).

82. The Excursion and Information Bureau was set up at the end of 1925 in part no doubt to accommodate displaced excursionists. The bureau does not seem to have conducted excursions or run seminars itself. It assembled bibliographies, provided consultations, and collected statistical information on provincial excursion work. "Doklad o deiatel'nosti Tsentral'nogo Biuro Kraevedeniia za period 1 ianvaria 1925 g. –1 marta 1927 g.," *Biulleten' Tret'ei vserossiiskoi konferentsii po kraevedeniiu*, 1:19–21.

CHAPTER 7

1. A. I. Dzens-Litovsky, "K voprosu o predmete i metode kursa 'kraevedenie,'" *Kraevedenie*, no. 2 (1923): 113.

2. Such programs and activities are occasionally mentioned in the "chronicle" section of the journal *Kraevedenie*. See, for instance, *Kraevedenie*, no. 1 (1923): 61; no. 2 (1923): 156, 165, 170–73.

3. Piksanov had been working to develop and popularize the theory of cultural nests since at least 1913. However, he did not speak to an audience of *kraevedy* about his research until the 1924 conference. See N. K. Piksanov, "Oblastnoi printsip v russkom kul'turovedenii. K razrabotke kul'turno-istoricheskoi skhemy," *Iskusstvo*, no. 2 (1925): 82–99.

4. For the abstract, see *Dnevnik Vtoroi vsesoiuznoi konferentsii po kraevedeniiu*, 1:13. The paper was published in the journal *Iskusstvo* in 1925 in what Piksanov called "a very abridged form." Later it formed the basis for the book *Oblastnye kul'turnye gnezda*. In commentary and introductions to his work, Piksanov repeatedly insisted that all of his publications and lectures on the subject of "cultural nests" essentially represented versions of a single paper, differing more in length and thoroughness of exposition than in the substance of the ideas set forth. At least for the abstract and the publications from 1925 and 1928, this does appear to be the case. Hence, it seems reasonable here to use later works to reconstruct the main points of Piksanov's talk at the 1924 conference. N. K. Piksanov, "Oblastnoi printsip v russkom kul'turovedenii," 82–99; N. K. Piksanov, *Oblastnye kul'turnye gnezda* (Moscow: Gosizdat, 1928), 3.

5. N. K. Piksanov, "Oblastnoi printsip v russkom kul'turovedenii," 88. As should be obvious from this quote, Piksanov generally uses the adjective "Russian" in a somewhat expansive sense, meaning by it the combined heritage of the Eastern Slavs—the Ukrainians, the Belarusians, and the Russians.

6. Ibid., 85, 86.

7. Lomonosov was from the Kholmogory area, S. T. Aksakov lived in Kazan, and Gorky was from Nizhni-Novgorod. Piksanov, *Oblastnye kul'turnye gnezda*, 20–28.

8. Piksanov, "Oblastnoi printsip v russkom kul'turovedenii," 94.

9. Ibid., 98.

10. The term *raznochintsy* literally means "people of various ranks." In the nineteenth century it was used to refer to university educated, professional intellectuals of nonnoble origin.

11. Ibid., 99.

12. Ibid., 60, 63.

13. While Piksanov was serving as the Director of the Saratov Teachers' Institute from 1918 to 1921, he organized a "Society of Literature and Ethnography" for students and faculty. It is possible that the group may have been interested in local issues. By late 1921, however, Piksanov had relocated to Moscow. His name does not appear in the publications issued by the Central Bureau of *Kraevedenie* until 1924, so one must assume that he was either uninvolved or, at least, not particularly prominent in the *kraevedenie* movement during the early 1920s. R. I. Kuz'menko, comp., *Nikolai Kir'iakovich Piksanov, Materialy k biobibliografii uchenykh SSSR* (Moscow: Nauka, 1968), 4.

14. The periodical *News of the TSBK* began to appear in July 1925.

15. Grevs attended the Second Conference on *Kraevedenie* and gave a paper at the same session as Piksanov, so he in all likelihood heard the speech. *Dnevnik Vtoroi vsesoiuznoi konferentsii po kraevedeniiu*, 1:8–9.

16. I. M. Grevs, "Istoriia v kraevedenii," *Kraevedenie*, no. 4 (1926): 502.

17. Antsiferov, *Teoriia i praktika literaturnykh ekskursii*, 91–92.

18. Antsiferov opens *The Soul of Petersburg* with a discussion of Pascal's view of human history. His 1927 article "Belletristy-kraevedy" contains an explanation of Bergson's theory of intuition. *Dusha Peterburga*, in *Nepostizhimyi gorod*, 27; "Belletristy-kraevedy," *Kraevedenie*, no. 1 (1927): 31.

19. In 1929, the well-known *kraeved* V. Zolotarev claimed to have invented the popular term "nest" himself, declaring that it first appeared in the 1916 edition of his book *Literatura v tsifrakh i skhemakh*. Piksanov's claim to the term is stronger: he used it in print in 1913. Zolotarev's assertion, however, was probably entirely sincere. The term "cultural nest" seems so natural that it is not difficult to imagine two people arriving at it independently. N. K. Piksanov, "Pis'mo v redaktsiiu," *Literaturnaia gazeta*, no. 8 (July 1929): 4.

20. For information on Piksanov's polemics with the formalists, see Kuz'menko, comp., *Nikolai Kir'iakovich Piksanov*, 11–12. For Piksanov's attack on the Academy of Sciences, see N. K. Piksanov, "V otvet na mnenie akademika V. M. Istrina. (K vyboram novykh akademikov)," *Izvestiia*, February 5, 1929, 1. In 1931 Piksanov was made a corresponding member of the Academy of Sciences himself, despite the fact that he had never written a dissertation. In 1934 he received the degree of Doctor of Philological Sciences on the basis of his prior publications.

21. I. M. Grevs, "Istoriia v kraevedenii," *Kraevedenie*, no. 4 (1926): 502–3.

22. N. P. Antsiferov, "Kraevednyi put' v istoricheskoi nauke," *Kraevedenie*, no. 6 (1928): 336–37; I. M. Grevs, "Ocherednaia zadacha kraevogo kul'turovedeniia," *Kraevedenie*, no. 6 (1928): 368–76; I. M. Grevs, "Pamiatniki kul'tury i sovremennost'," *Kraevedenie*, no. 6 (1929): 311–20.

23. Although it is possible to argue that in this period Leningrad was slowly becoming a part of the provinces, this does not mean that students of the region's culture saw themselves or the topics they explored as "provincial." On the contrary, residents of the northern city even now often insist that it remains Russia's capital in terms of culture.

24. See, for instance, A. N. Svobodov, *V Nizhnem Novgorode na zare XX veka. K kharakteristike kul'turnogo i literaturnogo gnezda*, Nizhegorodskii kraevedcheskii sbornik, vol. 1 (Nizhni Novgorod: n.p., 1925); N. N. Fatov, "O kraevedcheskom izuchenii istorii literatury," in *Rodnoi iazyk v shkole*, vol. 9 (Moscow: Rabotnik prosveshcheniia, 1926).

25. E. Gollerbakh, *Gorod muz: Tsarskoe Selo v poezii* (St. Petersburg: Art-Liuks, 1993), 35, 172.

26. See, for instance, the account of the revival given in: N. A. Milonov, *Literaturnoe kraevedenie* (Moscow: Prosveshchenie, 1985), 40–51.

27. See, for instance, N. Milonov, *Pisateli Tul'skogo kraia* (Tula: Tul'skoe knizhnoe izdatel'stvo, 1963); N. Milonov, *Russkie pisateli v Saratovskom Povolozh'e* (Saratov: Privolskoe knizhnoe izdatel'stvo, 1964); I. T. Trofimov, *Pisateli Brianskogo kraia* ([Briansk]: Brianskii rabochii, 1963); P. Beisov, *Svobodnoe slovo bessmertno* (Saratov: Privolzhskoe knizhnoe izdatel'vo, 1966).

28. N. P. Antsiferov, "1919-i god," OR RNB f. 27, l. 7, cited in A. M. Konechny and K. A. Kumpan, "Peterburg v zhizni i trudakh N. P. Antsiferova," the introduction to Antsiferov, *Nepostizhimyi gorod*, 16. This passage is omitted from the published edition of Antsiferov's memoirs, *Iz dum o bylom*. In the citation Antsiferov refers to Anna Akhmatova's 1915 poem "Ved' gde-to est' prostaia zhizn' i svet." Anna Akhmatova, *Stikhotvoreniia i poemy*, ed. V. M. Zhirmunsky, 2nd ed., Biblioteka poeta, Bol'shaia seriia (Leningrad: Sovetskii pisatel', 1979), 99.

29. Antsiferov, *Dusha Peterburga*, in Antsiferov, *Nepostizhimyi gorod*, 170. In *The Soul of Petersburg* Antsiferov was working from the 1916 edition of Bely's *Petersburg*. For the context in which this quote appears, see Andrei Bely, *Sobranie sochinenii. Peterburg: Roman v vos'mi glavakh s prologom i epilogom*, ed. V. M. Piskunov (Moscow: Respublika, 1994), 5.

30. Antsiferov, *Dusha Peterburga*, in Antsiferov, *Nepostizhimyi gorod*, 173.

31. Ibid.

32. Even if the dates included at the end of *The Soul of Petersburg* were inserted for literary effect and do not reflect the text's compositional history with perfect accuracy, their presence indicates that Antsiferov wanted readers to perceive the last three sections of his work in the context of particular moments in history.

33. Ibid., 174.

34. Ibid., 173. Northern Palmyra is a traditional epithet for St. Petersburg in Russian poetry. Petropol is another popular appellation for the city. In the original Russian text, the word "destruction" appears in Latin.

35. Mstislav Dobuzhinsky, *Peterburg v dvadtsat' pervom godu*, introduction by S. Iaremich ([Petrograd]: Komitet populiarizatsii khudozhestvennykh izdanii pri Rossiiskoi akademii istorii material'noi kul'tury, 1921); *Peterburg: Avtolitografii A. P. Ostroumovoi* (1922), introduction by Alexander Benois, reprinted as a supplement to N. Antsiferov, *Dusha Peterburga* (St. Petersburg: Detskaia literatura, 1990). For an example of comments by Benois, see page 2 of the latter volume. See also the engravings by Ostroumova-Lebedeva that were used to illustrate the original edition of *Dusha Peterburga*.

36. Antsiferov, *Dusha Peterburga*, in Antsiferov, *Nepostizhimyi gorod*, 48,30.

37. Ibid., 30, 31, 44.

38. Vernon Lee, *Genius Loci: Notes on Places* (London: Grant Richards, 1899), 3–4. Antsiferov includes this citation, minus the parenthetical remark, in *Dusha Peterburga*, in Antsiferov, *Nepostizhimyi gorod*, 30.

39. Sculptural representations of eight French cities form part of the architectural ensemble of the Place de la Concorde in Paris: images of Brest and Rouen by Cortot, of

Lille and Strasbourg by Pradier, of Lyon and Marseille by Petitot, and of Bordeaux and Nantes by Caillouette.

40. Ibid., 5. There were monuments to the *genius loci* in Tsarskoe Selo in the early nineteenth century. Engelgardt, the director of the Lyceum, had a cube built out of turf in his garden. A marble plaque was placed on top bearing the inscription "genius loci." Later on a similar monument appeared in the garden of the Lyceum itself. It became a kind of shrine for the students; they left small notes at it, recounting their worries and hopes for the future. Lee might have found these monuments less objectionable than the ladies on the Place de la Concorde, because they were so abstract. Antsiferov certainly found nothing exceptionable in them; he mentions this piece of trivia repeatedly in his later books. *Teoriia i praktika literaturnykh ekskursii*, 52; *Pushkin v Tsarskom Sele*, ed. Vlad. Bonch-Bruevich, Gosudarstvennyi literaturnyi muzei (Moscow: Gosizdat, 1950), 70.

41. *Genius Loci*, 6.

42. *Dusha Peterburga*, in Antsiferov, *Nepostizhimyi gorod*, 30.

43. The sphinxes on the Neva represent authentic Egyptian artifacts. Found at Luxor in 1820 and brought to Russia in 1832, they have the facial features of Pharaoh Amunhotep III, who ruled during Egypt's golden age (1417–1379 B.C.). The rostral columns on St. Basil's Island were designed by the architect Thomas de Thomon at the beginning of the nineteenth century. Modeled after monuments erected in Rome to celebrate naval victories, they are decorated with personified representations of Russia's four major rivers and carvings of boat prows. The two statues of the Shih Tza, a mythological creature resembling a lion, were brought to St. Petersburg in 1907 from Manchuria. Catherine the Great commissioned the equestrian monument to Peter I, known popularly as the Bronze Horseman. As I noted in Chapter 2, in the statue, Peter I wears a costume that in some respects seems Roman.

44. *Dusha Peterburga*, in Antsiferov, *Nepostizhimyi gorod*, 35–37.

45. Ibid., 44.

46. Ibid.

47. Ibid., 48.

48. Ibid., 170.

49. See, for comparison, Sofiia Snessoreva, *Zemnaia zhizn' presviatoi bogoroditsy i opisanie sviatykh chudotvornykh ee ikon, chtimykh pravoslavnoiu tserkov'iu, na osnovanii sviashchennogo pisaniia i tserkovnykh predanii, s izobrazheniiami v tekste prazdnikov bozhiei materi*, 2nd ed. (1898; Iaroslavl: Verkhne-Volozhskoe knizhnoe izdatel'stvo, 1993).

50. *Dusha Peterburga*, in Antsiferov, *Nepostizhimyi gorod*, 48.

51. Antsiferov devoted approximately nine pages to Pushkin, nine to Gogol, eight to Dostoevsky, fourteen pages to Blok, and nine to Bely. My count is based on the *Nepostizhimyi gorod* edition.

52. *Dusha Peterburga*, in Antsiferov, *Nepostizhimyi gorod*, 58–59.

53. Ibid., 47.

54. Ibid., 68. Antsiferov is speaking specifically about Gogol's St. Petersburg in the passage I cite. The line about "a foreigner to its own fatherland" is taken from Gogol's "Peterburgskie zapiski 1836 goda."

55. Ibid., 47.

56. Ibid., 123. Antsiferov uses the word "image" (*obraz*) in several different ways in *The Soul of Petersburg*. Sometimes it obviously refers to the independent entity I describe here; in other cases it indicates either the image of the city in the work of a specific author or a literary image (concrete representation). In the first case, the word only appears in the singular; in the latter two cases, it may be in the plural.

57. Ibid., 47.

58. References to Soloviev and later symbolists abound in Antsiferov's published and unpublished autobiographical writing. See Nikolai Antsiferov, *Iz dum o bylom*, ed. A. I. Dobkin (Moscow: Feniks, 1992), 29, 58, 70, 99, 171, 213, 368–69, 378, 426.

59. See, for instance, Antsiferov, *Dusha Peterburga*, in Antsiferov, *Nepostizhimyi gorod*, 47.

60. Ibid., 30.

61. *Liubov' Gertsena*, OR RNB, f. 27, ed. khr. 108; "Istoricheskaia nauka kak odna iz form bor'by za vechnost'," RNB OR f. 27, ed. khr. 72.

62. Vladimir Sergeevich Solov'ev, "Obshchii smysl iskusstva," in *Sobranie sochnenii*, ed. S. M. Solov'ev and E. L. Radlov, 10 vols. (St. Petersburg: Prosveshchenie, 1886–94), 6:84. This passage is partially cited in an article by Irina Paperno. I have built on her translation. Irina Paperno, "The Meaning of Art: Symbolist Theories," in *Creating Life: The Aesthetic Utopia of Russian Modernism*, ed. Irina Paperno and Joan Delaney Grossman (Stanford: Stanford University Press, 1994), 14.

63. Solov'ev, "Obshchii smysl iskusstva," 82, cited in Paperno, "The Meaning of Art," 14.

64. Solov'ev, *Sobranie sochnenii*, 6:85.

65. As noted in Chapter 6, Antsiferov adopted a trope strongly associated with nineteenth-century physiological sketches in many of the works he wrote during the 1920s: elaborate comparisons between specific parts of the city and the organs of the human body. See, for instance, N. P. Antsiferov, *Puti izucheniia goroda, kak sotsial'nogo organizma: Opyt kompleknogo podkhoda*, 2nd ed. (Leningrad: Seiatel', 1926), 15–28.

66. *Dusha Peterburga*, in Antsiferov, *Nepostizhimyi gorod*, 36.

67. Ibid., 35. For other passages where Antsiferov equates the genius loci with Falconet's statue, see pages 124, 145, and 146 of the same volume.

68. As cited in the notes to Andrei Bely, *Petersburg*, ed. and trans. Robert A. Maguire and John E. Malmstad (Bloomington: Indiana University Press, 1978), 324. The translation of the Pushkin passage is by Maguire and Malmstad.

69. Ibid., 64.

70. *Dusha Peterburga*, in Antsiferov, *Nepostizhimyi gorod*, 58–67, 73, 145–46.

71. Ibid., 170.

72. Gollerbakh published both editions at his own expense. The first edition of *City of Muses* was illustrated with silhouettes by other Russian artists. O. S. Ostroi and L. I. Iuniverg, *Erikh Fedorovich Gollerbakh kak kollektsioner i izdatel'* (Leningrad: Leningradskaia organizatsiia dobrovol'nogo obshchestva knigoliubov, 1990), 48–58.

73. I cite from a post-Soviet facsimile edition of *City of Muses: Gorod muz* (1930; St. Petersburg: Art Liuks, 1993), 34.

74. Ibid., 206–8, 162.

75. See the Pushkin poem "19 oktiabria," in A. S. Pushkin, *Polnoe sobranie sochinenii v desiati tomakh*, 6th ed. (Leningrad: Nauka, 1977), 2:245.

76. Gollerbakh, *Gorod muz* (1993), 44.

77. Antsiferov, *Dusha Peterburga*, in Antsiferov, *Nepostizhimyi gorod*, 48.

78. The two writers use the term genius loci in somewhat different ways. Gollerbakh clearly connects the phrase, first and foremost, with the monument on the grounds of the Lyceum. He apparently believed that one of the primary functions of the god of locality was to "protect poetry." In his book, the genius loci is strongly associated with the muses. Gollerbakh, *Gorod muz*, 198–99. See also Gollerbakh's introduction to *Tsarskoe Selo v poezii*, ed. N. O. Lerner (St. Petersburg: Parfenon, 1922), 3.

79. Gollerbakh, *Gorod muz*, 161, 162–63, 178, 174.

80. Ibid., 200, 166, 163.

81. O. S. Ostroi, "'Gorod muz' v zhizni E. F. Gollerbakha," in Dobkin and Kobak, eds., *Antsiferovskie chteniia*, 45.

82. "Nepostizhimyi gorod: Peterburg v poezii A. Bloka," in *Ob Aleksandre Bloke: Sbornik statei* (Petersburg: n.p., 1921), 285–325; "Peterburg Dostoevskogo: Opyt literaturnoi ekskursii," *Ekskursionnoe delo*, nos. 2–3 (1921): 49–68.

83. Gollerbakh might well have garnered most of this basic information from a brief brochure published by Innokenty Annensky in 1899. "Pushkin i Tsarskoe Selo," in *Knigi otrazhenii*, Literaturnye pamiatniki (Moscow: Nauka, 1979), 304–21.

84. A second revised version of *Pushkin's Petersburg* appeared in 1935. It was, unfortunately, seriously marred by the addition of Marxist rhetoric. My comments here are based on the 1931 text, as reprinted in A. Iatsevich, *Pushkinskii Petersburg* (St. Petersburg, Petropol', 1993).

85. Ibid., 4.

86. See the correspondence between the two men in OR RNB, f. 741, op. 1, ed. khr. 361.

87. Iatsevich thanks Stolpiansky specifically for his help in the preface to *Pushkin's Petersburg*. He also refers to his publications repeatedly throughout the book, either citing them as sources or disputing minor facts. See, for instance, Iatsevich, *Pushkinskii Petersburg*, 4, 120.

88. See, for instance, P. N. Stolpiansky, *Staryi Peterburg. Dvorets truda: Istoricheskii ocherk* (Petrograd: Gosizdat, 1923).

89. In the works he wrote from the 1930s on, Antsiferov even moved toward this kind of historical account. Antsiferov, *Peterburg Pushkina,* in Antsiferov, *Nepostizhimyi gorod,* 258–93; N. Antsiferov, T. Ivanova, N. Liubovich, A. Khramov, V. Kornilov, E. Iakovkina, and D. Giveev, *Po lermontovskim mestam,* ed. S. I. Aralov (Moscow: Gosudarstvennyi literaturnyi muzei, 1940); N. Antsiferov, *Pushkin v Tsarskom Sele,* ed. Vlad. Bonch-Bruevich, Gosudarstvennyi literaturnyi muzei (Moscow: Goskul'tprosvetizdat, 1950).

90. *Besedy o russkoi kul'ture: Byt i traditsii russkogo dvoriantsva (XVIII-nachalo XIX veka)* (St. Petersburg: Iskusstvo-SPb, 1994); *Velikosvetskie obedy,* Byloi Peterburg (St. Petersburg: Pushkinskii fond, 1996). Both books appeared posthumously.

91. Lotman, *Besedy o russkoi kul'ture,* 9.

92. This term was first used by Vladimir Nikolaevich Toporov—"O strukture romana Dostoevskogo v sviazi s istoricheskimi skhemami morfologicheskogo myshleniia *(Prestuplenie i nakazanie)*"—in *Structure of Texts and Semiotics of Culture,* ed. Jan Van der Eng and Grygar Mojmír (The Hague: Mouton, 1973), 277. I am particularly interested here in the way the theory was later developed by Z. G. Mints, M. V. Bezrodny, and A. A. Danilevsky in their article, "'Peterburgskii tekst' i russkii simvolizm," in *Semiotika goroda i gorodskoi kul'tury: Peterburg,* Trudy po znakovym sistemam XVIII v., Uchenye zapiski Tartuskogo gosudarstvennogo universiteta (Tartu: Tartuskii gosudarstvennyi universitet, 1984), 78.

93. Mints, Bezrodny, and Danilevsky, "'Peterburgskii tekst' i russkii simvolizm," 79, 81.

94. Ibid., 78.

95. Ibid., 80.

96. This quotation is from the first line of R. D. Timenchik's "Poetika Sankt-Peterburga epokhi simvolizma/postsimvolizma," in *Semiotika goroda i gorodskoi kul'tury: Peterburg,* 117. The article by Mints, Bezrodny, and Danilevsky from the same volume opens with a reference to Antsiferov's work as the ultimate source for the idea of a "single text." "'Peterburgskii tekst' i russkii simvolizm," 78. In "Mif o Peterburge i ego preobrazovanie v nachale veka," in *Na rubezhe vekov* (Leningrad: Sovetskii pisatel', 1985), Dolgopolov mentions Antsiferov five times.

CONCLUSION

1. Lenoir, "The Discipline of Nature and the Nature of Disciplines," in Messer-Davidow, Shumway, and Sylvan, eds., *Knowledges,* 76.

2. Joseph C. Kiger, "Discipline," in *Encyclopedia of Education* (New York: Philosophical Library, 1971), 3:99, cited in Wolfram W. Swoboda, "Disciplines and Interdisciplinarity," in *Interdisciplinarity and Higher Education,* ed. Joseph J. Kockelmans (University Park: Pennsylvania State University Press, 1979), 52.

3. Michel Foucault, *The Order of Things: An Archeology of the Human Sciences* (New York: Vintage, 1994); *Discipline and Punish: The Birth of the Prison*, trans. Alan Sheridan (New York: Vintage, 1977).

4. Belinsky, introduction to *Fiziologiia Peterburga*, 6–8.

5. Belinsky, "Peterburg i Moskva" in *Fiziologiia Peterburga*, 6–37; Alexander Herzen, "Moskva i Peterburg" and "Novgorod Velikii i Vladimir-Na-Kliaz'me," in Alexander Herzen, *Sobranie sochinenii v tridtsati tomakh* (Moscow: AN SSSR, 1954), 2:33–48; Kontastantin Aksakov, "Semisotletie Moskvy," in Konstantin Aksakov, *Sochineniia*, ed. E. A. Liatsky (St. Petersburg: n.p., 1915), 1:598–605.

6. See, for instance, the following textbook, which is designed for use in middle and high school *kraevedenie* classes: A. V. Darvinsky and V. I. Startsev, *Istoriia Sankt-Peterburga. XX vek* (St. Petersburg: Glagol, 1997), 127, 132–41, 151. The cover shows a view of the Peter and Paul Fortress, glimpsed through the arch over the Winter Canal. The sky, the water in the canal, the buildings, and the words "twentieth century" in the title are all in places painted red, as though spattered with blood. A hammer and sickle floats in the sky next to the Peter and Paul cathedral.

7. In recent years St. Petersburg publishing houses have released a substantial number of textbooks and workbooks for schools and classes employing the localized method. See Z. A. Serova, *Peterburgskii zadachnik dlia malyshei* (St. Petersburg: MiM, 1998); *Uprazhneniia po russkomu iazyku dlia peterburgskikh shkol'nikov*, 2nd enl. and rev. ed., Peterburgskaia tetrad' (St. Petersburg: Khimera, 1999); E. A. Sukharnikova, *Muzykal'nyi Sankt-Peterburg: Uchebnik-tetrad'*, 2nd rev. ed. (St. Petersburg: SpetsLit, 2000).

8. See, for instance, S. A. Prokhvatilova, ed., *"Gorod pod morem" ili blistatel'nyi Sankt-Peterburg: Vospominaniia, rasskazy ocherki, stikhi* (St. Petersburg: Lenizdat, 1996); L. L. Reshetnikova, ed., *Dusha Peterburga: Peterburg v proizvedeniiakh russkikh pisatelei XIX veka*, Shkol'naia biblioteka (St. Petersburg: Lenizdat, 1996); M. G. Kachurin, G. A. Kudyrskaia, and D. N. Murin, *Sankt-Peterburg v russkoi literature: Uchebnik—khrestomatiia dlia 9–11 kl. srednikh shkol, gimnazii, litseev, kolledzhei*, 2nd rev. and enl. ed., 2 vols. (St. Petersburg: Svet, 1996); *Sankt-Peterburg. 1703–1917*, ed. A.V. Darvinsky (St. Petersburg: Glagol, 2000); *Sankt-Peterburg. XX vek. Chto? Gde? Kogda?* (St. Petersburg: Paritet, 2000).

9. See, for instance, D. Zolotarev, "Rodinovedenie i narodnyi uchitel'," *Russkii ekskursant*, nos. 5–6 (1914): 6; Milonov, *Literaturnoe kraevedenie*, 3.

10. Confino, *The Nation as Local Metaphor*, 9–13.

11. See, for instance, *Metodologiia regional'nykh istoricheskikh issledovanii: Materialy mezhdunarodnogo seminara, 19–20 iunia 2000 goda, Sankt-Peterburg*, ed. Alexander Kobak, Stefan Kotkin, and Alla Sevast'ianova (St. Petersburg: Notabene, 2000).

12. See Antsiferov's *The Soul of Petersburg* for a discussion of this aspect of the image of St. Petersburg. *Dusha Peterburga*, in Antsiferov, *Nepostizhimyi gorod*, 68

SELECTED BIBLIOGRAPHY

ARCHIVES

Arkhiv Akademii nauk (AAN), St. Petersburg
Otdel rukopisei Rossiiskoi natsional'noi biblioteki (OR RNB), St. Petersburg
Tsentral'nyi gosudarstvennyi arkhiv literatury i iskusstva (TsGALI), St. Petersburg

JOURNALS

Ekskursionnoe delo
Ekskursionnyi vestnik (1914–16)
Ekskursionnyi vestnik (1922)
Iskusstvo i khudozhestvennaia promyshlennost'
Izvestiia Tsentral'nogo biuro kraevedeniia
Khozhdenie po Rusi i za rubezh
Khudozhestvennye sokrovishcha Rossii
Kraevedenie
Mir iskusstva
Muzei
Pedagogicheskaia mysl'
Russkii ekskursant
Shkol'nye ekskursii i shkol'nyi muzei
Sovetskoe kraevedenie
Sputnik ekskursanta
Starye gody

BOOKS AND ARTICLES

Akademicheskoe delo 1929–1931 gg. Issue 1. St. Petersburg: Biblioteka Rossiiskoi akademii nauk, 1993.
Aksakov, Konstantin, and Ivan Aksakov. *Literaturnaia kritika.* Moscow: Sovremennik, 1981.

Aleksandrov, Iurii. *Moskva: Dialog putevoditelei*. Moscow: Moskovskii rabochii, 1986.
Andrews, James T. "Local Science and Public Enlightenment: Iaroslavl Naturalists and the Soviet State, 1917–1930." In *Provincial Landscapes: Local Dimensions of Soviet Power, 1917–1953*, ed. Donald J. Raleigh, 105–24. Pitt Series in Russian and East European Studies. Pittsburgh: University of Pittsburgh Press, 2001.

———. *Science for the Masses: The Bolshevik State, Public Science, and the Popular Imagination in Soviet Russia, 1917–1934*. Eastern European Studies, no. 22. College Station: Texas A&M University Press, 2003.

Annensky, Innokenty. "Pushkin i Tsarskoe Selo." In *Knigi otrazhenii*, 304–21. Literaturnye pamiatniki. Moscow: Nauka, 1979.

Antsiferov, Nikolai. "Nepostizhimyi gorod: Peterburg v poezii A. Bloka." In *Ob Aleksandre Bloke: Sbornik statei*, 285–325. Petrograd: n. p., 1921.

———. *Puti izucheniia goroda, kak sotsial'nogo organizma: Opyt kompleksnogo podkhoda*. 2nd ed., rev. and enl. Leningrad: Seiatel', 1926.

———. *Teoriia i praktika ekskursii po obshchestvovedeniiu*. Leningrad: n. p., 1926.

———. *Teoriia i praktika literaturnykh ekskursii*. Leningrad: Seiatel', 1926.

———. *Pushkin v Tsarskom Sele (Literaturnaia progulka po Detskomu Selu)*. Ekskursionno- lektorskaia baza Oblono. V pomoshch' ekskursantu i turistu. Leningrad: Tipografiia Oblfo, 1929.

———. *Prigorody Leningrada*. Moscow: Gosudarstvennyi literaturnyi muzei, 1946.

———. *Metodika izucheniia i pokaza literaturnoi zhizni kraia v ekspozitsii kraevedcheskikh muzeev*. Moscow: Goskul'tprosvetizdat, 1949.

———. *Pushkin v Tsarskom Sele*. Ed. Vlad. Bonch-Bruevich. Gosudarstvennyi literaturnyi muzei. Moscow: Goskul'tprosvetizdat, 1950.

———. *Dusha Peterburga*. 2 vols. Leningrad: Lira, 1990.

———. *Dusha Peterburga. Peterburg Dostoevskogo. Byl' i mif Peterburga*. Reprint of 1922, 1923, and 1924 editions. Ed. E. B. Pokrovskaia. Moscow: Kniga, 1991.

———. *Nepostizhimyi gorod . . . Dusha Peterburga; Peterburg Dostoevskogo; Peterburg Pushkina*. Ed. M. B. Verblovskaia. Leningrad: Lenizdat, 1991.

———. *Iz dum o bylom: Vospominaniia*. Ed. A. I. Dobkin. Moscow: Feniks; Kul'turnaia initsiativa, 1992.

Antsiferov, Nikolai, and Tat'iana Antsiferova. *Kniga o gorode 1. Gorod kak vyrazitel' smeniaiushchikhsia kul'tur*. Leningrad: Brokgauz-Efron, 1926.

———. *Kniga o gorode 2. Sovremennye goroda*. Leningrad: Brokgauz-Efron, 1926.

———. *Kniga o gorode 3. Zhizn' goroda*. Leningrad: Brokgauz-Efron, 1927.

Antsiferov, Nikolai, and Georgy Petri. *Istoricheskie ekskursii po Ermitazhu*. Leningrad: Priboi, 1924.

Antsiferov, Nikolai, T. Ivanova, N. Liubovich, A. Khramov, V. Kornilov, E. Iakovkina and D. Giveev. *Po lermontovskim mestam*. Ed. S. I. Aralov. Putevoditel'

Gosudarstvennogo literaturnogo muzeia. Moscow: Gosudarstvennyi literaturnyi muzei, 1940.
Applegate, Celia. *A Nation of Provincials: The German Idea of Heimat*. Berkeley and Los Angeles: University of California Press, 1990.
Bakhtiarov, Anatoly. *Briukho Peterburga: Ocherki stolichnoi zhizni*. St. Petersburg: Fert, 1994.
Bashutsky, Alexander. *Panorama Sankt-Peterburga*. 3 vols. St. Petersburg: Tipografiia vdovy Pliushara, 1834.
———. *Nashi spisannye s natury russkimi*. St. Petersburg: Ia. A. Isakov, 1841–42. Facsimile edition with extensive commentary. 2 vols. Moscow: Kniga, 1986.
Becher, Tony, and Paul R. Trowler. *Academic Tribes and Territories*. 2nd ed. Buckingham: The Society for Research into Higher Education and Open University Press, 2001.
Bely, Andrei. *Petersburg*. Ed. and trans. Robert Maguire and John Malmstad. Bloomington: Indiana University Press, 1978.
Benois, Alexander [A. Benua]. *Tsarskoe Selo v tsarstvovanie imperatritsy Elisavety Petrovny*. St. Petersburg: R. Golike and A. Vil'borg, 1910.
———. *Aleksandr Benua razmyshliaet*. Ed. I. S. Zil'bershtein and A. N. Savinov. Moscow: Sovetskii khudozhnik, 1968.
———. *Moi vospominaniia v piati knigakh*. 2nd ed., enl. 2 vols. Literaturnye pamiatniki. Moscow: Nauka, 1993.
———. *Vozniknovenie "Mira iskusstva"*. Reprint of 1928 edition. Staraia kniga po iskusstvu. Moscow: Iskusstvo, 1994.
Bespiatykh, Iu. N ed. *Peterburg Petra I v inostrannykh opisaniiakh: Vvedenie, teksty, kommentarii*. Panorama istorii. Leningrad: Nauka, 1991.
———. *Peterburg Anny Ioannovny v inostrannykh opisaniiakh: Vvedenie, teksty, kommentarii*. St. Petersburg: BLITS, 1997.
Bezbakh, S. *K istorii kraevedcheskoi raboty v Leningrade: Obshchestvo "Staryi Peterburg—Novyi Leningrad". Otdelenie obshchestva v severnykh okrestnostiakh*. Leningrad: [Obshchestvo "Staryi Peterburg—Novyi Leningrad"], 1926.
Biulleten' Tret'ei vserossiiskoi konferentsii po kraevedeniiu. 6 issues. Moscow: TSBK, 1927.
Blinov, A. M. "Eti liudi byli podvizhnikami. . . ." *Leningradskaia panorama*, no. 9 (1988): 38–39.
Bogdanov, Andrei I. *Istoricheskoe, geograficheskoe i topograficheskoe opisanie Sanktpeterburga ot nachala zavedeniia ego s 1703 po 1751 god*. Ed. and suppl. Vasily Ruban. St. Petersburg: n.p., 1779.
———. *Opisanie Sanktpeterburga. Polnoe izdanie unikal'nogo rossiiskogo istoriko-geograficheskogo truda serediny XVIII veka*. Ed. K. I. Logachev and V. S. Sobolev. St. Petersburg: Severo-Zapadnaia Bibleiskaia Komissiia, Sankt-Peterburgskii filial Arkhiva RAN, 1997.

Bogdanov, V. V., ed. *Voprosy kraevedeniia: Sbornik dokladov, sdelannykh na Vserossiiskoi konferentsii nauchnykh obshchestv po izucheniiu mestnogo kraia v Moskve v dekabre 1921 goda sozvannoi Akademicheskim tsentrom.* Petrograd: Nizhpoligraf, 1923.

Bourdieu, Pierre. "The Specificity of the Scientific Field and the Social Conditions of the Progress of Reason." *Social Science Information* 14 (1975): 19–47.

Bowlt, John. *The Silver Age: Russian Art of the Early Twentieth Century and the "World of Art" Group.* Newtonville, Mass.: Oriental Research Partners, 1982.

Bozherianov, I. *Nevskii prospekt, 1703–1903. Kul'turno-istoricheskii ocherk dvukhvekovoi zhizni S.-Peterburga.* 2 vols. St. Petersburg: Tip. A. I. Vil'borga, 1903.

Buckler, Julie A. *Mapping St. Petersburg: Imperial Text and Cityshape.* Princeton: Princeton University Press, 2005.

Bur'ianov, Viktor. *Progulka s det'mi po S.-Peterburgu i ego okrestnostiam.* 3 vols. St. Petersburg: Tipografiia Glavnogo upravleniia putei soobshcheniia i publichnikh zdanii, 1838.

Butin, I. A., ed. *Leningrad: Kraevednyi sbornik (Posobie dlia shkol I-oi i II-oi stup.).* Leningrad: Izdanie Leningradskogo oblono, 1928.

Clark, Burton R. *The Higher Education System: Academic Organization in Cross National Perspective.* Berkeley and Los Angeles: University of California Press, 1983.

Clark, Katerina. *Petersburg: Crucible of Cultural Revolution.* Cambridge: Harvard University Press, 1995.

Clowes, Edith, Samuel D. Kassow, and James L. West, eds. *Between Tsar and People: Educated Society and the Quest for Public Identity in Late Imperial Russia.* Princeton: Princeton University Press, 1991.

Confino, Alon. *The Nation as Local Metaphor: Württemberg, Imperial Germany, and National Memory, 1871–1918.* Chapel Hill: University of North Carolina Press, 1997.

Cracraft, James. "St. Petersburg: The Russian Cosmopolis." In *Russia Engages the World, 1453–1825*, ed. Cynthia Hyla Whittaker, 24–49. Cambridge: Harvard University Press, 2003.

David-Fox, Michael, and György Péteri, eds. *Academia in Upheaval: Origins, Transfers, and Transformations of the Communist Academic Regime in Russia and East Central Europe.* Westport, Conn.: Bergin & Garvey, 2000.

Danilov, V. "Dedushka russkikh istoricheskikh zhurnalov: 'Otechestvennye Zapiski' P. P. Svin'ina." *Istoricheskii vestnik* (July 1915): 109–29.

Darvinsky, A. V., ed. *Sankt-Peterburg. 1703–1917.* St. Petersburg: Glagol, 2000.

Darvinsky, A. V., and V. I. Startsev. *Istoriia Sankt-Peterburga. XX vek: Uchebnoe posobie.* St. Petersburg: Glagol, 1997.

Dnevnik Vserossiiskoi konferentsii nauchnykh obshchestv po izucheniiu mestnogo kraia sozyvaemoi Akademicheskim tsentrom Narkomprosa v Moskve, 10–20 dekabria, 1921. 5 issues. Moscow: Pechatnyi tekhnik, 1921–22.

Dnevnik Vtoroi vsesoiuznoi konferentsii po kraevedeniiu. 4 issues. Moscow: Mospoligraf, 1924.

Dobkin, A. I., and A. V. Kobak, eds. *Antsiferovskie chteniia: Materialy i tezisy konferentsii (20–22 dekabria 1989 g.).* Leningrad: Leningradskoe otdelenie Sovetskogo fonda kul'tury, 1989.

Dobuzhinsky, Mstislav. *Peterburg v dvadtsat' pervom godu.* [Petrograd]: Komitet populiarizatsii khudozhestvennykh izdanii pri Rossiiskoi akademii istorii material'noi kul'tury, 1921.

———. *Vospominaniia.* Ed. G. I. Chugunov. Literaturnye pamiatniki. Moscow: Nauka, 1987.

Dolgopolov, Leonid. "Peterburg Aleksandra Benua." In *Leningradskaia panorama,* ed. Ia. A. Gordin, 385–405. Leningrad: Sovetskii pisatel', 1984.

———. "Mif o Peterburge i ego preobrazovanie v nachale veka." In *Na rubezhe vekov: O russkoi literature kontsa XIX-nachala XX veka,* 150—94. Leningrad: Sovetskii pisatel', 1985.

Downing, David B. "The 'Mop-Up' Work of Theory Anthologies: Theorizing the Discipline and the Disciplining of Theory." *Symplokë* 8, no. 1–2 (2000): 129–50.

Easton, David, and Corrine S. Schelling, eds. *Divided Knowledge: Across Disciplines, Across Cultures.* Newbury Park, Calif.: Sage Publications, 1991.

Eliashevich, I. Ia., ed. *Sputnik bezbozhnika po Leningradu.* Leningrad: Priboi, 1930.

Ely, Christopher. *This Meager Nature: Landscape and National Identity in Imperial Russia.* Dekalb: Northern Illinois University Press, 2002.

Etkind, Mark. *Aleksandr Nikolaevich Benua, 1870–1960.* Moscow: Iskusstvo, 1965.

———. *A. N. Benua i russkaia khudozhestvennaia kul'tura kontsa XIX–nachala XX veka.* Leningrad: Khudozhnik RSFSR, 1989.

Fanger, Donald. *Dostoevsky and Romantic Realism.* Chicago: University of Chicago Press, 1965.

Fitzpatrick, Sheila. *The Commissariat of Enlightenment.* Cambridge: Cambridge University Press, 1970.

———. *The Cultural Front: Power and Culture in Revolutionary Russia.* Ithaca: Cornell University Press, 1992.

Fitzpatrick, Sheila, Alexander Rabinowitz, and Richard Stites, eds. *Russia in the Era of NEP: Explorations in Soviet Society and Culture.* Bloomington: Indiana University Press, 1991.

Fiziologiia Peterburga. Literaturnye pamiatniki. Moscow: Nauka, 1991.

Foucault, Michel. *The Order of Things: An Archaeology of the Human Sciences.* Vintage Books, 1970.

———. *The Archeology of Knowledge and the Discourse on Language.* Trans. A. M. Sheridan Smith. New York: Pantheon Books, 1972.

———. *Discipline and Punish: The Birth of the Prison*. Trans. Alan Sheridan. New York: Vintage Books, 1977.

Franklin, Simon, and Emma Widdis, eds. *National Identity in Russian Culture: An Introduction*. Cambridge: Cambridge University Press, 2004.

Gatchina pri Pavle Petroviche Tsesareviche i Imperatore. Mramornaia seriia. St. Petersburg: Liga, 1995.

Geirot, A. *Opisanie Petergofa*. St. Petersburg: Tipografiia Imperatorskoi akademii nauk, 1868. Reprint. Leningrad: Aurora, 1991.

Gellner, Ernest. *Nations and Nationalism*. New Perspectives on the Past. Ithaca: Cornell University Press, 1983.

Georgi, I. G. [Johann Gottlieb]. *Opisanie rossiisko-imperatorskogo stolichnogo goroda Sankt-Peterburga i dostopamiatnostei v okrestnostiakh onogo s planom*. Mramornaia seriia. St. Petersburg: Liga, 1996.

Gilenson, A. B., ed. *V pomoshch' rabotniku muzeia: Zakony, rasporiazheniia, raz"iasneniia po muzeinomu stroitel'stvu*. Moscow: Narkompros RSFSR, 1936.

Gollerbakh, Erikh. *Detskosel'skie dvortsy-muzei i parki: Putevoditel'*. St. Petersburg: Gosizdat, 1922.

———. "Tsarskoe Selo v poezii." In *Tsarskoe Selo v poezii*, ed. N. O. Lerner, 3–14. St. Petersburg: Parfenon, 1922.

———. *Dioskury i kniga: Bibliofil'skii difiramb (1920–1930)*. Leningrad: Izdanie avtora na pravakh rukopisi, 1930. Facsimile edition. Moscow: DOK RSFSR. Vserossiiskaia assotsiatsiia bibliofilov, 1990.

———. *Gorod muz: Tsarskoe Selo v poezii. Prilozhenie k faksimil'nomu izdaniiu*. Article and commentary by O. S. Ostroi and L. I. Iuniverg. Moscow: Kniga, 1990.

———. *Gorod muz: Tsarskoe Selo v poezii*. 1930; reprint, St. Petersburg: Art-liuks, 1993.

Gollerbakh, Erikh, and N. Lansere [Lanceray], eds. *Charl'z Kameron: Sbornik*. Moscow: Gosizdat, 1924.

Golovin, N. *Peterburg v petrovskoe vremia: Istoricheskii ocherk*. St. Petersburg: M. O. Vol'f, 1903.

Golubeva, I. A. "Istorik-peterburgoved Petr Nikolaevich Stolpianskii (1872–1938): Biograficheskii ocherk." *Zhurnal liubitelei iskusstva*, no. 8–9 (1997): 74–82.

———. "Neizvestnyi P. N. Stolpianskii." In *Fenomen Peterburga: Trudy mezhdunarodnoi konferentsii sostoiavsheisia 3–5 noiabria 1999 goda vo Vserossiiskom muzee A. S. Pushkina*, ed. Iu. N. Bespiatykh, 166–77. St. Petersburg: BLITS, 2000.

Gordin, A., and M. Gordin. *Puteshestvie v Pushkinskii Peterburg*. Leningrad: Lenizdat, 1983.

———. *Pushkinskii vek. Byloi Peterburg*. St. Petersburg: Pushkinskii fond, 1995.

Grabar', Igor'. *Peterburgskaia arkhitektura v XVIII i XIX vekakh*. Reprint of vol. 3 of *Istoriia russkogo iskusstva*. St. Petersburg: Lenizdat, 1994.

Grevs, Ivan, ed. *K teorii i praktike "ekskursii," kak orudiia nauchnogo izucheniia istorii v universitetakh.* St. Petersburg: Senatskaia tipografiia, 1910.

———. "V gody iunosti (za kul'turu)." *Byloe*, no. 12 (1918): 2–88; 13 (1918): 137–66.

———, ed. *Ekskursii v kul'turu: Metodicheskii sbornik.* Moscow: Mir, 1925.

———. "Turgenev i Peterburg." In *Turgenev i Italiia*, 105–25. Leningrad: Brokgauz i Efron, 1925.

———, ed. *Kraevedenie v sovremennoi germanskoi shkole: Materialy dlia reformy ucheniia.* Leningrad: Brokgauz-Efron, 1926.

———, ed. *Po ochagam kul'tury: Novye temy dlia ekskursii po gorodu. Metodicheskii sbornik.* Leningrad: Seiatel', 1926.

Gurvich, L. M. *Ocherednye zadachi turistskogo dvizheniia.* 2nd ed. Biblioteka proletarskogo turista. Moscow: Ogiz."fizkul'tura i turizm," 1931.

Harkins, William E. "The Literary Context of 'The World of Art.'" In *Literary Journals in Imperial Russia*, ed. Deborah A. Martinsen, 197–206. Studies of the Harriman Institute. Cambridge: Cambridge University Press, 1997.

Heard, George Hamilton. *The Art and Architecture of Russia.* The Pelican History of Art. New York: Penguin, 1983.

Iatsevich, A. *Krepostnye v Peterburge.* Leningrad: Obshchestvo "Staryi Peterburg— Novyi Leningrad," 1933.

———. *Pushkinskii Peterburg.* St. Petersburg: Petropol', 1993.

Ionova, O. V. "Sozdanie seti kraevedcheskikh muzeev RSFSR v pervye desiat' let Sovetskoi vlasti." In *Ocherki iz istorii muzeinogo dela v SSSR*, issue 1, Trudy Nauchno-issledovatel'skogo instituta muzeevedeniia, 37–72. Moscow: Gosizdat kul'turno-prosvetitel'noi literatury, 1957.

———. "Iz istorii stroitel'stva kraevedcheskikh muzeev RSFSR." In *Ocherki istorii muzeinogo dela v SSSR*, issue 5, Trudy Nauchno-issledovatel'skogo instituta muzeevedeniia, 80–175. Moscow: Sovetskaia Rossiia, 1961.

Kachurin, M. G., G. A. Kudyrskaia, and D. N. Murin. *Sankt-Peterburg v russkoi literature: Uchebnik- khrestomatiia dlia 9 -11 kl. srednikh shkol, gimnazii, litseev, kolledzhei.* 2nd ed., rev. and enl. 2 vols. St. Petersburg: Svet, 1996.

Kagan, Moisei. *Grad Petrov v istorii russkoi kul'tury.* St. Petersburg: Slavia, 1996.

Kaganovich, B. S. "I. M. Grevs—istorik srednevekovoi gorodskoi kul'tury." In *Gorodskaia kul'tura srednevekov'ia i nachala novogo vremeni*, ed. V. I. Rutenburg, 216–35. Leningrad: Nauka, 1986.

Kanevskaia, Marina. "Nikolai Pavlovich Antsiferov: 'Teacher of Human Science.'" *East/West Education* 14, no. 2 (1993): 139–55.

Karatygina, V. A. "Staryi Peterburg v tvorchestve P. N. Stolpianskogo: Bibliografiia. (Knigi, stat'i iz knig i zhurnalov, zametki, retsenzii)." Manuscript. Leningrad: Gosudarstvennaia publichnaia biblioteka im. M. E. Saltykova-Shchedrina, Otdel fondov i obsluzhivaniia, 1957.

Karnovich, E. *Sanktpeterburg v statisticheskom otnoshenii*. St. Petersburg: Voennaia tipografiia, 1860.
Kasparinskaia, S. A., ed. *Muzei i vlast'*. Part 1. Moscow: NIIK, 1991.
Kenez, Peter. *The Birth of the Propaganda State: Soviet Methods of Mass Mobilization, 1917–1929*. Cambridge: Cambridge University Press, 1985.
Kennedy, Janet. *The "Mir iskusstva" Group and Russian Art, 1898–1912*. New York: Garland Publishing, 1977.
Khorkhordina, T. *Istoriia otechestva i arkhivy: 1917–1980-e gody*. Moscow: RGGU, 1994.
Kobak, Alexander, Stefan Kotkin, and Alla Sevast'ianova, eds. *Metodologiia regional'nykh istoricheskikh issledovanii: Materialy mezhdunarodnogo seminara, 19–20 iunia 2000 goda, Sankt-Peterburg*. St. Petersburg: Notabene, 2000.
Koblents, I. N. *Andrei Ivanovich Bogdanov, 1692–1766*. Moscow: Izdatel'stvo AN SSSR, 1958.
Kockelmans, Joseph J., ed. *Interdisciplinarity and Higher Education*. University Park: Pennsylvania State University Press, 1979.
Kon, F. Ia., ed. *Sbornik postanovlenii po muzeinomu stroitel'stvu RSFSR, 1931–1934 gg.* Moscow: Izdanie muzeinogo otdela NKP RSFSR, 1934.
Konechny, A. M. "Obshchestvo 'Staryi Peterburg—Novyi Leningrad', 1921–1938. Po materialam Gosudarstvennoi publichnoi biblioteki imeni M. E. Saltykova-Shchedrina." In *Muzei*, vol. 7, 249–52. Moscow: Sovetskii khudozhnik, 1987.
———. "N. P. Antsiferov—issledovatel' Peterburga." In *Peterburg i guberniia: Istoriko-etnograficheskie issledovaniia*, ed. N. V. Iukhneva, 154–61. Leningrad: Nauka, 1989.
———. "K istorii gumanitarnogo otdela Petrogradskogo nauchno-issledovatel'skogo ekskursionnogo instituta (1921–1924)." In *Etnografiia Peterburga-Leningrada: Materialy ezhegodnykh nauchnykh chtenii*, issue 3, ed. N. V. Iukhneva, 50–63. St. Petersburg: Muzei antropologii i etnografii im. Petra Velikogo (Kunstkamera); Rossiiskaia akademiia nauk, 1994.
Konradi, V. G. *Ekskursiia na gosudarstvenni farforovyi zavod*. Leningrad: Priboi, 1924.
Kovachev, Aleksandur. *Bulgarskoto kraeznanie v perioda 1878–1912 g.* Veliko Turnovo: n.p., 1999.
Kurbatov, Vladimir. *Pavlovsk: Khudozhestvenno-istoricheskii ocherk i putevoditel'*. St. Petersburg: Izdanie obshchiny Sv. Evgenii Krasnogo Kresta, 1912.
———. *Sady i parki*. St. Petersburg: M. O. Vol'f, 1916.
———. *Detskoe Selo*. Progulki po okrestnostiam Leningrada. Leningrad: LGSPS, 1925.
———. *Gatchina*. Progulki po okrestnostiam Leningrada. Leningrad: LGSPS, 1925.
———. *Pavlovskii dvorets i park*. Progulki po okrestnostiam Leningrada. Leningrad: LGSPS, 1925.
———. *Petergof*. Progulki po okrestnostiam Leningrada. Leningrad: LGSPS, 1925.

———. *Strel'na i Oranienbaum*. Progulki po okrestnostiam Leningrada. Leningrad: LGSPS, 1925.

———. *Peterburg: Khudozhestvenno-istoricheskii ocherk*. St. Petersburg: Lenizdat, 1993.

Kuz'menko, R. I., comp. *Nikolai Kir'iakovich Piksanov*. Materialy k biobibliografii uchenykh SSSR. Moscow: Nauka, 1968.

Kuznetsov, N. A., and K. V. Polzikova-Rubets, eds. *Ekskursii v sovremennost'*. Ekskursionnaia praktika Leningradskogo Gubsotsvosa. Leningrad: Izdanie knizhnogo sektora Gubono, 1925.

Lapshin, V. P. *Khudozhestvennaia zhizn' Moskvy i Petrograda v 1917 godu*. Moscow: Sovetskii khudozhnik, 1983.

Lapshina, N. *Mir iskusstva: Ocherki istorii i tvorcheskoi praktiki*. Moscow: Iskusstvo, 1977.

Lee, Vernon [Vernon Li]. *Genius Loci: Notes on Places*. London: Grant Richards, 1899.

———. *Italiia: izbrannye stranitsy*. Ed. P. Muratov. Trans. E. Urenius. 2 vols. Moscow: Tipografiia M. and S. Sabashnikovykh, 1914–15.

Levykin, K. G., and V. Kherbst, eds. *Muzeevedenie: Muzei istoricheskogo profilia*. Moscow: Vysshaia shkola, 1988.

Limonov, Iu. A., ed. *Rossiia XVIII v. glazami inostrantsev*. Biblioteka "Stranitsy istorii otechestva." Leningrad: Lenizdat, 1989.

———, ed. *Rossiia pervoi poloviny XIX v. glazami inostrantsev*. Biblioteka "Stranitsy istorii otechestva." Leningrad: Lenizdat, 1991.

Logachev, K. I., and Sobolev, V. S. *Opisanie Sanktpeterburga: Preprint*. Leningrad: LO AN SSSR, 1987.

Lomonosov, Mikhail. *Izbrannye proizvedeniia*. Ed. A. A. Morozova. Biblioteka poeta. Bol'shaia seriia. 2nd ed. Moscow: Sovetskii pisatel', 1965.

Lotman, Iurii M. "Simvolika Peterburga i problemy semiotiki goroda." In *Iu. M. Lotman: Izbrannye stat'i*, 3 vols. 3:9–21. Tallinn: Aleksandra, 1992.

———. *Besedy o russkoi kul'ture: Byt i traditsii russkogo dvoriantsva (XVIII–nachalo XIX veka)*. St. Petersburg: Iskusstvo-SPb, 1994.

Lotman, Iurii M., and E. A. Pogosian. *Velikosvetskie obedy*. Byloi Peterburg. St. Petersburg: Pushkinskii fond, 1996.

Lotman, Iurii M., and Boris A. Uspensky. "Otzvuki kontseptsii 'Moskva—tretii Rim' v ideologii Petra Pervogo." In *Iu. M. Lotman: Isbrannye Stat'i*, 3 vols., 3:201–12. Tallinn: Aleksandra, 1993.

Lukomsky, Georgy. *Sovremmenyi Petrograd: Ocherk istorii vozniknoveniia i razvitiia klassicheskogo stroitel'stva, 1900–1915 gg.* Petrograd: Svobodnoe iskusstvo, [1916].

———. *Staryi Peterburg: Progulki po starinnym kvartalam*. 2nd ed. Petrograd: Svobodnoe iskusstvo, [1916].

———. *Sankt-Peterburg (Istoricheskii ocherk arkhitektury i razvitiia goroda)*. Munich: Orchis-Verlag, 1923.

---. *Starye gody.* Berlin: E. A. Gutnov, 1923.
Lur'e, Lev, and Alexander Kobak. "Rozhdenie i gibel' peterburgskoi idei." *Muzei i gorod.* Special issue of *Ars,* no. 2 (1993): 23–31.
Merkul'ieva, K. *Gorod Lenina.* 2nd ed. Kraevaia biblioteka shkol'nika. Moscow: Uchebno-pedagogicheskoe izdatel'stvo, 1931.
Messer-Davidow, Ellen, David R. Shumway, and David J. Sylvan, eds. *Knowledges: Historical and Critical Studies in Disciplinarity.* Knowledge: Disciplinarity and Beyond. Charlottesville: University of Virginia Press, 1993.
Mikhnevich, V. O. *Peterburg ves' na ladoni, s planom Peterburga, ego panoramoi s ptich'ego poleta, 22 kartinkami i s pribavleniem kalendaria.* St. Petersburg: Izdanie knigoprodavtsa N. N. Plotnikova, 1874.
Milonov, N. A. *Literaturnoe kraevedenie.* Moscow: Prosveshchenie, 1985.
Monas, Sidney. "St. Petersburg and Moscow as Cultural Symbols." In *Art and Culture in Nineteenth-Century Russia,* ed. Theofanis George Stavrou, 27–39. Bloomington: Indiana University Press, 1983.
Morson, Gary Saul. *The Boundaries of Genre: Dostoevsky's Diary of a Writer and the Traditions of Literary Utopia.* Evanston: Northwestern University Press, 1981.
Mudrov, Iu. V., ed. *Pavlovsk: Imperatorskii dvorets, stranitsy istorii.* St. Petersburg: Artpalas, 1997.
Muzei Goroda k oktiabriu 1927. Leningrad: Muzei Goroda, 1928.
Obshchestvo "Staryi Peterburg", 1921–1923 g. Petrograd: Gos. uchebno-prakticheskaia shkola, 1923.
Okrestnosti Leningrada: Samoobrazovatel'naia ekskursiia. V pomoshch' ekskursantu. Leningrad: Priboi, 1927.
Omel'chenko, B. F. *Ekskursionnoe obshchenie: Poznanie, vospitanie, otdykh.* Moscow: Nauka, 1991.
Ostroi, Ol'ga. "S chego nachinalas' peterburgiana. Opisanie putevoditelei po gorodu s momenta ikh vozniknoveniia do serediny XIX stoletiia." In *Nevskii arkhiv: Istoriko-kraevedcheskii sbornik,* issue 3, ed. A. I. Dobkin and A. V. Kobak, 481–91. St. Petersburg: Atheneum-Feniks, 1997.
---. "'Peterburgiana' v Rossiiskoi Natsional'noi Biblioteke i ee Sozdatel' P. N. Stolpianskii." Forthcoming.
Ostroi, Ol'ga, and L. I. Iuniverg. *Erikh Fedorovich Gollerbakh kak kollektsioner i izdatel'.* Leningrad: Leningradskaia organizatsiia dobrovol'nogo obshchestva knigoliubov, 1990.
Otradin, M. V., ed. *Peterburg v russkom ocherke XIX veka.* Leningrad: Izdatel'stvo Leningradskogo universiteta, 1984.
---. *Peterburg v russkoi poezii XVIII–nachalo XX veka.* Leningrad: Izdatel'stvo Leningradskogo universiteta, 1988.
Pamiatnaia knizhka Tenishevskogo uchilishcha v S.-Peterburge za 1900/1901 uchebnyi god. God pervyi. St. Petersburg: Obshchestvennaia pol'za, 1902.

Paperno, Irina, and Joan Delaney Grossman. *Creating Life: The Aesthetic Utopia of Russian Modernism.* Stanford: Stanford University Press, 1994.
Pavelkina, Al'bina. "Muzei Starogo Peterburga." *Muzei i Gorod.* Special issue of *Ars*, no. 2 (1993): 10–15.
Perchenok, F. F. "Akademiia Nauk na 'velikom perelome.'" In *Zven'ia: Istoricheskii al'manakh,* issue 1, 163–235. Moscow: Progress-Feniks-Atheneum, 1991.
Peris, Daniel. *Storming the Heavens: The League of the Militant Godless.* Ithaca: Cornell University Press, 1998.
Petrov, P. N. *Istoriia Sankt-Peterburga s osnovaniia goroda do vvedeniia v deistvie vybornogo gorodskogo upravleniia, po uchrezhdeniiam o guberniiakh, 1703–1782.* St. Petersburg: Tipografiia Glazunova, 1884.
Petrov, Vsevolod. "The World of Art Movement." In *The World of Art Movement in Early 20th-Century Russia* by Vsevolod Petrov and Alexander Kamensky. Leningrad: Aurora, 1991.
Piksanov, Nikolai. "Oblastnoi printsip v russkom kul'turovedenii. K razrabotke kul'turno-istoricheskoi skhemy." *Iskusstvo,* no. 2 (1925): 82–99.
———. *Oblastnye kul'turnye gnezda. Istoriko-kraevednyi seminar.* Moscow: Gosizdat, 1928.
Polzikova-Rubets, K. V., ed. *Ekskursionnaia praktika. Sbornik 1: Temy "rynok", "kooperativ" i "khlebozavod."* Sborniki Leningradskoi shkol'noi ekskursionnoi stantsii. Leningrad: Seiatel', 1926.
———. *Ekskursionnaia praktika. Sbornik 2: Tema transport v shkolakh 1-oi stupeni.* Sborniki Leningradskoi shkol'noi ekskursionnoi stantsii. Leningrad: Seiatel', 1926.
———. *Ekskursionnaia praktika. Sbornik 3: Gorod, byt i proizvodstvo.* Sborniki Leningradskoi shkol'noi ekskursionnoi stantsii. Leningrad: Seiatel', 1926.
Popova, Galina. "Muzei Goroda." *Muzei i Gorod.* Special issue of *Ars*, no. 2 (1993): 16–22.
Pressman, A. P. *Peterburg-Leningrad v proshlom i nastoiashchem (Posobie dlia ekskurantov i turistov).* Leningrad: Leningradskoi oblastnoi otdel narodnogo obrazovaniia Politprosvet, 1928.
Prokhvatilova, S. A., ed. *"Gorod pod morem" ili blistatel'nyi Sankt-Peterburg: Vospominaniia, rasskazy ocherki, stikhi.* St. Petersburg: Lenizdat, 1996.
Pushkarev, Ivan. *Opisanie Sanktpeterburga i uezdnykh gorodov S. Peterburgskoi gubernii.* 4 vols. Vols. 1 2, St. Petersburg: privately published, 1839; vols. 3–4, St. Petersburg: Tipografiia S. Peterburgskogo gubernskogo pravleniia, 1841–42.
———. *Putevoditel' po Sanktpeterburgu i okrestnostiam ego.* St. Petersburg: Departament vneshnei torgovli, 1843.
———. *Istoricheskii ukazatel' dostopamiatnostei Sanktpeterburga.* St. Petersburg: Konrad Vingeber, 1846.

Putevoditel' po S.-Peterburgu: Obrazovatel'nye ekskursii. 1903. Reprint, St. Petersburg: IKAR, 1991.

Pyliaev, Mikhail. *Staroe zhit'e: Ocherki i rasskazy.* 2nd ed. 1879. Reprint, Moscow: Kniga, 1990.

———. *Staryi Peterburg.* 1889. Reprint, Mramornaia seriia, Leningrad: Titul, 1990.

———. *Zabytoe proshloe okrestnostei Peterburga.* St. Petersburg: Lenizdat, 1996.

Raikov, Boris, ed. *Shkol'nye ekskursii, ikh znachenie i organizatsiia.* Pedagogicheskii ezhegodnik izdavaemyi pri S.-Peterburgskom Lesnom kommercheskom uchilishche. Vol. 2. St. Petersburg: Tipografiia B. M. Vol'fa, 1910.

———. *Shkol'nye ekskursii, ikh znachenie i organizatsiia: Sbornik nauchno-pedagogicheskikh statei.* 2nd ed., rev. and enl. Petrograd: Gosizdat, 1921.

———. *Voprosy ekskursionnogo dela. Po dannym petrogradskoi ekskursionnoi konferentsii 10–12 marta 1923 g.* Petrograd: Nachatki znanii, 1923.

Ravikovich, D. A. "Muzei mestnogo kraia vo vtoroi polovine XIX–nachala XX veka (1861–1917 gg.)." In *Ocherki istorii muzeinogo dela v Rossii,* issue 2, Trudy Nauchno-issledovatel'skogo instituta muzeevedeniia, 145–224. Moscow: Sovetskaia Rossiia, 1960.

Raymond, James C., ed. *English as a Discipline; or, Is There a Plot in the Play?* Tuscaloosa: University of Alabama Press, 1996.

Razumovsky, V. V. "V. Ia. Kurbatov (K 70-letiiu so dnia rozhdeniia i 50-letiiu nauchnoi deiatel'nosti)." *Priroda* (January 1949): 88–90.

Reshetnikova, L. L., ed. *Dusha Peterburga: Peterburg v proizvedeniiakh russkikh pisatelei XIX veka.* Shkol'naia biblioteka. St. Petersburg: Lenizdat, 1996.

Rubinshtein, N., and M. Zelensky, eds. *Protiv vreditel'stva v kraevedcheskoi literature.* Moscow: Ogiz RSFSR, 1931.

Said, Edward W. *Orientalism.* New York: Vintage Books, 1994.

Sanktpeterburg. Issledovanie po istorii, topografii i statistike stolitsy. Izdanie Tsentral'nogo komiteta Ministerstva vnutrennikh del. St. Petersburg: Tipografiia V. Bezobrazova, 1870.

Sankt-Peterburg. XX vek. Chto? Gde? Kogda? St. Petersburg: Paritet, 2000.

Sbornik postanovlenii po muzeinomu stroitel'stvu RSFSR, 1931–1934. Moscow: Narkompros muzeinyi otdel, 1934.

Semevsky, Mikhail. *Pavlovsk: Ocherk istorii i opisanie, 1777–1877.* 1877. Mramornaia seriia. Reprint, St. Petersburg: Liga Plius, 1997.

Semiotika goroda i gorodskoi kul'tury: Peterburg. Trudy po znakovym sistemam XVIII v., Uchenye zapiski Tartuskogo gosudarstvennogo universiteta. Tartu: Tartuskii gosudarstvennyi universitet, 1984.

Seregny, Scott. *Russian Teachers and Peasant Revolution: The Politics of Education in 1905.* Bloomington: Indiana University Press, 1989.

Serova, Z. A. *Peterburgskii zadachnik dlia malyshei.* St. Petersburg: MiM, 1998.

Shreder, F. *Noveishii putevoditel' po Sankt-Peterburgu s istoricheskimi ukazaniiami.* St. Petersburg: Pervyi kadetskii korpus, 1820.
Shumway, David R., and Ellen Messer-Davidow. "Disciplinarity: An Introduction." *Poetics Today* 12, no. 2 (1991): 212.
Siegelbaum, Lewis H. *Soviet State and Society Between Revolutions, 1918–1929.* Cambridge: Cambridge University Press, 1992.
Sindalovsky, N. A. *Peterburgskii fol'klor.* St. Petersburg: Maksima, 1994.
———. *Istoriia Sankt-Peterburga v predaniiakh i legendakh.* St. Petersburg: Norint, 1997.
Skaz o Sankt-Peterburkhe: Iz istorii goroda Sankt-Peterburga v bytnost' ego stolitseiu gosudarstva rossiiskogo sbornik podlinnykh povestvovanii sostavlennykh dlia pol'zy i udovol'stviia pochtennykh gorozhan i uvazhaemykh gospod puteshestvennikov. Leningrad: Biblioteka Zvezdy, 1991.
Skrzhinskaia, E. Ch. "Ivan Mikhailovich Grevs: Biograficheskii ocherk." In *Tatsit,* by I. M. Grevs, 223–47. Moscow: AN SSSR, 1946.
Slukhovsky, M. I. "K biografii pervogo russkogo knigoveda A. I. Bogdanova." In *Kniga: Issledovaniia i materialy,* vol. 26, 191–212. Moscow: Kniga, 1973.
Snessoreva, Sofiia. *Zemnaia zhizn' presviatoi bogoroditsy i opisanie sviatykh chudotvornykh ee ikon, chtimykh pravoslavnoiu tserkov'iu, na osnovanii sviashchennogo pisaniia i tserkovnykh predanii, s izobrazheniiami v tekste prazdnikov bozhiei materi.* 2nd ed. 1898. Reprint, Iaroslavl: Verkhne-Volozhskoe knizhnoe izdatel'stvo, 1993.
Sobolev-Tomilin, N. *Sputnik turistu po Leningradu i okrestnostiam.* Leningrad: Ogiz fizkul'tura i turizm, 1932.
Solov'ev, Vladimir. *Sobranie sochnenii.* Ed. S. M. Solov'ev and E. L. Radlov. 10 vols. St. Petersburg: Prosveshchenie, 1886–94.
Solzhenitsyn, A. *Arkhipelag Gulag.* 6 vols. Moscow: Novyi Mir, 1990.
Stites, Richard. *Revolutionary Dreams: Utopian Vision and Experimental Life in the Russian Revolution.* New York: Oxford University Press, 1989.
Stolpiansky, Petr. *Revoliutsionnyi Peterburg: U kolybeli russkoi svobody.* Petrograd: Kolos, 1922.
———. *Staryi Peterburg: Kolybel' russkoi svobody (Delo 1 marta 1881 g.).* Petrograd: Gosizdat, 1922.
———. *Staryi Peterburg. Dvorets Truda: Istoricheskii ocherk.* St. Petersburg: Gosizdat, 1923.
———. *Lenin v Peterburge.* Leningrad: Gozisdat, 1924.
———. *Staryi Peterburg. U mednogo Petra.* Leningrad: Gublit, 1924.
———. *Zhizn' i byt peterburgskoi fabriki za 210 let ee sushchestvovaniia, 1704–1919 gg.* Leningrad: Lengubsovetprofsoiuzov, 1925.
———. "Bibliografiia Sankt-Piter-Burkha (Nyne Leningrada). Vypusk pervyi. Opisaniia i plany. Po ekzempliaram Publichnoi Biblioteki." Manuscript. Leningrad: Gosudarstvennaia publichnaia biblioteka, 1926.

———. *Peterburg: Kak voznik, osnovalsia i ros Sankt-Piterburkh.* Liki goroda. 1918. Reprint. St. Petersburg: Nega, 1995.

Sukharnikova, E. A. *Muzykal'nyi Sankt-Peterburg: Uchebnik-tetrad'.* 2nd rev. ed. St. Petersburg: SpetsLit, 2000.

Surozhsky, P. *V gorode Lenina: Putevka pervaia.* Po zemle sovetskoi. Moscow: Molodaia gvardiia, 1925.

Svin'in, Pavel. *Sketches of Moscow and St. Petersburg.* Philadelphia: Thomas Dobson, 1813.

———. *Dostopamiatnosti Sanktpeterburga i ego okrestnostei.* 5 vols. Vols. 1–4: St. Petersburg: Tipografiia V. Plavil'shchikov, 1816–21. Vol. 5: St. Petersburg: A. Smirdin, 1828.

———. *Dostopamiatnosti Sanktpeterburga i ego okrestnostei.* Ed. A. A. Alekseev. St. Petersburg: Liga Plius, 1997.

Titov, A. A., ed. *Dopolnenie k istoricheskomu, geograficheskomu i topograficheskomu opisaniiu Sanktpeterburga s 1751 po 1762 goda sochinennoe A. Bogdanovym.* Izdanie glasnogo Sankt-Peterburgskoi gorodskoi dumy P. A. Fokina v pamiat' dvukhsotletnego iubileia. Moscow: Tipo-litografiia I. M. Mashistova, 1903.

Tolz, Vera. *Russian Academicians and the Revolution: Combining Professionalism and Politics.* Studies in Russian and East European History. New York: St. Martin's Press, 1997.

Toporov, V. N. "O strukture romana Dostoevskogo v sviazi s istoricheskimi skhemami morfologicheskogo myshleniia (*Prestuplenie i nakazanie*)." In *Structure of Texts and Semiotics of Culture,* ed. Jan Van der Eng and Grygar Mojmír. The Hague: Mouton, 1973.

Traveling Across North America, 1812–1813: Watercolors by the Russian Diplomat Pavel Svinin. Ed. Yuri Pamfilov. Trans. Kathleen Carroll. New York: Harry N. Abrams, 1992.

Uprazhneniia po russkomu iazyku dlia peterburgskikh shkol'nikov. 2nd ed., rev. and enl. Peterburgskaia tetrad'. St. Petersburg: Khimera, 1999.

Vialova, S. O. "K tvorcheskoi biografii professora I. M. Grevsa." In *Iz istorii rukopisnykh i staropechatnykh sobranii (Issledovaniia. Obzory. Publikatsii.). Sbornik nauchnykh trudov,* ed. L. L. Al'bina, I. N. Kurbatova, and M. Ia. Stetskevich, 128–41. Leningrad: Gosudarstvennaia publichnaia biblioteka, 1979.

Vigand, M. G., ed. *Putevoditel' po Leningradu s prilozheniem novogo plana g. Leningrada.* Leningrad: Lenoblispolkom i Lensovet, 1933.

Vil'chkovsky, S. N. *Tsarskoe Selo: Reprintnoe vosproizvedenie izdaniia 1911 goda.* St. Petersburg: Titul, 1992.

Vraskaia, O. B. "Arkhivnye materialy I. M. Grevs i N. P. Antsiferova po izucheniiu goroda." In *Arkheograficheskii Ezhegodnik za 1981,* 303–16. Moscow: Nauka, 1982.

Weiner, Douglas. *Models of Nature.* Bloomington: Indiana University Press, 1988.

Wellek, René. "Vernon Lee, Bernard Berenson, and Aesthetics." In *Discriminations: Further Concepts of Criticism,* 164–86. New Haven: Yale University Press, 1970.

Wortman, Richard. "Moscow and Petersburg: The Problem of Political Center in Tsarist Russia, 1881–1914." In *Rites of Power: Symbolism, Ritual and Politics since the Middle Ages,* ed. Sean Wilentz, 244–71. Philadelphia: University of Pennsylvania Press, 1985.

———. *Scenarios of Power: Myth and Ceremony in Russian Monarchy.* Vol. 1. Princeton: Princeton University Press, 1995.

Zaks, A. B. "Opyt izucheniia i propagandy istorii revoliutsionnoi Moskvy v 20-e gody XX v." In *Iz istorii ekonomicheskoi i obshchestvennoi zhizni Rossii. Sbornik statei k 90-letiiu akademika Nikolaia Mikhailovicha Druzhinina,* ed. L. V. Cherepnin, 273–86. Moscow: Nauka, 1976.

Zhivotov, N. N. *Peterburgskie profili.* 4 vols. St. Petersburg: n.p., 1894–95.

Zhukov, Iu. N. *Stanovlenie i deiatel'nost' sovetskikh organov okhrany pamiatnikov istorii i kul'tury, 1917–1920 gg.* Ed. I. M. Katuntseva. Moscow: Nauka, 1989.

INDEX

PAGE NUMBERS IN *italics* REFER TO ILLUSTRATIONS.

Abramtsevo group, 85
Academic Center of Narkompros (Aktsentr), 91, 94, 117, 119, 157–59. *See also* Narkompros (Commissariat of Enlightenment)
Academy of Arts, 52, 65, 67, 75, 243 n. 5
Academy of Sciences, 4, 11, 12, 158, 159–60, 170; Library, 20, 21, 22; resistance to Soviet state, 174–75, 188; Stalinist purges and, 174–76. *See also* Central Bureau of *Kraevedenie* (TsBK)
activism, 4, 6, 8, 68, 176, 217
Admiralty, 25, *42,* 48, 136
Admiralty Side, 23
Akhmatova, Anna, 192
Aksakov, Konstantin, 36, 236 n. 60
Aksakov, Sergei, 184
alcohol, excursions as alternative to, 115, 147
Alexander Column, 86, 149
Alexander I, Tsar, 45, 46, 56, 64, 136
Alexander II, Tsar, 39
Alexander III, Tsar, 48, 79, 150
Alexandrine Theater, 48
amateurs, 6, 115, 118, 159, 221

Andrews, James T., 91, 94
Anichkov Palace, 60, 82, 83, 113, 245 n. 34
Anna Ioannovna, Empress, 18, 42, 233 n. 24
Annensky, Innokenty, 206, 207
anthropology, 2, 3, 5, 159
antiquities, export of, 67
Antsiferov, Nikolai, 11, 96, 113, 120, 209; arrests and imprisonment of, 174, 180, 181, 264 n. 77; books written by, 97–98; Central Bureau and, 181; on decentralization of culture, 165; *Dostoevsky's Petersburg,* 97, 133, 137–39; Excursion Institute and, 121; Grevs as mentor of, 105, 126; guidebooks and, 218; legacy of, 180–82; *Petersburg in Reality and Myth,* 97, 126–28, 133–35, 137, 138; "regional cultural nests" and, 187–90; Society of Old Petersburg and, 145–46; *Soul of Petersburg,* 182, 189–90, 192–204, 206–8; on strolls as self-education, 145; studied in Russian schools, 224; Tartu semioticians and, 211–12, 213; Tenishev School and, 250 n. 10; *Theory and Practice of Literary Excursions,* 129–33
Antsiferova, Tatiana, 181, 192
Anuchin, Dmitrii, 159

Applegate, Celia, 9
Archeological Commission, 67
architects, 13, 49, 57, 60, 63, 179
architecture, 10, 24, 46, 83, 209;
    baroque and classical styles, 64, 79;
    destruction of landmarks, 222;
    Empire style, 48, 64, 65; excursionism
    and, 104, 122; neoclassical, 44, 75;
    neo-Gothic, 64; Petrine period,
    128; pseudo-Renaissance, 64;
    revolutionary government and, 75,
    76; Russia's heritage in, 66, 67, 68;
    in *Soul of Petersburg*, 196, 202; at
    Tsarskoe Selo, 206; in *World of Art*, 52
Architect [Zodchii] (journal), 92
archives, 56, 57, 69, 166, 183
Argutinsky-Dolgoruky, Vladimir, 69
aristocracy, 75, 80
"Arkhangelskoe" estate, 61
Art and Art Industry (journal), 52
art and artists, 33, 43–44, 46, 83; artists'
    union in Petrograd, 76–77, 78;
    art journals, 51–64; collections, 63,
    69, 77; exhibits, 62, 66; landscape
    painting, 20; modernist styles, 44
art criticism, 9, 43, 57
art history and historians, 3, 57, 113, 161
Artistic-Historical Commission for
    Inventorying the Movable Property
    of Petrograd Palaces of the Former
    Palace Administration, 78
art lovers, societies of, 66
Art Treasures of Russia (journal), 53–54,
    56–57, 59–64, 82
Askoldov, Sergei, 262 n. 57
autocracy, 29, 32, 75, 150

Baedeker guides, 58
Bakhtin, Mikhail, 262 n. 57
Bakst, Leon, 43, 61
Ballets Russes, 43

baroque style, 64, 79
Bashutsky, Alexander, 31, 36, 57, 235 n.
    47, 236 n. 55
Batiushkov, Konstantin, 200
Bedny, Demian, 150
Belinsky, Vissarion, 35–36
Bely, Andrei, 193, 200, 203–4, 212
Benois, Alexander, 11, 43, 67, 68, 97,
    195; *Art Treasures of Russia* and, 53–54,
    56–57, 59–61, 63–64; Bolshevik
    regime and, 81; *Bygone Years* and, 62;
    emigration from Russia, 81; Gorky
    Commission and, 73, 74, 75, 77;
    guidebooks and, 218; legacy of, 180;
    memoirs, 45, 60, 61–62, 62; Museum
    of Old Petersburg and, 69; October
    Revolution and, 82; on Petersburg as
    work of art, 47–50; post at Hermitage,
    244 n. 18; Pushkin's "Bronze
    Horseman" and, 239 n. 14; Society
    of Old Petersburg and, 89; studied
    in Russian schools, 224; *World of Art*
    and, 46, 51–54, 56, 63–64
Bespiatykh, Iurii, 17
Bestuzhev Women's Courses, 99, 100
Bilibin, Ivan, 73
Blok, Alexander, 200, 206, 208
Bogdanov, Andrei, 20–22, 25, 27, 40, 57
Bolshevik regime, 70, 79, 95; educational
    policy, 111; excursionism and, 110,
    111, 143; intelligentsia and, 80–81, 86,
    244 n. 17; status of Leningrad and,
    178. *See also* October Revolution;
    socialism; Soviet Union
Book about the City, A (Antsiferov), 181
Boundaries of Genre, The (Morson), 32–33
Bozherianov, Ivan, 56
Bronze Horseman monument (Falconet),
    48, 150, 198, 203–4, 268 n. 43
Bronze Horseman, The (Pushkin), 29–30,
    51, 126, 128, 141; Benois's illustrations

for, 239 n. 14; literary excursions and, 133; mythic elements in, 134–37; spirit of St. Petersburg and, 203–4; Tartu semioticians and, 211

Buckler, Julie, 234 n. 41, 238 n. 7

bureaucracy, 106, 109, 119, 172

Burianov, Victor, 33

Bygone Years [Starye gody] magazine, 56–58, 62–66, 69, 78, 81, 85, 92, 108; preservationism and, 66–68; retrospectivist exhibits and, 78; veteran contributors, 73, 80, 82

canals, 127

Capital and Estate [Stolitsa i usad'ba] (journal), 92

Catherine II ("the Great"), Empress, 23, 46, 205, 233 n. 24; architectural style under, 64, 238 n. 9; growth of St. Petersburg and, 24; opulence of court life under, 45

"Cave, The" (Zamiatin), 195

censorship, Soviet, 97, 181, 210

censorship, tsarist, 38, 76

Central Bureau of *Kraevedenie* (TSBK), 11, 99, 132, 153, 217, 220; as affiliate of Glavnauka, 164, 166, 171; Excursion and Information Bureau, 181, 264 n. 82; Grevs and, 155; legacy of, 180; Moscow conference (1921) and, 158, 159; Narkompros chain of command and, 164–65; network of affiliates, 162, 163–64; *putevoditeli* and, 12, 14, 15; regional culture and, 186–87, 190; resistance to centralism by, 166; rivalry between capital cities and, 166–72; Stalinist purges and, 173–76, 263 n. 70. *See also* Academy of Sciences

centralization, 184, 222–23, 241 n. 46

Central Station for Excursions in the Humanities, 113, 245 n. 23

charitable groups and institutions, 23, 24, 66

Chinese Palace (Oranienbaum palace), 56

Chukovsky, Lydia and Nikolai, 250 n. 10

churches, 23, 108, 149, 177, 201

cities, 104, 218, 219; "biography" of, 103; excursionism and urban studies, 121–23; as living organisms, 99

City of Muses: Tsarskoe Selo in Poetry (Gollerbakh), 191, 192, 205–8

civil society, 66, 71, 111, 176–77

Civil War, 70, 81, 85; destruction of, 206; end of, 143; excursionism during, 111, 112; Petrograd's ordeal in, 122, 192–204, 235 n. 49; recovery from, 157

Clark, Katerina, 96, 241 n. 46

classes, social, 27, 28, 31, 40; Bolshevik regime and, 95; culture and, 66; elementary education for lower classes, 105; excursionism and, 107; excursion primers and class struggle, 144; lower classes as local color, 31; Soviet organizations and, 87

classicism, 79, 238 n. 9

collectors, 69

Comenius, John, 102

Commissariat of Enlightenment. *See* Narkompros (Commissariat of Enlightenment)

Commission for the Study and Description of Old Petersburg, 68, 89, 242 n. 57

Commission on Artistic Affairs (Gorky Commission), 73

Commission on Artistic Issues, 74

Committee to Assist the Society, 90

Communist Party, 92

Confino, Alon, 7, 9

Conversations about Russian Culture (Lotman), 211

crime, 27, 31, 37, 93
Crime and Punishment (Dostoevsky), 138–40
"Cultural Nests in the Provinces" (Piksanov), 184
cultural revolution, 81, 86
cultural workers, 86, 94, 115; imperial symbols interpreted by, 149–50; *kraevedy* as, 165; meanings of *kraevedenie* and, 192
culture, 4, 14, 35; crossing of international boundaries and, 1; decentralization of, 165; differences in pursuit of knowledge and, 227; identity and, 217; literary *kraevedenie* and, 211; October Revolution and, 81; in post-Soviet period, 223; provinces as "nests" of, 184–89; social classes and, 66; state-society relations and, 67–71; urban history and, 122

Dante Alighieri, 105, 198
Decembrist rebellion, 29, 210
Department for the Preservation of Art and Antiquities, 204
Derzhavin, Gavrila, 28, 50, 131, 200
Description of St. Petersburg and the Chief Towns of the Regions of the St. Petersburg Gubernia (Bashutsky), 31
Description of the Russian Imperial Capital City St. Petersburg and the Memorable Sites in Its Suburbs, with a Map (Georgi), 22
Detskoe Selo, 112, 113, 114
Diaghilev, Sergei, 43–44, 53, 56, 61, 75
"Diary of a Madman" (Gogol), 30
disciplines, academic, 1–3, 215–17
Dobuzhinsky, Mstislav, 43, 61, 68; Civil War artwork, 195; Gorky Commission and, 73, 75, 77
Dolgopolov, Leonid, 239 n. 14

Dostoevsky, Fyodor, 50, 200, 208; *Crime and Punishment*, 138–40; literary excursions and, 133; *Poor Folk*, 30, 235 n. 45
Dostoevsky's Petersburg (Antsiferov), 97, 133, 137–39
Dzeiver, A. Ia., 141

"Echoes of the Conception 'Moscow—the Third Rome' in the Ideology of Peter I" (Lotman and Uspensky), 133
ecology, 6, 221, 222, 223
economics, 3, 5, 117, 129
education, progressive, 100–103, 108; *Heimatkunde* as influence, 220; literary *kraevedenie* and, 191; localization and, 143; Narkompros and, 110–17; post-Soviet, 224
ekskursii (excursion primers), 13, 98, 125
Elizabeth Petrovna, Empress, 20–21, 41, 45
English language, guidebooks in, 12, 13
Esenin, Sergei, 130
ethnic studies, 1, 5, 6, 225
ethnographers, 159, 221
Ethnographic Museum, 114, 131, 149
Europe, Western, 1, 10, 27, 53, 99; architects from, 49; arts periodicals in, 52–53; description of St. Petersburg and, 17, 18; guidebooks in, 235 n. 5; loss of contacts in, 221; as rival of Russia, 29; Russian diplomats in, 19; stereotypes of Russia in, 42
Europeanization, 20
Europeanness, 19–20
everyday life, 143
Excursion Herald (journal), 18, 106, 109, 120, 251 nn. 24, 28, 31
excursionism, 12, 98–100; academic agenda and, 118–23; collapse of movement, 162; journals devoted

to, 106–10; in Moscow, 252 n. 39; museums and, 151–52; Narkompros and, 110–17, 120; nationalism and, 107; political content in Soviet era, 149–52; *putevoditeli* (guidebooks) and, 14, 15, 98, 217; recreational value in, 147–49; Tenishev School and, 100–107. *See also* Petrograd Excursion Institute

Excursion Matters (journal), 162

excursion primers, 120, 125–26, 151; everyday life and, 143; on individual sites, 141–42; interdisciplinary approaches in, 142; literary texts and, 128–41; *Petersburg in Reality and Myth,* 126–28; socialism emphasized in, 143–44

"Excursion to the Domain of Financial Capitalism, An" (Fedorov), 141

factories, 106, 109, 115, 129; closed during Civil War, 157; excursion primers on, 142; workers on excursions, 147, 148–49

Falconet, Étienne-Maurice, 48, 137, 198, 203, 204

February (1917) Revolution, 67, 83

Fedorov, Vladimir, 141

Fenomenov, Mikhail, 168, 260 n. 37

Fersman, Alexander, 159, 259 n. 29

feuilletons, 32–35, 37

Filosofov, Dmitrii, 43, 61

First Conference of Scientific Studies for the Study of Local Regions (1921), 157–59, 161, 183, 220

Fitzpatrick, Sheila, 111

Five-Year Plans, 19, 87, 148, 176

floods, 18, 29–30, 136

Fomin, Ivan, 64, 68, 69, 73, 75

Fontanka River, 82, *195*

Forgotten Past of the Suburbs of Petersburg (Pyliaev), 40–41

Formalism, campaign against, 188

Foucault, Michel, 215, 218, 230 n. 6

Garshin, Vsevolod, 200

Gatchina palace-park complex, 56, 78

gay and lesbian studies, 5

Geirot, Alexander, 39–40

gender studies, 1, 3, 5, 225, 227

"General Meaning of Art, The" *[Obshchii smysl iskusstva]* (Soloviev), 201–2

genius loci, 188, 197–98, 201, 202, 210; *Bronze Horseman* and, 204; poetry and, 270 n. 78; at Tsarskoe Selo, 268 n. 40

geography, 4, 14, 32, 221; of cities, 121; excursionism and, 106; exploration of geographic space, 33–34; functional analysis of, 35; geographic clubs, 157; guidebooks and, 25; literary, 184, 187, 208; Russia's vastness, 49; St. Petersburg and, 11; Tenishev School and, 101

Georgi, Johann, Gottlieb, 22–25, 27, 28, 32, 40, 57

glasnost, 97, 152, 221–22

Glavnauka (Central Scientific Administration), 91, 93, 164; Central Bureau under, 164, 166, 171; Museum of the City and, 87

Glavprofobr (Central Administration for Professional Education), 119

Gogol, Nikolai, 30, 50, 131, 200, 211, 235 n. 45

Gollerbakh, Erikh, 191–92, 204–8, 209, 213, 270 n. 78

Golovin, F. A., 78, 80

Gordin, A. and M., 210

Gorky, Maxim, 73, 77, 80, 130, 184

Gorky Commission, 74–78, 243 n. 5

Grabar, Igor, 57–58, 64, 238 n. 8

gradovedenie (city studies), 123, 181

"grand tour," nineteenth-century, 107
Granin, Daniil A., 250 n. 10
Grevs, Ivan, 11, 99–106, 111, 147;
  Bolshevik education programs and,
  117, 119, 120; disciples of, 141, 144, 253
  n. 49; on education, 110; excursions
  to Italy with students, 103–5;
  imprisoned in Stalinist purges, 174,
  262 n. 56; on *kraevedenie*, 156, 258 n.
  7; LOIMK and, 162–63; "Monumental
  City and Historical Excursions,"
  121, 122–23, 126, 127, 181; Museum
  Department (Narkompros) and, 113;
  Petrograd Excursion Institute and,
  155–56; "regional cultural nests" and,
  187–90; revolutionary cause and, 249
  n. 7; Tenishev School and, 102, 103,
  250 n. 13; urban studies of, 121–23,
  126; works republished in post-Soviet
  era, 152
Guash, A. F., 69
Gubernia Executive Committee
  (Gubispolkom), 91, 93, 248 n. 63
guidebooks, 30–31, 57, 58, 96, 120, 219;
  composition of, 156; fictional works
  as, 33; genres of, 32–34; in late
  Soviet period, 222; in Moscow, 237
  n. 63; panegyric tendencies, 32; post-
  Soviet, 223; preservationism and, 59;
  Romanov patronage and, 39–40. See
  also *putevoditeli* (guidebooks)

Haymarket district, 139, 140
Heimatkunde (homeland studies), 4–5, 7,
  9, 158; emergence of *kraevedenie* and,
  220–21; in Prussian school curriculum,
  107; role in German unification, 225;
  Russian excursionism and, 118
Hermitage, 23, 41; *Art Treasures of
  Russia* and, 54; catalogues of, 58; as
  conservative institution, 52; excursion
  primer on, 141–42; pedagogical
  excursionism and, 114; Petrine gallery,
  56
Herzen, Alexander, 43, 200
High Society Dinners (Lotman and
  Pogosian), 211
historians, Russian, 38–39, 56, 99, 100,
  118, 159
*Historical Herald, The [Istoricheskii
  vestnik]* (newspaper), 40
historical societies, 157
history, 3, 14, 187, 209, 219; academic
  disciplines outside United States and,
  2; geographic factors in, 4; regional, 6
History of the Emperor Peter the Great
  (Prokopovich), 18
Hotel Angleterre, 179
humanities, 103, 113, 116, 120

Iaremich, Stepan, 61
Iatsevich, Andrei, 96, 191–92, 208–10
icons, 199
identities, 14, 15; excursionism and
  Soviet identity, 150–52; post-Soviet, 8;
  regional and ideological, 226; Russian,
  10
identity disciplines, 5–6, 7, 215–27
Ilin, Lev, 82, 83, 85, 113
imperialism, 76, 192, 194, 198
industrialization, 87, 148, 169, 186, 190
Industrial Party *(Prompartiia)*, 175
In Lenin's City [V gorode Lenina]
  (children's book), 150–51
Institute of Art History, 74
Institute of Scientific Pedagogy, 146–47
Institute of World Literature, 180
intellectuals/intelligentsia, 43, 92, 219,
  225, 235 n. 49; Bolshevik regime and,
  80; Stalinist purges and, 176
"In the Footsteps of Peter the Great"
  (Tumim), 129

Iudenich, Gen. Nikolai, 112, 192
Iusupov mansion, 114, 139
Ivan IV ("the Terrible"), Tsar, 223
Ivanov, Viacheslav, 133, 203
Izvestiia (Soviet newspaper), 188

journalism, 33, 34, 36, 38
journals, literary, 38–39
Journey to Pushkin's Petersburg, A (Gordin and Gordin), 210

Kaigorodov, Dmitri, 111
Kalinin, Mikhail, 170
Kamennoostrovsky Prospect, 141
Kantemir, Antiokh, 18–19
Karlova, Countess, 85
Kassow, Samuel D., 70
Kenez, Peter, 143
Khrushchev, Nikita, 177
Khrushchev Thaw, 176–78
Kiger, Joseph, 216
Kobak, Alexander, 177
Kolomna region, 208
Koni, Anatoly, 113
Konradi, V. G., 121, 142
Konstantin Nikolaevich, Grand Prince, 39, 163
Kraevedenie (journal), 160, 161, 184, 261 n. 46
kraevedenie (regional or local studies), 3–5, 82, 132, 164; city studies and, 123; definition of, 153, 156–57, 163–64, 167–68, 191–92; excursionism and, 96, 98, 118; in *glasnost/perestroika* era, 221–22; history of, 8–9, 158–59, 163–64, 220–23; identity disciplines and, 6, 215–27; influence of *Heimatkunde* on, 4–5, 220–21; literary, 183, 191–92, 209–11; Narkompros conference (Moscow, 1921), 157–59; Petersburg as theoretical center of, 10–12; Petrograd Excursion Institute and, 155–57; popularity of, 7; in post-Soviet Russia, 222–27; in post-Stalin years, 177–78; preservationism and, 43, 96; *putevoditeli* and, 15; "regional cultural nests" and, 186–89, 189; in capital cities of Russia, 162–72; Stalinist purges and, 173–77, 263 n. 70; *kraevedy* (practitioners of *kraevedenie*), 3–4, 8, 10, 159, 161–62; as amateur scholars, 160; Central Bureau and, 165, 167, 220; guidebooks and, 218; *Heimatkunde* and, 221; literature and, 183; Petrograd Excursion Institute and, 155; in post-Soviet Russia, 153; post-Thaw, 179–80; provincial, 167, 169, 185, 187; self-conception of, 11, 12; Soviet state and, 172, 177–78; as victims of purges, 173–77, 261–62 n. 54; Yeltsin's liberal reforms and, 222–23
krai (region or district), 3, 10–11, 156, 164, 168, 174
Krasnukha, Emma, 117, 119, 146
Krupskaia, Nadezhda, 119, 170
Kurbatov, Vladimir, 58, 61, 64, 68, 96, 244 n. 21; excursionism and, 113; guidebooks and, 218; legacy of, 180; on Museum of Alexander III, 85; Museum of Old Petersburg and, 69; Museum of the City and, 84; Narkompros projects and, 82–83; Society of Old Petersburg and, 89; studied in Russian schools, 224

Lanceray, Evgeny, 55, 61
Lanceray, Nikolai, 64–65, 73, 76
landmarks, 37, 51; destruction of, 67, 222; literary excursions and, 138, 140
landscapes, 3, 31, 43, 130; design of, 82; landscape painting, 20; literary, 122, 199; suburbs of St. Petersburg, 40

League of the Militant Godless, 95
Le Blond, Jean-Baptiste, 127
lectures, public, 95
Lee, Vernon, 196–98
legends, 42
Lenin, V. I., 86
Leningrad, 91, 153, 230 n. 14; Central Bureau in, 166–73; children's excursion guide to, 150–51; German siege in World War II, 178, 179; in *glasnost* period, 97; Gubernia Department of Communal Management (Gubotkomkhoz), 86, 91; *kraevedenie* movement in, 162–83; provinces and, 266 n. 23; reemergence as center of *kraevedenie*, 178–80. *See also* Petrograd; St. Petersburg
Leningrad Society for the Study of the Local Region (LOIMK), 162–63
Lenoir, Timothy, 215–16
Lermontov, Mikhail, 30, 200, 210
Lesnoe Commercial School, 111, 129, 162, 252 n. 37
libraries, 8, 20, 21, 22, 57
"life-creation" *(zhiznetvorchestvo)*, 201
Liteinaia District, 23
literary criticism, 9, 219
"Literary Excursions" (Sokolov), 129
literature, 24, 33, 209; excursion primers and literary texts, 128–41; *kraevedenie* and, 183, 187; negative depiction of Petersburg in, 29–30; *putevoditeli* (guidebooks) as, 231 n. 17
"little men," 30, 31, 50
Lomonosov, Mikhail, 28, 50, 163–64, 184, 200
Lomonosov Square, 48
Lotman, Iurii, 133, 211
Lovers of Russian Fine Editions, 62

Lukomsky, Georgy, 73, 75, 76, 243 n. 5; *Bygone Years* and, 58, 78; emigration from Russia, 81
Lunacharsky, Anatoly, 79, 80, 83, 110, 170, 252 n. 38
Lure, Lev, 177, 230 n. 12
Lyceum, at Tsarskoe Selo, 205–6, 208, 268 n. 40

Makovsky, Sergei, 62, 242 n. 48
Mandelstam, Osip, 250 n. 10
maps, 57, 99, 104, 163; "biography" of cities and, 103; Grevs's Italian excursions and, 105; historic, 121
Marble Palace, 60
Maria Fyodorovna, Grand Princess, 32, 60
Maria Tenisheva, Princess, 240 n. 29
Marr, Nikolai, 259 n. 29
Marser, Pavel, 52
Mayakovsky, Vladimir, 76, 130, 199
Meier, Alexander, 174, 201, 262 n. 57
Meklenberg-Strelitsky, Duke G. G., 85
Menzhinskaia, Ludmila, 110
Menzhinskaia, Vera, 82–83, 84
Merievo, F. I. Iankovich de, 102
messianism, 20, 28
Meyerhold, Vsevolod, 76
middle class, 107
Mikhailovsky Palace, 48
Mikhailovsky Theater, 76
military, Russian (Soviet), 18, 116
Ministry of Court, 56, 60, 69
modernization, 9, 87, 95
Mokrushi region, 137, 140
"Monumental City and Historical Excursions, The" (Grevs), 121, 122–23, 126, 127, 181
monuments, 10, 13, 40; accurate documentation of, 57; aesthetic valuation of, 46–47; excursionism

and, 109, 129; genius loci and, 197; government's failure to protect, 66–67; imperial, 149–50; lost to Stalinist construction projects, 178; October Revolution and, 79, 80; Petersburg anniversaries and, 51; preservation of, 44, 62, 67–69, 158; Society of Old Petersburg and, 89, 90; Soviet-era, 222; study of, 101; in Tsarskoe Selo, 204. *See also* Bronze Horseman monument (Falconet)

Morson, Gary Saul, 32–33

Moscow, 14, 18, 50, 219; as center of state power, 184; Central Bureau rivalry with Leningrad, 166–72; central role in Russian culture, 223; classicism in, 61; in *glasnost* period, 97; guidebook tradition in, 237 n. 63; Kremlin, 108; as new capital in Soviet Union, 193; in post-Soviet era, 222–23, 226; as Slavophile stronghold, 35; as "Third Rome," 19, 28; in World War II, 178

Moscow Letters, 19

Moscow School District, 106, 108

Moscow State University, 184, 186

Muscovite, The [Moskvitianin] (periodical), 36

Museum Department, Excursion Section at, 111, 113–14, 116, 121, 180

Museum of Alexander III (Russian Museum), 77, 85

Museum of Old Petersburg, 69–70, 77, 83, 84, 242 n. 57, 243 n. 8

Museum of the City, 82, 83–86, 91, 96, 113, 245 n. 26; *kraevedenie* and, 157, 161; legacy of, 179; LOIMK and, 163; renaming of, 246 n. 45

Museum of the Society for the Encouragement of the Arts, 77

museums, 63, 69–70, 93, 223; curatorship, 81; employees of, 115; excursionism and, 108–9, 114, 120; in Germany, 220; provincial, 157, 158; Soviet state policies and, 95, 151–52 myths, 4, 14, 30, 42, 126, 128, 131, 133–34, 218, 227 "image" of St. Petersburg and, 213

Nabokov, Vladimir, 250 n. 10

nagliadnost' (visuality), 101

Napoleonic Wars, 29, 45, 107

Narkompros (Commissariat of Enlightenment), 81, 82, 83, 90, 120, 189; budget cuts at, 145; excursion method endorsed by, 98, 110–17, 120; *kraevedenie* movement and, 164–65, 171, 172, 261 n. 48; museum tours and, 151–52. *See also* Academic Center of Narkompros (Aktsentr)

nationalism, 27, 42, 107, 118

natural sciences, 101, 112, 117, 187

nature lovers, societies of, 66, 157, 159

Neva River, 28, 30, 127; building of St. Petersburg and, 135; excursions on, 148; in mythology, 135; sphinxes on embankment of, 198, 203, 268 n. 43

Nevsky, Alexander, 238 n. 7

Nevsky Prospect, 82, 141

"Nevsky Prospect" (Gogol), 30

New Economic Policy (NEP), 87, 90, 95, 194; cultural revolution following end of, 86, 96; origins of propaganda state and, 143

Newest Guidebook to St. Petersburg (Shreder), 26

News of the Central Bureau of Kraevedenie [Ivzestiia TSBK] (journal), 160, 172

New Times [Novoe vremia] (newspaper), 40

Nicholas I, Tsar, 32, 38, 64, 79, 241 n. 45

Nicholas II, Tsar, 48, 73, 150

Nizhni-Novgorod, 102, 184

Northern War, 18

"Nose" (Gogol), 30
nostalgia, 42, 43, 46–47, 75, 177
Notes of the Fatherland (Otechestvennye zapiski), 35, 234 n. 36
Noteworthy Sights in St. Petersburg and Its Environs (Svinin), 26
Novgorod, 122, 223
Novikov, Nikolai, 102

ocherk (sketch), 13, 32–38, 219, 236 n. 55
October Revolution, 10, 66, 70, 92, 144, 205, 206; artistic-historical commissions and, 79; decentralization of culture and, 165; excursionism and, 98, 99; imperial palaces and, 78. *See also* Bolshevik regime; socialism; Soviet Union
Odessa, 106, 227
Odoevsky, Vladimir, 30, 200
Old Believers, 134, 246–47 n. 48
Oldenburg, Sergei, 159, 170, 249 n. 7, 259 n. 29
"old Petersburg," 43, 45, 46, 52, 60; architecture of, 61; changing definition of, 65; cult of, 62; literary *kraevedenie* and, 209; memories of, 193; preservation of, 64, 67–70
Old Petersburg [Staryi Peterburg] (Pyliaev), 40–41
opisanie (description), 13, 25–26, 27, 35, 125
Oranienbaum palace-park complex, 56, 76, 146, 247 n. 49
Orientalism, 41
Ostroi, Olga, 25
Ostroumova-Lebedeva, Anna, 195
Our Folk Sketched from Nature by Russians (anthology), 236 n. 55
"Overcoat, The" (Gogol), 30, 235 n. 45
palace-park complexes, 25, 39–40, 41, 53; Bolshevik education programs and, 120; under Provisional Government, 76–77, 78; transformed into museums, 79, 83. *See also specific palaces*
Palace Square, 48, 149
Pallas, Peter Simon, 22
panegyrics, 29, 32, 50
Panorama of St. Petersburg (Bashutsky), 31, 36, 235 n. 47
panoramic views, 25, 26, 32, 57, 105, 121
parks, 24, 39, 41, 53, 82, 201
patriotism, 27–28, 107, 118, 224
Paul I, Tsar, 32, 64, 79, 238 n. 9
Pavlov-Silvansky, N. N., 168, 171–72, 261 n. 48
Pavlovsk palace-park complex, 39, 40, 61, 91, 264 n. 74; *Art Treasures of Russia* issues dedicated to, 60, 240 n. 31; Bolshevik educational policy and, 112, 113, 114, 146, 247 n. 49; October Revolution and, 84
peasants, 40, 43, 77, 122
Pedagogical Thought (journal), 110, 252 n. 36
perestroika, 179, 221
Peris, Daniel, 95
Peter and Paul Fortress, 52, 55, 127, 128, 148, 272 n. 6
Peterhof palace-park complex, 39, 40, 91; *Art Treasures of Russia* issue dedicated to, 56; Bolshevik educational policy and, 112, 113, 114, 146, 247 n. 49; Monplaisir, 46; October Revolution and, 79, 84; restored after World War II, 179; Russian revolutions and, 76, 78
Peter I ("the Great"), Tsar, 9, 17, 18, 37, 64, 79; construction of St. Petersburg and, 128, 200; death of, 38, 136, 233 n. 24; as demigod, 32, 128, 135; denounced as Antichrist, 30; face mask of, 56; growth of St. Petersburg and, 24; homage paid

to, 19, 21; mythology surrounding, 134–35; popular attitudes toward, 126; portraits and statues of, 20, *48*, 203, 238 n. 7; reforms of, 47–48, 219
Petersburg (Bely), 203–4, 212
Petersburg in Reality and Myth (Antsiferov), 97, 126–28, 133–35, 137, 138, 144–45
Petersburg Tales (Gogol), 211
Petri, Georgy, 120, 121, 141–42, 146
Petrograd, 73, 75, 88, 96, 120, 230 n. 14; as educational center, 111; *kraevedy* in, 161–62; life during Civil War, 192–204; palaces transformed into museums, 79; preservationism in, 80; schools in, 112; Soviet of Workers' and Soldiers' Deputies, 74, 77, 80; suburbs, 145; teachers' colleges, 119. *See also* Leningrad; St. Petersburg
Petrograd Excursion Conference (1923), 156
Petrograd Excursion Institute, 11, 98, 119, 120–21, 123, 152; closure of, 165, 181, 187; humanities division, 99; *kraevedenie* and, 161, 163; legacy of, 179; Polisprovet and, 146–47; reputation of, 192. *See also* excursionism
Petrograd Municipal Authority: Cultural Enlightenment Department, 82
Petrograd Side, 127, 138, 139
Petrov, Petr, 57–58
Petrov-Vodkin, Kuzma, 73
photography, 54, 56, 57; inventory work and, 78; preservationism and, 68; Soviet excursionism and, 149
Physiology of St. Petersburg, A (Belinsky), 35–36
"Picturesque Petersburg" *[Zhivopisnyi Peterburg]* (Benois), 47, 49–50, 51, 52

Piksanov, Nikolai, 132, 184–90, 265 nn. 3–5, 266 n. 20
pilgrimage, tradition of, 131
Pinkevich, Albert, 167–68, 169
Platonov, Sergei, 15, 159, 262 n. 63
poets and poetry, 28–29, 34–35, 50, 126, 199, 234 n. 41
Pogosian, Elena, 211
Pokrovsky, Mikhail, 119, 170
Poliansky, I. I., 111, 162
Politprosvet, Excursion Subdepartment of, 91, 114–17, 145–46
Polonsky, Yakov, 200
Polzikova-Rubets, Kseniia, 121
Poor Folk (Dostoevsky), 30, 235 n. 45
Potemkin, Prince Grigory, 40, 41
poverty, 31, 38, 95
Prakhov, Adrian, 59–61, 62, 239 n. 21, 240 n. 29
preservationists, 12, 43–44, 157, 177, 221; "apolitical" attitude of, 80–81; Bolshevik regime and, 87; centralized power and, 241 n. 46; in Germany, 220; government's failure to protect monuments and, 66–67; in Khrushchev Thaw, 179; Museum of the City and, 88; October Revolution and, 79; plan for ministry of fine arts and, 75; pre-Revolutionary organizations, 67–69; *putevoditeli* (guidebooks) and, 14, 15, 59, 217
private sphere, 9
progulka (stroll), 13
Prokopovich, Feofan, 18
proletariat, dictatorship of the, 110
Proletkult, 164, 259 n. 25
propaganda, 115
Provisional Government, 74, 76, 77–78, 79, 80
Pskov, 122
Public School Code (1786), 102

public sphere, 9
publishing houses, 97, 222
purges, of Stalin era, 8, 94, 153, 173–77, 263 n. 70
Pushchin, Ivan, 206
Pushkarev, Ivan, 31
Pushkin, Alexander, 50, 137, 141, 200, 203–4; life of, 208–9; monument in Tsarskoe Selo, *205*; Peter the Great viewed by, 134–35; "Queen of Spades," 211; at Tsarskoe Selo, 206, 207; *World of Art* issue dedicated to, 52. See also *Bronze Horseman, The* (Pushkin)
Pushkin House, 175
Pushkin's Petersburg (Iatsevich), 191, 192, 208–10, 270 n. 84
putevoditeli (guidebooks), 12–15, 25–27, 34, 125, 217, 231 nn. 17–18. See also guidebooks
Pyliaev, Mikhail, 40–43, 45, 46, 57, 209

Quarenghi, Giacomo, 49
"Queen of Spades, The" (Pushkin), 211

Raikov, Boris, 110, 111, 114, 147, 172
Rastrelli, Bartolomeo Carlo, 49, 238 n. 7
Ratkov-Rozhnov, Iakov, 62
raznochintsy (intellectuals of nonnoble origin), 185, 265 n. 10
"real" school movement, 101, 108
reforms: of cultural institutions, 44; in nineteenth century, 38, 39; Petrine, 47–48, 49, 66, 219
Regional Cultural Nests (Piksanov), 189
regionalism, 7, 9, 132, 225
regions, 4, 13, 170; "cultural nests" in, 184–89, 190, 265 n. 3; historic role or destiny of, 218; as holistic units, 118; literary heritage of, 132; regional exploration, 31; regional identity, 164

religion, excursions as alternative to, 147, 149
Rescue *(Spasenie)*, 179
research activity, 10, 156
rodinovedenie (homeland studies), 4, 108, 123, 153; educational program based on, 118; relationship to *kraevedenie*, 158, 159, 258 n. 7
Roerich, Nikolai, 68, 73
Romanov dynasty, 19, 24, 27, 37, 38, 40, 66; Petrine legacy and, 232 n. 9; praise of, 28, 32; preservationist organizations and, 70; Soviet tourism and, 149; three-hundred-year jubilee (1913), 64, 107. See also Russia, tsarist; tsars
romanticism, 27
Rosenberg, William G., 87
Rossi, Carlo, 48, 49, 238 n. 8
Rousseau, Jean-Jacques, 102
Rozanov, Vasily, 204, 207
Ruban, Vasily, 21, 22
Russia, post-Soviet, 9, 152–53, 222–27
Russia, tsarist, 9, 49, 70; civil society in, 66; diverse regions of, 219, 236 n. 60; as European power, 17–18; European stereotypes of, 42; Napoleonic invasion (1812), 27, 107; progressive education in, 102–3. See also Romanov dynasty; tsars
Russian Archive, The [Russkii arkhiv] (journal), 18
Russian Excursionist, The (journal), 106, 108–9, 118, 251 n. 31
Russian Museum, 114, 131, 204, 253 n. 49
Russianness, 7, 10, 14, 219; Europeanness and, 19–20; imperial and popular identity blended in, 28
Russian North, 120
Russian Olden Times [Russkaia starina] (journal), 38–39, 40, 42, 43, 46

Russians, 7, 36; educated society (*obshchestvennost'*), 66; as ethno-cultural group, 27–28; interest in national history, 39; in post-Soviet period, 223; regional commonalities shared by, 164
Russo-Japanese War, 61
Rykov, Alexei, 170
Ryndina, O. M., 121

Sadovaia Street, 141
St. Isaac's bridge, *42*
St. Isaac's Cathedral, 126, 135, 136, 149
St. Petersburg, 9–10, 85, 230 n. 1; anniversaries of founding, 51, *55*; architecture, 24, 32, 37, 48–49, 61; as center of state power, 184; as city of tsars, 21; during Civil War, 192–204; dark and gloomy aspect, 50; European look of, 28, 59; foreign travelers in, 17–18, 26; founding of, 18, 20–21, 127; in graphic arts, *42*; guidebook tradition of, 15; as historic city, 43, 49; history of, 29, 127–28; *kraevedy* in, 161; literary tours in, 133; in literature, 29–30, 113; mythology and, 134; in poetry, 28–29; in post-Soviet era, 226; Public Library, 57, 179; Pushkin and, 208–10; suburbs, 39, 40, 58, 82; as "theoretical center" of *kraevedenie*, 10–12; topographic description of, 17–27; as Westernizers' stronghold, 36–37, 219; as "window on the West," 49. *See also* Leningrad; "old Petersburg"; Petrograd
St. Petersburg Religious-Philosophical Society, 43, 201
St. Petersburg University, 54, 99, 100, 162, 249 n. 4
Sapozhnikova, Tatiana, 146

School Excursions: Their Significance and Organization (Raikov), 114, 129
School Excursions and the School Museum (journal), 106, 107–8
science, 9, 110, 116, 188, 227; natural sciences, 101, 112, 117, 187; social sciences, 103, 122
Science for the Masses (Andrews), 94
Sector of Social Education, 116–17, 147
self-education, 66, 145, 151
self/selfhood, 5, 7, 217, 227
Semenov-Tian-Shansky, Petr, 56
Semevsky, Mikhail, 38, 39, 40, 42
semiotics, 133, 210–13
Senate Square, 29, *42*
Seregny, Scott, 105
serfdom, 38, 210
Shakhty case, 86, 87, 175
Shaliapin, Fyodor, 73
Shchuko, Vladimir, 68, 69
Shenberg, G. G., 162
show trials, 86–87
Shreder, Fyodor, 26–28, 233 n. 30
Shuvalov mansion, 114
sightseers, 31, 34, 58, 107, 235 n. 47
"Sirius" publishing house, 62
Siuzor, Pavel, 70, 77
Sketches from the History of Roman Landownership (Principally in the Time of the Empire) (Grevs), 100
Slavophiles, 9, 20, 219; Moscow as center of, 35, 36–37; Petersburg disliked by, 30, 43; Petrine reforms and, 48; sketches and, 35
Smidovich, P., 176
Smolensk Cemetery, 194
Sobranie raznykh sochinenii i novostei (journal), 21
socialism, 143–44, 169–70, 179, 241 n. 46
social sciences, 103, 122

Society for the Encouragement of the Arts, Imperial, 52, 53, 59
Society for the Study, Popularization, and Artistic Preservation of Old Petersburg, 11, 82, 88–89, 192, 209
Society of Architect-Artists, 68, 70, 89
Society of Old Petersburg, 89–96, 120; Division of the Northern Environs, 162; excursionism and, 115, 145–46; *kraevedenie* and, 157, 161, 162, 163, 191; legacy of, 179; targeted by Politprosvet, 145–46
Society of Proletarian Tourism and Excursions (OPTE), 148–49
sociology, 3, 31, 218
Sokolov, Boris, 168, 260 n. 37
Sokolov, N. M., 111, 129
Soloviev, Vladimir, 201–2
Solovki labor camp, 180, 181, 264 n. 77
Somov, Konstantin, 43, 68, 75
Son of the Fatherland [Syn Otechestva] (journal), 22
Soul of Petersburg, The (Antsiferov), 182, 189–90, 192–204, 269 n. 56; *City of Muses* in comparison with, 206–8; Tartu semioticians and, 211–12
Sovietization, 96
Soviet Union, 3, 86, 221; collapse of, 7, 8, 226; *glasnost* and *perestroika* era, 97, 152, 221–22; institutions of, 143–44; liberalization of Khrushchev era, 176–79; power balance between Moscow and Leningrad, 166–72; recovery from Civil War, 157; voluntary associations in early period, 91, 95; in World War II, 178, 223. *See also* Bolshevik regime; October Revolution; socialism
Sovnarkom, 171, 175
space, geographical, 3, 15, 35, 49

Special Advisory Board on Artistic Affairs, 74, 77
specialization, academic, 2, 5, 6, 216
"Sphinxes on the Neva, The" (Ivanov), 203
Stakhanovite movement, 94
Stalin, Joseph, 8, 87, 170, 178, 223
Stalinism, 71, 177, 178, 241 n. 46
State Academic Council *[Gosudarstvennyi uchenyi sovet]* (GUS), 117, 119
State Duma, 62, 67
State Literary Museum, 180
State Publishing House *(Gosizdat)*, 186, 204
Stites, Richard, 77
Stolpiansky, Petr, 58, 89, 92–93, 96, 147, 209; guidebooks and, 218; legacy of, 180, 224; Society of Old Petersburg and, 146
Storming the Heavens (Peris), 95
stranovedenie (country studies), 4, 158
Stroganov Palace, 56, 114, 146
strolls, 102, 105, 107, 133
Stroll with Children Through St. Petersburg and the Surrounding Regions, A (Burianov), 33
Studitsky, K., 109, 251 n. 31
Sub-Department of Adult Education (Narkompros), 111, 114–17
suburbs, 113, 141, 178
Sumarokov, Alexander, 28, 199
Summer Gardens, 41
Sviatsky, D. O., 174
Svinin, Pavel, 26–28, 32, 40, 57, 234 n. 36
symbolism, 20, 44, 51, 52, 104; religious philosophy and, 201; Tartu semioticians and, 211
"Symbolism of Petersburg and the Problems of a Semiotics of the City, The" (Lotman and Uspensky), 133

Tarle, Evgenii, 175
Tartu school of semiotics, 133, 210–13
Tauride Palace, 41
Tenishev, Prince Viacheslav, 100
Tenishev School, 98, 100–107, 108, 110, 114, 250 n. 10
Theory and Practice of Literary Excursions (Antsiferov), 129–33
"Third Rome" idea, 19, 28, 133
Thomon, Thomas de, 49
Tolz, Vera, 174
Tomashevsky, V. B., 168
topography, 15, 104, 189, 211
totalitarianism, 71
tourism, 13, 95, 103, 107, 108, 148–49
Towards the Theory and Practice of Excursions as a Tool in the Scientific Study of History in Universities (Grevs), 103, 104, 106
tradespeople, 31, 41
trade unions, 115, 116, 147
transportation routes, 35, 121, 126–27
Tretiakov, Pavel, 85
Trinity Bridge, 127
Trinity Square, 127, 128, 138
Troinitsky, Sergei, 62, 89, 113, 241 n. 48
Trubetskoi, Pavel, 150
Trubnikov, Alexander, 62
tsars, 21, 24, 39, 41. *See also* Romanov dynasty; Russia, tsarist; *specific tsars*
Tsarskoe Selo in Poetry (Gollerbakh), 208
Tsarskoe Selo palace-park complex, 60, 61, 78; Artistic and Historical Commission at, 204; Catherine Palace and Park, 79, 132, 179; genius loci monuments in, 268 n. 40; in Gollerbakh's description, 204–8; October Revolution and, 79, 84; Pushkin monument, *205*
Tuchkov Bridge, 138
Tumim, G., 129

Union of Militant Atheists, 115
United Labor School, Excursion Department of, 111, 112–13, 116, 252 n. 42
urbanizm (urban studies), 123, 181
urban planning, 65, 81
Uspensky, Alexander, 56, 60, 64
Uspensky, Boris, 133

vandalism, 59, 63, 67, 68, 178
Vasilievsky, V. G., 100
Vasilievsky Island, 23, 127, 247 n. 48
Veiner, Petr, 62, 65, 67, 78, 244 n. 18; arrested, 84; on cooperation with Bolshevik regime, 80; excursionism and, 113; Museum of Old Petersburg and, 69; Society of Old Petersburg and, 89
Vereshchagin, Vasily, 62, 78, 80, 243 n. 14, 244 n. 18
Versailles, court of, 28, 75
Vishnevsky, B. N., 160
Vliadikh, Ia. A., 121
Voskresen'e circle, 201, 262 n. 57
Vrangel, Baron Nikolai, 62, 67–68, 69, 241 n. 45, 241–42 n. 48
Vyborg Side, 23

Ways of Studying the City as a Social Organism (Antsiferov), 181
Westernizers, 9, 20, 30, 219; *Notes of the Fatherland*, 35; Petersburg as stronghold of, 36–37; Petrine reforms and, 48
White Sea Canal, 180, 181, 264 n. 77
Winter Palace, 60, 78, 115, 136, 193
working class, 77, 147–49
World of Art [Mir iskusstva] (journal), 44, 46, 81, 82; Benois and, 51–54, 55, 56–59, 61; Petersburg issue, 52,

55; retrospectivist exhibits and, 78; veteran contributors, 73, 80
World of Art Circle *(Mir iskusstva)*, 11, 43–44, 54; *Art Treasures of Russia* and, 61; Gorky Commission and, 73, 75, 77; nostalgia and, 46–47
World War I, 65, 107, 118
World War II, 3, 88, 176, 178, 223
Wortman, Richard, 232 n. 9

Yaroslavl, 106, 108, 109
Yeltsin, Boris, 222
Young Communists' League (Komsomol), 152
Young Pioneers, 150

Zakharov, Adrian, 48
Zamiatin, Evgeny, 195
Zdanevich, I., 76
zemstvos (local assemblies), 66, 109; reform of, 110; schools, 108; zemstvo teachers, 105, 106, 107
Zharnovsky, S. N., 88–89, 92, 93
Zhukovsky, Vasily, 206
Zolotarev, D., 108
Zuev, V. F., 102

www.ingramcontent.com/pod-product-compliance
Lightning Source LLC
Chambersburg PA
CBHW021355290426
44108CB00010B/245